SIMPLICITY IN MUSIC APPRECIATION

Second Edition

———

by

ANTHONY J. APICELLA

Director of Music
Cambridge Public Schools
Cambridge, Massachusetts

ATTILIO J. GIAMPA

Supervisor of Music Education
Boston Public Schools
Boston, Mass.

MARGARITA B. APICELLA

Teacher of Physical Science and Chemistry
Bedford High School
Bedford, Massachusetts

Parker Publishing Company, Inc.
West Nyack, New York

Library of Congress Cataloging in Publication Data

Apicella, Anthony J
    Simplicity in music appreciation.

    Includes discographies.
    Bibliography: p.
    1. Music—Analysis, appreciation. I. Giampa,
Attilio J., joint author. II. Apicella, Margarita
B., joint author. III. Title.
MT6.A65S5 1974   780'.15   74-3295
ISBN 0-13-810150-7

A WORD FROM THE AUTHORS
ABOUT THIS NEW EDITION

The many changes and happenings in the field of music over the past decade have necessitated a new edition of our book "Simplicity in Music Appreciation". In the process of updating the book, the authors have added some innovative and relevant material that will appeal to the interests of the youth of today. The composers of rock, electronic, aleatoric, popular and black music along with informative descriptions of their works are a significant addition to the original book. The relationship of this music to present-day art forms is made possible through concise and informative descriptions that are easy to comprehend.

All recordings, biographical information, bibliographies, composers and styles of composition have been updated and revised so as to provide the reader with a more comprehensive view of all phases of music.

In this book, the authors have tried to present a practical approach to the understanding and appreciation of music. The aim of this book is to present functional lesson plans so that music appreciation can be correlated with other subjects of the curriculum, thus providing an interesting stimulus for learning through aesthetic enjoyment. Motivation being the key to all learning, we have attempted to present an interesting, informative and simplified approach to music appreciation.

We have not attempted to make a complete or comprehensive study of each composer, but have endeavored to touch upon some of the important highlights of his life and his art. This will allow the teacher to present more composers during the year, thus making the lessons more interesting and providing for the students a broader coverage of the history of music.

We have tried to present a lesson outline that can be adapted, with some supplementary material, to any grade level, varying accommodations for musical material and equipment, time allotted for music and almost any type of musical background or educational experience. The outline is flexible so that teachers and students will be able to expand upon the given material according to the amount of time available.

iii

Included with information about each composer is an excerpt taken from one of his major works. The melody, harmony and rhythm of many of these excerpts have been altered somewhat, in order to achieve a smooth and complete-sounding phrase. This is intended to serve as a beginning in the presentation of listening exercises in music.

The authors suggest that this book be used as a student text and teacher resource book for music appreciation. The material need not be presented in a chronological order. The contents may be presented over a period of several years and may be adapted to any music curriculum.

The individual adult who wishes to obtain a broader cultural background through the study of music and develop the ability to listen to music intelligently will find this a useful text.

This format for teaching music appreciation has been successfully used by the authors in the teaching of all grade levels. It is hoped that this book will prove to be a valuable aid to the classroom teacher and an interesting and informative text for the student.

Anthony J. Apicella
Attilio J. Giampa
Margarita B. Apicella

Dedicated to the classroom teachers whose unselfish devotion to the children and enthusiasm for music, have provided the authors with the inspiration to write this book.

Anthony J. Apicella
Attilio J. Giampa
Margarita B. Apicella

TABLE OF CONTENTS

BIBLIOGRAPHY

ILLUSTRATIONS
    Composers: Pictures of the composers are included with
        the descriptions of their lives and music.
    Musical Instruments: Photographs of the instruments of
        the symphony orchestra are shown with each descrip-
        tion.

ACKNOWLEDGMENTS

Grateful acknowledgment is made to the following:

Mary R. Geiger for proof reading of the manuscript and invaluable suggestions in the preparation of the first edition.

Gilbert Prentiss for editing of the manuscript and suggesting the use of pertinent material in the first edition.

James Landrigan of Cambridge High & Latin School for editing revisions of second edition.

RCA Victor and American Society of Composers, Authors and Publishers (ASCAP) for pictures of the composers.

Conn, "World's largest manufacturer of band instruments", for photographs of brass and woodwind instruments.

Ludwig Drum Company, Chicago, Ill., for photographs of percussion instruments.

Roth Violins (Scherl & Roth, Inc.), Cleveland, Ohio, for photographs of string instruments.

M. Steinert & Sons, Boston, Mass., for photograph of piano.

Lyon & Healy, Inc., Chicago, Ill., for photograph of harp.

Custom Music Company, Detroit, Mich., for photographs of Contra-Bassoon (Puchner-Cooper) and English Horn.

Fender Musical Instruments, Fullerton, California, for photographs of electric guitars.

Boston Symphony Orchestra for photograph of orchestra.

CHAPTER 1

SUGGESTED PROCEDURES
FOR MUSIC APPRECIATION LESSONS

Introduction: In the following outline the authors have
suggested many activities and educational experiences that
will contribute to the development of a good music appreciation program. The student and teacher should try to include
as many of the activities and experiences as possible within
this course of study. The procedure for the presentation of
printed themes and recorded material may be adapted to the
varying musical background of the class. A knowledge of the
historical background of the period in music history is
essential to an intellectual approach to music appreciation.
An understanding of the cultural accomplishments and the
related liberal arts areas will make the study of music
appreciation a more meaningful experience. The following
outline includes a complete program of educational activities and tested procedures for the presentation of listening sessions.

    A. Preparatory work assigned previous to scheduled day
       for listening lesson:

      1. Research by class in the following areas:
        a. Composer: Biographical material, etc.
          (1) General education: schools attended and
             academic achievements.
          (2) Musical training: teachers and schools.
          (3) Musical activities: positions held and pro-
             fessional endeavors.
          (4) Non-musical experiences: activities partici-
             pated in outside the realm of music.
          (5) General information about the composer's
             music.
          (6) Interesting anecdotes concerning composer.
        b. Music History: History of the development of
          music during the period (Polyphonic, Baroque,
          Classical, etc.) in which the composer lived.
          (1) General advancements in the development of
             vocal and instrumental composition.
          (2) Progress made in the improvement of existing
             instruments and invention of new instruments.
          (3) Improvements made in the various areas of
             musical production such as opera, oratorio,
             ballet, etc.

        (4) Opportunities available to composers and
            musicians of each period and social position
            attained by them.
   c. General History and Cultural Accomplishments:
      (1) Study of the most important developments in
         the history of the period.
      (2) Acquiring of a knowledge of the cultural
         achievements of the prominent figures of
         the period.

B. Discussion of the above assignments on day of listening
lesson:

  1. Discussion of the composer:
    a. Biographical information about composer.
    b. Composer's contribution to the art of music.
    c. Discussion of composition to be played:
      (1) Musical form of the composition.
      (2) Program or absolute music.
      (3) Instrumentation.
    d. Discussion of the conductor and performing group
       of the recording to be presented.
  2. Correlation with other subjects of the curriculum:
    a. Social Studies:
      (1) Discussion of the historical background of
         the period during which the composer lived.
      (2) Political figures and developments during
         this period.
      (3) Reports on the geographical location of the
         composer's place of birth.
    b. Physical Sciences:
      (1) Discussion of famous scientists of the period,
         and their relationship, if any, to the com-
         poser.
      (2) Discussion of the fundamentals of acoustics.
      (3) Scientific explanation of the principles of
         tone production of the various musical in-
         struments.
      (4) Scientific inventions and discoveries that
         might have influenced the music of the period.
    c. Literature:
      (1) Assigned readings on famous authors and their
         writings that were popular during the life-
         time of the composer.
      (2) Oral reports and discussion about the compos-
         er.
      (3) Written reports on the composer and his music.
      (4) Creative writing of lyrics to musical compo-
         sitions.

        (5) Writing of interpretive essays on musical compositions.

        (6) Relating poetic meter to musical rhythm.

  d. Philosophy:

        (1) The influence of philosophical thought upon the type of music of the period.

        (2) A study of the philosophers who wrote about music.

        (3) A study of educational philosophy, its origin and development, its influence upon music.

  e. Fine Arts:

        (1) Drawing pictures that the music or title suggests.

        (2) Painting or sketching a picture of the composer.

        (3) Discussion of art and architecture of the period in music history.

        (4) For sculpture, creating clay models of musical subjects.

        (5) Making a comparison of the art and music forms of the period.

  f. Mathematics:

        (1) Discussion of time signatures and note values in music, and their relationship to mathematics.

        (2) Research on the mathematical principles involved in equal-tempered tuning of the piano.

        (3) Selection of musical instruments and research on the mathematical dimensions of these instruments.

  g. Physical Education:

        (1) Folk dances from the country of the composer performed by the students.

        (2) American versions of the above dances.

        (3) Calisthenics performed with a musical background.

        (4) Discussion of famous athletic events and athletes of the country of the composer.

  h. Foreign Language Studies:

        (1) Learning and singing folk songs of the composer's country (words in foreign language learned phonetically).

        (2) Learning and singing some of the American adaptations of the foreign songs.

        (3) Preparing and presenting a play in the language of the composer.

i. Vocal and Instrumental Music:
   (1) Singing selections of the composer by the class.
   (2) Setting a poem of this period to music.
   (3) Performance of a selection of the composer for the class by an instrumental student.

C. Presenting and playing of printed theme on the piano by the teacher or student - suggested procedure:

1. Write title and composer's name on the blackboard.
2. Write musical theme on the blackboard.
3. Play theme twice and have class listen.
4. Play theme twice and ask the class to hum the melody following the notes of the theme written on the blackboard.
5. Suggest to the class that they memorize the melody of the theme, so that later on they might have fun playing the Radio and Television game called "Name That Tune"or "Musical Baseball".
6. Try to play this theme as many times as possible during this and other days, so that the class will become familiar with the melody.
7. The following are suggested questions for discussion of the piano theme:
   a. Who has heard this melody before?
   b. Where have you heard it?
   c. What instrumental groups, chorus, or soloists performed this theme?
   d. Is this a pretty melody that you might easily memorize?
   e. What type of rhythm does it have?
   f. Is it a waltz, march, polka, minuet, gavotte, etc.?
   g. Is it a lively song that suggests running, dancing, marching, skipping, etc.?
   h. Is it a sad or quiet song? Does it suggest a lullaby?
   i. What does this song suggest to you?
   j. Can you draw a picture of a scene suggested by this melody?
   k. Can you make up a dance that would fit this song?
   l. Can you make up words to fit this melody?
   m. Does the music suggest the meaning of its title?
   n. What other title might be appropriate for this theme?
   o. Who thinks that they might be able to play this melody on a musical instrument?
   p. How does this song compare with the popular melodies of today?

D. Presenting and playing suggested recordings of composer's music:

1. Write title and composer's name on the blackboard.
2. Play a substantial part of the composition (Complete composition to be played later).
3. Discuss the selection played (sometimes this discussion may precede the first playing of the selection):
    a. Type of composition (symphony, opera, concerto, etc.).
    b. Performing group (vocal, instrumental, or solo).
4. Play recording again, bringing to the attention of the class the main theme (or themes).
5. Discuss the musical structure (play section that would illustrate the following):
    a. Repetition of themes.
    b. Contrasting themes.
    c. Variation of themes:
        (1) Melodic variation.
        (2) Rhythmic variation.
        (3) Harmonic variation.
    d. Use of contrapuntal devices:
        (1) Similar to a "round" or "canon".
6. Play the entire composition (if not too long, so that the interest of the class might be retained).
7. The following are suggested questions for the above recording:
    a. Can you tell me what this music suggests to you?
        (1) What kind of story does it suggest to you?
        (2) Does it bring to mind any mental image or picture?
    b. What mood does it suggest?
        (1) Sad, quiet, mysterious, thoughtful, dreamy, melancholy, somber, (add to these).
        (2) Happy, lively, gay, joyful, ecstatic, spirited, saucy, full of play, jaunty, rollicking, (add to these).
    c. What type of rhythm does it have?
    d. Is it a waltz, march, polka, minuet, gavotte, etc.?
    e. Does this song suggest any of the following rhythmic activities:
        (1) Running, dancing, marching, skipping, etc.?
    f. What instrument or instruments did you recognize in this composition?
    g. Is this title appropriate for this music or can you suggest another title?

       h. Where might this composition be used?
         (1) Concert stage, film background music,
            parade, circus, etc.?
       i. How does this selection compare with others you
         have heard?

E. Other listening, performance, educational activities
   and experiences that would help to achieve a higher
   level of music appreciation:

   1. Melody: Analyze the development of melody histori-
      cally in its relationship to the various periods
      in music history. Make comparisons of the nation-
      alistic styles of music used in the various coun-
      tries of the world. Perform these melodies on solo
      instruments.
   2. Harmony: Study the advances achieved in harmony
      over the centuries. Play the harmonic accompani-
      ments on piano, autoharp, guitar, etc.
   3. Rhythm: Study and demonstrate the rhythmic charac-
      teristics of music through the performance of
      folk dances and songs. Play accompaniments on
      rhythm instruments.
   4. Form: Develop the ability to analyze the structural
      patterns of musical form, such as repetition, con-
      trast, and variation.
   5. Instrumental Music: Trace the invention and develop-
      ment of musical instruments and compare this to
      technological accomplishments in other areas. Play
      or listen to performances of the various instru-
      ments. Make a study of the mechanics and tone pro-
      ducing qualities of these instruments.
   6. Vocal Music: Do research on the development of
      choral music in music history. Compare religious
      and secular vocal music. Sing some of the more
      prominent songs of each era of music history.
   7. Miscellaneous Activities:
      a. Field Trips: Attend community musical perform-
        ances at the local concert hall, churches,
        colleges, public schools, radio and television
        stations. Visit local conservatories, music
        exhibits at museums, and colleges of music.
      b. Lectures: Attend music lectures given at the
        local colleges or invite professional people
        to lecture to your class about their music
        specialty.
      c. Performance: Apply for membership in community
        choirs and instrumental organizations. Join
        local dance groups which encourage the perform-
        ance of folk, art, and social dancing.

d. Research: Select areas of music that interest you; do research and write reports on these topics.

e. Audio-Visual Aids: Make use of audio-visual equipment available in your school and public libraries, which would include recordings, film-strips, films, slides, music illustrations, photographs and charts.

F. Suggested recordings that are pertinent to subjects used in correlation with music:

1. Social Studies:

   a. Title: *Music of the World's Peoples*
      Performers: Compiled by Henry Cowell
      Record No.: Folkways Records FE 4504
      Grade Level: 4 - 12

   b. Title: *National Anthems of the World*
      Performers: Band of the Grenadier Guards
      Record No.: London PS 120
      Grade Level: 4 - 12

2. Physical Sciences:

   a. Title: *Switched-On Bach* (Electronic Production)
      Performers: Walter Carlos
      Record No.: Columbia MS 7194
      Grade Level: 7 - 12

   b. Title: *Sounds of New Music* - Electronic
      Performers: Unusual instruments and sound equipment
      Record No.: Lyons LB 5810
      Grade Level: 4 - 12

3. Literature:

   a. Title: *Songs of Robert Burns*
      Performers: Vocal
      Record No.: London SW 99228
      Grade Level: 7 - 12

   b. Title: *Tom Sawyer*
      Performers: Readings - Ed Begley
      Record No.: Caedmon DC 1205
      Grade Level: 4 - 12

4. Fine Arts:

   a. Title: *Background Music for Home Movies*
      Performers: Orchestra
      Record No.: Folkways FS 6110
      Grade Level: 4 - 12

   b. Title: *Impressionism in Art and Music*
      Performers: Orchestral Music and Filmstrip
      Record No.: EAV 98RF311
      Grade Level: 4 - 12

5. Physical Education:

   a. Title: *Music for Physical Fitness*
      Performers: Orchestral Music
      Record No.: Bowmar 135
      Grade Level: 4 - 8

   b. Title: *Folk Dance* (with instructions)
      Performers: Instrumental Music
      Record No.: Monitor 900
      Grade Level: 4 - 12

6. Foreign Language Studies:

   a. Title: *Let's Learn Spanish Songs*
      Performers: Vocal-Instrumental
      Record No.: EAV 92T701
      Grade Level: 7 - 12

   b. Title: *A World of Song*
      Performers: Vocal-Instrumental
      Record No.: Angel 36296
      Grade Level: 4 - 8

CHAPTER 2

THUMBNAIL SKETCH
OF THE HISTORY OF EARLY MUSIC

I. Ancient Music Up to the Birth of Christ: The history of
ancient music is uncertain due to the lack of notated
records of this period. Many sculptured pieces and
etchings have been found that depict musical activities
and musical instruments. Musicologists have interpreted
the meaning of these archeological findings and have
concluded that music was an integral part of the culture
of all ancient civilizations.

   A. Sumerians 4000 - 2300 B.C. Music played an important
   part in the religious, political and social activities
   of this culture.
      1. The musicians belonged to religious groups and
      occupied a high position in the social order.
         a. The religious music consisted of the chanting
         of prayers and hymns.
         b. Reed-pipe, lyre and drums supplied the accom-
         paniment for the singers.

   B. Egyptians 3000 - 200 B.C. The music and religion of
   the Egyptian culture were closely related. Most vocal
   music was part of the religious service and all instruments invented during this period were considered
   symbolic of the power of their Gods. Egyptian music
   was quite extensive and influenced the music of later
   periods, especially Greek music.
      1. Egyptian music was subject to religious laws.
      2. Female dancers and choruses performed in religious
      worship.
      3. Secular music for social diversion of the royalty
      and noblemen was a later development.
      4. Egyptian instruments:
         a. Strings: Cithera, lute, harp.
         b. Wind: Oboe, flute, trumpet (used for military
         purposes).
         c. Percussion: Sistrum, drums.

   C. Babylonians and Assyrians 2300 - 500 B.C. Music played
   an important part in the religious culture of these
   civilizations. Sacred hymns sung and played by musicians were the most important part of their services.
   Secular music began to emerge among the upper classes.

1. The Babylonians and Assyrians were influenced by
   the music of the Sumerians and continued the development of this art.
2. Choruses and orchestras were formed at this time.
3'. Larger instruments were developed:
   a. Strings: Harp, cithara, lute.
   b. Winds: Single and double flutes, reeds.
   c. Brass: Trumpets.
   d. Percussion: Drums, cymbals, tambourines.

D. Hebrews 1000 B.C. The Hebrews had developed a highly
   organized religious service in which music played an
   important part. Their religious music had a great influence upon the church music of the Christians,
   especially in antiphonal singing and plainsong.
   1. The Jews believed that music possessed miraculous
      power.
   2. Secular music developed in the Hebrew culture:
      a. War songs.
      b. Work songs.
      c. Songs of sadness and joy - emotional music.
   3. Instruments used (borrowed from Assyrians):
      a. Strings: Harp, psalteries, sistra, lyre.
      b. Winds: Trumpets, pipes, flutes.
      c. Percussion: Drums, cymbals.
   4. Large choirs of voices and instrumental groups were
      used for religious services.

E. Greeks 1000 - 300 B.C. The Greeks associated the
   origin of music with mythology. Poetry and drama based
   upon the various myths were combined with music for
   religious and cultural enrichment. Greek music is the
   most important of all ancient music because it had the
   most imfluence upon succeeding civilizations.
   1. Greek theory influenced musical theory of the mid-
      dle ages.
   2. The Greeks developed poetry recitations accompanied
      by the lyre, syrinx or Paneau pipe.
   3. They developed the tragedy or music drama:
      a. Music used as a medium of expression.
      b. Greek tragedy influenced opera of the future.
   4. The ancient Greeks had two types of notation: in-
      strumental and vocal notation.
   5. Pythagorus founded the science of mathematical
      acoustics:
      a. He discovered the acoustical properties of the
         octave, the perfect fifth, and other intervals.
   6. The Greek scale was founded on the tetrachord (four-
      tone scale).

7. Greek modes: A mode is a linear arrangement of pitches within an octave, with a definite pattern of whole-steps and half-steps. The Greek modes include the following:
a. Dorian
b. Lydian
c. Phrygian
d. Ionian
e. Aeolian
f. Hypodorian
g. Hypophrygian
h. Mixolydian

F. Romans 500 B.C. - 150 A.D. The Romans obtained their music from the Greeks. They developed a smoother melodic line in which the rhythm was more easily adapted to the lyric.
1. Roman culture was borrowed from the Greeks.
2. Greek drama was not imitated:
a. Artistry was suppressed because the Romans were not interested in drama.
3. Use of musical instruments for warfare:
a. Winds: Cornu and tuba.
4. Change of attitude towards music in the first century A.D.
a. Music cultivated and sought after by the nobles and people.
b. Music for the aesthetic and sensual uses.

II. Early Christian Era: 1 - 800 A.D. The early Christian church adopted the music of the Hebrews for their services. They used antiphonal singing (solo voice with congregational response or divided choirs), unison singing, chant and plainsong. The church of this period made much progress in the development of liturgical music.

A. The Beginnings of Christianity:
1. Hebrew chant adopted by the Roman Catholic Church.
2. Adaptation of some Greek hymns:
a. *Hymn of Jesus*, 160 A.D.
3. First choir school founded by Pope Sylvester in the year 320 A.D.

B. St. Ambrose, Bishop of Milan 333 - 397 A.D.
1. Collected and edited music for the church.
a. Set standards for church music.
2. Adopted four modes (scales) which were used for church singing:
a. He called these modes "Authentic".

11

b. St. Ambrose insisted on a simple form of hymn which became popular because the congregation could join in the singing.

c. He wrote many of these hymns as examples.

C. Pope Gregory the Great 540 - 604 A.D.
1. Adopted the plagal modes.
2. Created the form for the musical setting of the liturgy:
a. Psalmody
b. Antiphons
c. Responds
d. Hymns
3. Established choir schools that set definite standards for church music.
4. Gregorian Chant: It is the official liturgical chant of the Roman Catholic Church and is named after Pope Gregory who guided its codification. Another name for Gregorian chant is plainsong. It consists of a pure melodic line in free rhythm. Church music still contains Gregorian chant melodies. Gregorian chant makes use of eight modes (scales), each of which expresses certain emotions and feelings:
a. First and second modes: seriousness, contemplation.
b. Third and fourth modes: glorification, ecstacy.
c. Fifth and sixth modes (most like our own major scale): brightness, confidence.
d. Seventh mode: solemn affirmation.
e. Eighth mode: tranquility, content, calm.

III. Music of the Middle Ages: 800 - 1300 A.D. The music of this period can be divided into two main categories: sacred and secular. Obviously sacred music included the liturgical music of the church. Secular music was composed and performed by various groups including the Troubadours of southern France, the Trouveres of northern France, the Minnesingers and Meistersingers from Germany. Music theory was further developed during the Middle Ages.

A. Hucbald of Flanders 840 - 930 Flemish monk.
1. Created use of parallel lines to indicate difference of pitch.
2. Tried to establish harmony through the scientific basis of tone relationships.
a. Wrote book: *De Harmonica Institutione*.

B. Guido D'Arezzo 995 - 1050
   1. His greatest contribution was the establishment of
      a practical system of musical notation.
      a. He is credited with developing the two line
         staff into a staff of four lines.
      b. He placed neumes (notes) on specific lines of
         the staff representing fixed pitches.
   2. Guido's method of teaching Solfeggio (sight sing-
      ing) is still used today.
C. Franco of Cologne - 13th century.
   1. He developed a system of measuring time:
      a. He wrote the treatise *The Art of Measurable
         Music* around 1250 A.D.
      b. He assigned time values to notes.
      c. He established binary and ternary meter.

D. Secular Music - Minstrel singers:
   1. Early minstrels of France - 12th and 13th
      centuries:
      a. Troubadours - French knights who sang to their
         court ladies.
      b. Jongleurs - Performed among the common people;
         acrobats, jugglers, play actors.
      c. Most famous troubadour was Adam de la Halle:
         (1) Wrote medieval play with music: *Robin et
             Marion*.
   2. Early minstrels of Germany - 12th and 13th
      centuries:
      a. Minnesingers (singers of love songs); German
         equivalent of the Troubadours.
   3. Meistersingers of Germany - 14th to 16th
      centuries:
      a. Were trades people, not aristocrats.
      b. Were members of music guilds which became power-
         ful and influential in Germany.
   4. Most famous Meistersinger was Hans Sachs:
      a. He was the leader of the Meistersingers in
         Nuremburg.
      b. Wagner immortalized Hans Sachs in his opera
         Die Meistersinger von Nürnberg.

E. Some Important Medieval Schools of Music:
   1. Paris University: the establishment of a school of
      music in 1100 A.D.
      a. Music was given the same status as a science.
   2. Notre Dame School of Music: established in 1150.
      a. Leo Magister Leonin 1175 A.D.
         (1) Wrote two-part organum book: *The Great Book
             of Organum*.
      b. Magnus Perotin 1183 A.D.
         (1) Expansion of organum to three and four parts.

CHAPTER 3

THE POLYPHONIC PERIOD (1100-1600)

Historical Background of the Polyphonic Period:

I. The Ars Antiqua (1100-1300) (the Late Middle Ages or the Gothic Period):

   A. Political Conditions in Europe:

      1. Until the 14th century, the feudal system was the major form of the political organization of England, France, Italy and Germany.

      2. Royal power became supreme during this period. Centralized government was achieved through the establishment of monarchies which controlled the courts, armies, taxation and appointment of civil officials.

   B. The Roman Catholic Church:

      1. The Roman Catholic Church exerted a great deal of influence during the Middle Ages.

      2. Medieval universities were created by the church for the study of theology, law, medicine and liberal arts. The church developed great scholars. The monks performed civic duties and were responsible for keeping civil records.

   C. The Crusades:

      1. From 1095 to 1291 there were eight Crusades. Christian armies fought the Moslems but the Holy Land was never liberated from Moslem control.

      2. The Crusades resulted indirectly in such developments as the exchange of goods between the Moslems and Europeans, and the exchange of intellectual and social ideas that benefited the Christians.

   D. The Roman Empire:

      1. The great Roman Empire survived during the Middle Ages. The Eastern half of the Roman Empire endured until 1453 when it fell to the Turks after the

capture of Constantinople, the capital city. The Roman Empire of the West continued to exist until Napoleon dissolved it in 1806.

E. Moslem Arabia:

1. The civilization of Moslem Arabia was at its most advanced state of development during this period.

2. The Arabians developed a highly civilized culture by means of their industrial skills, successful irrigation techniques in agriculture, and their commercial trade with Europe and the Far East.

II. The Ars Nova (1300-1500) ("The New Art" - transition from the Middle Ages to the Renaissance):

A. Political Conditions in Europe:

1. At the beginning of the 15th century, the rulers of Europe attempted to establish themselves as absolute monarchs so that by 1500, a number of dynastic states had developed in Western Europe -- England, Spain, France and Portugal.

2. The monarchs achieved territorial unification by marriage, inheritance, military conquest or by purchase.

3. The rulers of these countries were supported by the middle classes, for the kings fostered commerce and instituted laws that were beneficial to them.

B. The Hundred Years' War:

1. A series of battles took place between England and France from 1337 to 1453 that was known as the Hundred Years' War.

2. As a result of this war, England lost all of her possessions in France.

3. In 1429 Joan of Arc, the "Maid of Orleans", led the French army to victory over the English at Orleans.

C. The Black Death:

1. In 1349 and throughout the remainder of the 14th century, bubonic plague was responsible for the death of millions of people. This catastrophe is known as The Black Death.

2. As a result of this plague, labor became increasingly scarce and the workers demanded more rights. By the end of the 15th century, serfdom no longer existed in most of France, Italy and England, although it remained in central Europe.

D. Italy:

1. Italy was the commercial center of Europe in the 14th century and hence was in contact with many cultures. This commerce fostered the growth and exchange of new ideas.

2. The increased economic opportunities resulted in the rise of wealthy families (such as the Medici of Florence) who became "patrons of the arts." This is the chief reason for the birth of the Renaissance in Italy.

3. By the end of the 15th century Italy was divided into five states: Duchy of Milan, The Venetian Republic, Republic of Florence, Papal States, and Kingdom of Naples which varied in size, wealth and government.

E. Exploration:

1. In the 15th century a great period of exploration began. In 1471 the equator was crossed by Portuguese sailors.

2. Christopher Columbus, believing that the earth was a sphere, set sail for his first voyage in 1492 and discovered the West Indies.

3. In 1497, the Portuguese explorer, Vasco da Gama, sailed around Africa to reach India.

4. John Cabot, an Italian navigator, reached Nova Scotia in 1497 and Florida in 1498, which he believed was part of India.

III. The Renaissance (1500-1600):

A. Political Conditions in Europe:

1. Portugal began to colonize Brazil, her most valuable possession in the New World. In 1580 Portugal was annexed to Spain.

2. In 1588 Sir Francis Drake with thirty British ships defeated the Spanish Armada, and Britain became the dominant sea power. As a result, Spain lost some of her overseas possessions to England and Holland.

3. Ivan IV (The Terrible) (1533-1584) of Russia, established the first "zemski sobor" which was an advisory assembly of nobles, clergy and important townsmen. When the nobles tried to revolt, the "oprichnika" (first Russian secret police) destroyed those whom Ivan considered disloyal, and administered the land.

B. Protestant Reformation:

1. The Protestant Reformation was a movement which occurred during the Renaissance and was brought about by economic, political, social, intellectual as well as religious factors.

2. In France, Civil War between the Huguenots (French Protestants) and Catholics raged from 1560 to 1589. In 1589 Henry IV gave freedom of worship and full political rights to the Protestants by the Edict of Nantes.

3. Calvinism (Protestant movement led by John Calvin) spread to Switzerland, France, Holland, Scotland and England (Puritanism).

4. Lutheranism (Protestant movement led by Martin Luther) spread throughout Germany and led to open revolt in the Knights' War (1522) and the Peasants' Rebellion (1524-1525).

5. Lutheranism spread to Sweden, Finland, Norway and Denmark.

C. Catholic Counter Reformation:

1. The Council of Trent (1545-1563) was established to institute reforms that would win converts and redeem heretics.

2. The "Society of Jesus" (the Jesuits) and other religious orders were formed to help combat Protestantism through education and missionary work. The influence of the Catholic religious orders spread throughout Europe, Asia and America.

D. Exploration:

1. Ponce de Leon (Spanish) discovered Florida in 1513.

2. Vasco Nunez de Balboa (Spanish) led an expedition across the Isthmus of Panama and discovered the Pacific Ocean in 1513.

3. Hernando Cortez (Spanish) discovered Mexico in 1518.

4. Ferdinand Magellan (Spanish) circumnavigated the earth during this period.

5. Jacques Cartier (French) made a series of voyages between 1534 and 1541 and discovered and explored the valley of the St. Lawrence River in Canada.

6. Sir Walter Raleigh (English) made two unsuccessful attempts to colonize Virginia between 1584 and 1590.

Studies in Cultural Correlation - Polyphonic Period:

I. <u>Cultural Achievements</u> - <u>Social Studies</u>:

From the latter part of the Middle Ages through the Renaissance, practical economic and commercial theories evolved. Scholars wrote significant treatises on pricing, profit, interest and monopoly. Economic theories were developed which would reflect Christian morality, (e.g. The economic theory of St. Thomas Aquinas in *Summa Theoligica*).

European nations arose under strong political authorities and trade systems grew to encompass world-wide markets. The European economy changed from a feudal system to a commercial system. There was a growth of cities and towns, and new citizen classes developed -- the wealthy and influential, and also the serfs who had become free peasants and a source for cheap labor.

By 1500 the important commercial centers of Italy, England, Spain, France, Germany, Scandinavia and Russia had been established. This meant that the problem of population shifts had to be solved, new laws had to be formulated, and the divisions of a new working class had to be organized. The solutions set patterns for the future.

The outstanding political and sociological figures of the Polyphonic Period are:

1. <u>King John</u> (1167-1216) - English King: Ruled England from 1199 to 1216. In 1215 the nobles rebelled and defeated him. He was forced to sign the *Magna Carta (Great Charter)* at Runnymede, England in 1215. This document has served as one of the bases of English constitutional freedom.

2. <u>Marco Polo</u> (1256-1323) - Venetian explorer and author: Polo made journeys from Venice, Italy to China, India and other far eastern countries, and helped Kublai Khan, the Mongol ruler, destroy the Chinese Sung armies by directing the building of catapults and artillery. His vivid accounts (*Travels*) of the Far East helped to motivate exploration and discovery.

3. <u>Sir Thomas More</u> (1478-1535) - English author and statesman: More was the author of *Utopia* (the kingdom of nowhere), which attacked the evils of his society and described an ideal state modeled after *Plato's Ideal Commonwealth*. He believed in an enlightened treatment of men and women brought about through liberty, fraternity and equality. His term "utopia" has been used since to represent an ideal social or economic organization.

4. Martin <u>Luther</u> (1483-1546) - German leader of the <u>Protestant Reformation</u>: Luther initiated a movement which became involved in the political and economic development of Germany. For about sixty years, Germany was beset by civil war over religious issues until the Peace of Augsburg. This treaty settled religious differences of the German people by "who rules, his religion" (e.g. The people would automatically have to adopt their rulers' religion as their own).

5. John <u>Calvin</u> (1509-1564) - French Protestant theologian: Calvin believed that religion should be integrated with the social structure. He is sometimes called the "Protestant Pope." Calvinism spread from Switzerland to France (Huguenot Church), to Germany (Reformed Church), Scotland (Presbyterian Church) to England and America (Puritans).

II. <u>Cultural Achievements</u> - <u>Physical Sciences</u>:

Renaissance scientists developed theories based on experimentation and observation rather than the acceptance of the authority of the ancient Greeks and Romans. The outstanding scientists and inventors of the Polyphonic Period are:

1. Johannes <u>Gutenberg</u> (1398-1468) - German inventor: Gutenberg is credited with the invention of printing by use of movable type.

2. Leonardo <u>da Vinci</u> (1452-1519) - Italian scientist: Leonardo was a scientist as well as an artist. His notebook studies of astronomy and anatomy were ahead of his time and contain sketches of bridges, naval vessels, artillery, tanks, submarines and aircraft, and drawings of meteorological and geographical formations.

3. Nicholas <u>Copernicus</u> (1473-1543) - Polish astronomer: Copernicus developed the theory that the sun was the center of our solar system. His theory was a landmark for science since he was the first to use inductive reasoning (scientific method) to arrive at the truth.

4. Andreas <u>Vesalius</u> (1514-1564) - Flemish anatomist: Vesalius was the first man to describe correctly the structure of the human body. The science of anatomy as we know it today began with his studies.

5. Galileo <u>Galilei</u> (1564-1642) - Italian astronomer and physicist: Galileo improved the telescope and with it proved that the Copernican theory was correct. He experimented with falling bodies, and also derived the law of pendulum vibration.

become empirical (knowledge that is derived from experience) forming the basis for the development of modern scientific theory.

The outstanding philosophers of the Polyphonic Period are:

1. Peter Abélard (1079-1142) - French scholastic philosopher, teacher and theologian: Abélard's philosophical thinking was influenced by Aristotle. He believed that universal truths existed only as concepts of the human mind.

2. Averroes (1126-1198) - Arabian philosopher: Averroes was the last of the great Islamic philosophers. He defended the philosophy of Aristotle. Averroes was called "the Commentator" by scholastic writers. His theory of "double truth" was concerned with the possible conflict between religious and philosophical truths. He believed that religion and nature were separate and distinct.

3. Albertus Magnus (1193-1280) - German Dominican philosopher: Magnus, a tutor of Thomas Aquinas, was the first of the prominent Schoolmen. He endeavored to keep philosophy and theology distinct, and believed that the basic doctrines of Christianity could not be proved by logic alone.

4. Roger Bacon (1214-1294) - English Franciscan philosopher and scientist: Bacon considered that scientific empiricism was essential for the understanding of theology and philosophy. He taught that human experience depended on the senses and that mystical knowledge was based on divine inspiration from within.

5. Thomas Aquinas (1225-1274) - Dominican theologian and philosopher: Aquinas taught the theory of two sources of knowledge or truth -- Revelation and reason which must be harmonized. The rational theological philosophy of Aquinas replaced Augustinian theology as the official philosophy of the Roman Catholic Church during the papacy of Leo XIII.

6. Desiderios Erasmus (1466-1536) - Dutch theologian and humanist philosopher: Erasmus was the author of many theological works including the translation of the New Testament from the Greek. His *In Praise of Folly* attacked, by witty satire, the hypocrisy of his society. Erasmus' works against bigotry and intolerance were read throughout Europe.

V. Cultural Achievements - Fine Arts:

The cathedral was the most important building in the Medieval and early Renaissance Periods, for it was a place of worship, a school, and a public meeting place. In the 12th and 13th centuries the gothic style of architecture was predominant. It was characterized by ribbed vaults, thin walls, buttresses, flying buttresses, piers, pointed arches, and large stained glass windows. The structure was held erect by a perfect design of a counter-balanced framework. Gothic architecture expressed the spiritual yearning of the people.

The subjects of the paintings of the Renaissance were mainly religious although some of the German and Dutch masters painted scenes depicting everyday life. The Italian Renaissance artists received a well-rounded education which enabled them to become architects, sculptors, as well as painters.

The following artists were prominent during the Polyphonic Period:

1. Giotto di Bandone (1266-1337) - Italian painter, sculptor and architect: Giotto designed the bell tower of the Cathedral of Florence. During his time all other pictures were two dimensional in appearance, but Giotto's pictures give an illusion of three dimensional space. His paintings emphasized simplicity, dramatic feeling, and a sculptural concept of the human figure: e.g. *St. Francis Preaching to the Birds,* and *The Flight into Egypt.* He is known as the father of Italian Renaissance painting.

2. Filippo Brunelleschi (1377-1446) - Florentine architect: Brunelleschi designed and directed the construction of the octagonal and pointed dome of the Cathedral of Florence. He was the first to use the theory of optics as a basis for the artistic portrayal of space in perspective.

3. Lorenzo Ghiberti (1378-1455) - Florentine sculptor and painter: Ghiberti created twenty panels of the baptistry doors of the Cathedral of Florence (1452), called the *Gates of Paradise.* They depict biblical events.

4. Jan van Eyck (1390-1440) - Dutch painter: Van Eyck developed the method of oil painting by using varnish and oil mixtures which resulted in clear glazes. He painted religious subjects.

5. Michelangelo Buonarroti (1475-1564) - Italian painter, architect, sculptor and poet: Michelangelo was one of the world's famous sculptors. His works include the

statues of *Moses*, *David*, and his marble *Pietà*. As an architect he modified Bramante's St. Peter's in Rome. He is also famous for his frescoes in the Sistine Chapel.

6. Raphael Sanzio (1483-1520) - Italian painter: Raphael painted the tapestries of the Papal Chapel. He is famous for his paintings of the Madonna: *Sistine Madonna*, *Madonna of St. Cecilia*, and *Madonna Della Sedia*. His art reveals his great ability to organize and balance pictorial elements on a flat surface.

7. Tiziano Vecellio (Titian) (1477-1576) - Venetian painter: Titian perfected the use of rich colors in his works. He painted numerous religious and mythological pictures as well as life-like portraits. He used chiaroscuro effects and dramatized landscapes.

8. Albrecht Dürer (1471-1528) - German painter, engraver and wood-cut designer: Dürer is regarded as the inventor of etching. His woodcuts and engravings showed mythological fantasies, realistic subjects as well as philosophical ideas. His engravings, which symbolized social and religious ideas of his day, include: *The Knight, Death and the Devil*, *Melancholia*, and *Saint Jerome*.

9. Tintoretto (Jacopo Robusti) (1518-1594) - Venetian painter: Although Tintoretto was influenced by Titian (color) and Michelangelo (drawing), he developed his own style of painting. His numerous, rather elongated figures enhance the dramatic effects of his art which anticipated the Baroque style.

Music of the Polyphonic Period:

Developments Which Contributed to the Musical Culture:

General Characteristics: The music of Western Civilization became highly developed during the Polyphonic Period. A scientific approach to music composition resulted in the development of a modern style of harmony, highly integrated polyphony, the creation of many new vocal and instrumental forms, and enhanced melodic innovations through the use of chromaticism. New schools of composition appeared during this time. Religious music achieved its greatest prominence during the Polyphonic Period. At the same time, the knowledge and practice of secular music became widespread among the general public.

A. Subdivisions of the Polyphonic Period: The music of the Polyphonic Period is generally divided into three eras:

1. Ars Antiqua (1100-1300)
2. Ars Nova (1300-1500)
3. Renaissance (1500-1600)

B. Schools of Composition: The schools of composition which flourished during this period were:

1. Notre Dame School: Leading composers and theorists: Leonin (c. 1150), Perotin (1183-1236) and Franco of Cologne (1220- 1280).
2. Burgundian School: Leading composers: Guillaume Dufay (c. 1400-1474), Gilles Binchois (c. 1400-1460), and John Dunstable (c. 1370-1453).
3. Flemish School: Leading composers: Johannes Ockeghem (c. 1420-1495), Jacob Obrecht (1430-1505), Josquin des Pres (1450-1521), Jean Mouton (1475-1522), Heinrich Isaac (1450-1517), and Orlando di Lasso (1530-1594).
4. Venetian School: Leading composers: Adrian Willaert (1485-1562), Andrea Gabrieli (1510-1586), Giovanni Gabrieli (1557-1612), Cipriano de Rore (1516-1565), and Jacques Arcadelt (c. 1504-1570).
5. Roman School: Leading composers: Marc Antonio Ingegneri (1545-1592), Giovanni Pierluigi da Palestrina (1525-1594), and Felice Anerio (1560-1614).
6. Spanish School: Leading composers: Cristobal Morales (1500-1553) and Tomas Luis de Victoria (1548-1611).
7. English School: Leading composers: Thomas Tallis (1505-1585), William Byrd (1543-1623), John Bull (1562-1628), and Orlando Gibbons (1583-1625).
8. German School: Leading composers: Jacob Gallus (Handl) (1550-1591), and Ludwig Senfl (c. 1492-1555).

C. Elements of Music: The elements of music underwent various stages of development. The characteristics of this development are as follows:

1. Melody: Melodic movement of Renaissance polyphony was freer as compared to the strict parallel motion of the voice parts used during the Middle Ages. The use of the five line music staff and solfa syllables occurred during this period. Imitative writing (rounds) was popular in choral singing.

2. Harmony: The texture of polyphonic music during the Renaissance was horizontal. Towards the end of this period, vertical relationships of harmony came into use when triads were introduced in the accompaniment. Lutheran chorales also revealed harmonic relationships. Major and minor modes began to be emphasized in the development of a more tonal style of harmony.
3. Rhythm: Regular meter was not observed in early polyphonic music. Gradually, measured time was brought into use. One of the most important developments in rhythm was the use of the isorhythmic principle (repeated pattern of note values). Time signatures and bar lines came into regular use at a later period.

D. Vocal Music: Polyphonic vocal music in the modal style achieved the highest degree of perfection during this period. Some of the most important types of vocal composition of the Polyphonic Period are:

1. Mass: Setting of the Liturgy - developed in polyphonic style - themes taken from plain chant (a sacred melody in free rhythm).
2. Motet: Sacred non-liturgical composition - often makes use of imitation with a different melody for each line of the text.
3. Madrigal: A secular dramatic composition for a small group of singers.
4. Chanson: A secular French song often written in three-part form.
5. Chorale: A hymn sung by the congregation during the Lutheran Church service.
6. Rondel: A type of round which was later developed into the canon.
7. Anthem: A sacred English composition, which developed from the motet.
8. Frottola: An Italian secular song in homophonic style with the melody in the upper part.

E. Instruments of the Polyphonic Period: Instruments of the early Polyphonic Period were primarily used to accompany singing or dancing. When used with singing, the instruments often duplicated the voice parts. The instruments used at this time are as follows, with the modern equivalents shown in parenthesis:

1. Keyboard Instruments: The two most prominent keyboard instruments of this era included the clavichord and harpsichord. They originated in the latter half of the 14th century and came into general use in the 15th century.

2. String Instruments: The most common string instruments of this era included the lute (similar to the
   guitar) and instruments of the viol family: viola
   da braccio (viola), viola da gamba (cello) and the
   basso di camera (double-bass).
3. Wind Instruments: The most prominent woodwind instruments of this period included the oboe, the
   shawm, transverse flute and the recorder. The brass
   instruments included the valveless trumpets and
   horns.

F. Instrumental Music Forms: During the Polyphonic Period
   music composed for instruments alone were called
   sonatas. Among the important instrumental compositions
   are:

   1. Pavane: A slow dance in 4/4 time.
   2. Galliard: A fast dance in 3/4 time.
   3. Allemande: A medium fast dance in 2/4 time.
   4. Fantasia: A dance in free form with embellishments.
   5. Toccata: A composition which displays technical
      agility.
   6. Estampie: A dance form with variations in metrical
      rhythm.

GUILLERMUS DUFAY

Composer: Guillermus Dufay
    Born: Hainault, Holland 1400
    Died: Cambrai, Holland 1474

Aural Recognition of Themes:
    Composition: *L'Homme Armé Mass* (1450)

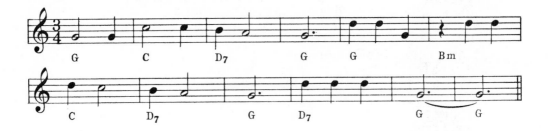

General Information about Composer and Compositions:

1. In his youth Guillermus Dufay sang in the choir of the
   Cathedral at Cambrai and was later transferred to the
   Papal Choir in Rome. While he was a choir member at the
   Cathedral of Cambrai, he composed a song celebrating
   the court marriage of two celebrities Charles Malatesti
   and Vittoria di Lorenzo Colonna which took place in 1416.

2. He studied for the priesthood and was ordained at Paris
   in 1436. He became Canon of the Cathedral of Cambrai in
   1437. He was later appointed Canon of the Cathedral of
   Bruges. He lived in Savoy from 1438 to 1444. In 1445 he
   again accepted the post of Canon of the Cathedral at
   Cambrai which he held until his death in 1474.

3. In 1443 he was engaged as music tutor to the son of
   Phillipe le Bon, Duke of Burgundy. During this period
   he composed the motet *Ave Regina Coelorum* which was
   performed in the chapel after his death.

4. Dufay was considered the leader and founder of the early
   Flemish school of polyphonic music. He improved the
   musical notation as it existed at that time.

5. His music consisted mainly of contrapuntal pieces. He composed masses, magnificats, motets, and was especially famous for his chansons.

Composer's Main Contribution to the Art of Music:

1. Guillermus Dufay substituted the more appealing secular melodies of that time for the Gregorian chants of the Mass. Some of these melodies were adopted from folk tunes. By the use of a simpler method of writing harmony and counterpoint, he improved vocal polyphony. This resulted in more interesting and colorful four-part choral and instrumental composition. The teachings of Dufay and his contemporaries of the early Flemish school of polyphonic music made a marked impression on the culture of northern Europe.

Suggested Listening:

1. Title: *Hymns, Choruses and Songs, Sacred and Secular*
   Performers: Capella Cordina - Planchart
   Record No.: Lyrichord 7233
   Grade Level: 4 - 8

2. Title: *Motets*
   Performers: Capella Cordina - Planchart
   Record No.: Lyrichord 7233
   Grade Level: 7 - 12

Optional Assignments:

1. Guillermus Dufay was especially noted for his chansons. Do some research on this music form and explain it to the class.

2. Choose one of the topics we have discussed under general information and see what you can find out about it in other books. Give an oral report of your findings to the class.

3. After doing some research, write a report on some of the historical events taking place in Europe during the lifetime of the composer.

4. Make up words for the melody of the composer notated in the section, Aural Recognition of Themes, and sing as a solo for the class.

5. Using only a skeleton outline, tell the class about an interesting musical event you have attended recently.

JOHANN OCKEGHEM

<u>Composer</u>: Johann Ockeghem
    Born: Termonde, Flanders 1430
    Died: Tours, Flanders 1495

<u>Aural Recognition of Themes</u>:
    Composition: Agnus Dei from the Mass
                Missa Mi-mi (1467)

General Information about Composer and Compositions:

1. In 1444, as a youth, Johann Ockeghem sang in the choir of Antwerp Cathedral. He became a member of the court of Duke Charles of Bourbon at Moulins, France in 1446. In 1449 he studied composition with Dufay. From 1454 to 1461 he was the first Chaplain to the King of France. He was a favorite composer of the royal family and is said to have provided musical services for three kings of France over a period of forty years.

2. He was the founder of the new Netherlands School of Composition, and was its first great teacher. Josquin des Pres was one of his well-known pupils.

3. He invented many contrapuntal devices and developed the canon to a high degree of perfection. His works were a large contribution to the advancement of the music of that period.

4. Since music printing was not invented until the beginning of the sixteenth century, Ockeghem's music was not printed until after his death.

5. Ockeghem's high degree of contrapuntal achievement is displayed in all his compositions, which include masses, motets, chansons and canons.

Composer's Main Contribution to the Art of Music:

1. Ockeghem contributed to the development of polyphony (the combination of two or more independent melodies). He and his pupils of the Netherlands School of composition developed contrapuntal techniques such as imitation, obbligato counterpoint, inversion, augmentation, diminution, and canonic imitation which are still used today. His fame as a teacher is unparalleled. His composing techniques were disseminated throughout Europe by his pupils and followers.

Suggested Listening:

1. Title: *Chansons, Missa Caput*
   Performers: Capella Cordina - Planchart
   Record No.: Lyrichord 7213
   Grade Level: 4 - 8

2. Title: *Missa Mi-mi* and *Chanson Fors Seulement*
   Performers: Berkeley Choral Singers - Zes
   Record No.: Lyrichord LYR 108
   Grade Level: 7 - 12

Optional Assignments:

1. Lead a class discussion on the composer's life and music. Prepare an outline for this purpose.

2. During the life span of Johann Ockeghem, America was discovered by Christopher Columbus. Write a paper on the events leading up to and following the discovery of America.

3. After you have studied the references available at your library, write a report on the famous scientists of the Polyphonic Period.

4. Create a musical crossword puzzle or make up a quiz using information about the composer and his works.

5. Let a member of the class who belongs to a church choir learn a hymn and sing it for the class. Teach this hymn to the class and have them sing it.

JOSQUIN DES PRES

Composer: Josquin des Pres
    Born: Conde, Burgundy 1445
    Died: Brussels, Belgium 1521

Aural Recognition of Themes:
    Composition: Motet *Tu Pauperum Refugium* (1502)

General Information about Composer and Compositions:

1. Josquin des Pres' early training in music was received at the Collegiate Church of St. Quentin and he later continued his studies privately with the great Flemish composer Johann Ockeghem.

2. He was idolized by his contemporary composers. Martin Luther said: "Josquin des Pres is the master of the notes". His achievements in music were compared with Michelangelo's accomplishments in art.

3. In the composing of religious compositions, Josquin des Pres sometimes used secular tunes that were popular at that time. The composers of this period had no qualms about using beautiful and melodious themes, although they were not original.

4. He spent much of his life in the service of royalty, composing and performing for them. He performed at the court of the Sforza family in Milan in 1475; was a member of the Papal Choir from 1486 - 1494; then was commissioned by Duke Hercules of Ferrara to compose the *Miserere* in 1495; and served Louis XII of France in 1515.

5. He composed masses, motets and secular songs. Some of his compositions are: *Mater Patris* (1516) from third book of masses, and *Stabat Mater* (1502) from book of motets.

Composer's Main Contribution to the Art of Music:

1. Josquin des Pres was the leading composer of the Flemish school of polyphonic composition. He was a master of the art of melodic and contrapuntal writing. His music is typical of the Renaissance in its sensitive expression of warmth, beauty and emotion. His use of simple, clear, concise, yet expressive melodies and harmonic devices contributed to the beauty of polyphonic music. That musicians and composers of his time referred to him as the "Father of Musicians" is a great tribute to his genius. The development of contrapuntal writing reached a high degree of perfection in his music.

Suggested Listening:

1. Title: *Motets and Instrumental Pieces*
   Performers: New York Pro Musica - Greenberg
   Record No.: Decca 9410
   Grade Level: 4 - 8

2. Title: *Choral Works*
   Performers: Dessoff Chorus - Boepple
   Record No.: Turnabout 34437
   Grade Level: 7 - 12

Optional Assignments:

1. Investigate and write a report on the qualifications and training required of a choir boy in a church.

2. Josquin des Pres was compared to the great artist Michelangelo. Prepare an outline and give an oral report to the class on the life and works of Michelangelo.

3. The composers of the polyphonic period often used melodies that were not original. How does the copyright law of today protect the music of a composer? Write a report on this subject.

4. Using only a skeleton outline, tell the class about an interesting musical event that you attended recently.

5. After listening to a selection by Josquin des Pres, write a critique, and compare his music with another composer of the polyphonic period.

MARTIN LUTHER

Composer: Martin Luther
    Born: Eisleben, Germany 1483
    Died: Eisleben, Germany 1546

Aural Recognition of Themes:
    Composition: Christmas Carol *Away In A Manger* (1524)

General Information about Composer and Compositions:

1. As a youth, Martin Luther studied for the priesthood and was ordained in 1507. He was appointed professor of theology at the University of Wittenberg. He became a reformist and in 1517 broke away from the Roman Catholic Church. He introduced the Protestant Reformation and was the founder of the Lutheran Church.

2. Martin Luther had an excellent voice; he was a self-educated musician. His hymns and chorales contain old folk tunes as well as original melodies.

3. Luther played original melodies for his chorales on his flute and his contemporary Johann Walther notated the melodies. With this collaboration they wrote and adapted hymns for church services.

4. He felt that music was an important part of the church service. He believed that the congregation should take a more active part in the music of the church service.

5. He was a famous composer of hymns, he initiated the use

of church chorales. His first book of chorales was published in 1524, and his best known chorale A *Mighty
Fortress* was published in 1529.

Composer's Main Contribution to the Art of Music:

1. Martin Luther, the founder of the Lutheran church, was
   noted as the originator of congregational singing during
   the church service. Using his ability as a singer and
   composer, he wrote many hymns that are still performed
   today as part of the Protestant church service. Many of
   the melodies of his chorales are adaptations of the
   secular and folk songs of the period. He composed his
   chorales and hymns to be sung in unison, without accompaniment. At a later time his hymns were arranged for
   four part singing.

Suggested Listening:

1. Title: *A Mighty Fortress*
   Performers: Robert Shaw Chorale
   Record No.: R.C.A. Victor LM-2199
   Grade Level: 4 - 8

2. Title: *Great Lutheran Hymns*
   Performers: The Festival Singers - Dale Warland
   Record No.: Lutheran Records RF 6903
   Grade Level: 7 - 12

Optional Assignments:

1. Johann Walther collaborated with Martin Luther in writing
   hymns. Do some research on the life and music of Johann
   Walther, prepare an outline, and give an oral report to
   the class.

2. From the historical point of view, write a report on the
   Lutheran Reformation.

3. Do some research on the chorale and hymn; describe these
   music forms and their characteristics to the class.

4. If you sing or play a musical instrument, select a composition of Luther and perform it for the class.

5. Luther played the lute, which was a string instrument of
   the polyphonic period. Make a notebook of pictures and
   information about the lute and other instruments of this
   period.

GIOVANNI PIERLUIGI DA PALESTRINA

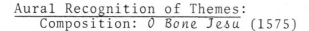

Composer: Giovanni Pierluigi da Palestrina
    Born: Palestrina, Italy 1526
    Died: Rome, Italy 1594

Aural Recognition of Themes:
    Composition: *O Bone Jesu* (1575)

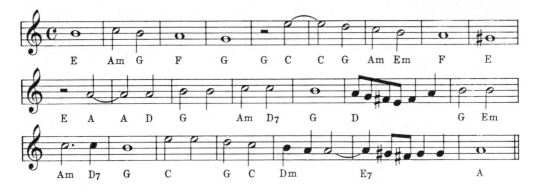

General Information about Composer and Compositions:

1. Historical records concerning Palestrina's youth are very
   skimpy. It is believed that he studied music at the
   Frenchman Goudemel's school in Rome around 1540. In 1544
   he became music director of the Cathedral in his native
   town where he sang, taught and played the organ.

2. In 1555 he became choirmaster at St. John Lateran Church
   (Rome) and Julian Chapel. He was a member of the Sistine
   Choir, and later was appointed composer for the Sistine
   Chapel.

3. Palestrina was the greatest composer of the Renaissance
   period, having composed a large amount of liturgical
   music for the Roman Catholic Church. He is credited with
   the perfection of sacred polyphonic music.

4. Previous to Palestrina's time, the Church used secular
   (popular) melodies to accompany religious services. Pope
   Gregory XIII commissioned Palestrina to compose appropriate liturgical music for the Church Mass.

5. Palestrina is noted for his masses. He composed about one
   hundred of them. His most famous Mass was *Missa Papae*

36

Marcelli (Pope Marcellus Mass), (1567), dedicated to that pontiff. He also composed over five hundred motets, several books of madrigals, and many other religious compositions.

Composer's Main Contribution to the Art of Music:

1. Giovanni Pierluigi da Palestrina was known as "The Prince of Music" by his contemporaries. He achieved the perfection of church music. He was an adherent of the Roman school of polyphony which advocated strict liturgical style of writing. He avoided the use of secular and folk melodies. His conservative, systematic and formal style of composition gave his music the purity of style required by the church.

Suggested Listening:

1. Title: *Missa Papae Marcelli*
   Performers: Wagner Chorale
   Record No.: Angel S 36022
   Grade Level: 4 - 8

2. Title: *Choral Works*
   Performers: Wagner Chorale
   Record No.: Angel S 36013
   Grade Level: 7 - 12

Optional Assignments:

1. Write a report on the historical developments of the Mass of the Roman Catholic Church.

2. The churches of Italy are architectural masterpieces. Prepare an outline and give an oral report on the art and architecture of one of the churches in which Palestrina worked.

3. Write a report on the Renaissance period in general. Explain the political and economic conditions which prevailed during this period of revival.

4. Palestrina is credited with the perfection of sacred polyphonic music. Select another composer of polyphonic music and lead a class discussion of his works.

5. List some events in the field of art and poetry during this period.

ORLANDO DI LASSO

Composer: Orlando di Lasso
   Born: Mons, Belgium 1530
   Died: Munich, Germany 1594

Aural Recognition of Themes:
   Composition: Chanson *Bon Jour, Mon Coeur* (1555)

General Information about Composer and Compositions:

1. As a young boy Orlando di Lasso possessed a beautiful
   voice and sang in the choir of St. Nicholas Church at
   Mons, Belgium. At the age of nine, he was taken to the
   court of Ferdinand Gonzaga, the Viceroy of Sicily, in
   whose choir he sang.

2. In 1543 he became choirmaster at St. John Lateran Church
   in Rome for one year. Later he was appointed director of
   choral music (1557-1594) for Duke Albert of Munich. He
   trained a group of singers, composing for them and providing music for evening concerts and Sunday chapel
   services.

3. Orlando di Lasso was a contemporary of Palestrina who
   also wrote polyphonic music. He was the last and most
   important of the Flemish composers.

4. Palestrina's music consisted of a smooth, flowing interpretation of the text, while Lasso's music gave emphasis
   displaying sudden changes in melody and harmony to
   climactic words of the text.

5. Lasso is credited with the composition of over twenty-five hundred works. He composed motets, madrigals, and songs (Italian canzones and French chansons). His greatest work is the musical setting of the *Seven Penitential Psalms* (1563).

Composer's Main Contribution to the Art of Music:

1. Orlando di Lasso was a master of the polyphonic style used by the composers of several countries. He composed French chansons, Italian madrigals and German secular songs. His great talent enabled him to write over fifteen hundred compositions of both secular and religious music. He was considered the most prolific and representative composer of the Flemish school.

Suggested Listening:

1. Title: *Motets*
   Performers: Hahn
   Record No.: Nonesuch 71084
   Grade Level: 4 - 8

2. Title: *Madrigals*
   Performers: Pro Musica- Greenberg, N.Y.
   Record No.: Decca 79424
   Grade Level: 7 - 12

Optional Assignments:

1. Orlando di Lasso was a Flemish composer. Write a report on another well-known Flemish composer.

2. After a study, write a report on the type of musical activities in which Lasso was engaged for Duke Albert of Munich.

3. Lasso is credited with developing the Munich Library. Give an oral report to the class on this development.

4. Write a composition on the history and development of the French chanson.

5. Lasso received honors from the Pope and other people. Do some research and give an oral report on this topic.

WILLIAM BYRD

Composer: William Byrd
    Born: Lincoln, England 1543
    Died: Stondon, England 1623

Aural Recognition of Themes:
    Composition: *Ave Verum* (1588)

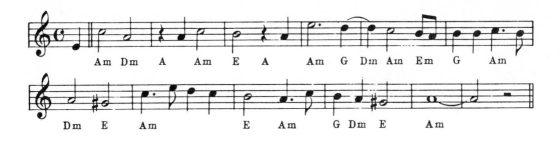

General Information about Composer and Compositions:

1. As a youth, William Byrd attended St. Paul's School in Lincolnshire. He was a protege of Thomas Tallis (his godfather) who was a famous composer of the Polyphonic period. Byrd was a contemporary of Palestrina and was considered the foremost English composer and organist of his time.

2. At the age of twenty he was appointed organist at Lincoln Cathedral. He attained fame also as a teacher of the organ, and Queen Elizabeth was one of his pupils. She was so impressed with his compositions that she granted him the exclusive right to print and sell music.

3. He became known as the "English Palestrina" because of the excellence of his liturgical compositions. He was well known for his madrigals and keyboard arrangements of English music. Byrd was probably the first Englishman to compose madrigals.

4. Byrd was also one of the first composers to give atten - tion to keyboard music for harpsichord and virginal. Among the more famous of these compositions are: Fantasia *The*

Leaves Be Green for harpsichord (1589) and *The Bells* for virginal (1612).

5. He developed the idea of theme with variations; also he was probably the first composer to write violin, viola and cello music. He paved the way for chamber music composition.

Composer's Main Contribution to the Art of Music:

1. Although William Byrd wrote a large amount of church music, he is known today for his madrigals and keyboard pieces. He was the founder of the English School of madrigal composers. He was known as the "Parent of British music".

Suggested Listening:

1. Title: *William Byrd Suite*
   Performers: Eastman Wind Ensemble - Fennell
   Record No.: Mercury 50197
   Grade Level: 4 - 8

2. Title: *Mass in Three Parts*
   Performers: King's College Chorus - Willcocks
   Record No.: Argo 5362
   Grade Level: 7 - 12

Optional Assignments:

1. Make a notebook on the life and music of William Byrd; include original illustrations and a written report.

2. Byrd was one of the first composers to write madrigals. Do some research and write a report on the madrigal in general, and discuss another composer of madrigals.

3. Create a musical crossword puzzle, or make up a quiz, using information about the composer.

4. Do some research into the exclusive patent for printing music that Byrd received from Queen Elizabeth; give an oral report to the class on this subject.

5. Byrd paved the way for the writing of chamber music. Give an oral report to the class on chamber music; include well-known composers of this type of composition.

TOMÁS LUIS DE VICTORIA

<u>Composer</u>: Tomás Luis de Victoria
   <u>Born:</u> Avila, Spain 1548
   <u>Died:</u> Madrid, Spain 1611

<u>Aural Recognition of Themes:</u>
   Composition: *O Magnum Mysterium* (1572)
           excerpt from motet

<u>General Information about Composer and Compositions:</u>

1. Tomás Luis de Victoria received his early musical training as a choirboy in the Cathedral of Avila. In 1565 he
   went to Rome where he studied composition with Palestrina
   and was markedly influenced by him. He became a Roman
   Catholic priest who devoted his life to the composition
   of church music. He became music director of the Roman
   Seminary, a post which Palestrina originally held.

2. In 1566 he was engaged both as chaplain and as a singer
   at the Collegium Germanicum in Rome. During this period
   he composed masses, magnificats, and motets, some of
   which he dedicated to Duke Ernest of Bavaria. This enhanced
   Victoria's prestige and reputation as a composer in
   Germany.

3. In 1595 he became chaplain to Empress Maria of Spain. He
   dedicated many works to the Empress, and he composed the
   famous *Requiem Mass* for her funeral in 1603.

4. His style of composition is like that of Palestrina, but
   has much dramatic quality in it, a typical Spanish trait.
   A good example of this is heard in his motet *O Vos Omnes*.
   It is often said that the music of Palestrina can be

compared to the art of Raphael, whereas Victoria's music can be compared to the artistic works of El Greco.

5. Victoria composed many types of religious music, including masses, motets, magnificats, hymns, psalms and sequences.

Composer's Main Contribution to the Art of Music:

1. Although he was a Spanish composer by birth, Tomás Luis de Victoria belonged to the Roman school of polyphonic music. Like Palestrina, he directed his efforts towards the perfection of church music. He added an emotional and dramatic quality to his music that can be attributed to his Spanish origin. His music is more dramatic, vivid and imaginative than the music of Palestrina.

Suggested Listening:

1. Title: *Motets and Choral Works*
   Performers: Saint John's College Choir
   Record No.: Argo ZRG-620
   Grade Level: 4 - 8

2. Title: *O Magnum Mysterium*
   Performers: Hill Chorus
   Record No.: Orion 7022
   Grade Level: 7 - 12

Optional Assignments:

1. After a study, write a report on the qualifications and educational training required to become a Roman Catholic priest in the United States.

2. Write an historical background of the period during which Victoria lived.

3. Make a study of the music required for Roman Catholic Church services and give an oral report to the class on this subject.

4. Listen to a recording of Victoria and listen also to a recording of Palestrina. Write a report comparing the styles of these two composers.

5. Make an historical investigation of the Papacy in Rome from its inception to the present day. Prepare an outline and present an oral report to the class.

GIOVANNI GABRIELI

Composer: Giovanni Gabrieli
  Born: Venice, Italy 1557
  Died: Venice, Italy 1612

Aural Recognition of Themes:
  Composition: excerpt from sacred song
          Jubilate Deo (1597)

General Information about Composer and Compositions:

1. Giovanni Gabrieli's early musical training consisted of music lessons with his famous uncle, Andrea Gabrieli, who was one of the leaders of the Venetian school of composition. From 1575-1579 he lived in Munich where he assisted and studied with Orlando de Lasso. He became the first organist at St. Mark's in Venice in 1585. He was a renowned organ teacher, and one of his pupils was the famous organist Heinrich Schuetz.

2. He was a notable composer of the Venetian school. He composed both vocal and instrumental music. His vocal music was antiphonal (composed for from two to five choirs combined). The architecture of St. Mark's Church facilitated the performance of antiphonal choirs.

3. Although Gabrieli never left Venice during his lifetime, his music became well known throughout the world through the efforts of his pupils and followers.

4. He was the first composer to indicate dynamics (loud, soft etc.) in his musical scores. He was also the first to combine choral groups and orchestra. He wrote separate parts for the instruments of the orchestra, although it

was the custom of that period for the instrumentalists to read from the choral parts.

5. He composed madrigals, motets, and sonatas. Some of his better-known compositions are: *Sonata pian'e forte* (1587) motet for instruments, and *Sacrae symphoniae* (1597) for both voices and instruments.

Composer's Main Contribution to the Art of Music:

1. Giovanni Gabrieli was known, during his time, as "The Father of Orchestration" by the composers of the Venetian school. He devised a new style of instrumental writing that was completely independent of the style of vocal writing. His musical genius is displayed in his antiphonal style, combining four or five choruses with instrumental accompaniment. He was the first composer to assign dynamic markings to his compositions. Gabrieli achieved another first in the composition of secular and religious music for the organ.

Suggested Listening:

1. Title: *Canzoni for Brass Choirs*
   Performers: New York Brass Quintet
   Record No.: Golden Crest S-4023
   Grade Level: 7 - 12

2. Title: *Music for Organ and Brass*
   Performers: N.E. Brass Ensemble - Biggs, Burgin
   Record No.: Columbia MS 6117
   Grade Level: 4 - 8

Optional Assignments:

1. Make a study of the architecture and historical background of the famous churches of Italy. Write a report and include pictures and illustrations.

2. Gabrieli was one of the greatest composers of the Venetian school of musicians. Make a study of other composers of this period who were members of the Venetian school.

3. The brass instruments of this period did not have valves for the playing of chromatic pitches (similar to present day bugles). Study and give an oral report to the class.

4. Make up words for the above composition and sing as a solo for the class.

5. Make a study of the historical background of this period and write a report on the cultural achievements in areas other than music.

JOHN BULL

Composer: John Bull
    Born: Somersetshire, England 1562
    Died: Antwerp, Belgium 1628

Aural Recognition of Themes:
    Composition: Harpsichord piece
                 The King's Hunt (1623)

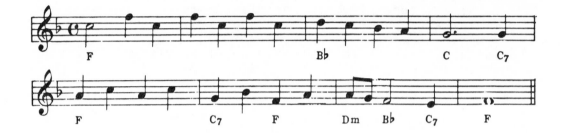

General Information about Composer and Compositions:

1. As a boy, John Bull studied music at the Chapel Royal
   under the tutelage of William Blitheman. He later studied composition at Oxford University in England and
   received his bachelor and doctorate degrees in music.
   On the recommendation of Queen Elizabeth he was assigned
   the post of professor of music at Gresham College.

2. He was appointed organist at the Hereford Cathedral in
   1582, and later became choir director. From 1617-1628
   he was organist at Notre Dame Cathedral in Antwerp.

3. Historians have called John Bull "The Franz Liszt of the
   Polyphonic Period" because of his great contribution to
   the virtuosity of harpsichord music. Many of his compositions are contained in the *Fitzwilliam Virginal Book*
   (1620). Ornamentation in composition was his forte.

4. He travelled extensively in Europe and performed for
   royalty. He left England in 1601 because of ill health
   and eventually settled in Antwerp, Belgium where he died
   in 1628. He was buried at Notre Dame Cathedral in
   Antwerp.

5. He wrote both vocal and instrumental compositions consisting of anthems, canons, organ music, and also music for the virginal and harpsichord.

Composer's Main Contribution to the Art of Music:

1. John Bull was an excellent performer on the virginal and organ, and he composed a prodigious amount of virtuoso music for these instruments. He contributed immensely to the development of the technique for the playing of the virginal and organ. A well-coordinated and fascile technique is required to perform his works which include animated scale passages, complex rhythms, and many other technical innovations.

Suggested Listening:

1. Title: *Keyboard Music*
   Performers: Dart - Harpsichord Soloist
   Record No.: Oiseau 255
   Grade Level: 4-8

2. Title: *Works for Viols, Virginal, Organ*
   Performers: Jeans
   Record No.: Archive 198472
   Grade Level: 7 - 12

Optional Assignments:

1. John Bull earned a doctor's degree in music. Do some research and write a paper containing the requirements for a doctorate at our American universities.

2. Make a study of the organ and explain to the class the mechanism of this instrument and how it produces musical sounds.

3. Make an historical survey of the Church of England during this period, and write a paper on this subject.

4. Make a list of composers who wrote music for the organ and list their most famous compositions.

5. Make a study of the famous literary geniuses of this period and write a composition on this topic.

CHAPTER 4

THE BAROQUE PERIOD (1600-1750)

Historical Background of the Baroque Period:

I. Introduction: The term "Baroque Age" came from the language of art and it refers to the type of culture of that period. In the arts, "baroque" (from the Portuguese language meaning "an irregular shaped pearl") is characterized by its theatrical, elaborate, and grandiose style.

In the 17th century trends were being established which would culminate in the development of democracy. Two things stand out in this historical period: the rise of England as a world power through her acquisition of colonies and territories, and the growth of France as the cultural center of Europe.

A. France:

1. Cardinal Richelieu, minister of King Louis XIII (1610-1642), increased the King's power and decreased the authority of the nobles and French Huguenots. France became the leading power of Europe by aiding the Protestant centers during the Thirty Years' War.

2. Under the guidance of his minister Cardinal Mazarin, King Louis XIV (1643-1715) destroyed the power of the nobles in the War of the Fronde and became an absolute ruler with no check on his power. Jean Baptiste Colbert, financial minister, made France prosperous by his direction of economic development.

3. Classical culture reached its height during the reign of Louis XIV. He encouraged the development of painting, architecture, music, and literature by giving royal commissions and pensions to his court to men of achievement from France, Italy, and other European countries. The French court became the center of the arts during his reign.

4. In 1685, King Louis XIV revoked the Edict of Nantes which had protected the Huguenots, causing many to leave France and go to England, Germany, and

America. The French industry and economy suffered because the Huguenots were the skilled laborers.

5. Louis XIV, through the encouragement of his war minister, Louvois, proceeded to wage a series of aggressive wars involving many countries of Europe. This left France with her revenues depleted and no longer a dominant power in Europe.

B. Germany:

1. At the beginning of the 17th century the German Empire was completely disorganized. The strife between those who favored Lutheranism and those who supported the Catholic Counter-Reformation resulted in a Civil War, the Thirty Years' War (1618-1648). The treaty of the Peace of Westphalia (1648) was significant for it confirmed the political changes which occurred during the war.

2. The German state of Brandenburg was ruled by the Hohenzollern line of rulers called Electors. They developed a centralized government and the most powerful and best disciplined army in Europe. Frederick William Hohenzollern I (1640-1688), the Great Elector, obtained control of the region between Brandenburg and Prussia. His son, William II, united all the various states and called them Prussia.

3. In the War of the Austrian Succession (1740-1748), Frederick the Great (1740-1786) seized Silesia from Austria. He fought off attempts by Austria to regain it in the Seven Years War (1756-1763) which involved England, Prussia, France, and Austria.

4. Frederick the Great made Prussia one of the most powerful countries of Europe. He developed education, industry and public works. Many philosophers, artists, and composers visited his court. Germany now became the center of culture.

C. Russia:

1. Peter Romanov, or Peter the Great (1682-1725), succeeded in making Russia a great empire. He tried to Europeanize or modernize Russia and introduced many new reforms in dress, industry, science, commerce, agriculture, education, and military science. He built a new westernized capital of Russia, St. Petersburg (1703).

D. **England**:

1. With the death of the Tudor Queen Elizabeth (1603), James VI of Scotland (or James I of England) became king establishing the Stuart line of rulers. Both England and Scotland were now ruled by the same king.

2. The Puritan Revolution (1642-1648) caused by religious, political, economic, and social conditions broke out in England. The Puritans, led by Oliver Cromwell, defeated the Cavaliers (the forces of the king). Cromwell gradually assumed military and religious dictatorship of the country and dissolved Parliament. The Puritan austerities were very unpopular with the people. As a result, on the death of Cromwell, the English people restored the Stuart line of Kings by making Charles II king. The staid Puritan social life became transformed to a happy and gay one. Music, literature, and the drama of the theater reflected a merry England.

3. James II, who followed Charles II as king, was replaced by William of Orange and Mary of Scotland as rulers of England as requested by Parliament. A major political revolution took place with no bloodshed and was called the "Glorious Revolution". Parliament passed the Bill of Rights (1689) which limited the powers of the king and gave rights to the people. The civil liberties from this bill are included in the first ten amendments of the United States Constitution. The Glorious Revolution resulted in the establishment of Parliament as the governing body of England which has endured to this day.

E. **Italy**:

1. During the Baroque Period, the Italian peninsula was subdivided into areas that were ruled by Spain, Austria, and other small independent states that had allied themselves with various European countries.

2. Chronologically the development of the Baroque style coincided with the Catholic Counter Reformation. The Catholic Church attempted a spiritual revival. Instrumental in this movement was the Jesuit order which founded churches, schools, and used the arts to inspire religious feeling. The Roman baroque style followed the Jesuits and spread to all parts of Europe.

3. In Florence a group of poets, philosophers and musicians assembled and developed the early opera,
recitative and oratorio. This group was known as
the Florentine Camerata.

4. Despite Italy's political chaotic state she exerted
a tremendous influence on the development of art,
music, literature and science. Bologna, Florence
and Venice were art centers during the 17th century.
Rome was also important in influencing sacred music,
operas, cantatas, literature and other arts.

F. Colonization:

1. By the 17th century Spain's and Portugal's colonization began decreasing because of the fading political and economic conditions.

2. The Dutch set a standard for colonization in the
New World by their development of New Amsterdam
(1604) which had the best harbor. They had great
commercial skill but failed in colonization because
prosperity reigned in the Netherlands and a suf-
ficient number of settlers could not be encouraged
to migrate to the colonies.

3. The French failed in the colonization of the New
World because they picked an unfavorable position.
In 1608 the French founded Quebec in the St.
Lawrence River Valley and confined themselves to
this area because of the friendly Huron Indians.
The Huron and Iroquois Indians were mutual enemies.
If the French had been friendly with the Iroquois
they could have blocked the English settlements.

4. The English succeeded in colonization because of
friendly aid from the Indians. Englishmen, who were
motivated by religious persecution, sheer love of
adventure and also by economic and political re-
wards, migrated to the American continent where they
founded thirteen colonies along the Atlantic coast.

Studies in Cultural Correlation - Baroque Period:

I. Cultural Achievements - Social Studies:

The Age of Louis XIV marked the Baroque Period in
France. The court life of Louis XIV put an end to crude-
ness, for the noblemen of the French court were polished

and refined. Every court in Europe and even the colonial planter aristocracy tried to imitate the social graces of the French court.

Women played a prominent part in the court of Louis XIV. Elegantly dressed and famous women presided over the important social institution of France - the salon which had been imported from Italy. At these gatherings music, poetry, drama, prose and art were cultivated in the grand and exaggerated Baroque style. This style was inspired by Italian classical themes, ideas and methods.

The Baroque Period was also a period of war and dissension. The many political problems such as the relation of the king to the government, the development of a cabinet system of government with a party system produced new and different political theories.

The following men influenced social and political development:

1. Thomas Hobbes (1588-1679) - English philosopher: Hobbes was the political philosopher of the Stuarts. His political philosophy was completely materialistic. His social philosophy taught that if man were uncivilized he would be in a state of war. Since man could not tolerate lawlessness and feared it to avoid destruction, he would make a social contract to protect himself. This stable society, which he called the "Leviathan" would have only the necessary powers which a government would need to maintain order. Hobbes' principal works include: *Leviathan* (1651), and *On Man* (1658).

2. Hugo Grotius (1583-1645) - Dutch statesman and writer: Grotius wrote the first treatise on international law: *On the Law of War and Peace*. This was based on Roman laws and established a theory of certain natural rights. Grotius believed that the fundamental purpose of the natural law of man was concerned with the protection of his social life.

3. Jean Baptiste Colbert (1619-1685) - French statesman: Colbert became controller general of finances in 1661, under King Louis XIV. He is most famous for his system of mercantilism which was used to increase commerce and industry, and help regulate the economy. His policies helped France to become a leading power. He influenced King Louis XIV in subsidizing the arts and men of literature which helped to make the French court the most cultured in Europe.

4. John Locke (1632-1704) - English philosopher: Locke was a great philosophical crusader for democracy. He wrote *Two Treatises of Government* (1690) which justified the English Glorius Revolution of 1688. He believed in freedom of thought and speech, and in the natural rights of man including individual liberties. He influenced the great philosophers Berkeley, Hume, Rousseau, Voltaire and the American Founding Fathers. The *Declaration of Independence*, was based on Locke's *Two Treatises of Government*.

5. Baron Charles de Montesquieu (1689-1755) - French political writer and philosopher: Montesquieu preferred a limited government with a system of checks and balances as in the British Constitution which prevents either the king or the people from gaining absolute control or power. He influenced many thinkers of Europe and also the framers of the United States Constitution. His most famous work was the *Spirit of the Laws*, in which he made a study of the various European political systems.

II. Cultural Achievements - Physical Sciences:

During the Baroque Period the scientific theories that were developed concerning natural laws were sounder than earlier ones, for they were now based upon careful observation, measurement, and analysis. Scientists began questioning old beliefs and creating new conclusions based on the logical evaluation of information they collected. Faith in human reason, as emphasized by the philosopher and scientist Descartes, was the basis for this evolution in science. From this grew the symbolic tool of mathematics which was developed in order to make the rational observations more accurate and workable.

Scientific academies, libraries, schools and laboratories were founded so that scientific knowledge could be shared. Italy founded a scientific academy (1600), England, the Royal Society (1660), and France, l'Académie (1662).

The outstanding scientists of the Baroque Period included:

1. Sir Isaac Newton (1642-1727) - English physicist, mathematician, astronomer and philosopher: Newton laid the foundation for modern physical science in his treatise *Principia* (1687). His theories of motion and mechanics have remained almost unquestioned up to the present time. His discoveries include the law of gravitation, reflecting telescope, calculus, the three laws

of motion, and the corpuscular theory of light. Newton's theories influenced philosophy as well.

2. Edmund Halley (1656-1742) - English astronomer and mathematician: Halley discovered "Halley's comet" in 1682 and predicted its correct return in 1759. He made the first correct predictions of stellar motion and published the first map of the winds of the earth.

3. William Harvey (1578-1657) - English physician and physiologist: Harvey discovered the exact pattern of circulation of the blood (1616) and proved that the heart contracts and dilates. His discoveries helped to develop modern biological science.

4. Robert Boyle (1637-1691) - English chemist: Boyle is called the "father of chemistry" for he was the first to distinguish the difference between a chemical element and a compound, and to explain chemical reaction and analysis. He proved that sound could not travel in a vacuum. He is famous for Boyle's Law which states that the volume of a gas at constant temperature is inversely proportional to the pressure. He was also the founder of the Royal Society of England.

5. Christian Huygens (1629-1695) - Dutch astronomer, mathematician and physicist: Huygens designed the pendulum clock and developed the theory of the compound pendulum. He improved the telescopic lenses which made possible his discovery of a satellite of Saturn and additional rings. He is famous for the wave (undulatory) theory of light which he used to explain reflection and refraction of light.

III. Cultural Achievements - Literature:

In the Baroque Age, the accomplishments of science over-shadowed those in literature. The classical French literature of the age of King Louis XIV was imitated and considered to be the model for perfect values. Only in England did the geniuses of literature build a different form of expression. There arose a desire for freedom of expression by the "Moderns" from the formal rules and convention of the ancient classical tradition of literature.

Italian literature was of low calibre during this period for most of the poetry was artificial and verbose, and Italian drama lacked vitality.

Germany was nearly depopulated during the Thirty
Years' War (1618-1648). The sparsity of young talent and
the demoralization that followed prevented creativity in
literature.

Among the famous men of letters of this period were:

1. Pierre Corneille (1606-1684) - French tragedy writer:
   Corneille's *Le Cid* began the great Neo-classical period
   of the French theater (which can be compared to the
   English Elizabethan period). He re-emphasized the rules
   of the classical drama by adhering to three unities of
   time, place and action. His works include *Horace* (1640)
   and *Le Menteur* (1644).

2. Jean Baptiste Racine (1639-1699) - French dramatist:
   Racine brought the classical French drama to its high-
   est point of perfection. His masterpieces of classical
   French tragedy include *Andromoque* (1667) and *Phedre*
   (1677). He also wrote the religious dramas *Esther* and
   Athalie (1690).

3. Molière (Jean Baptiste Poquelin) (1632-1673) - French
   comedy writer: Moliere refined a slap-dash buffoonery
   type of humor to thoughtful comedy which was unrivaled
   until the time of George Bernard Shaw. His famous
   pieces include: *Tartuffe, le Misanthrope* and *Le Malade
   imaginaire.*

4. Jean de La Fontaine (1621-1695) - French poet: Fontaine
   was one of the great figures in the French classical
   movement. He is famous for his twelve books of *Fables*,
   which are still studied by all in France. His mastery
   of form, moralizing, wit and graceful verse are said to
   form the purist canon of literary style.

5. John Milton (1608-1674) - English poet: Milton became
   involved in the political and religious controversies
   of his day, and became a crusader for the Puritans,
   writing about freedom of the press and speech: *Areopa-
   gitica* (1644). He became blind in 1652. He completed
   his famous *Paradise Lost* in 1663, the great epic poem
   which embodied his philosophy and theology.

6. John Dryden (1631-1700) - British dramatist, poet and
   critic: Dryden was a supporter of Oliver Cromwell whom
   he eulogized in his *Heroic Stanzas*. His *Essay of Drama-
   tick Poesy* (1668) set a moderate position between
   French classicism and the freedom of the English
   Elizabethans.

7. Jonathan Swift (1667-1745) - British satirist: Swift is considered to be the most famous of the British satirists and one of the most brilliant men of his time. His masterpiece was *Gulliver's Travels* (1726), which was a great satire on man's weaknesses and vices and was concerned with education, politics, social institutions and philosophy.

8. Alexander Pope (1688-1744) - British poet: Pope was one of the leading literary figures of the 18th century. His famous works include his much quoted *An Essay on Man*. His translations of Homer's *Iliad* and *Odyssey* made him wealthy. He developed the heroic couplet which reflected the preciseness demanded by his age.

IV. Cultural Achievements - Philosophy:

In the Baroque Age, the growth of the scientific method resulting in a systematized body of knowledge, collection of information, and emphasis upon human reason brought about a more secular and man-centered philosophy. The philosophers sought what was reasonable and natural in religion, ethics, and politics. They believed that civilization could be improved by man's use of reason.
Among the illustrious philosophers of this age are:

1. René Descartes (1596-1650) - French philosopher and mathematician: Descartes has been called the founder of modern philosophy. The basis of his philosophy is found in the words "Cogito, ergo sum" (I think, therefore, I exist). His method consisted of accepting only those concepts as true that were absolutely certain; analyzing problems completely, section by section; and building knowledge from the simple to the complex.

2. Benedict Spinoza (1632-1677) - Dutch philosopher: In 1663 Spinoza published a criticism of the Cartesian philosophy which presents his system of pantheism (the belief that God and Nature are identical). He is considered a great writer on morals and a rigid determinist. His philosophy was part rational and part emotional. He believed that all events are determined (rational) and man should accept this fact (emotional). His book, *Ethics*, was published after his death.

3. George Berkeley (1685-1753) - Irish philosopher: Berkeley was an idealist who believed that only spirits and their ideas exist. In his *Treatise Concerning the Principle of Human Knowledge* (1710) he postulates that

man only knows his own ideas. The reality of matter de-
pends on it being perceived and that God perceives
things when they are not understood by us.

4. David Hume (1711-1776) - Scottish philosopher and his-
   torian: Hume was a prominent skeptical and empirical
   philosopher. In his *Treatise of Human Nature,* he reduced knowledge to impressions (sensory experiences and
   feelings) and ideas (images which occur through reasoning). He denied all knowledge that could not be reduced
   to an impression or an idea. He believed that all man
   can know is that which he directly experiences.

5. Gottfried Wilhelm Leibnitz (1646-1716) - German histo-
   rian, mathematician and philosopher: Leibnitz was a
   German idealist and rationalist who believed that reality consists of monads. In his book *Monadology,* he devised a new philosophical system in which he postulated
   theories that have now been developed by scientific
   studies. He believed that the simple things of the
   universe are simple monads which unite and form complex
   monads. Leibnitz's monads can be compared to our present scientific idea of atoms which have electrons
   whose energy never runs down, and of living cells that
   can develop into high forms of life.

6. Blaise Pascal (1623-1662) - French philosopher and
   mathematician: Pascal contributed Pascal's Law (a fluid
   in a closed system exerts equal pressure in all directions) to physics. His *Lettres Provinciales* (1656) defended Jansenism against Jesuit attack. His *Pensees*
   (thoughts) bases the defense of religion on "the heart",
   as opposed to reason and nature.

V. Cultural Achievements - Fine Arts:

   Baroque Art was typified by an exuberant and dynamic
design - twisting forms and exaggerated ornamentation. The
architecture had elaborate monumental facades which reflected the spirit of the newly formed nationalistic
countries of Europe. This was an age of royal and religious pageantry which affected art.
   The architecture of the churches consisted of a series
of curves and waves which appear irrational because there
are no measurable surfaces or straight lines. Space, is
unmeasurable with no beginning or ending. Curves appear
to go in and out and windows were placed in weird places.
   Baroque sculpture had extreme concave and convex treatment of marble, elaborate draping effects, and made use of
richly colored marble.

In painting there was an extravagant display of rich-
ness in color and style. They were characterized by curves,
voluminous figures, open space, illusions and de-emphasis
of balanced perspective. The vanishing point in the paintings doesn't appear to stop, but gives one the imaginary
feeling of being drawn upward - as if there were no law of
gravity. Baroque art in general was theatrical and elaborate but also rich and magnificent.

The well-known artists of this period included:

1. El Greco (Dominico Theotocopuli) (1548-1625) - Spanish
   painter: Greco was moved by the religious turmoil at
   the time (Inquisition), so his paintings were spiritual
   and portrayed a mood of disquiet. This mood was characterized by his use of unearthly hues. Among his famous
   works are: *Burial of Count Orgaz, View of Toledo,* and
   Jesus Bearing the Cross.

2. Peter Paul Rubens (1577-1640) - Flemish painter: Rubens
   used a painterly technique in his earthy and sumptuous
   paintings. He was exuberant and dynamic in his art. His
   paintings include: *Venus and Adonis* and *Judgement of
   Paris.* Rubens' favorite subject for his paintings included a story concerned with human conflict; landscape
   settings full of space, light, and growths of nature;
   and idealized feminine physical beauty.

3. Nicholas Poussin (1594-1665) - French painter: Poussin
   was commissioned by Cardinal Richelieu to paint the
   Louvre gallery. He developed the formalized style of
   the Baroque Period. His paintings were cold, severe,
   intellectual and architectural, having a linear quality.
   Many of his paintings were concerned with historical
   subjects and showed lessons in classical ideals like
   courage and heroism: *Achilles on Skyros.*

4. Anthony Van Dyck (1599-1641) - Flemish artist: In his
   early period Van Dyck developed a formal portrait style
   that included graceful poses, rich interior settings
   and formal landscapes. His art reflected English aristocratic society. His style influenced English painters
   of the 17th and 18th centuries.

5. Diego Rodriquez de Silva y Velazquez (1599-1660) -
   Spanish painter: Velazquez was court painter under King
   Philip IV and received many honors. His court portrai-
   ture was never glamorized but painted in a penetrating
   detached manner. He had great technical versatility and
   was a master in the use of simultaneous contrast and
   paintrily technique. His wide range of subject matter

included: *The Water Carrier of Seville, The Surrender of Breda, Philip IV of Spain,* and *Pope Innocent X.* Velazquez used darkened foregrounds, spatial recessions, bright colors, and textures to create his classic Baroque paintings.

6. Rembrandt Harmensoon van Rijn (1606-1669) - Dutch etcher and painter: Rembrandt carried humanism in his paintings and drawings to a profound degree. He is compared to Beethoven and Shakespeare. His paintings were coloristic; he used a limited number of colors in a subtle interlocking way. His controlled mastery of light was so infinitely graded that even the shadows were illuminated. Some of his famous works are: *Anatomy Lesson, The Night Watch, The Three Crosses, Self-Portrait,* and *The Prodigal Son.*

7. Giovanni Lorenzo Bernini (1598-1680) - Italian sculptor and architect: Bernini's sculpture and architecture is considered the most outstanding of the Baroque Period. He made excessively ornate and dramatic religious statues. Much of his sculpture was architectonic (designed as part of the architecture such as fountains, facades and monuments). His sculpture of *David* and *Ecstacy of St. Teresa* are famous examples of Baroque art. His architectural works include: *The Fountain of the Four Rivers* located in the Piazza Navona in front of St. Peter's Church in Rome.

Music of the Baroque Period:

Developments Which Contributed to the Musical Culture:

A. General Characteristics: The Baroque Period gave rise to many new and important developments in both vocal and instrumental music.

   1. The scope of instrumental music broadened from the composition of music mainly for dance and vocal accompaniment during the Renaissance to the writing of instrumental pieces in all idioms for musical performance.

   2. The gradual development of nationalism in music was brought about by the various schools of composition which advanced characteristic idioms of musical style peculiar to the national culture.

   3. The old church modes were gradually replaced with the major and minor modes reflecting a greater emphasis upon tonality.

4. At the beginning of the Baroque Period, the Italians dominated the musical scene with the introduction of opera, while at the end of the period German music predominated.
5. Secular music attracted more attention and interest, and as a result began to take precedence over the religious music of this period.

B. Elements of Music:

1. Melody: Homophonic music (a single melody line with chordal accompaniment) replaced the Polyphonic style of the Renaissance Period. Great attention was given to the melody which included repetitions and variations, and was ornamented with many embellishments.
2. Harmony: During this period a theory of chords and their use in accompaniment and composition was developed that forms the basis of our modern harmonic system. At the end of the Baroque Period, Johann Sebastian Bach brought tonal polyphony to the greatest height ever achieved in the 18th century.
3. Rhythm: In most of the music of this time, the use of accented rhythm was prominent. Consistent rhythmic patterns were developed to reflect a single mood. Single time signatures, accents, measures and bar lines were introduced during this period. Free rhythm was used in narrative and declamatory passages to suggest speech in operas, oratorios and cantatas.

C. Secular Vocal Music: Vocal music developed into a true art form. The Baroque opera was performed for the general public requiring paid admissions (for the first time in history), a custom which was to continue to the present day. Concerts and operas were also performed for and supported by the nobility and royalty. Schools of opera composition flourished in the various countries of Europe during this period.
   Composers of opera contributed to the advancement of vocal music and style in the following ways:

1. Arias: They wrote arias (solo songs) in which the singers displayed their virtuosity. The true measure of a vocal soloist or virtuoso was determined by his success in improvising the parts from a melodic outline indicated by the composer. More attention and popularity was accorded the soloist than the other performers.
2. The opera composers took cognizance of the quality of pleasant tone and stressed the vocal expression of the emotional content of the story along with tuneful melodies.

D. Sacred Vocal Music: Church music prior to this period was mainly vocal. During the Baroque Period, instrumental music assumed a more prominent role in the church service. During the Renaissance Period, church music had an almost universal style. The Baroque saw the rise of more individual nationalistic styles as found in the church music of Italy, France, Germany and England. Among the popular forms of church music are oratorios, cantatas and anthems.

1. Oratorio: The oratorio was a sacred composition for soloists, chorus and orchestra - the religious counterpart of opera. It achieved its highest state of development in the music of George Frederick Handel at the end of the Baroque Period.
2. Cantata: The cantata, an important type of composition in the Baroque Period, was similar to the oratorio, but much shorter and less elaborate. The cantata consisted of several movements including arias, recitatives, duets and choruses. There were two main types of cantatas in the Baroque Period:
   a. Secular Cantata: Its form was as mentioned above. It was developed in Italy where it was called "cantata da camera".
   b. Church Cantata: It was developed in Germany and was frequently part of a religious service. The choral cantata was an important example of the chorale and it was based on the chorale melody and text. The Lutheran Chorale became very popular during this period. Johann Sebastian Bach composed many cantatas and harmonized chorales for the Protestant Church.

E. Musical Inventions: The following revolutionary inventions in the field of music took place during the Baroque Period:

1. The Pianoforte (Piano), with an improved hammer mechanism, was invented in 1711 by Bartolommeo Cristofori of Padua, Italy. The Harpsichord, a predecessor of the piano, achieved its highest state of popularity during this period.
2. The Violin, as it exists today, was designed in 1600 by Gaspar da Salo from Brescia, Italy. The famous Cremona School of violin makers includes the following:
   a. Niccolo Amati (1596-1684)
   b. Antonio Stradivari (1644-1737)
   c. Giuseppi Guarneri (1698-1744)

3. The Organ was the most important solo keyboard instrument of this period. Andreas Silbermann (1678-1734) and other members of his family made improvements on the organ which extended the range of possibilities for organ composition.
4. "Equal Temperament" - dividing octaves of the clavier and organ into twelve equal semi-tones. Andreas Werkmeister from Germany wrote a treatise on this subject in 1691 and is known to be one of its inventors.

F. Instrumental Music and Instrumental Music Forms: Many developments in instrumental music and instruments took place during this period:

1. Instrumentation: The instrumentation of the Baroque orchestra was expanded and was determined by the desire of the composer. It usually included flutes, oboes, bassoons, strings, keyboard and sometimes brass instruments.
2. Virtuoso Performers: With the perfection of musical instruments and the development of new ones, there arose the instrumental virtuoso and the composition of music (concertos) for these soloists.
   a. The violinist with his great technical proficiency became a popular soloist and orchestral performer.
   b. The harpsichord became one of the most important instruments of the opera orchestra; it was played by the orchestra conductor who was usually the composer. The harpsichordist usually improvised the chords and accompaniments from a figured bass (number shorthand to denote chord positions), very much as the dance band pianist uses today.
   c. The very popular organ virtuoso of this period was able to display great technical and improvisational skill.
3. Chamber Music: Compositions written for a small ensemble with one instrument for each part. Chamber music was very popular during this period and included the following forms:
   a. Solo Sonata: A composition for instrumental soloist; usually with accompaniment.
   b. Trio Sonata: A composition for two violins and keyboard accompaniment, or two violins, viola da gamba, and harpsichord. The trio sonata was the most popular form of chamber music.
   c. Chamber Sonata: (sonata da camera): A suite composed for small ensembles. It was one type of trio sonata.

d. Sonata da Chiesa (Church sonata): A variation of the trio sonata. It was a composition for a chamber group made up of four movements with tempo indicated: (e.g.: slow, fast, slow, fast).
4. Baroque Suite: A composition in three movements consisting of various dances as follows:
   a. Allemande: 1st movement, 4/4 time, moderate, German dance.
   b. Courante: 2nd movement, 3/2 time, moderate, French and Italian dance.
   c. Sarabande: 3rd movement, 3/4 time, slow, of Oriental origin.
5. Other Dance Forms: Other dance forms that were used as optional movements of the suite are:
   a. Minuet: 3/4 time, moderate, became 3rd movement of the symphony in the Classical Period.
   b. Gavotte: 4/4 time, moderate, a French dance.
   c. Bourrée: 4/4 time, fast, similar to the Gavotte.
   d. Pavan: 4/4 time, slow, French and English.
   e. Galliard: 3/4 time, fast, sometimes combined with Pavan.
   f. Gigue: 6/8 time, fast, from Irish Jig or Scottish dance, usually last movement of suite.
6. Instrumental Contrapuntal Form: Contrapuntal music achieved its highest state of popularity during the Baroque Period.
   a. Fugue: The fugue was an important instrumental and vocal form of the Baroque Period. It is a highly developed contrapuntal composition based on one or more themes which are imitated by the several parts.
7. Keyboard Music Forms: Keyboard instruments of the Baroque Period included the organ, harpsichord, virginal, spinet and clavichord. Keyboard music of this period included the following types:
   a. Invention: A short contrapuntal piece written in two or three parts.
   b. Toccata: An improvisatory keyboard piece with elaborate ornamentation.
   c. Prelude: A short piece in free form, originally an introductory piece; sometimes used as a keyboard exercise piece.

CLAUDIO MONTEVERDI

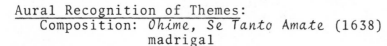

Composer: Claudio Monteverdi
    Born: Cremona, Italy 1567
    Died: Venice, Italy 1643

Aural Recognition of Themes:
    Composition: *Ohime, Se Tanto Amate* (1638)
          madrigal

General Information about Composer and Compositions:

1. Claudio Monteverdi received an excellent education in composition from Ingegneri, a famous teacher of that time. At the age of sixteen he published his first composition, a four-part madrigal.

2. Monteverdi was the most celebrated Italian composer of the first part of the seventeenth century. Other accomplishments included: singing, mastery of the viola and the violin, bandmaster at Mantuan Court (1589-1590), also choirmaster at St. Mark's, Venice (1613-1643).

3. He was the first eminent composer of opera. He also composed madrigals, masses, and motets. Two of his best known operas are: *Orfeo* (1607) and *L'Incoronazione di Poppea* (1642).

4. Monteverdi introduced the use of special instrumental effects in opera. He was the originator of the violin tremolo and string pizzicato. He used these special sound effects for the first time in his opera, *Il Combattimento di Tancredi e Clorinda,* composed in 1624.

5. He belonged to the Venetian school of opera and was master of the dramatic style. In opera he created a new

style of composition. He developed new techniques in the use of rhythm, harmony, modulations and instrumentation in order to represent better dramatic action and interpretation of the characters of the opera.

Composer's Main Contribution to the Art of Music:

1. Claudio Monteverdi was the first composer to achieve the proper balance between drama and music in opera writing. He used many innovations to achieve this union, among which were discords, key and rhythm changes, and tonal timbre. He used the orchestra to portray the moods, characters and action of the drama. This technique has been used up to the present day, thus accounting for the name given to him, "Music's Prophet". In his opera he made his characters realistic and true to life whereas previously the opera composers created abstract and stereotyped characters.

Suggested Listening:

1. Title: *Motets*
   Performers: Monteverdi Chorus
   Record No.: Argo ZRG 645
   Grade Level: 4 - 8

2. Title: *Madrigals*
   Performers: Monteverdi Chorus
   Record No.: Argo ZRG 645
   Grade Level: 7 - 12

Optional Assignments:

1. The opera was an important type of composition during the Baroque period. Give an oral report to the class on the development of opera during this period.

2. Do some research and write a report on the historical background of the Baroque period.

3. The violin was developed and introduced by the Italians during this period. Make up a notebook on the history of the violin. Include illustrations and give a report to the class.

4. During this period the American Colonies were formed. Give an oral report on the Colonial period and music in America at that time.

5. Monteverdi introduced violin tremolo and pizzicato. If you play a string instrument, demonstrate the use of tremolo and pizzicato to the class.

HEINRICH SCHUETZ

Composer: Heinrich Schuetz
    Born: Köstritz, Germany 1585
    Died: Dresden, Germany 1672

Aural Recognition of Themes:
    Composition: *The Christmas Story* (1664)
           overture

General Information about Composer and Compositions:

1. Heinrich Schuetz's early education revealed his talents not only in music but also in other academic subjects. He studied law at the University of Marburg and music at Venice, Italy under the great composer Giovanni Gabrieli. Schuetz published a book of five madrigals dedicated to Gabrieli.

2. In 1613 he was a chorister and organist for the chapel of the Landgraf Maurice of Cassel. In 1615 he became kapellmeister to the Elector of Saxony at Dresden, a position which he held until his death.

3. Schuetz was known as "The Father of German Music". He was the author and composer of the first German opera, and he was also influential in the development of church music.

4. Schuetz was the connecting link between Palestrina and Bach. He developed the semi-dramatic style of Monteverdi, and thus paved the way for the music of Johann Sebastian Bach. He brought about a renaissance in German music comparable to the musical reform in Italy during that period.

66

5. He was a prolific composer and wrote madrigals, psalms, operas, oratorios, motets and passions.

Composer's Main Contribution to the Art of Music:

1. Heinrich Schuetz is commonly referred to as one of the three most famous composers of the Protestant church. The other two composers are Bach and Handel. Schuetz wrote the first German opera *Dafne* in 1627. It was his only opera. He was known as the "Father of German Music" because he established the main characteristics of German music in the Baroque period. He achieved an ultimate renown in the fusion of Italian and German styles of composition during his lifetime. His style of composition was an outstanding model and an inspiration to Johann Sebastian Bach and other German composers of the late Baroque.

Suggested Listening:

1. Title: *Psalms*
   Performers: Telemann Society - Schulze
   Record No.: Vox 760
   Grade Level: 4 - 8

2. Title: *German Passion Music*
   Performers: Vocal-Orchestra
   Record No.: RCA - LM-6030
   Grade Level: 7 - 12

Optional Assignments:

1. After a study, write a report about the music of the German church of this period.

2. Make a list of interesting facts about the composer and his music, and present an oral report to the class developing one of these facts.

3. After a study, write a report about the famous artists and painters of this period.

4. After listening to a recording of the composer's music, write a critique, compare the work with other compositions you have heard, or make up an appropriate story that the music might suggest to you.

5. If you have attended a concert recently, present an oral report to the class on the music you have heard.

GIACOMO CARISSIMI

Composer: Giacomo Carissimi
    Born: Marino, Italy 1604
    Died: Rome, Italy 1674

Aural Recognition of Themes:
    Composition: excerpt from the introduction to the
            oratorio *Judicum Salomonis* (1669)

General Information about Composer and Compositions:

1. Giacomo Carissimi received his early training in music
   as a choir boy and later as organist at the Cathedral of
   Trivoli. He became choirmaster at Assisi in 1624, and
   also at the church of St. Apollinare in Rome in 1628.
   Although he had less preparation than other composers,
   he was gifted with a wonderful imagination which contributed to his modern outlook and creativity.

2. He was a renowned teacher whose famous pupils include
   Cesti, Buononcini and Alessandro Scarlatti. He influenced
   the oratorio style of Handel and Schuetz.

3. Carissimi is known as the "Father of the Modern
   Oratorio". He is also known to have perfected the
   recitative. He developed the sacred cantata to great
   perfection and beauty, and supplied a dramatic quality
   to sacred music.

4. He was one of the first to write instrumental accompaniments to be used with the voices in church services. He
   had a feeling for modern style, lightness and variety
   in his accompaniments.

5. He is best known for his oratorios and cantatas. He also composed motets and other sacred music. His most popular oratorios are: *Jepthe* (1660) and *Jonah* (1664).

Composer's Main Contribution to the Art of Music:

1. Giacomo Carissimi is recognized as the first master of modern oratorio. He developed and set the standards of oratorio composition which future composers were to follow. He was the first oratorio composer who did not require his performers to wear costumes during the performance. This custom of dispensing with costumes and scenery during the performance of oratorios is still kept today. He perfected the recitative (singing imitation of the speaking voice) and originated the use of the narrator in the oratorio. Though he composed other works, his contribution to the modern techniques of oratorio writing was his greatest achievement.

Suggested Listening:

1. Title: *Jepthe* - Oratorio (selections)
   Performers: Rilling, Kantorei
   Record No.: Turnabout 34089
   Grade Level: 4 - 8

2. Title: *Jepthe* - Oratorio
   Performers: Rilling, Kantorei
   Record No.: Turnabout 34089
   Grade Level: 7 - 12

Optional Assignments:

1. Giacomo Carissimi was well known for his oratorios. Do some research on the oratorio form; name other composers of this form, and explain the oratorio to the class.

2. Make a study of the famous philosophers of the Baroque period, and write a report on this subject.

3. Listen to a recording of an oratorio and write a critique about it.

4. Compare a typical sacred song of this period with some of the church music of today. Listen to a recording of each.

5. Make a study of the famous literary geniuses of this period and write a composition on this subject,especially noting their contribution to the culture of the Baroque period.

JEAN-BAPTISTE LULLY

Composer: Jean-Baptiste Lully
    Born: Florence, Italy 1633
    Died: Paris, France 1687

Aural Recognition of Themes:
    Composition: *L'Amour Medecin* (1672)
        Overture from the Ballet

General Information about Composer and Compositions:

1. At an early age, Jean-Baptiste Lully learned to play the
   guitar from a monk, and later taught himself to play the
   violin. He was discovered, at fourteen years of age, by
   a Parisian nobleman who took him to Paris for further
   music study. He became a musician in the orchestra of
   King Louis XIV.

2. Lully was so proficient as a violinist, that he surpassed
   in ability all the violinists of that period. King Louis
   XIV was so impressed that he organized an orchestra called
   "Les Petits-Violons" for Lully to direct.

3. Lully was a ballet dancer and composed thirty ballets
   for performance at the Court of Louis XIV, for which he
   was awarded many honors.

4. In 1672 he became director of the Paris Opera. He composed operas and founded a national French opera style.
   To insure success of opera he worked diligently as composer, director and stage manager.

70

5. He was one of the few composers to amass a great personal fortune. He was a prolific composer of operas, ballets, overtures and chansons.

Composer's Main Contribution to the Art of Music:

1. Although Jean-Baptiste Lully was of Italian birth, he became famous as the creator of the French opera. He developed the importance of the accompanied recitative in his operas. His recitatives expressed emotion and mood, and depicted characters. He fitted the music to the libretto. Italian composers of this period usually adapted the libretto to the music thus losing the dramatic effect. He limited the use of long arias (vocal solos). He used the orchestra much more effectively than previous composers. He also used a larger variety of instrumentation than his contemporaries.

Suggested Listening:

1. Title: *Marches, Fanfares*
   Performers: Paris College of Music - Douatte
   Record No.: Nonesuch 1009
   Grade Level: 4 - 8

2. Title: *Ballet Music from Xerxes*
   Performers: Andre, Menardi
   Record No.: Turnabout 34376
   Grade Level: 7 - 12

Optional Assignments:

1. After a study, write a report about the famous court of Louis XIV of France.

2. Compare a typical composition of the Polyphonic period with a composition of the Baroque period.

3. Make a list of composers who composed music for the violin and list their most famous compositions.

4. Lully was the director of the Paris Opera. Do some research on the duties of an opera director, and present an oral report to the class on the subject.

5. If you are artistic, draw a picture or paint a portrait of the composer, and present it to the class for bulletin board display.

71

ARCANGELO CORELLI

Composer: Arcangelo Corelli
  Born: Fusignano, Italy 1653
  Died: Rome, Italy 1713

Aural Recognition of Themes:
  Composition: *Violin Sonata, Op. 5, No. 9* (1700)

General Information about Composer and Compositions:

1. Arcangelo Corelli studied violin with Benvenuti and counterpoint with Matteo Simonelli. He became the most celebrated violin virtuoso of this period. He published many works for the violin.

2. He traveled to Munich, Germany and was attached to the court of the Elector of Bavaria as a performer and composer. From 1685 until his death he lived in Rome where he composed and performed for high society. One of his best friends and music patrons was Cardinal Ottoboni.

3. Although Corelli achieved great fame, he was very humble in his manner and dress, and he lived very simply. The famous composer Handel said of him "He likes nothing better than seeing pictures without paying for it, and saving money".

4. He was the founder of chamber music and orchestral composition, and he laid the foundation for the solo sonata and concerto grosso. Bach and Handel further developed these forms.

5. His compositions displayed good violin technique. He composed concerti grossi, sonatas, gavottes and sarabandes. His best known work is *Les Folies d'Espagne*.

Composer's Main Contribution to the Art of Music:

1. Although Arcangelo Corelli was known as "The father of modern violin playing", his greatest contribution to music was the development of two instrumental forms: the sonata and the concerto. Previous to his time the sonata was developed from the canzona and cantata which were vocal forms. Corelli developed the sonata as an independent instrumental form. His mastery of the violin helped him in the composition of the excellent violin sonatas for which he is renowned today. In his *Twelve Concerti Grossi, Op. 6*, (1682-1710), he established the form and style for the concerto.

Suggested Listening:

1. Title: *Gigue in B Flat*
   Performers: R.C.A. Victor Symphony Orchestra
   Record No.: E 74 R.C.A. Basic Record Library, Vol. 4
   Grade Level: 4 - 8

2. Title: *Concerto Grosso in G, Op. 6, No. 8*
   Performers: Philadelphia Symphony Orchestra - Ormandy
   Record No.: Columbia MS 6081
   Grade Level: 7 - 12

Optional Assignments:

1. Arcangelo Corelli composed many concerti grossi and sonatas. Look up these terms and prepare a brief outline explaining their structure.

2. Corelli, Handel and Alessandro Scarlatti performed together in Rome and Naples. Do some research on their performances and write a paper describing them.

3. Study Corelli's life as described in the World Book or any other encyclopedia, and present an oral report to the class.

4. After a study, write a report on the historical background of the Baroque period.

5. Make a study of the major performing instrument of the composer and collect literature and pictures of this instrument for your notebook.

HENRY PURCELL

Composer: Henry Purcell
    Born: London, England 1658
    Died: London, England 1695

Aural Recognition of Themes:
    Composition: *Dido and Aeneas* (1689) - opera

General Information about Composer and Compositions:

1. Henry Purcell was the son of the famous musician, Thomas Purcell, who was a choirmaster at Westminster Abbey in London. Henry became a choirboy at the Chapel Royal and there was trained in singing, violin, lute and organ as well as in general academic subjects. He studied organ with John Blow, a famous organist of that time.

2. When his voice changed in 1673 he was given the position of "caretaker of the king's instruments". In 1667 he became the composer for the king's orchestra which performed at royal functions of the court. In 1679 he replaced John Blow as organist of Westminster Abbey. In 1682 he was appointed organist of the Chapel Royal.

3. He was a master of contrapuntal devices. He studied composition with the composer John Bull. Purcell was greatly influenced by George Frederick Handel. He composed sonatas, anthems, church music, songs, stage scores, organ and harpsichord music. He composed several church compositions dedicated to St. Cecilia (Patron saint of musicians): *Te Deum* (1688) and *Jubilate in D* (1688).

4. He was an outstanding English composer and organist. He was the only great English operatic composer. He is famous for his opera *Dido and Aeneas*. He wrote incidental music for plays and dramas: *King Arthur* (1691) and *Fairy Queen* (1692).

74

5. Purcell composed music for royalty to celebrate special occasions. He composed an anthem, *My Heart Is Inditing of a Good Matter*, for the coronation of King James II. He was buried under the organ at Westminster Abbey.

Composer's Main Contribution to the Art of Music:

1. Henry Purcell's opera *Dido and Aeneas* is his most famous work. It is the only opera of note written by an English composer before World War II. Alfred Einstein called this opera "a pinnacle by itself, a model of pure and profound expression achieved by modest means". Purcell showed the influence of the Italian opera composers in his recitatives and instrumental accompaniments. The influence of the French composer Jean-Baptiste Lully is displayed in the elaborate combination of music, dancing and spoken drama. He achieved perfection in the expression of the accents of the English language in dramatic vocal music.

Suggested Listening:

1. Title: *Music for the Theatre*
   Performers: Bath Festival Orchestra
   Record No.: Angel S 36332
   Grade Level: 4 - 8

2. Title: Opera - *Dido and Aeneas*
   Performers: Vocal and Orchestra - Thomas
   Record No.: Vanguard S 279
   Grade Level: 7 - 12

Optional Assignments:

1. Henry Purcell wrote incidental music for plays. Give a report on the use today of incidental and background music for plays or movies.

2. Make a study of the famous artists of this period and write a composition about their lives and works.

3. Learn a basic dance used during Purcell's time and present this dance for the class.

4. Do some research about the major performing instruments of the Baroque period and collect literature and pictures of these instruments for your notebooks.

5. Purcell was buried at Westminster Abbey. Give an oral report on this historical place.

ALESSANDRO SCARLATTI

Composer: Alessandro Scarlatti
   Born: Palermo, Sicily 1659
   Died: Naples, Italy 1725

Aural Recognition of Themes:
   Composition: *O Cessate di Piagarmi* (1706)

General Information about Composer and Compositions:

1. Alessandro Scarlatti, as a child, studied with the composer Carissimi in Rome. He is known as the foremost master of the Italian school of composition during the seventeenth century. His early compositions were influenced by the composers Legrenzi and Stradella.

2. He was a famous teacher and several of his pupils achieved fame as operatic composers in Europe. He held the position of music professor at three conservatories of music: San Onofrio Conservatory, de'Poveri di Gesu Christi Conservatory, and Loret Conservatory.

3. In 1694 he was appointed Choirmaster to the viceroy of Naples. In 1703 he moved to Rome where he became assistant musical director at the church of Santa Maria Maggiore. He later became private Choirmaster to Cardinal Ottoboni.

4. He was the founder of the famous Neopolitan school of opera which established the Italian operatic style of the 18th century. In his opera composition he introduced the following innovations: orchestral ritornello (instrumental refrain), recitative obbligato (accompaniment for narrative part of the opera), and the aria (opera vocal solo) form.

5. Scarlatti produced more than one hundred and fifteen operas. He composed five hundred chamber cantatas, two hundred masses, fourteen oratorios and a string quartet. His best known opera is *Pompeo* (1683).

Composer's Main Contribution to the Art of Music:

1. Alessandro Scarlatti was one of the most influential composers of the Neopolitan school of opera. He established the rules and the style of opera composition not only for his contemporaries, but for the future composers of opera in all of Europe. He established the use of the Italian Overture. Under his guidance, the aria (vocal solo) achieved an important position in opera composition.

Suggested Listening:

1. Title: *Arias*
   Performers: Berganza
   Record No.: London 25726
   Grade Level: 4 - 8

2. Title: *Concerti Grossi*
   Performers: Paris College
   Record No.: Monitor S 2102
   Grade Level: 7 - 12

Optional Assignments:

1. In order to become more familiar with the opera, do some research on the various parts of the opera, such as: aria, recitativo, libretto etc.

2. Write a report about the qualifications, training and education needed to become an operatic singer.

3. Choose one of the topics we have discussed under general information, do research on it in other books, then give an oral report to the class.

4. Collect some information about the Metropolitan Opera in New York or the Boston Opera Group, and report your findings to the class.

5. Listen to a recording of an opera, or watch an opera on television, or see an opera performance on stage. Write a critique on the performance and tell the class about it.

FRANÇOIS COUPERIN

Composer: François Couperin
   Born: Paris, France 1668
   Died: Paris, France 1733

Aural Recognition of Themes:
   Composition: *Les Fastes de la Grande et Ancienne
      Menestrandise* for Harpsichord (1725)

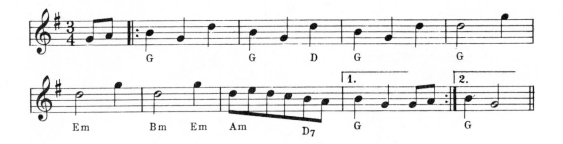

General Information about Composer and Compositions:

1. Like Bach, François Couperin came from a family of musicians. He was the most renowned in the family. To distinguish him from the rest of his family, he was called
   "Couperin Le Grand". His father was an organist with
   whom François studied. Other Couperins were violinists,
   organists and harpsichordists. Many of them performed
   at the French Court.

2. Couperin was organist to Louis XIV at the Chapel Royal.
   He was also an accomplished performer on the harpsichord.

3. Bach's keyboard style was influenced by Couperin's
   harpsichord compositions. Couperin's textbook "The Art
   of Playing the Harpsichord" (1716) was studied thoroughly
   by Johann Sebastian Bach.

4. Couperin, along with Rameau, was a pioneer in the field
   of program music. Some of his keyboard pieces are of a
   highly descriptive character. Beethoven and Liszt developed this style more fully later.

5. Francois Couperin was a prominent figure in the field of keyboard composition. He was perhaps the most important composer of Baroque harpsichord music. His music is composed in typical French style. He started a new era of light, delicate and ornamental keyboard playing. Good examples of this style are: *Pièces de Clavecin* (1713-1730) and *Suites for Harpsichord* (1722-1725).

Composer's Main Contribution to the Art of Music:

1. Francois Couperin was recognized as one of the earliest masters of the harpsichord. He achieved such remarkable virtuosity that he was given the title of "Le Grand" (the great). He developed techniques of playing and a method of fingering that is still used today. He created a style of keyboard playing that is noted for its expressive beauty, balance and precision.

Suggested Listening:

1. Title: *Harpsichord Music*
   Performers: Fuller
   Record No.: Nonesuch 71265
   Grade Level: 4 - 8

2. Title: *Pièces de Clavecin*
   Performers: Fuller
   Record No.: Nonesuch 71265
   Grade Level: 7 - 12

Optional Assignments:

1. François Couperin wrote a great deal of music for the harpsichord. Make a list of other composers of harpsichord music.

2. In the field of science, Isaac Newton was active during Couperin's time. Tell the class about some of his laws and inventions.

3. The harpsichord was a popular instrument of the Baroque period. Make up a notebook about the harpsichord, including pictures, reports, magazine articles and other sources of information about this instrument.

4. Couperin and Rameau were pioneers in the field of program music. Do some research and explain the term "Program Music" to the class.

5. King Louis XIV encouraged cultural activities. Give an oral report about Louis XIV and some composers and musicians who performed in his court.

JOHANN SEBASTIAN BACH

Composer: Johann Sebastian Bach
   Born: Eisenach, Germany 1685
   Died: Leipzig, Germany 1750

Aural Recognition of Themes:
   Composition: *Bourrée* (1726)

General Information about Composer and Compositions:

1. Johann Sebastian Bach came from a musical family and had
   a long line of musical ancestors. His father was a vio -
   linist. Bach himself had a large family; he had twenty
   children, several of whom became musicians.

2. Bach started his musical training by studying the violin,
   and later transferred to the organ. He became court organist and violinist to the Duke of Weimar.

3. He was the foremost composer of polyphonic music. He
   brought polyphony to its climax. He is still considered
   by many to be the foremost composer and musician of all
   time.

4. Bach's music has been a great source of study and inspi -
   ration to composers, students and musicians of later
   periods. He developed tempered tuning of the piano, a
   technique which is still used today.

5. Bach composed cantatas, preludes, fugues, masses, orato -
   rios, sonatas, concertos and chorales. He wrote the
   following compositions for organ, piano, violin, orches -
   tra, woodwind and string ensembles: *The Well Tempered
   Clavier* (48 preludes and fugues) (1722), *Christmas*

Oratorio (1734), *St. Matthew Passion* (1729), *St. John Passion* (1723), *Art of Fugue, Brandenburg Concertos* (1721), *Italian Concerto* (1735) *and* chorales: *Sleepers Awake* (1739) *and Jesu, Joy of Man's Desiring* (1721).

Composer's Main Contribution to the Art of Music:

1. Johann Sebastian Bach achieved the most perfect development of polyphony. This amazing genius exhausted all techniques of composition and possibilities of growth in the style of the Late Baroque. He composed a large collection of music for the harpsichord and the clavichord. The piano was not invented until Bach was sixty years of age. Many of his works have been transcribed for the piano including his composition *Well Tempered Clavier,* which demonstrated the feasibility of equal temperament in the tuning of keyboard instruments.

Suggested Listening:

1. Title: *French Suites (6) for Harpsichord, S.81217*
   Performers: Backhaus - Piano
   Record No.: London STS 15065
   Grade Level: 4 - 8

2. Title: *Passion According to St. Matthew*
   Performers: New York Philharmonic - Bernstein
   Record No.: Columbia M3S-692
   Grade Level: 7 - 12

Optional Assignments:

1. Bach came from a musical family. Do some research and write a report on the musical talent in his own family.

2. The piano was invented during Bach's time. Make up a notebook on the history of the piano.

3. If you play a musical instrument, select a composition by Bach and play it for the class.

4. Select a musical form mentioned in number five above and write briefly on it.

5. Create a musical crossword puzzle, or make up a quiz, using information about Bach.

GEORGE FREDERICK HANDEL

Composer: George Frederick Handel
   Born: Halle, Germany 1685
   Died: London, England 1759

Aural Recognition of Themes:
   Composition: *Where'er you Walk* (1744) from opera *Semele*

General Information about Composer and Compositions:

1. In his youth, George Frederick Handel studied composition, harpsichord, organ, violin and oboe with Frederick Zachan who was the organist at Maria Church in Halle, Germany. In 1696 he attended the University in Berlin where he studied law for a brief period.

2. He accepted a position as violinist in the Hamburg Opera Orchestra, and in 1705 produced his first operas: *Almira* and *Nero*. In 1710 he accepted the position of court orchestra leader for the Elector of Hanover.

3. He went to London where his opera *Rinaldo* was performed at the Haymarket Theater in 1711 with complete success. He taught music and played concerts in Germany, Italy and England. He became Director of the Royal Academy of Music in England in the year 1720.

4. He was engaged by various members of the royal court for musical services. Queen Anne of England gave him a lifetime pension. Another patron of Handel was King George I of England. Handel was buried in Westminster Abbey, a great honor reserved for royalty.

5. Handel's music has influenced many composers, and his oratorios have prompted the formation of choral societies: (Ex.: Handel and Haydn Society located in Boston, Mass.). He is considered the greatest composer of oratorios. His works also include operas, cantatas, concertos, anthems,

suites, instrumental and orchestral music. *The Messiah* (1742) is the most famous of all oratorios. It is often performed during the Christmas season. The first performance was given at Dublin, Ireland. At a London performance, during the *Hallelujah Chorus*, the audience which included King George was so thrilled by the performance that it stood up during the performance. This custom of standing during the *Hallelujah Chorus* is still observed today.

Composer's Main Contribution to the Art of Music:

1. George Frederick Handel was famous for both his operas and oratorios. He was admired by Beethoven who said: "Handel was the greatest and the most skilled composer who ever lived. I can still learn from him." Handel's opera style reflects largely that of the Italians rather than that of his own German contemporaries. His ornate and grand style of oratorio writing also reveals the Italian influence. His oratorio style established the highest standards for composition in this form because of his genius.

Suggested Listening:

1. Title: *Water Music: Suite*
   Performers: Philadelphia Orchestra - Ormandy
   Record No.: Columbia MS 7515
   Grade Level: 4 - 8

2. Title: *Messiah* (selections)
   Performers: Philadelphia Orchestra - Ormandy
   Record No.: RCA LSC-3226
   Grade Level: 7 - 12

Optional Assignments:

1. Give an oral report to the class about one selected example of Handel's works, using a recording.

2. Bach and Handel were born in the same year. Name other things common to these composers.

3. Handel's *Water Music* was written for a special occasion. Do some research and tell the class about this event.

4. Make up a notebook on the life and music of Handel, including pictures, newspaper and magazine articles, concert programs, thematic excerpts, original illustrations and a written report.

5. The Baroque period had some famous scientists. Make a study of them and write a composition on this subject.

223 Flute, lute and drone; Johannes Steen (1626—1679). National Gallery, Prague.

CHAPTER 5

THE CLASSICAL PERIOD (1750-1820)

Historical Background of the Classical Period:

I. Introduction: The effect of the American Revolution against autocracy was significant for it meant the formation of the republic of the United States with its separate executive, judicial, and legislative branches, and a bill of rights which protected the American people. It helped persuade the British officials to modify their colonial policies. It also acted as an impetus towards inspiring the French Revolution. The French Declaration of the Rights of Man significantly parallels the Declaration of Independence.

The French Revolution (1789-1799) left its mark on western civilization, but whether it had a good or bad effect is still debated today. The revolution overthrew an absolute monarchy and formed a republic which became a military dictatorship. It also changed economic and social conditions, and subsequently affected cultural patterns of the day.

A new Classical Period emerged; an era too troubled and serious after the tribulations of the French Revolution to care for the delicate and ornate form of Baroque art. A search for new art forms became an essential part of 18th century civilization. In this search, man once more became attracted to classical thought. Germany was the leader in this movement. The rebirth of classical antiquity through German genius is one of the most significant facts of this period.

A. The American Revolution (1775-1781):

   1. The American colonists believed that they were deprived of their rights as Englishmen. They protested by a boycott of British goods.

   2. In 1774 the First Continental Congress convened to try to repeal unfair laws. In 1775 the Second Continental Congress convened and planned armed resistance. George Washington was selected as Commander-in-chief of the Army.

   3. On July 4, 1776 Congress announced the Declaration of Independence. Their grievances included their dislike of German soldiers hired by the British and

quartered in the colonies and the Prohibitory Acts which withdrew their protection from the Indians.

4. In 1781, General Cornwallis surrendered at Yorktown and this resulted in the end of the Revolutionary War. The victory of the American colonists stunned the whole world and inspired Frenchmen to gain freedom from tyranny.

B. Causes of the French Revolution:

1. Royal extravagance with its colorful pageantry and luxury made the hungry and oppressed common people rebel. Certain classes were privileged, taxes were unjust, and inequality in religion resulted in the violence of the people.

2. The absolute and corrupt government was ruled by King Louis XVI. The nobility blocked legislative reform and forced Louis XVI to call the Estates-General (1789). It represented three estates or classes -- (1) the clergy, (2) the nobility, and the (3) professional men, artisans and peasants.

C. The French Revolution:

1. On July 14, 1789 a Parisian mob stormed the Bastille, an old prison. A panic known as the "Great Fear" swept over France.

2. On October 5th a Parisian mob stormed Versailles and brought the King back to Paris. Reforms of the organized National Assembly, formed after the third estate had left the Estates General, included the Declaration of the Rights of Man. The Civil Constitution of the Clergy was drawn up, and a limited monarchy was organized. Later a National Convention was elected to govern France which established the First French Republic. It also founded the Louvre and the Institute of France.

3. The French Republic lasted from 1792 to 1804. In 1793 Louis XVI and Marie Antoinette were beheaded on the guillotine, and a reign of terror prevailed.

4. From 1799 to 1802 France was governed by the Directory. France was under the rule of consuls, one of whom was Napoleon Bonaparte.

D. The Period of Napoleon:

1. Faced with the Austrian War, the Directory sent Napoleon, a French General, with a small army to Italy (1796) where he succeeded in driving out the Austrians. By a "coup d'etat" (seizure of power), Napoleon overthrew the Directory (1799) and gained control of the government. In 1804 he became Emperor.

2. Napoleon established the Code Napoleon (which emphasized equality before the law), the Bank of France, the Concordat with the Pope, the University of France, and the "Continental System".

3. By 1808 Spain, Germany and Italy were under Napoleon's control. Austria, Prussia and Russia were his allies, but England remained free. At Trafalgar, Lord Nelson's victory established British naval supremacy.

4. During the Napoleonic Wars, the United States became involved in the War of 1812 with England over the impressment of seamen and the rights of neutral trade.

5. Napoleon's defeat was due to the failure of his "Continental System", the British naval blockade, and the fact that he over-extended himself. He invaded Russia and was defeated at Leipzig. He raised another army but was defeated by a union of allied armies at Waterloo. In 1821 Napoleon died in exile.

6. The Congress of Vienna (1815) re-established France within the area which she had possessed in 1790. Germany was reconstituted as a federation of states with an Austrian president, and Austria regained her Italian holdings. In general, the Congress attempted to restore former domains to rulers of the period before the wars or give them adequate compensation.

Studies in Cultural Correlation - Classical Period:

I. Cultural Achievements - Social Studies:

Science had made possible the theory that the universe was governed by the laws of Nature. Soon philosophers became interested in natural man and humanitarians were concerned with natural rights. The new movements of thought gave rise to the English "Enlightenment", the French "Illumination", and the German "Aufklärung". In the United States it was known as the "Age of Reason".

The political revolutionary movements of this period were given an intellectual and emotional impetus through the writings of the critics and social philosophers. These include the following:

1. Francois Marie Arouet Voltaire (1694-1778) - French writer: Voltaire was a chief figure of this Age of Enlightenment. His belief in free speech and religious tolerance was made evident in *Candide* and *The Philosophical Letters on the English*.

2. Jean-Jacques Rousseau (1712-1778) - French philosopher, political thinker, and novelist: Rousseau's *Social Contract* (1726) was a modification of Locke's idea concerning popular government. He believed that the government should be an expression of the general will of the people.

3. Adam Smith (1723-1790) - British economist: Smith founded the classical school of British political economy. He was one of the strongest objectors to mercantilism of his time. His *Inquiry into the Nature and Causes of the Wealth of Nations* emphasized the laissez-faire (policy of non-interference) management of economic affairs.

4. Denis Diderot (1713-1784) - French philosopher and social scientist: Diderot's most famous work, *Encyclopedia* (1751-1772), was a very significant scientific and informative piece of literature. He stressed rationalism in solving social and political problems.

5. Thomas Jefferson (1743-1826) - American statesman, third President of the United States: Jefferson was the author of the *Declaration of Independence*. He believed in the rights of the states, but was opposed to a strong centralized government.

II. Cultural Achievements - Physical Sciences:

This period, two centuries after Newton, was not as brilliant as the one before it, but it was one of steady progress. A single mind could still carry a substantial working knowledge of all the sciences. Gradually science began to form detached units which one day would emerge into single specialized fields of knowledge for the whole field of science would become too vast and complicated for any one mind to comprehend.

The following are some of the prominent scientists of the Classical Period:

1. Joseph Priestley (1733-1804) - British chemist: Priestley discovered oxygen. He discovered photosynthesis, the process by which the leaf manufactures carbohydrates in the presence of sunlight. He was persecuted for his religious and political views and came to the United States in 1794.

2. Count Alessandro Volta (1745-1827) - Italian physicist: Volta began the research on electricity which resulted in the invention of the electric battery (the voltaic pile) and the electric condenser. The unit of electrical potential was called the volt in honor of Volta.

3. Edward Jenner (1749-1823) - British physician: Jenner developed the cowpox vaccination for the prevention of smallpox in 1796.

4. Antoine Laurnet Lavoisier (1743-1794) - French chemist: Lavoisier was a member of the French commission responsible for establishing the metric system. He was one of the founders of modern chemistry and stated that matter is neither created or destroyed in a chemical reaction (Law of Conservation of Matter).

5. John Dalton (1766-1844) - English scientist: Dalton's research led to the fundamental ideas of modern chemistry including the atomic theory. He discovered colorblindness (Daltonism).

6. Eli Whitney (1765-1825) - American inventor: Whitney's cotton gin, used to separate the seed from the cotton plant (1793), greatly influenced cotton agriculture and industry. He also contributed to mass production by introducing division of labor and standardization of parts in manufacturing.

7. Baron Georges Leopold Cuvier (1769-1832) - French naturalist: Cuvier developed the system of classification in zoology and founded comparative anatomy. His best known work is the *Animal Kingdom Arranged According to Its Organization* (1816).

8. James Watt (1736-1819) - Scottish engineer: Watt designed some basic improvements for the Newcomen steam engine. He introduced the term "horsepower". The watt, the metric unit of power, is named after him.

III. Cultural Achievements - Literature:

At the beginning of the 18th century, literature strove for the classical perfection of style and form. Toward the end of this century there was a gradual breaking away from classicism towards a new liberalism. Many writers took up the cause against social changes. The late Classical and early Romantic poets attacked formal art and aristocratic values, and sympathized with the popular causes of that age. The Romanticists' themes also dwelt on the past for they glorified romance and mystery in settings of ancient churches and castles of the Middle Ages. They also attacked the ideals of the 18th century. The cold formal aristocratic society of this age could not satisfy the poetic souls who searched for and wrote of the ideals of nature. Reason and science were censured by them for their cold analytical evaluation of life. The literature was predominantly philosophical, political and satirical. Some of the literary giants of this period are discussed below:

1. Robert Burns (1759-1796) - Scottish poet: Burns' poems, written in the Scottish dialect, became famous. His poetry portrayed humanity, tenderness, humor, love of nature, and the joys of life. He rebelled against the repression imposed by the politics and religion of his day. His works include the folksongs of Scotland *Auld Lang Syne* and *My Love is Like a Red, Red Rose* and the poems *Tam O'Shanter* and *To a Mouse*. He led the way for Moore and Scott in his use of dialect and for Coleridge and Wordsworth in his portrayal of nature.

2. William Wordsworth (1770-1850) - British poet: Wordsworth lived in the Lake Country and his depiction of Nature was superb. His famous *The Prelude* (autobiographical poem) and *The Excursion* are reflections on man, Nature and society. He became poet laureate in 1843.

3. Johann Wolfgang von Goethe (1749-1832) - German poet and writer: Goethe is acclaimed in Germany and elsewhere as one of the great men of letters; he invented the term, world literature. He is renowned chiefly through his famous dramatic poem *Faust* which is based on a medieval legend about a German magician. This piece of literature, with its world thought, knowledge and history, became an inspiration for both literary and musical selections.

4. Sir Walter Scott (1771-1832) - Scottish poet and novelist: Scott is famous for his *The Lay of the Last Minstrel*, *Marmion* and *The Lady of the Lake*. He invented

the historical novel in his *Waverley* novels. This
literary type spread throughout Europe and has remained
a popular type up to the present time.

5. Percy Bysshe Shelley (1792-1822) - English poet:
    Shelley's works include *The Cenci* (1819) which was con-
    cerned with freedom and love, and *Prometheus Unbound*
    (1820) in which he combined philosophy, morality, his-
    tory and economics. His famous shorter lyrics include
    To a Skylark and *Ode to the West Wind*. He believed that
    a poet was a "law-giver" whose destiny was to show
    humanity the way to obtain liberation. He is considered
    to be one of the greatest of the Romantic poets.

IV. Cultural Achievements - Philosophy:

   The spirit of modern philosophy developed during this
age of enlightenment. This period saw the glorification of
knowledge in the sciences and arts, and the progress of
achievements in civilization. The philosophers of this age
primarily used reason to examine every sacred tradition.
   Among the most illustrious philosophers of this era
are:

1. Immanuel Kant (1724-1804) - German philosopher: Kant
    analyzed the various interests of his age -- Enlighten-
    ment, skepticism, empiricism, mysticism, the will, and
    morals. He felt that the senses of man furnished the
    basis for knowledge. He stressed duty and loyalty. In
    the *Critique of Pure Reason*, he concluded that our
    intellect imposes laws on Nature rather than deriving
    laws from it.

2. Johann Gottleib Fichte (1762-1814) - German philosopher:
    Fichte's basic philosophy dealt with freedom or "duty
    for duty's sake". He believed that man's moral duty
    consisted of respect for one's self as a free being, and
    one's obligation to act without violating the freedom of
    others. His *Address to the German Nation* had great po-
    litical influence.

3. Friedrich Schleiermacher (1768-1834) - German philoso-
    pher and theologian: Schleiermacher tried to correlate
    religion with the rationalistic views of his time. He
    believed that religious ideas were an impetus towards a
    life of virtue. One of his most influential works was
    Soliloquies.

4. George Wilhelm Hegel (1770-1831) - German philosopher: Hegel made significant contributions to the philosophy of history, art, religion, logic and politics. He was extremely influential although he was not recognized in Germany until many years after his death. He developed the dialectic system of reasoning. This consisted of a thesis and antithesis which was resolved by the formation of a new synthesis. His chief works include the *Science of Logic* and the *Encyclopedia of the Philosophical Sciences*.

V. Cultural Achievements - Fine Arts:

European art was dominated by the neo-classicists of the Academy of France until the downfall of Napoleon. With the fall of the French emporer and the introduction of the concept of democracy in France and the United States, no one country dominated the field of art. This was the age of the revival of styles from other eras and it was also the age of the "individual". The style of the Romanticist and neo-Classicist dominated art as well as literature from 1750 to 1820. The neo-Classicists stressed order, reason and balance whereas the Romanticists stressed emotions, senses and subjective imagination. Nature was idealized by both groups. The neo-Classical style favored balanced composition, smoothly modeled figures and muted colors. The Romantic style stressed the sensual effect of color, movement and individual expressions.
The following include some of the major painters of this period:

1. Sir Joshua Reynolds (1723-1792) - British painter: Reynolds was one of Britain's greatest portrait painters. He was the founder of the Literary Club of England. He was the first president of the Royal Academy of Arts where he presented his theories of art in *Discourses*. His famous paintings include *Mrs. Siddons as the Tragic Muse*.

2. Thomas Gainsborough (1727-1788) - British portraitist and landscape painter: Gainsborough was one of the most popular painters of the 18th century. He was influenced by Rubens and Van Dyck, but had a rococo touch. His most famous work is the *Blue Boy*.

3. John Singleton Copley (1738-1815) - American painter: Copley was a member of the Royal Academy. His portraits of British royalty include, *Death of Lord Chatham*. He is known for his originality in his paintings of historical subjects.

4. Jean Antoine (1740-1828) - French sculptor: Antoine is famous for his busts of Voltaire, Franklin, Rousseau, etc. He was invited to the United States and he created the statue of Washington (now at Richmond, Virginia).

5. Francisco Goya (1746-1828) - Spanish painter and engraver: Goya's paintings showed the beginning of modern art and he was considered to be one of the great Spanish masters. He was court painter for Charles IV of Spain. His famous works include: *The Executions of the Third of May* and *Caprichos*. He lived in exile in Bordeaux, France because of his political views.

6. Jacques Louis David (1748-1825) - French painter: David was the most important painter of the French Revolution and French school of painting during Napoleon's rule. One of his most famous paintings includes the *Portrait of Mme. Recamier*. Many of his paintings were inspired by classical and historical figures.

7. Pierre Charles L'Enfant (1754-1825) - French engineer and architect: L'Enfant fought in the American Revolution under Lafayette. In 1792 he drafted a plan for Washington, D.C. consisting of a series of radial avenues. His plan was not used until its expansion in 1901.

8. Gilbert Stuart (1755-1828) - American painter: Stuart painted many famous portraits of prominent men of the Revolutionary War Period. He also did portraits of King George III and the Prince of Wales. His portrait of George Washington is considered a masterpiece.

9. John Trumbull (1756-1843) - American artist: Trumbull served in the Revolutionary War. His famous paintings include the *Battle of Bunker Hill* and *Death of Montgomery before Quebec*. He was commissioned by Congress in 1817 to paint four works for the rotunda of the Capitol in Washington, D.C.

10. Charles Bulfinch (1763-1844) - American architect: Bulfinch traveled and studied architecture in Europe and then returned to the United States where he designed many buildings. His works include the completion (after 1817) of the United States Capitol.

Music of the Classical Period:

Developments Which Contributed to the Musical Culture:

A. General Characteristics: During the Classical Period, definite patterns and rules of composition were established. Some of the important characteristics of this period are:

   1. Clarity of form, objectivity in composition, simplicity of harmony, and clarity of melody were definitely established during this period.
   2. The objectivity of the Classical Period is more apparent in instrumental music than in vocal composition. The organization of instrumental choirs contributed to a better balance in instrumentation of the orchestra.
   3. Variations of dynamics and symbols to indicate levels of dynamics were used by the Classical composers.
   4. Vienna became the center of music at this time. The music of Bach, and Polyphonic music in general, became very distasteful during the Classical Period.
   5. Musical instruments were constantly being improved as to pitch, range, flexibility and tonal coloration. The piano was accepted as the most important keyboard instrument by the end of this period.
   6. Public concerts and the printing and publishing of music gave rise to a new era of patronization of music by the people.

B. Elements of Music:

   1. Melody: The emphasis on tonality and the use of the diatonic scale was an important step in creation of classical melodies. The long and embellished melodic line of the Baroque Period was replaced by more concise and symmetrical melodic structure.
   2. Harmony: The harmony of this period was marked by the use of a simple chord structure and the departure from contrapuntal forms. The instrumentation was used in such a way as to enhance the unusually refined harmonic effect.
   3. Rhythm: A simple, light and regular pulse is characteristic of the rhythm of this period. The rhythmic flow, created through the alternation of accented and unaccented beats was further articulated by rests and cadences.

C. Secular Vocal Music:

1. Opera: Opera composition underwent a tremendous
   growth and development during the Classical Period.
   The most important styles of opera composition are:
   a. Neapolitan Style - Italy: The Neapolitan style of
      opera composition was an extension of the Neapoli-
      tan opera of the Baroque Period, and its influence
      spread throughout Europe. The most important re-
      presentative composer of this period was Alessan-
      dro Scarlatti (1659-1725).
   b. Reformed Style - Germany: In this style the music
      was subordinated to the dramatic content of the
      opera. The music was simplified and the recitative
      became more important than the aria. An overture
      was included to create the mood for the opera. The
      opera libretti were influenced by Classical Greek
      drama. The most important representative composer
      was Christoph Willibald von Gluck (1714-1787).
   c. Reformed Style - Austria: Wolfgang Amadeus
      Mozart's opera style shows the influence of many
      schools of opera composition, especially the
      Italian school. He is considered the greatest
      opera composer of the 18th century, and his operas
      are the only ones of this period produced today,
      with the exception of Gluck's *Orfeo*.

D. Sacred Vocal Music: Generally speaking, sacred music of
   the Classical Period was mainly dramatic in style, and
   was more fit for the concert hall rather than the
   church. Religious music of this period consisted of the
   following: masses, motets, litanies and vespers.

1. Mass: The mass of this period, like other religious
   music, was not necessarily intended for church
   services. These masses are sometimes called concert
   masses. The most prominent composers of church music
   in the Classical Period were Haydn and Mozart.
2. Oratorio: The oratorio continued to be a popular
   vocal form during this period, especially in England.
   It is sometimes called a religious opera without
   scenery, costumes, and dancing. It has a religious
   text and uses orchestral accompaniment. The leading
   composer of oratorios in the Classical Period was
   Haydn, who wrote *The Creation* (1798) and *The Seasons*
   (1801).

E. Development of the Symphony Orchestra: The size of the
   symphony orchestra was increased during this period.

Instrumental choirs were established within the orchestra by Haydn. His plan established the practice which is used in our symphony orchestras today. The divisions are:

1. String choir: violin, viola, cello, and double-bass.
2. Brass choir: trumpet, French horn, trombone, and tuba.
3. Woodwind choir: flute, oboe, clarinet, and bassoon.
4. Percussion instruments: tympani, snare and bass drums, cymbals, etc.

F. Instrumental Music and Instrumental Forms: The instrumental music of the Classical Period attracted much more attention than the vocal music. The most important instrumental forms developed in this period are:

1. Classical Sonata: It has three or four movements. The most important form developed in the Classical Period was the sonata. It serves as the basis for most of the instrumental music of the period including the concerto, keyboard sonata, symphony and chamber music pieces. An analysis of the sonata is as follows:
   a. First movement: (Fast): It is written in sonata-allegro form which is made up of three main sections:
      (1) Exposition: The principal themes of the composition are presented in this section.
      (2) Development: This section develops the themes presented in the exposition with certain variations.
      (3) Recapitulation: This section restates the themes and material of the exposition in a different key sequence.
   b. Second movement: (Slow): The structure of this movement varies. A commonly used form is the ternary (A-B-A) song form.
   c. Third movement: (Minuet): It is played moderate or fast in 3/4 time. This is an optional movement in the sonata but is used in four-movement symphonies and quartets. It is in three-part song form with a trio.
   d. Fourth movement: (Finale - Fast): This movement is frequently written in rondo form. It is often similar to the first movement.

2. Classical Symphony: The symphony is one of the most outstanding contributions of the Classical Period, for it is the basis of most of the instrumental music of this period. It embodies the classical sonata form described above. It is usually in four movements, patterned after the sonata, with the third movement (minuet) sometimes omitted. Beethoven brought the symphony to its highest development in the Classical Period.
3. Classical Concerto: This is a sonata for solo instrument and orchestra.
4. Overture and Prelude: Both forms are instrumental introductions to a sonata, symphony, opera etc.
5. Divertimento: This form is similar to the suite. It has from four to ten movements.
6. String Quartet: It followed the same form as the classical sonata and was scored for two violins, viola and cello. The string quartet was the most popular type of chamber music groups of this period.
7. Keyboard Sonata: Its form varies according to the composer and includes from two to four movements.

JEAN-PHILIPPE RAMEAU

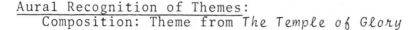

Composer: Jean-Philippe Rameau
   Born: Dijon, France 1683
   Died: Paris, France 1764

Aural Recognition of Themes:
   Composition: Theme from *The Temple of Glory*

General Information about Composer and Compositions:

1. Jean-Philippe Rameau played harpsichord music at sight when he was only seven years old. He also studied the organ and violin. His father was a church organist. Later he studied music in Paris under the tutelage of the famous organist Louis Marchand.

2. He toured Italy with a French opera group as a violinist. In 1727 he became the organist at St. Paul's Church in Paris. In 1732 he received the post of organist at Saint-Croix de la Britonnerie, and in 1736 he joined the staff of a Jesuit College.

3. Rameau is noted as the founder of modern harmony. In 1726 he published a treatise on harmony called *The New System of Music Theory*. In his system, all chords were based on intervals of a third. He simplified and classified all chords and their inversions.

4. In 1745 the King of France appointed Rameau chamber-composer to the King, and bestowed upon him the rank of Nobleman prior to his death. Rameau was given a solemn funeral befitting a nobleman at his death.

5. Besides being a prolific composer, Rameau was a prominent author of several outstanding books on music theory. He composed operas, ballets, cantatas, motets, harpsichord suites, and arrangements for violin and piano. He composed the opera *La Princesse de Navarre* (1745) for the wedding of the Dauphin and Infanta of Spain, using the libretto written by the author Voltaire.

Composer's Main Contribution to the Art of Music:

1. Jean-Philippe Rameau continued the development of the French classical opera that was founded by Lully. He was considered an excellent theorist as a result of the publication of his treatise on harmony. He applied his ability to write enriched harmony to his orchestrations. The overtures to his operas are very popular today because of their beautiful melodies, pulsating rhythms and rich harmonies. His ability as a dramatist and orchestrator far surpassed that of any of his predecessors.

Suggested Listening:

1. Title: *Pièces de Clavecin*
   Performers: Leonhardt
   Record No.: Telefunken S-9422
   Grade Level: 4 - 8

2. Title: *Ballet Suite - The Temple of Glory*
   Performers: Orchestra - Budd
   Record No.: Candide 31012
   Grade Level: 7 - 12

Optional Assignments:

1. Write the name, city of origin, and conductor of the important symphony orchestras in the United States.

2. Do some research and make a chart of "dynamics", listing the symbols and meanings. Ex. (f) forte - loud.

3. Rameau was a church organist. Find out the duties of a church organist and make a report on your findings to the class.

4. Make a biographical sketch of the composer's life.

5. Write a paper on the subject of the necessity of studying the music of the past in order to comprehend better the music of today. Conduct a class discussion of this subject.

DOMENICO SCARLATTI

Composer: Domenico Scarlatti
    Born: Naples, Italy 1685
    Died: Madrid, Spain 1757

Aural Recognition of Themes:
    Composition: *Toccata in D Minor* (1730)

General Information about Composer and Compositions:

1. Domenico Scarlatti was the son of the famous composer Alessandro Scarlatti, who was his first music teacher. In 1708 Domenico studied music in Venice with the famous theorist Gasparini.

2. Domenico met George Frederick Handel in Venice where a competition was arranged to decide who was the more proficient in the playing of the harpsichord and organ. The result was a tie in harpsichord playing; Handel won the organ contest. The two men became very good friends.

3. He became court composer for Marie Casimire, Queen of Poland, writing many operas for her private performances in Rome. He also held court positions in Naples, Lisbon and Madrid where he served until his death in 1757.

4. He is known as the founder of modern piano technique. He developed the clavier sonata form which was later perfected by Franz Joseph Haydn. His piano style influenced such great composers as Mendelssohn and Liszt.

5. Domenico Scarlatti wrote more than six hundred sonatas and other pieces for the harpsichord. He composed operas, fugues, compositions for voices and organ, and a *Salve Regina* for a solo voice. He also wrote a collection of exercises for the piano.

Composer's Main Contribution to the Art of Music:

1. Domenico Scarlatti, a virtuoso harpsichordist, was a composer of music for this instrument. His works for keyboard instruments are excellent for developing technique. All phases of technical proficiency are required for the performance of his sonatas. Some of the technical devices are scale passages in parallel motion and contrary motion, arpeggios, trills and broken chords. His music has been transcribed for piano and is included today in the repertoire of most concert artists.

Suggested Listening:

1. Title: *Sonata for Piano*
   Performers: Horowitz
   Record No.: Columbia MS 6658
   Grade Level: 4 - 8

2. Title: *Sonatas for Harpsichord*
   Performers: Payne
   Record No.: Turnabout 34434
   Grade Level: 7 - 12

Optional Assignments:

1. Make a list of the various contemporary piano teaching methods for the beginning student.

2. Make a comparison of Domenico Scarlatti and his father Alessandro with reference to type of music they wrote and their contribution to music composition and performance.

3. If you are able to play the piano, perform for the class a composition by Domenico Scarlatti.

4. If you are artistic, draw or paint a picture of the harpsichord or organ.

5. Write a composition on the famous literary geniuses of this period.

GIUSEPPE TARTINI

Composer: Giuseppe Tartini
    Born: Pirano, Italy 1692
    Died: Padua, Italy 1770

Aural Recognition of Themes:
    Composition: *Concerto in D* (1745) for Violin and
                 Orchestra

General Information about Composer and Compositions:

1. Giuseppe Tartini was born of wealthy parents, who, though
   they realized that Giuseppe was musically talented, per-
   suaded him to study for the priesthood at the Pirano
   School of Oratories and later to study law at the University of Padua. He studied music at the Franciscan Monastery at Assisi. He was not only a famous composer and
   violin virtuoso, but was also an eminent scientist.

2. He became solo violinist at the Chapel of San Antonio in
   Padua in 1721. In 1723 he was appointed conductor of the
   court orchestra of Count Kinsky in Prague. He returned
   to Padua in 1723 where he founded a famous school for
   violin virtuosos.

3. He wrote treatises on music theory and acoustics. He was
   the discoverer of the harmonic sound effects of double-
   stops in violin playing. He made innovations in the
   physical structure of the violin bow and increased the
   thickness of the strings.

4. Tartini was an outstanding success as a teacher and
   author. He wrote a book for the use of his violin pupils
   called *The Art of Bowing*. His pupils included the most
   renowned violinists of the period.

102

5. Tartini composed one hundred and forty violin concertos, fifty string trios, one hundred and fifty sonatas for violin and harpsichord, and a trio for two violins and a bass. His *Miserere* was performed during Holy Week of 1758 in the Sistine Chapel.

Composer's Main Contribution to the Art of Music:

1. Giuseppe Tartini was one of the most important composers of music for the violin. He continued the work of Corelli who had first developed the solo sonata and concerto grosso. Through his music and technical innovations, Tartini achieved many improvements in violin playing.

Suggested Listening:

1. Title: *The Devil's Trill*
   Performers: Szeryng - violin
   Record No.: R.C.A. Victor, VIC-1037
   Grade Level: 4 - 8

2. Title: *Concerto in D for Violin*
   Performers: Francescatti
   Record No.: Columbia MS 6953
   Grade Level: 7 - 12

Optional Assignments:

1. Make a study of the famous violinists of today and list their names, native country and musical education, and report on their current performances.

2. Make a study of the string instruments of the symphony orchestra, and using a skeleton outline, present an oral report to the class.

3. If you can play the violin, perform a solo for the class. Demonstrate and explain the physical and tonal make-up of the violin to the class.

4. If you have attended a concert recently, tell your class about some of the selections on the program.

5. Tell the class about an historical or interesting event during the life of the composer.

KARL PHILIPP EMANUEL BACH

Composer: Karl Philipp Emanuel Bach
   Born: Weimar, Germany 1714
   Died: Hamburg, Germany 1788

Aural Recognition of Themes:
   Composition: *Concerto in D* (1745)

General Information about Composer and Compositions:

1. Karl Philipp Emanuel Bach was the son of the famous composer Johann Sebastian Bach, from whom he received most of his musical training. He studied law at the University of Frankfurt. He taught and performed his compositions at the Musik-Akademie and Collegium Musicum in Frankfurt.

2. He conducted and composed for a choral society in Frankfurt. From 1746 to 1757 he was chamber-musician and clavicinist to Frederick the Great of Prussia. Frederick the Great was an accomplished flutist and Bach was his accompanist. From 1767 until his death he served as director of church music at Hamburg.

3. He was one of the best clavier players of the period and established an impressive reputation as a virtuoso and teacher. He wrote a famous book on the art of keyboard playing, *Essay on the True Art of Playing Keyboard Instruments* (1753). This book is still used today in the study of the classic harmonic style.

4. He contributed a modern style to the sonata and symphony forms, and his development of orchestration foreshadowed modern techniques.

104

5. K.P.E. Bach composed two hundred and ten solo pieces for the clavier, fifty-two concertos with orchestra, sonatas, minuets, polonaises, fugues, marches etc. He also composed eighteen symphonies, instrumental compositions, oratorios, passions, motets, cantatas and other sacred songs.

Composer's Main Contribution to the Art of Music:

1. Karl Philipp Emanuel Bach is famous for his development of the piano sonata form. He is sometimes referred to as the composer that linked polyphony with homophony (single melody with harmonic accompaniment). His piano music had an immeasurable influence on Haydn, Mozart and Beethoven. He introduced a dramatic style of expression in his piano music. During his lifetime he was more renowned than his father, Johann Sebastian Bach.

Suggested Listening:

1. Title: *Concerto in D for Harpsichord*
   Performers: Collegium Anreum - Leonhardt
   Record No.: RCA VICS-1463
   Grade Level: 4 - 8

2. Title: *Orchestral Symphonies*
   Performers: Munich Bach Orchestra - Richter
   Record No.: DG, ARC-2533050
   Grade Level: 7 - 12

Optional Assignments:

1. The Bach family (twenty children) was very musical. After a study, write a report on the musicians and composers of this noted family.

2. There is another famous family of musical performers living today called the Trapp family. Do some research and give an oral report to the class on this family, living today in the United States.

3. Write a report on Benjamin Franklin who lived during this time, noting his contribution to the knowledge of electricity.

4. If you are a pianist, play a composition by the composer or another member of the Bach family for the class.

5. Do some research on the qualifications and training necessary for becoming a member of a professional choral society.

CHRISTOPH WILLIBALD VON GLUCK

Composer: Christoph Willibald von Gluck
    Born: Weidenwang, Germany 1714
    Died: Vienna, Austria 1787

Aural Recognition of Themes:
    Composition: *Dance of the Furies* from the opera
                 Orpheus and Eurydice (1762)

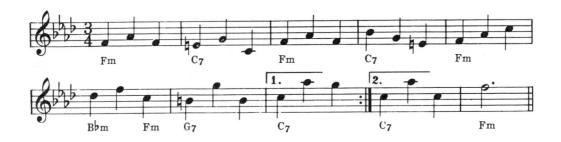

General Information about Composer and Compositions:

1. At the age of twelve, Christoph Willibald von Gluck went to Bohemia where he studied voice, organ, harpsichord and violin at the Jesuit School. In 1732 he went to Prague where he continued his study of music. While there, he also played professionally at peasant dances and sang in church choirs.

2. Gluck is one of the most important reformers of opera. He is sometimes called the "Father of Modern Opera". Gluck and Mozart are considered the two greatest composers of opera in the Classical Period. Gluck wrote his first opera *Artaserce* in 1741 which was so successful that he wrote seven other operas in a short period of time.

3. Gluck believed that music should assist the action of the story. He thought that the music was more important than the showmanship of the performer. Opera should not be the occasion for the singer merely to display her technical ability or virtuosity. He achieved a perfect blend of the lyrical and dramatic elements in opera.

4. In 1776, during the American Revolution, an operatic war broke out in Paris between the supporters of the traditional Italian opera style (headed by Piccinni) and the

106

followers of Gluck's reforms. Gluck's ideas triumphed. His operatic style was adopted by Mozart and others.

5. Gluck was great orchestrator. He made the orchestra a vital part of the drama instead of being merely a mechanical support as it had formerly been. His overtures are closely related to the opera itself. Many of his operas are based on Greek mythology: *Orfeo ed Euridice* (1762), *Alceste* (1767), *Paride ed Elena* (1770) and *Iphigenie en Tauride* (1779).

Composer's Main Contribution to the Art of Music:

1. Christoph Willibald von Gluck was one of the first composers to reform the opera. In his early period he followed the traditional Italian style of opera composition. In 1750 he joined a movement to reform this style. He created a perfect blend of the orchestra, drama and singing. He gave to the world an international style of operatic composition.

Suggested Listening:

1. Title: *Caprice on Airs de Ballet* from *Alceste*
   Performers: R.C.A. Victor Symphony Orchestra
   Record No.: Victor Basic Record Library E80, Vol. 4
   Grade Level: 4 - 8

2. Title: *Don Juan* - ballet
   Performers: Westminster Symphony Orchestra - Bernard
   Record No.: Everest 3188
   Grade Level: 7 - 12

Optional Assignments:

1. Play a recording of the composition listed under Aural Recognition of Themes for the class and give an oral report on the selection.

2. Write a report on the Revolutionary War and include the story and origin of the song *Yankee Doodle*.

3. Make up a notebook on the history of opera, including clippings related to the current opera season.

4. Make a list and diagram of the instruments of the orchestra of Gluck's time.

5. Write a biographical sketch of Gluck's life.

FRANZ JOSEF HAYDN

Composer: Franz Josef Haydn
  Born: Rohrau, Lower Austria 1732
  Died: Vienna, Austria 1809

Aural Recognition of Themes:
  Composition: *Symphony No. 94 in G* ("Surprise") (1791)

General Information about Composer and Compositions:

1. Franz Josef Haydn came from a musical family and at the age of five he studied music with his cousin Johann Frankh, a professional musician. In 1740 he became a choir boy at the Cathedral of St. Stephen in Vienna. In 1755 he conducted the orchestra for Prince Furnberg. From 1758 to 1761 he served as Kapellmeister to Count Morzin. In 1761 he accepted the position of Kapellmeister to the court of Prince Esterhazy.

2. Haydn believed that knowledge of the voice was an important requirement for a composer. He said that the human voice was the most beautiful of all musical instruments. Haydn was one of the best composers of religious music. He composed masses, motets, offertories and oratorios. Oratorios: *The Creation* and *The Seasons* (1801). Masses: *Missa Solemnis in B Flat Major* (1801).

3. Haydn was known as the "Father of the Symphony Orchestra" (Papa Haydn). He was the first composer to develop the use of choirs of instruments in the physical arrangement of the symphony orchestra: (1) String choir, (2) Brass choir, (3) Woodwind choir, (4) Percussion group.

4. His symphonies portray clearness of style, grace and playfulness. A good example of this playfulness is the humorous use of an explosive chord in the *Surprise Symphony* supposedly to awaken those in the audience who fell asleep during the Andante movement of the symphony.

108

5. Most of Haydn's symphonies were composed of four movements: (1) *Introduction - Allegro*, (2) *Andante*, (3) *Minuet*, (4) *Finale*. He was a very prolific composer, and he composed one-hundred and twenty-five symphonies, in addition to many other types of compositions.

Composer's Main Contribution to the Art of Music:

1. Franz Josef Haydn established the pattern of structure for the symphony orchestra, and set the form of symphonic composition for later composers. He revised sonata form as it existed at that time, introduced the minuet as the third movement, and also perfected the other movements.

Suggested Listening:

1. Title: *Surprise Symphony - Andante*
   Performers: R.C.A. Victor Symphony Orchestra
   Record No.: R.C.A. Basic Record Library, E-80, Vol. 4
   Grade Level: 4 - 8

2. Title: *The Creation* - oratorio
   Performers: N.Y. Philharmonic and Camarata Singers
   Record No.: Columbia M2S 773
   Grade Level: 7 - 12

Optional Assignments:

1. Make a seating plan of the modern symphony orchestra of today.

2. Write words to the main theme of the *Surprise Symphony*, keeping in mind the element of humor that Haydn injected into this composition.

3. Make a comparison of the above theme with the popular song of today. Conduct an oral discussion of this subject in class.

4. After a study, give an oral report on the historical background of this period.

5. If you play a musical instrument, select a composition of the composer and perform it for the class.

LUIGI BOCCHERINI

Composer: Luigi Boccherini
    Born: Lucca, Italy 1743
    Died: Madrid, Spain 1805

Aural Recognition of Themes:
    Composition: *Menuetto* (1802)

General Information about Composer and Compositions:

1. Luigi Boccherini was taught the cello by his father who himself was a professional bass violinist. Luigi continued his musical education with Abbe Vanucci, who was choirmaster to the Archbishop. Boccherini was a well-known composer and also the most renowned cellist of the period.

2. From 1757 to 1767 he lived in Rome where he became famous as a composer and cello soloist. From 1764 to 1779 he played in the theatre orchestra and town band of Lucca. During this period he toured Europe with Filippo Manfredi, a renowned violinist, and his reputation was greatly enhanced by performances for royalty.

3. From 1779 to 1785 he was chamber-composer to the King of Spain. During this period he wrote six quartets which he dedicated to the Infante Don Luis, brother of the King. In 1787 he dedicated a composition to Friedrich Wilhelm II, King of Prussia, who awarded him the post of chamber-composer to the King with a comfortable salary.

4. Although Boccherini was an Italian, he was very much influenced by the Viennese style of composition. The

influence of Franz Josef Haydn was very apparent in his symphonies and chamber music.

5. Boccherini was a very prolific composer of chamber music having written four hundred and sixty-seven instrumental works. He composed twenty symphonies, one opera, concer- tos, string quartets, sonatas, one oratorio and one mass.

Composer's Main Contribution to the Art of Music:

1. Luigi Boccherini is noted for his development of chamber music for strings. He composed a large amount and variety of string music, and was the first composer to write music for string quintets and string sextets. Although he lived during the time of Haydn and Mozart and could have been easily overshadowed by their genius, Boccherini was recognized by his contemporaries as a master of the art of composition for strings.

Suggested Listening:

1. Title: *Minuet*
   Performers: R.C.A. Victor Symphony Orchestra
   Record No.: R.C.A. Basic Record Library, E-80, Vol. 4
   Grade Level: 4 - 8
2. Title: *Cello Concerto in B Flat Major*
   Performers: Giulini Philharmonic - Starker
   Record No.: Angel S 35725
   Grade Level: 7 - 12

Optional Assignments:

1. If you play the cello, or any other string instrument, perform a solo for the class and give a brief description and history of the instrument.

2. Do some research on chamber music and write a report about it.

3. Write a review of a chamber music concert you have heard either in concert, radio or television.

4. If you are artistic, draw or paint a picture of the composer and present it to the class for bulletin board display.

5. Tell the class about an historical or interesting event that took place during the life of the composer.

MUZIO CLEMENTI

Composer: Muzio Clementi
    Born: Rome, Italy 1752
    Died: Evesham, England 1832

Aural Recognition of Themes:
    Composition: *Sonata No. 2 in B Flat* (1773) - second
        theme

General Information about Composer and Compositions:

1. As a child Muzio Clementi was taught music by A. Buroni, a choirmaster at the local church. He later studied organ with the famous organist Condicelli. At the age of nine he was appointed church organist in Rome and when he became fourteen, several of his works, among which was a mass, were performed in public.

2. At the age of fourteen, Clementi went to London where he made a successfull debut as a pianist and composer. Except for his concert tours he spent all of his time in England as conductor, virtuoso and teacher. He formed his own company for publishing music and constructing pianos.

3. Clementi was a master in the development of piano technique. He was one of the first to develop a specific style of composition for the piano whereas previous composers wrote mainly for the harpsichord and clavichord. In 1773 he composed three sonatas which became models for the piano sonata form.

4. Clementi foreshadowed Beethoven in piano composition for he set the style for the piano sonata form. Beethoven

112

thought so highly of Clementi's piano sonatas that he recommended their use for all piano students and virtuosos of that era.

5. He composed one hundred sonatas, fugues, variations and waltzes for the piano. One of his most famous musical accomplishments in use today is the *Gradus ad Parnassum* (1817).

Composer's Main Contribution to the Art of Music:

1. Muzio Clementi was the first composer to take advantage of the perfected mechanism of the piano in his compositions. With the invention of the piano, it became possible to play sustained tones and various degrees of dynamics (loud and soft) therefore producing a more sonorous tone quality. He was the first composer to develop a specific style for piano composition and wrote several musical works which set the pattern for other composers.

Suggested Listening:

1. Title: *Clementi Sonatas*
   Performers: Crowson
   Record No.: Oiseau S-306
   Grade Level: 4 - 8

2. Title: *Concerto in* C, for piano and orchestra
   Performers: Prague Orchestra - Blumenthal
   Record No.: Turnabout 34375
   Grade Level: 7 - 12

Optional Assignments:

1. Make a list of composers who wrote piano music and list their most famous compositions.

2. Do some research on Carl Czerny and compare him with Muzio Clementi.

3. Describe the differences in construction of the piano, harpsichord and clavichord.

4. If you are a pianist, play one of the works or studies of Clementi for the class.

5. Write and present a report to the class about the various makers of musical instruments during Clementi's lifetime.

WOLFGANG AMADEUS MOZART

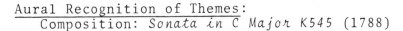

Composer: Wolfgang Amadeus Mozart
  Born: Salzburg, Austria 1756
  Died: Vienna, Austria 1791

Aural Recognition of Themes:
  Composition: *Sonata in C Major K545* (1788)

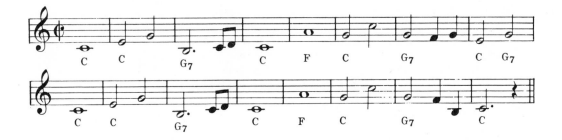

General Information about Composer and Compositions:

1. Wolfgang Amadeus Mozart was a child prodigy and a musical genius. His father, Leopold, was a professional musician and composer. Wolfgang played piano at the age of three. At five years of age he composed a concerto. At the age of six, he made his first concert tour of Europe. When he was only eight, his first four violin sonatas were published. At the age of nine his first symphonies were played in London. By the time he reached fourteen, he had completed two comic operas and one opera seria.

2. In 1770 he went to Rome where he performed the remarkable feat of genius. He notated from memory the entire score of Gregorio Allegris' *Miserere* after hearing it only once. His early reputation as a prodigy and musical genius actually hindered his career as a concert artist in later years. He had lost a great deal of his glamour and public appeal as an adult performer.

3. He expressed himself in his music with such a perfect blend of emotional and spiritual feeling that the listener is completely receptive to his art. Mozart was recognized as the greatest melodic genius of his time, as is exemplified in his operas and symphonies: Operas: *The Marriage of Figaro* (1786) and *Don Giovanni* (1787); Symphonies: *Jupiter* (1788) and *Prague* (1786).

4. Much of his piano music is included in the standard repertoire of all concert pianists. He composed many sonatas and concertos.

5. Mozart used more chromatic devices and embellishments than Haydn. The musical form of his symphonies was more refined than that of his contemporaries due partly to his superior musical training. He composed symphonies, operas, piano and violin concertos, sonatas, fantasies, masses, motets and chamber music.

Composer's Main Contribution to the Art of Music:

1. Wolfgang Amadeus Mozart was recognized as a genius in all areas of musical composition. His immense creative ability, his complete mastery of musical form, his genius in expressing human emotions and spiritual feeling, his versatility and universal understanding of human nature all contributed to the greatness of his achievement. His compositions were a culmination of much of the music that preceded his era and forshadowed most of the music of future composers.

Suggested Listening:

1. Title: *Divertimento No. 17*
   Performers: Esterhazy Orchestra
   Record No.: Vanguard C-10066
   Grade Level: 4 - 8

2. Title: *Symphony No. 41 in C (Jupiter)*
   Performers: Boston Symphony Orchestra - Leinsdorf
   Record No.: R.C.A. Victor LM 2694
   Grade Level: 7 - 12

Optional Assignments:

1. If you are a pianist, play a composition of Mozart for the class.

2. Do some research on Mozart's *Symphony in C Major* and give an explanation for the use of the name *Jupiter* for this symphony.

3. Prepare a skit involving interesting incidents in the life of Mozart.

4. Make a study of the major performing instruments of the composer and collect literature and pictures of these instruments for your notebook.

5. Write a paper about the scientists and the scientific developments of this period.

LUDWIG VAN BEETHOVEN

Composer: Ludwig van Beethoven
 Born: Bonn, Germany 1770
 Died: Vienna, Austria 1827

Aural Recognition of Themes:
 Composition: *Für Elise* (1810)

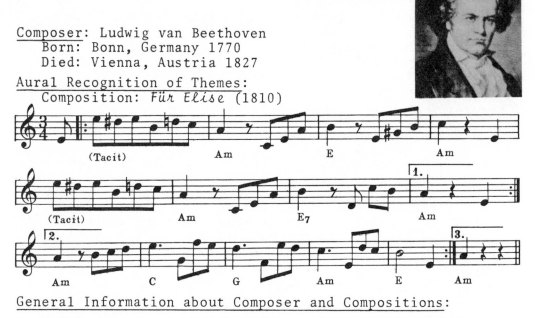

General Information about Composer and Compositions:

1. Ludwig van Beethoven came from a poor family and was exploited by his selfish father who, because of the boy's musical talents, wanted to make another Mozart of him. At the age of four his father began to teach him violin and piano. In 1781, he studied composition and harmony along with organ under the tutelage of the court organist, Christian Gottlob Neefe; and at the age of fifteen became Neefe's assistant. He was eleven years old when he composed three piano sonatas. At the age of fifteen, he played cembalo with the opera orchestra.

2. In 1795 he made his first concert appearance in Vienna as a pianist and was proclaimed one of the foremost pianists of that time. In 1800 he made his debut as a composer in Vienna with the performance of his first symphony. Beethoven was a pupil of Haydn and was influenced by both Haydn and Mozart in his earlier compositions.

3. It is the opinion of some that Beethoven is the most famous and important composer of all time. His music represents the peak of the Classical school of composition and the beginning of the Romantic school. The music of Beethoven contained great emotional expression, masterful style and form, and superb use and expansion of the instrumentation of the symphony orchestra. In his *Ninth Symphony* he used a chorus to help achieve the expression of his emotions and ideas.

4. During the last twenty years of his life he was completely deaf. Although physically handicapped and emotionally
disturbed by his loneliness, Beethoven achieved his most
creative musical output during this period. When he died
in 1827 he was paid homage by the musical world of Europe.
Franz Schubert was a pallbearer at his funeral and a
eulogy was delivered by the famous Austrian poet,
Grillparzer.
5. He composed symphonies, overtures, piano and violin concertos and sonatas, operas, masses and chamber music.
Among the most popular of these are: Symphony: *Symphonies
Nos. 1 to 9* (1800-1823); Opera: *Fidelio* (1805); Mass:
Missa Solemnis in D (1823).

Composer's Main Contribution to the Art of Music:

1. The music of Ludwig van Beethoven is probably performed
more and given greater recognition by musicians than that
of any other composer in history. His early compositions
expressed the traditionally stricter form of the Classical period while his later works established a freedom of
structure and expression typical of the Romantic era. His
greatness is displayed in his ability to transmit and
symbolize through his compositions the supreme expression
of the human spirit and nature at a high intellectual and
emotional level.

Suggested Listening:

1. Title: *Symphony No. 8* - second movement
   Performers: National Symphony Orchestra, Washington, D.C.
   Record No.: R.C.A. Victor LE 1009 Adventures in Music
   Grade Level: 4 - 8
2. Title: *Prometheus* - ballet music
   Performers: Boston Symphony Orchestra - Leinsdorf
   Record No.: RCA Victor LSC-3032
   Grade Level: 7 - 12

Optional Assignments:

1. Make up a notebook on the life and music of Beethoven.

2. Play a recording of a composition by Beethoven for the
   class, and conduct a discussion of this composition.

3. Learn a basic dance (Minuet) used during the composer's
   lifetime and perform it for the class.

4. Write a report on the history and development of the
   major instruments of this period.

5. Create a crossword puzzle, or make up a quiz using
   information about the composer.

Haydn rehearsing a quartet in the Esterházy castle.

CHAPTER 6

THE ROMANTIC PERIOD (1820-1900)

Historical Background of the Romantic Period:

I. Introduction: Since the end of the Middle Ages, nationalism had been developing in the Western countries. This development gained momentum with the rise and fall of Napoleon. With nationalism came the rise of liberalism and industrialization which were opposed by the conservative groups of the royalty, clergy and aristocracy. The new liberalism eventually brought about political equality and abolition of class distinction. The progressives, composed of idealists who promoted nationalism, liberal views, and new industrial production methods, began steadily gaining power.

During the period of 1848 to 1900, historical events took place which were of decisive importance to the culture of Russia, United States and Asia. The great strides achieved in science and industry forced a change in political events. The significant events that followed were: the emancipation of the slaves in America and serfs in Russia, and the opening of the Far Eastern ports to the Western nations.

A. Era of Metternich:

1. Following the defeat of Napoleon (1815), the European nations met in Vienna to form a peace treaty. Prince Klemens von Metternich represented Austria. The thirty years following the Congress of Vienna is called the Age of Metternich.

2. Metternich was one of the leaders of the Quadruple Alliance (Austria, Russia, Prussia and England) which suppressed democratic or nationalistic revolts. His system enforced censorship of speech, press and education. A spy system was used to uncover plots to overthrow the government.

3. In 1820, a revolt broke out in Spain and a French army was sent by the Quadruple Alliance to crush it. Spain then became an autocratic and backward state for about 100 years.

4. In Italy (1820) in the states of Piedmont and Naples, a revolt was led by the Carbonari ("charcoal burners").This secret organization demanded the limiting

of the absolute power of royalty.

5. After Napoleon's defeat, Spain tried to regain her colonies in South America. The American people sympathized with the South American colonies who were trying to obtain their freedom. In the Monroe Doctrine (1823) the United States warned Metternich and Spain that the European nations should not transgress and infringe on the rights of the governments of the Western Hemisphere.

6. In 1821 the Greeks revolted against the Turks. France, Russia and England, breaking with the Quadruple Alliance, gave aid to the Greeks which enabled them to win their freedom in 1829. This was another blow against the Metternich system.

B. French Revolution of 1830:

1. In Paris (July 1830) the bourgeois revolted against Charles X and Louis Philippe was elected King by the legislature. The "Citizen King" was opposed by liberal and democratic groups, for the workers who had fought were still not given the right to vote. Because this revolt succeeded, it led to revolts in other parts of Europe.

C. Revolutions of 1848:

1. In February 1848, riots broke out in Paris and Louis Philippe was dethroned. A provisional government under Louis Blanc was established. Soon, this government was eliminated and a Second French Republic under middle-class bourgeois was established.

2. The German states under the "Frankfurt Assembly" were not able to establish unity until the next generation because of disagreement over the type of government to be established.

3. Charles Albert of Sardinia attempted to unify Italy but was defeated by the Austrian armies in 1849. Constitutions were revoked and the liberals were jailed.

4. Democratic and nationalistic revolts swept through the Austrian Empire in 1848. Prince Metternich became a main target of these revolts because of the growing inefficiency of the Austrian government. He was exiled and the revolution was later suppressed by the Austrian army.

120

5. The supporters of nationalism had not yet won freedom and unity for the Italians, Germans, Czechs and Hungarians.

D. Crimean War (1854-1856):

1. The Crimean War reflected the rivalry between England and Russia. French, English, Italian and Turkish troops put an end to Russian aggression in Turkey.

E. American Civil War (1861-1865):

1. The cotton and rice plantation owners encouraged the use of slave labor and as a result Negro slavery spread throughout the South. From 1845 to 1860 the settlement of each new territory resulted in a controversy over slavery.

2. The firing on Fort Sumter resulted in Abraham Lincoln's issuing his proclamation of war in 1861. Much hardship and suffering was caused in the South particularly by Sherman's March to the Sea and the Union blockade of southern seaports. In 1865 General Lee surrendered to General Grant at Appomattox.

3. One of the effects of the war was the break up of the plantation system. The victory of the Union resolved the question of the supremacy of the Federal government over the state government. It abolished slavery in the nation.

F. Franco-Prussian War (1870)

1. To increase his faltering prestige, Napoleon III entered into a reckless war with Prussia (1870-1871). France was quickly defeated and Napoleon III was exiled to England. By the Treaty of Frankfurt, Prussia obtained Alsace Lorraine and was paid an indemnity of one billion dollars by France. The Franco-Prussian War completed the unification of the German Empire.

G. Industrial Revolution:

1. The invention of machines that could replace human labor introduced the First Industrial Revolution. The revolution began in England which had the skilled labor, water power, natural resources, overseas colonial markets, and the machinery necessary for manufacturing. The First Industrial Revolution

resulted in the development of the factory system, poor working conditions, child labor, the growth of industrial cities and a new class system. Manufacturing grew in England, United States, France and Belgium.

2. After 1870, the Second Industrial Revolution (or New Industrial Revolution) saw a period of very rapid growth in the number of countries becoming industrialized. The revolution was an impetus to the development of new forms of communication and transportation. In the United States railroads were built across the continent helping industry to grow and aiding in the settlement of pioneers across the country. Russia built the Trans-Siberian Railway (1895-1905) which connected European and Asiatic Russia. Many canals were built because the cost of transporting goods overland was high. The Suez Canal (1869) joined Europe to the Far East by way of the Mediterranean Sea.

3. Labor and governments acted to cope with the problems of industrialization. Labor unions were organized and government legislation was voted to improve working and living conditions of the worker. In England unions were legalized in 1825 and strikes were made lawful in 1875. Labor parties were formed to uphold the rights of workers and unions. In European countries they were called Socialist Parties. The revolution spread throughout Europe, America and Asia.

Studies in Cultural Correlation - Romantic Period:

I. Cultural Achievements - Social Studies:

The industrial revolution of the 19th century began to attract people to the cities resulting in the development of urban areas. An agricultural revolution was also taking place. Industry was dependent on agriculture for cotton, wool and other raw materials. Markets were created for the provision of food for the workers and the sale of manufactured products. Farming was thus becoming a big business. Industrial work replaced "small" farming as a chief means of employment.

Monotony in the repetitive type of work, long working hours, low pay, abuses of child labor and slum living conditions, created a wide gulf between laborers and the factory owner who supplied the capital. The workers strove to obtain better conditions by organizing trade unions.

The labor movement became involved in socialism and political democracy.

The following were prominent leaders in social developments:

1. Karl Marx (1813-1883) - German political philosopher: Marx was the founder of modern socialism or Marxism. With Friedrich Engels (1820-1895) he wrote *The Communist Manifesto* (1848). His chief work was *Das Kapital* (1867). He wrote about class struggle, surplus value, the economic systems' influence on history, internationalism of workers' unions, and his belief in the inevitability of socialism. Lenin's interpretation of Marx's theories were put into practice in Communist Russia after the Russian Revolution of 1917.

2. Andrew Carnegie (1835-1919) - American industrialist and philanthropist: Carnegie founded the United States Steel Corporation. His large grants of money promoted peace and aided scientific research, libraries, colleges and the fine arts. He gave funds for Carnegie Hall in New York. He was one of the wealthiest Americans. In his book *The Gospel of Wealth*, he wrote of the responsibility of rich men to society and the necessity for their creating social services.

3. Comte de Saint Simon (1760-1825) - French social philosopher: Saint Simon's idealistic social theory proposed and organized society which was scientifically planned to aid the poor through communal control of property. He taught that freedom resulted from serving the community and that economic conditions influenced spiritual values. His works included: *Système Industriel* (1820-1823) and *Nouveau Christianisme* (1825).

4. Robert Owen (1771-1858) - British utopian socialist and author: A textile factory owner, Owen remodeled the town of New Lamarck, Scotland creating a utopian colony by supervising education, housing, and giving his employees a share in management and profit. His cooperatives in both New Lamarck, Scotland and New Harmony, Indiana failed but his ideas influenced socialist and cooperative societies.

5. Benjamin Disraeli (1804-1881) - British statesman and novelist: Disraeli's famous works include *Coningsby* (1844) and *Lothair* (1820) which displayed his brilliant insight into the political and social issues of the day. He extended British imperialism by purchasing control of the Suez Canal, crowning Queen Victoria Empress of India,

by obtaining Cypress and stopping Russia from gaining control of Constantinople at the Congress of Berlin (1878).

II. <u>Cultural Achievements</u> - <u>Physical Sciences</u>:

Science had a profound influence on this age. The invention of machinery resulted in altering methods of labor. Technology caused new and changing social conditions which forced changes in government.

The work of the 18th century scientists that had been accomplished by the use of the scientific method was enlarged upon by research and then applied. Medical research began conquering deseases and providing better means of health. Improved means and methods of communication made important contributions to the spread of knowledge throughout the world.

The following people contributed to scientific progress:

1. <u>Michael Faraday</u> (1791-1867) - British physicist and chemist: Faraday discovered electromagnetic induction which laid the foundation for the invention of the telegraph and many types of industrial machinery.

2. <u>Samuel F. B. Morse</u> (1791-1872) - American artist and inventor: Morse as a portrait painter founded the National Academy of Design in New York City (1825). He invented the telegraph and developed the Morse code.

3. <u>Charles Darwin</u> (1809-1882) - British naturalist: On the basis of evidence that Darwin collected over a period of about twenty-five years as a naturalist, he published his: *Origin of the Species* (1859) and *The Descent of Man* (1871). He developed the theory of organic evolution.

4. <u>Gregor Mendel</u> (1822-1884) - Austrian biologist: Mendel, who was an Augustinian monk, established the laws of heredity through his experiments with plants.

5. <u>Louis Pasteur</u> (1822-1895) - French chemist and bacteriologist: Pasteur developed the germ theory of disease and is called "the father of modern bacteriology". He discovered the treatment of rabies and developed the method of pasteurization for destroying harmful bacteria in milk.

6. <u>William Morton</u> (1819-1868) - American dentist: Morton was the first to use ether as an anaesthetic in surgery.

7. Joseph <u>Lister</u> (1827-1912) - British surgeon: Basing his
   methods on work accomplished by Pasteur, Lister developed and introduced antiseptic methods in surgery, thus
   enormously reducing fatalities caused by infections.

8. Thomas Alva <u>Edison</u> (1847-1931) - American inventor:
   Edison obtained over thirteen hundred patents. His most
   well-known inventions include: the incandescent lamp,
   phonograph, motion picture machine, mimeograph machine,
   the carbon telephone transmitter and carbon microphone.

III. <u>Cultural Achievements</u> - <u>Literature</u>:

At the beginning of the 19th century literature was
characterized as being romantic. Romantic literature was
less restrained than the previous classical literature.
It was a revolt against the formal and rational thought of
the 18th century, the interest in ancient Greek and Roman
culture, and also against many of the social, moral and
political traditions of the period. Literature was influenced by the scientific advances along with the industrial and social unrest which created new ideas of thought.
In England, the works of this period were designated as
Victorian, named after the Queen who reigned from 1837 to
1901. In France, from 1840 to 1900, realism and naturalism
in literature emphasized the psychological approach to the
study of the problems of the individual and society. In
Germany, the literary style was nationalistic for the
unification of the country was not completed until 1871.
Significant writers of this period include:

1. Lord George Gordon <u>Byron</u> (1788-1824) - British poet:
   Byron's greatest poem *Don Juan* (1819-1823) was a witty
   satire on English society's corruption and hypocrisy,
   set in a framework of the adventures of Don Juan.
   Byron's style was imitated by many future poets.

2. Heinrich <u>Heine</u> (1797-1856) - German poet and critic:
   Heine wrote lyrical poetry of profound beauty. His
   satirical works *Travel Pictures* (1826-1831) and *Germany*
   (1844) stressed his disgust with the social and political conditions in Germany. He fought against bigotry
   and oppression. Schubert, Schumann and Brahms are among
   the famous composers who have set to music many of
   Heine's sentimental lyrics and ballads (e.g. *In the
   Lovely Month of May* and *The Loreley*).

3. Robert <u>Browning</u> (1812-1899) - British poet: Browning
   was an outstanding poet who portrayed a variety of
   characters through his famous dramatic monologues.

Among these are: *The Ring and the Book, My Last Duchess* and *Fra Lippo Lippi*. His wife, Elizabeth Barrett Browning (1806-1861), was also a famous poet noted for her celebrated love poems (e.g. *Sonnets from the Portuguese*).

4. Herman Melville (1819-1891) - American author: Melville's *White Jacket* (1850), dealt with the hardships suffered in the Navy and helped improve the conditions of life aboard ship in this service. His novel on whaling *Moby Dick*, is considered to be his masterpiece.

5. Walt Whitman (1819-1892) - American poet: Whitman developed a free verse style. In his writings he portrayed American democracy and also a deep sense of humanity. His works include: *Leaves of Grass* and *Democratic Vistas*.

6. Fedor M. Dostoevsky (1821-1881) - Russian novelist: Dostoevsky's works include: *Crime and Punishment, The Brothers Karamazov* and *The Possessed*. His novels are famous for his graphic portrayal of human motivation.

7. Leo Tolstoy (1828-1910) - Russian novelist: Tolstoy's *War and Peace*, is considered by many to be the greatest historical novel of the 1800's. It was concerned with Napoleon's invasion of Russia and the heroism of the common soldier. His novel *Anna Karenine*, criticized society through the unhappy love affair of the heroine. Tolstoy was a moral and spiritual leader of his time.

8. Emile Zola (1840-1902) - French novelist: Zola's works were concerned with political, social and psychological matters. His editorial masterpiece, *J'Accuse*, helped secure the release of an officer, Dreyfus, from a penal colony. His novels include: *L'Assommoir*, a study of alcoholism and *Germinal*, concerned with the hardships of miners.

9. Charles Dickens (1812-1870) - British novelist: Dickens' historical novel *A Tale of Two Cities*, dealt with the French Revolution. His *A Christmas Carol* (1843), is universally known. Among his other novels are: *David Copperfield* and *Oliver Twist*. His novels attacked the social evils of child labor and debtors' prisons.

10. Mark Twain (1835-1910) - American writer: Twain's works give a vivid insight into American character which includes individualism, love of fun, and the devotion to democratic ideals. Among his famous works are: *The*

Prince and the Pauper, Huckleberry Finn, The Adventures of Tom Sawyer and *A Connecticut Yankee in King Arthur's Court.*

IV. Cultural Achievements - Philosophy:

New philosophies emerged and materialistic theories began diminishing in influence during the 19th century. This was the age of the "individual" when romanticists stressed feeling and instinct as against the narrowness of over-intellectualism. The theory of utilitarianism which emerged placed the good or happiness of men above social and political interests.

Biological knowledge made great strides and the theory of biological evolution also dominated philosophic thought. The concept of evolution changed from a speculative to a scientific theory.

Prominent philosophers of this period include the following:

1. Auguste Comte (1798-1857) - French philosopher: Comte was the founder of modern sociology. He developed a new social science based on observation and experience. He called his social philosophy "positivism" or social physics. In *Course of Positive Philosophy*, he divided positivism into order (Social Statics) and progress (Social Dynamics).

2. Jeremy Bentham (1748-1832) - English philosopher: Bentham was interested in obtaining legislative reform in the extension of the ballot. He was the founder of utilitarianism and stressed this in his work *The Principles of Morals and Politics*. He believed that the good or evil of an act was determined by its usefulness in achieving the "greatest happiness of the greatest number", hence its utility.

3. John Stuart Mill (1806-1873) - British philosopher and economist: Mill sought in his *System of Logic* (1843) to find a place in the utilitarian theory for the feelings of man which consisted of more than the mere seeking of pleasure. In social philosophy he sought freedom of thought and speech for the individual (*e.g. On Liberty*).

4. Herbert Spencer (1820-1903) - British philosopher: Spencer was concerned with an evolutionary survey of man and nature. He correlated the principle of evolution to politics, society and all phases of life. His most famous work was *Synthetic Philosophy.*

5. Ernst Haeckel (1834-1919) - German biologist and philosopher: Haeckel supported the evolution theory of Darwin in his *Riddle of the Universe* (1899). He is known for his monistic (one kind of substance) philosophy of nature. His works became popular in Germany and throughout Europe.

6. Frederich Wilhelm Nietzsche (1844-1900) - German philosopher: Nietzsche attacked modern Christianity for its weakness or "morality of pity". He stressed the importance of the will and the need in life for the development of a powerful type of person which he called the "superman". His greatest works include: *Thus Spake Zarathustra* and *Beyond Good and Evil*. His philosophy influenced the development of Hitler's Nazism.

V. Cultural Achievements - Fine Arts:

Romanticism, Realism, Impressionism, Post-Impressionism and Symbolism are the various stages in the development of painting from 1820 to 1900. There were few sculptors during this period, for the main artistic expression was in painting. Rodin, an outstanding sculptor, was one of the few exceptions. Sculpture became the side line work of many artists, including Degas and Renoir.

The architecture of the period manifested the influence of earlier styles, e.g. Classic, Gothic, Renaissance and Baroque.

The art centers of this period became Paris, London, Vienna and Berlin. Although there was an outstanding English school of landscape painting at the beginning of the 19th century, the greatest center of European painting of this age was the School of Paris.

Some of the notable artists of this period include:

1. John Constable (1776-1837) - British landscape painter: Constable was the founder of the English school of landscape painting. He used the countryside of Southern England (*View of Stokes*) for almost all of his works. His technique of using the palette knife to apply color was later used by the Impressionists.

2. Pierre Auguste Renoir (1841-1919) - French painter: Renoir created his own personal style by combining the classical style with the achievements of his time. He re-introduced the method of making colors appear to be in a certain position by their relative warmth or coolness. He combined the classical color and form techniques with the Impressionistic portrayal of light

effects. *The Luncheon of the Boating Party*, includes his vivid play of color and subtle portrayal of individual human beings.

3. Edouard Manet (1832-1883) - French painter: Manet is called the originator of impressionistic painting. He was not concerned with the nature of the object he painted, but was more interested in its appearance at a certain moment of time and under certain atmospheric conditions. Hence, light activated the painting of his figures or landscape. One of his famous paintings is *L'Olympia*.

4. Auguste Rodin (1840-1917) - French sculptor: Rodin was one of the most original and bold artists of his day. His work fused naturalism, romanticsm and impressionism which he achieved through his use of contrasting surfaces and balance of mass and space. One of his famous pieces is *The Thinker*.

5. Paul Gauguin (1848-1903) - French painter: Gauguin, a painter of the post-impressionist school, left France and went to Tahiti where he painted Tahitian life. He painted his subjects in rich color accents such as pink, lemon, yellow and lilac. His famous paintings include his self-portrait and *Zahini with Gardenia*.

6. Henri de Toulouse-Lautrec (1864-1901) - French painter: Toulouse-Lautrec's portraits of singers and actors of Parisian cabarets were skilfully portrayed by his flat, two-dimensional Japanese type of prints. He is noted for the development of the lithographic process which he used for his poster reproductions. His famous paintings include: *Seated Girl* and *Back View*.

7. Paul Cézanne (1839-1906) - French painter: Cézanne attempted to combine classical techniques and impressionism. His still lifes and landscapes are noted for their vivid color and depth. His *Card Players* and *Oranges*, were examples of his style that influenced many outstanding artists of the 1900's.

8. James Whistler (1834-1903) - American artist, etcher and author: Whistler settled in London (1863) where he became known for his wit as an author and his use of impressionism in his painting. He became well-known in Paris and London also for his etchings. His most famous oil painting is the portrait of his mother.

9. Alexandre Gustave Eiffel (1832-1923) - French engineer:
   Eiffel's most famous works include the Panama Canal
   Locks and the Eiffel Tower of Paris (1887-1889). His use
   of compressed air caissons in bridge building, and
   studies in aerodynamics were significant contributions
   to the field of engineering.

Music of the Romantic Period:

Developments Which Contributed to the Musical Culture:

A. General Characteristics: Many far-reaching changes in
   musical expression and composition were brought about
   during the Romantic Period. Self-expression and freedom
   from strict form in the arts was the ideal for this
   period. The following musical developments and characteristics are notable:

   1. Music of the Romantic Period expressed emotion, mood
      and tension.
   2. Expression of individual freedom and subjectivity on
      the part of the composer, who felt somewhat hampered
      by the strictness of Classical form, was evident at
      this time.
   3. The Romantic composers were more intense and exciting
      in some ways, than the Classicists. Because of revo-
      lutionary conditions in which individual freedom was
      a primary consideration, the composer and artist of
      this period became more self-centered and egotisti-
      cal.
      a. In their efforts to break away from limiting
         structural patterns, composers experimented with
         extremes in musical expression.
      b. Some of the composers of this period used mytho-
         logical legends of the past for their themes in
         order to break away from the conventionalism of
         their world.
      c. Many **composers** were highly emotional and intense,
         and some of them developed physical and mental
         infirmities as a result of the emotional strain.
   4. Many of the composers of this period were infant
      prodigies who began to compose music at an early age.
   5. There was a definite correlation of music composi-
      tion with literature and the other arts, as expressed
      in the program music of the period.
   6. Development of nationalism in music was possible be-
      cause of freedom of expression in form, style, melody
      and harmony.
      a. Themes from native folk songs were used.

       b. Composers founded a style of music peculiar to
          their country.

B. Elements of Music:

   1. Melody: There developed a freedom of melodic writing
      featuring longer and more irregular phrases. A much
      greater use of chromaticism by the composer extended
      the possibilities of melodic expression. The compos-
      ers expressed their feelings in their melodies.
   2. Harmony: Romanticists were interested in music with
      rich color effects, and as a result, used more com-
      plicated harmonies than did the Classicists. Tonality
      became less distinct because of the use of disso-
      nance, chromaticism, modulation, new chords and pro-
      gressions. Orchestral effects with elaborate color-
      ation were achieved.
   3. Rhythm: This period gave rise to many instrumental
      virtuosi who extended the possibilities of melodic
      rhythm to a highly technical degree. Complicated
      rhythm and variety of rhythmic patterns are among the
      characteristics of Romantic music.

C. Vocal Music and Opera: Although the vocal music of this
   period is not as important as the instrumental music, it
   contains some of the finest art works of the period.

   1. Lied: The most important vocal form, the Lied, was
      created by Schubert. It is an art song for solo voice
      with piano accompaniment.
   2. Oratorio: In the field of oratorio, Felix Mendel-
      ssohn, inspired by Handel, composed some of his
      greatest works which include *St. Paul* and *Elijah*.
   3. Opera: The refinement of opera continued through the
      Romantic Period and three distinct schools of opera
      composition were formed:
      a. Italian: Vocal parts were more prominent than
         orchestral parts.
         (1) Opera seria - grand opera
         (2) Opera buffa - comic opera
      b. French:
         (1) Opéra-comique - comic opera (entertainment
             type)
         (2) Grand opera - (spectacular)
         (3) Lyric opera - (refined)
      c. German: Wagner was the greatest composer of German
         opera during the 19th century.
         (1) Wagner achieved the perfect fusion of music,
             poetry and stage performance.
         (2) Wagner wrote his own libretti.

131

(3) Wagner created the "leitmotiv" (themes which represent certain characters, ideas, places or things).

D. Instrumental Music: Great progress was made in the development of instrumental music during the Romantic Period. Orchestration was expanded and refined. Improvements in construction and addition of new instruments contributed to the growth of the symphony orchestra.

1. The virtuoso, with his showmanship in technical achievement, became popular.
   a. This was possible because of the improvement of the tone and flexibility of musical instruments.
2. Romantic composers became interested in wind instruments.
3. The trombone was used in the symphony orchestra for the first time during the Romantic Period.
4. Brass instruments:
   a. The use of valves was developed in the first half of the 19th century.
5. Woodwind instruments:
   a. Keys to open and close the holes were developed.
   b. Boehm perfected the flute.
6. The English horn gave a new color to the woodwind section of the orchestra.

E. Instrumental Music Forms: Symphonic music and forms were the most important achievements in composition during this era.

1. Symphony: It is similar in structure to the classical symphony except for the freer treatment of thematic material.
2. Symphonic Poem: A literary or descriptive orchestral composition in one movement.
3. Symphonic Suite: Programmatic work that is divided into several movements.
4. Program Symphony: A programmatic work that follows the scheme of a four-movement symphony.
5. Concerto: A three-movement composition for solo and orchestra often characterized by elaborate virtuosity.
6. Concert Overture: A concert piece with beautiful melodies and orchestration in sonata-allegro form.
7. Viennese Waltz: A popular dance of Vienna in 3/4 time.
8. Mazurka: A Polish national dance in 3/4 time.
9. Polonaise: A Polish dance in 3/4 time which is stately and majestic.

132

F. Keyboard Music: During the Romantic Period, greater emphasis was placed on short keyboard compositions. The piano became the most important keyboard instrument of this period. Some of the greatest composers of piano music lived at this time, including Beethoven, Schubert, Schumann, Mendelssohn, Chopin, Liszt and Brahms.

1. Piano music of this period included works for piano solo, chamber music and concerti.
2. Composers often used the piano keyboard to assist them in their composing. Many were virtuoso pianists.
3. The piano was greatly improved in the 19th century:
   a. A repeating action was invented by a Frenchman, named Erad.
   b. A steel frame replaced the wooden frame.
   c. Thicker strings were used to produce a stronger tone.
   d. Cross stringing of the piano was used.
   e. The pedal mechanism was improved.
4. Short piano pieces were composed in free form:
   a. Fantasy: It expresses a free and dreamlike mood.
   b. Etude: A composition requiring great technical facility.
   c. Arabesque: A composition with beautiful and decorative qualities.
   d. Nocturne: It usually expresses a lyrical, melancholy or reflective mood.
   e. Ballade: A dramatic piece.

NICCOLO PAGANINI

Composer: Niccolo Paganini
   Born: Genoa, Italy 1782
   Died: Nice, France 1840

Aural Recognition of Themes:
   Composition: *Concerto No. 1 in D Op. 6* (1811)
      for Violin and Orchestra

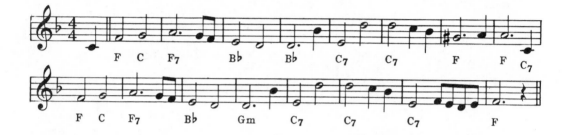

General Information about Composer and Compositions:

1. Niccolo Paganini is considered one of the greatest violin virtuosos that ever lived. At the age of nine he performed at a concert in Genoa with the famous singers of that era, Luigi Marchesi and Madame Albertinotti.

2. At an early age he made an intensive study of instrumentation and counterpoint. During this period he composed many difficult compositions.

3. He toured Europe extensively and on two separate occasions he was presented two priceless violins, a Guarnerius and a Stradivarius by two eminent admirers.

4. Paganini was a great showman. He performed many unbelievable feats such as continuing a concert by playing on three strings when one of the strings of his violin broke, and he employed some tricky bowing and many enharmonic effects.

5. Some of his violin compositions are so technically difficult that many present day violinists are unable to play them. He composed sonatas, concertos, caprices and miscellaneous other pieces.

Composer's Main Contribution to the Art of Music:

1. Niccolo Paganini is recognized as one of the best virtuoso violinists in the world. He was the inspiration for all virtuosi who were to follow. None were able to attain his great technical proficiency. Some of his compositions are too difficult for performance by some of the best living violinists. In his compositions for the violin, he created beautiful sonorities never before achieved by any other composer. His beautiful melodies are enriched by ingenious musical inventions while the harmony is comparably simple. He was admired by many of his contemporaries. Schumann said, "Paganini is the turning point in the history of virtuosity."

Suggested Listening:

1. Title: *Caprice No. 24*
   Performers: London Symphony - Friedman, violinist
   Record No.: RCA VICS-1647
   Grade Level: 4 - 8

2. Title: *Moto Perpetuo for Violin and Orchestra, Op. 11*
   Performers: Philadelphia Symphony - Ormandy
   Record No.: Columbia MS-7146
   Grade Level: 7 - 12

Optional Assignments:

1. Do some research on the history of the violin and its use in the symphony orchestra during the Romantic period.

2. If you play the violin, perform a solo (any selection) for the class.

3. Make a study of the string section of the symphony orchestra, listing instruments, seating plan and general characteristics of the instruments.

4. Make a study of the famous scientists of this period and list their accomplishments.

5. Write a biographical sketch of the life of Niccolo Paganini.

CARL MARIA VON WEBER

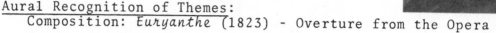

Composer: Carl Maria von Weber
  Born: Eutin, Germany 1786
  Died: London, England 1826

Aural Recognition of Themes:
  Composition: *Euryanthe* (1823) - Overture from the Opera

General Information about the Composer and Compositions:

1. Carl Maria von Weber came from a musical family. His father held various positions as bandmaster, theatrical director and choirmaster. Carl studied piano and composition with Michael Haydn in Salzburg. He also studied in Munich and Vienna with Abbe Vogler under whose tutelage he composed a set of six fughettas for the piano at the age of twelve. By the time he was fourteen he had written two operas. In 1813 he accepted the post of musical director of the German Opera in Prague and in 1817 became the director of the Dresden Opera to which he brought great fame.

2. Weber was the founder of the German romantic opera. He was the first composer to break away from the Italian style of opera composition, and he based his operas on German folk music and dances.

3. He was the first composer to use specific musical themes to describe the characters of his operas. This theme was the forerunner of the Leit-Motif used by Richard Wagner. Some of Weber's most popular and famous operas are: *Der Freischütz* (1821), *Euranthe* (1823) and *Oberon* (1826).

136

4. Weber was noted for his instrumentation. He composed excellent concertos for clarinet, horn, bassoon and flute. His concertos are among the finest ever written.

5. Besides operas, he composed masses, cantatas, symphonies, overtures, marches, concertos, sonatas and many smaller choral and piano works. One of his most popular piano compositions *Invitation To The Dance* (1819) is still performed, and has been arranged for orchestra.

Composer's Main Contribution to the Art of Music:

1. Carl Maria von Weber is known for his important contribution in the field of opera composition. He was dissatisfied with the Italian opera style and transformed it into the style of the music drama. He was the first composer to use the Leit-Motif (musical identification of a character or situation in an opera). He was a master of orchestration. He served as an inspiration to many other opera composers including Rossini, Meyerbeer and Wagner.

Suggested Listening:

1. Title: *Country Dance*
   Performers: R.C.A. Victor Symphony Orchestra
   Record No.: R.C.A. Basic Record Library, E-74, Vol. 4
   Grade Level: 4 - 8

2. Title: *Invitation to the Dance, Op. 65*
   Performers: Symphony Orchestra - Reiner
   Record No.: RCA LSC-2112
   Grade Level: 7 - 12

Optional Assignments:

1. Do some research on opera and make a comparison of the German and Italian styles of opera composition.

2. Make up words to the composition printed under the heading of Aural Recognition of Themes, and sing it for the class.

3. Select an opera that you have enjoyed on Television or radio and present an oral report on it to the class.

4. After listening to a selection by the composer, write a critique; compare the work with other selections you have heard, or make up an appropriate story that the music might suggest to you.

5. If you are a pianist, learn the *Invitation To The Dance* and perform it for the class.

GIOACCHINO ROSSINI

Composer: Gioacchino Rossini
  Born: Pesaro, Italy 1792
  Died: Ruelle, France 1868

Aural Recognition of Themes:
  Composition: *Overture* from Opera *William Tell* (1829)
              2nd Theme

General Information about Composer and Compositions:

1. Gioacchino Rossini's mother was a successfull prima donna in comic opera. His father played the trumpet in the opera orchestra. Rossini himself studied composition at the Conservatory of Bologna.

2. Rossini lived in France for a few years and studied the French style of opera composition. During this period he wrote the grand opera *William Tell* which takes five hours to perform. Although the opera itself is not played very often, the overture has become very popular (used as the theme of the Lone Ranger Television program).

3. Rossini was considered one of the best composers of Opera Buffa (Comic Opera). He developed a new light, melodious and enchanting opera style. His first comic opera *L'Italiana in Algeri* (1813), was a great success. It is saturated with enjoyable comedy and burlesque which appealed to the light-hearted people of Venice.

4. He was a very prolific composer of opera and at the age of twenty-one was known in all the theaters in Italy. Some of his best-known operas are: *Barber of Seville* (1815), *William Tell* (1829) and *Othello* (1816). (Verdi later wrote an opera based on Shakespeare's *Othello*).

5. He was also a composer of sacred music. One of the most famous of his sacred works is *Stabat Mater*. After he wrote the opera *William Tell*, he ceased composition altogether except for the writing of two religious songs: *Stabat Mater* (1842) and *Petite Messe Solennelle* (1864).

Composer's Main Contribution to the Art of Music:

1. Gioacchino Rossini's comic opera style was for many years an inspiration to all composers. He added many innovations to the instrumentation of the orchestra. He replaced the harpsichord with strings as the accompanying instrument. He added new instruments to the orchestra thus increasing its range and harmonic capabilities. He added the use of dynamics to create the effect of dramatic action.

Suggested Listening:

1. Title: *Overture to William Tell* - opera
   Performers: Boston Pops Orchestra - Arthur Fiedler
   Record No.: RCA LSC-2745
   Grade Level: 4 - 8

2. Title: *Music of Rossini*
   Performers: New York Philharmonic - Bernstein
   Record No.: Columbia N30305
   Grade Level: 7 - 12

Optional Assignments:

1. If you have a recording of one of Rossini's compositions, play it for the class, and give an oral report on the piece being played.

2. Make a study of the historical background of the Romantic period, and write a report on this subject.

3. Make a collection of current opera program notices for the class bulletin board and give a brief talk to the class about them.

4. After some research, give an oral report on comic opera, explaining how it differs from grand opera.

5. Opera includes music, drama, dancing and scenery. Write about these operatic components.

FRANZ PETER SCHUBERT

Composer: Franz Peter Schubert
   Born: Vienna, Austria 1797
   Died: Vienna, Austria 1828

Aural Recognition of Themes:
   Composition: *Unfinished Symphony* (1822)

General Information about Composer and Compositions:

1. Although Franz Peter Schubert's father was a school-teacher, Franz received little formal training. He was taught piano and violin by his father and brother. He also studied composition with Michael Holzer, the organist and choirmaster of the local church. In 1808 he was accepted at the "Konvict" School in Vienna where he was trained for membership in the Chapel Choir of the Imperial Court.

2. Schubert is reputed by many to be the greatest songwriter that ever lived. He had a natural talent for music and a great aptitude for writing melodies. He wrote over six hundred German Lieder (art songs), the most popular of which are *Ave Maria* (1825), *Who Is Sylvia* (1826) and *Serenade* (1828).

3. In composing his Lieder, Schubert made the accompaniment as important as the solo part. In his art songs he painted a musical picture or background and in many cases told a story.

4. He composed his *Symphony in D* (1813), at the age of sixteen. He wrote seven other symphonies including the very popular *Unfinished Symphony* which contains only two movements instead of the usual four.

140

5. In addition to his symphonies and songs, Schubert composed operas, masses, sonatas, choral works and chamber music. His most prolific year was 1815, during which he composed one hundred and ninety-five compositions.

Composer's Main Contribution to the Art of Music:

1. Franz Peter Schubert is recognized by very many as the greatest melody writer in the history of music. He could conceive melodies to fit any theme or emotion. In his larger works, he created beautiful variations of his main themes which he easily blended into the development of the structure. He created new harmonic progressions within the framework of tonality.

Suggested Listening:

1. Title: *Symphony No. 5 - First Movement*
   Performers: Chicago Symphony Orchestra - Reiner
   Record No.: RCA Victor LSC-2516
   Grade Level: 4 - 8

2. Title: *Symphony No. 8 (Unfinished Symphony)*
   Performers: Philadelphia Symphony - Ormandy
   Record No.: RCA LSC-3056
   Grade Level: 7 - 12

Optional Assignments:

1. Make up words that will fit the melody printed under the heading Aural Recognition of Themes, and sing it as a solo for the class.

2. Compare the art song of Schubert with the popular song of today.

3. Learn one of Schubert's songs, and sing it for the class. If you play a musical instrument, learn one of Schubert's melodies and perform it for the class.

4. Write a report on the recordings of the *Unfinished Symphony* and compare this work with other compositions you have heard.

5. Try to write a melody of sixteen measures with lyrics. This will test your ability to create beautiful melodies and will give you some idea of your talent as a composer.

VINCENZO BELLINI

Composer: Vincenzo Bellini
  Born: Catania, Sicily 1801
  Died: Puteaux, France 1835

Aural Recognition of Themes:
  Composition: *Grand March* (1831)

General Information about Composer and Compositions:

1. Vincenzo Bellini's father was a professional organist and was his first music teacher. Bellini was later sent to the Conservatory of Music at Naples where he graduated in 1827. Afterward, he studied privately with such famous composers as Haydn, Mozart and Pergolesi.

2. Bellini was subsidized in his study by a Sicilian nobleman who was very much impressed by his unusual talent. Bellini justified this confidence by composing a symphony, two masses and other compositions as a student.

3. He composed his first opera *Adelson and Salvini* (1825), which was performed by the Conservatory students. This work so impressed the manager of the San Carlo Theater, that he commissioned Bellini to write an opera *Bianca and Fernando* (1826), for his theater.

4. He was then commissioned by the director of La Scala, in Milan, to write operas for this world-famous center of opera. In 1827 he composed *Il Pirata* (*The Pirate*) and in 1829 wrote *La Straniera*.

5. In 1833 he went to Paris where he wrote *I Puritani* (*The Puritans*) for the Italian Theater. His most popular opera *Norma* was written in 1831. He died at the early age of thirty-four, from an illness caused by overwork and neglect of his health.

Composer's Main Contribution to the Art of Music:

1. Vincenzo Bellini is noted for his refinement of lyricism. In his arias, the harmony is subordinate and complementary to the melody. He is often referred to as "The aristocrat of his era" because of the nobility and purity of his works. His operatic arias are very popular because of their beauty and the emotional appeal which they afford to the listener.

Suggested Listening:

1. Title: *Norma* - selections
   Performers: Callas - vocal soloist
   Record No.: Angel 35666
   Grade Level: 4 - 8

2. Title: *Arias*
   Performers: Sutherland - vocal soloist
   Record No.: London 25940
   Grade Level: 7 - 12

Optional Assignments:

1. Bellini's musical education was subsidized by a member of the nobility. What other composer received financial assistance from either the nobility or the state?

2. Make a biographical sketch of the composer's life.

3. After listening to a selection by the composer, write a critique and compare his music with other compositions you have heard.

4. Do some research on the world-famous La Scala Theater, and give an oral report to the class on this topic.

5. Make a study of the famous artists and painters who were Bellini's contemporaries.

HECTOR BERLIOZ

Composer: Hector Berlioz
    Born: Grenoble, France 1803
    Died: Paris, France 1869
Aural Recognition of Themes:
    Composition: *The Corsair Overture, Op. 21* (1821)

General Information about Composer and Compositions:

1. Hector Berlioz was the son of a prominent physician. His father sent him to Paris to study medecine, but after three years Berlioz gave up this pursuit and entered the Paris Conservatory of Music in 1825. In 1825 he wrote his first large composition, *Messe Solennelle* which was performed by one hundred and fifty musicians.

2. Berlioz was a very good friend of Franz Liszt, who helped him receive recognition as a conductor and composer in Germany. As a writer for a Paris newspaper, he earned his living as a music critic, and became one of the most popular music critics in Europe.

3. Berlioz is particularly noted as the first great modern orchestrator. He created new tonal effects and colors through the use of instruments not utilized heretofore by the symphony orchestra, and greatly increased its size. He also created new rhythmic effects by using irregular beat patterns that are commonly used by composers today. He was known as "The inventive genius of composition." His textbook "Treatise on Orchestration" is still considered one of the best books on the subject.

4. He was one of the first composers to arrange public concerts which he conducted himself. The presentation of many of his own works at these public concerts helped him achieve popularity and recognition as a composer.

5. Berlioz composed symphonies, operas, a requiem, cantatas, overtures and other works. One of the most popular of his

symphonies is *Symphonie Fantastique* (1830). He dedicated a concerto for viola and orchestra, *Harold en Italie* (*Harold in Italy*) (1834), to Paganini.

Composer's Main Contribution to the Art of Music:

1. Hector Berlioz's music always had some literary inspiration. In order to make his works symbolize the realities of literature, he introduced many innovations in orchestration. He increased the size of the orchestra, developed new irregular rhythmic patterns, experimented with instrumentation to achieve new tonal colors, and devised new harmonic structures that have influenced the composers of today.

Suggested Listening:

1. Title: *Nuits d'été - song cycle, Op. 7*
   Performers: Chicago Symphony Orchestra - Reiner
   Record No.: RCA Victor LSC-2695
   Grade Level: 4 - 8

2. Title: *Symphonie Fantastique, Op. 14*
   Performers: N.Y. Philharmonic - Bernstein
   Record No.: Columbia MS-6607
   Grade Level: 7 - 12

Optional Assignments:

1. Investigate the music critics of today; collect some of their articles and present a digest of this information to the class.

2. Visit the administrative office of the Boston Symphony Orchestra and consult the person in charge about their system of organization and presentation of public concerts. Then give an oral report to the class on the information obtained from your interview.

3. After some research on the orchestra of Berlioz, present an oral report to the class on this subject, comparing his orchestra with the modern one of today.

4. Do some research on the qualifications, training and education needed for a person to become a symphonic conductor, and write a report on this topic.

5. Make a list of interesting facts about the composer and his music, and write a composition developing one of these.

FELIX MENDELSSOHN

Composer: Felix Mendelssohn
    Born: Hamburg, Germany 1809
    Died: Leipzig, Germany 1847

Aural Recognition of Themes:
    Composition: *Spring Song* (1830)

General Information about Composer and Compositions:

1. Felix Mendelssohn came from a very wealthy family of bankers and he received the best of musical training. Felix, as a youth, conducted many concerts in his home (his father would engage an orchestra for these occasions).

2. From 1835-1846 he was the director and conductor of the Leipzig Orchestra, and it was during this period that this orchestra became the best in Europe. He also founded the Leipzig Conservatory for the training of young musicians and composers.

3. Mendelssohn revived many of the works of Johann Sebastian Bach who was unrecognized in his time. He produced very successfully Bach's *St. Matthew Passion* (1829), in Berlin which brought deserved attention to the genius of Bach.

4. He travelled extensively and the countries he visited inspired some of his works: Scotland - *Fingal's Cave* (1832), *Scotch Symphony* (1842); Italy - *Italian Symphony* (1833); and England -Shakespeare's *A Midsummer Night's Dream* (1826).

5. Mendelssohn composed symphonies, overtures, chamber music, piano music, oratorios, cantatas, concertos and songs. His *Wedding March* (1843) is still played at many wedding services as the recessional march for the bridal party.

Composer's Main Contribution to the Art of Music:

1. Felix Mendelssohn was one of the originators of program music. The titles of his compositions established the scene for the listener. He had an amazing vocabulary of melodies that would create a musical picture of many varieties of fantasies, characters and scenery. He firmly believed that music could communicate the program intended by the composer.

Suggested Listening:

1. Title: Nocturne from *Midsummer Night's Dream*
   Performers: R.C.A. Victor Symphony Orchestra
   Record No.: R.C.A. Basic Record Library, E-80, Vol. 4
   Grade Level: 4 - 8

2. Title: *Symphony No. 4 in A, Op. 90* (Italian Symphony)
   Performers: New York Philharmonic Orchestra - Bernstein
   Record No.: Columbia N31819
   Grade Level: 7 - 12

Optional Assignments:

1. Make up words for the melody written under the section Aural Recognition of Themes, and sing it as a solo for the class.

2. Read Shakespeare's play A *Midsummer Night's Dream* and listen to Mendelssohn's overture based on this play. Then write a report describing the use of musical depiction by the composer.

3. Write a report comparing the music of Mendelssohn with that of other composers you have studied.

4. Do some research on the folk music of England and Italy. Write a report comparing the folk music of these countries.

5. Present an oral report to the class describing the ways in which travel might influence the music of a composer.

FRÉDÉRIC FRANÇOIS CHOPIN

Composer: Frédéric François Chopin
  Born: Warsaw, Poland 1810
  Died: Paris, France 1849

Aural Recognition of Themes:
  Composition: *Minute Waltz* (1847)

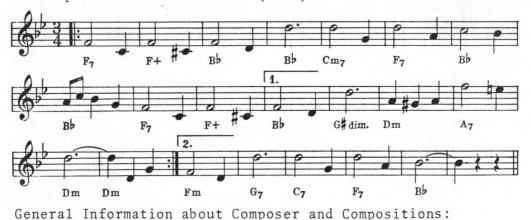

General Information about Composer and Compositions:

1. Frédéric François Chopin began the study of piano at the age of four with his sister. He took piano lessons from Albert Zywny at the age of six. When he was only seven years old his first *Polonaise* was published and performed by him on the concert stage. His father was a teacher of French at the Military Academy in Warsaw. He attended Warsaw High School and studied privately at the Warsaw Conservatory with Joseph Elsner.

2. Chopin, who became a concert pianist, composed chiefly for this instrument. He played mostly for small groups of the nobility in private salons. He developed an extensive literature for the piano, and became known as the "Poet of the Piano."

3. Franz Liszt introduced George Sand, the famous woman novelist, to Chopin who was so attracted by her brilliance and her self-confidence that he became completely dependent on her strong character. She assisted him financially and provided emotional inspiration for his most ambitious works.

4. Chopin used the dance forms of his native Poland in many of his compositions: The Polonaise - dance of the nobility, and The Mazurka - dance of the peasants.

5. He composed concertos, nocturnes, preludes and ballads, the beauty of which has never been surpassed. His music expresses his personality. His nationalism is expressed in his *Revolutionary Etude* (1831).

Composer's Main Contribution to the Art of Music:

1. Frédéric François Chopin was one of the originators of modern piano style and technique. He developed a style of piano music that was unique. He created techniques of piano composition that are used today by some composers. He was one of the first Romantic composers to use dynamics and idiomatic ornamentations in his piano compositions.

Suggested Listening:

1. Title: *Etude in G Flat Major (Butterfly Etude)*
   Performers: R.C.A. Victor Symphony Orchestra
   Record No.: R.C.A. Basic Record Library, E-81, Vol. 5
   Grade Level: 4 - 8

2. Title: *Polonaises*
   Performers: Artur Rubinstein - piano
   Record No.: RCA Victor LSC-7037
   Grade Level: 7 - 12

Optional Assignments:

1. If you are a pianist, select a composition of Chopin and play it for the class.

2. Make a list of composers who wrote music for the piano and list their most popular works in this idiom.

3. Write or call your local music school for schedules of piano recitals and post these notices on the class bulletin board.

4. Make a study of the folk music and customs of Poland and give an oral report to the class on this subject.

5. If you are artistic, make a drawing of a grand piano, showing the keyboard, pedals and general shape of this instrument.

ROBERT SCHUMANN

Composer: Robert Schumann
    Born: Zwickau, Saxony 1810
    Died: Endenich, Germany 1856

Aural Recognition of Themes:
    Composition: *Träumerei* (1840)

General Information about Composer and Compositions:

1. Robert Schumann's mother was a talented pianist. The boy studied composition at the age of seven and at eight years of age, took piano lessons with the local organist. At the age of eleven he composed choral and orchestral music. In high school, at the age of twelve, he formed and conducted an orchestra which played some of his own compositions.

2. Schumann was so eager to become a concert pianist that he devised a mechanical contraption that he hoped would help strengthen the weak fourth finger of his right hand. This device permanently damaged his finger, thus wrecking all hopes and ambitions for a career as a piano virtuoso. He then turned to composition as a career.

3. Schumann was the founder of a music magazine, "The New Journal of Music" (1844), and was successful as a journalist and critic. He was a rather controversial music critic, and promoted new composers and their music. Through his efforts Chopin and Brahms achieved recognition. In 1843 Schumann was appointed professor of piano and composition at the Conservatory of Music in Leipzig.

4. His wife, the former Clara Wieck, a famous pianist, did much to popularize his piano works. Schumann also composed vocal and orchestral music which was received enthusiastically by the public.

5. Schumann composed symphonies, overtures, concertos, chamber music and over one hundred songs. His piano se - lection *Träumerei* is still used today as background music for the benediction of many wedding ceremonies.

Composer's Main Contribution to the Art of Music:

1. Robert Schumann introduced the pure Romantic style of composition in many forms of music from the simple song to the more complex symphony. His zealous interest in poetry and literature influenced his compositions. He is noted for the poetic quality of his music. His knowledge of poetry enabled him to write lyrics that complemented his beautiful melodies.

Suggested Listening:

1. Title: *Scenes from Childhood - Träumerei*
   Performers: National Symphony Orchestra, Washington, D.C.
   Record No.: R.C.A. Victor, LE-1005
   Grade Level: 4 - 8

2. Title: *Carnaval, Op. 9*
   Performers: Artur Rubinstein - Piano
   Record No.: R.C.A. Victor LM-2669
   Grade Level: 7 - 12

Optional Assignments:

1. Write a brief review of a book you have read about Schumann, including biographer, title and interesting facts.

2. Schumann was a music critic. Read the articles printed by some of the music critics of today in your newspapers and magazines, and report to the class your evaluation of these criticisms.

3. Write lyrics to *Träumerei*, the song printed under the section Aural Recognition of Themes, and perform it as a solo for the class.

4. Write a paper on the qualifications, training and educa - tion required for a person to become a concert pianist.

5. After making a study of the music of Franz Schubert, com - pare his music with Schumann's work.

FRANZ LISZT

Composer: Franz Liszt
    Born: Raiding, Hungary 1811
    Died: Bayreuth, Germany 1886

Aural Recognition of Themes:
    Composition: *Liebesträume* (1850)

General Information about Composer and Compositions:

1. Franz Liszt took piano lessons from his father at the age of six and when he was nine, he made his debut as a concert pianist. In 1821 he studied piano with Karl Czerny. Two years later at another concert, Beethoven applauded him enthusiastically and kissed him on the forehead. He applied and was refused admittance to the Paris Conservatory because of a law which did not allow acceptance of foreigners.

2. Liszt was probably the most accomplished pianist that ever lived. He was noted for his fluent technique and dexterity at the keyboard. He was often called the "Paganini of the Piano."

3. In 1861 he gave up music, for a while, for the study of religion, philosophy and literature.

4. He became known as "Abbé Liszt" upon his entrance to a monastery near Rome, where for seven years he composed religious works. Some of the more popular of these are: *Hungarian Coronation Mass* and the Oratorio *Christus*.

5. His piano compositions require extreme technical facility of the performer. He wrote symphonies, concertos, symphonic poems and Hungarian rhapsodies. He transcribed works of many other composers for the piano.

Composer's Main Contribution to the Art of Music:

1. Franz Liszt is known as one of the most outstanding virtuoso pianists that ever lived. His most important musical contributions are the creation of the symphonic tone poem, and his modern treatment of the piano sonata and rhapsody form. His music was the inspiration of Wagner and the composers of music impressionism in the modern period of composition.

Suggested Listening:

1. Title: *Dance of the Gnomes*
   Performers: R.C.A. Victor Symphony Orchestra
   Record No.: R.C.A. Basic Record Library, E-82, Vol. 6
   Grade Level: 4 - 8

2. Title: *Les Preludes, Symphonic Poem No. 3*
   Performers: New York Philharmonic Orchestra - Bernstein
   Record No.: Columbia M30306
   Grade Level: 7 - 12

Optional Assignments:

1. Chopin and Liszt were two of the most noted pianists of the Romantic period. Make a comparison of their lives and works and give a talk on this subject to the class.

2. Liszt was born in Hungary. Write a report on the folk music of that country.

3. If you are artistic, draw or paint a picture of the composer and present it for bulletin board display.

4. After preparing an outline, lead a class discussion on the life and music of Liszt.

5. Prepare a skit involving interesting incidents in the life of Liszt.

GIUSEPPE VERDI

Composer: Giuseppe Verdi
   Born: Le Roncole, Italy 1813
   Died: Milan, Italy 1901

Aural Recognition of Themes:
   Composition: Selection from Opera *Aïda* (1871)

General Information about Composer and Compositions:

1. Giuseppe Verdi, at the age of eight, began organ lessons with the local organist, Baistrocchi. When he was ten years old he was appointed organist at the village church of Le Roncole. He received his early formal education in the town of Busseto. He was refused admission to the Milan Conservatory because he failed the entrance examination, but he studied composition and orchestration privately with Lavigna at Milan.

2. During his stay in Busseto he was employed by Barezzi, a local merchant, who was fond of music and became Verdi's benefactor. In 1836 Verdi married Barezzi's daughter.

3. In 1833 he was appointed conductor of the Philharmonic Society and organist at Busseto. In 1834 he conducted a choral society in Milan for the performance of Haydn's *Creation*.

4. Verdi brought Italian opera to its highest level of de - velopment in the nineteenth century. He created a beautiful fusion of drama and music. With this perfect unity he achieved an authentic representation of mood, charac - terizations, atmosphere, and emotion. His first opera *Oberto*, was produced in 1839 at La Scala Opera House in

Milan. Its performance was so successful that he received a contract from La Scala's impressario, Merelli, to write three new operas.

5. Verdi was a prolific composer of opera. He composed his last opera *Falstaff* (1893), at the age of eighty. He also composed a requiem mass, sacred pieces and a string quartet. Some of his best known operas are: *Rigoletto* (1851), *Il Trovatore* (1853), *La Traviata* (1853), and *Aida* (1871).

Composer's Main Contribution to the Art of Music:

1. Giuseppe Verdi, the Italian and Richard Wagner, the German, were the two most outstanding composers of opera in the nineteenth century. Verdi's main interest was the fusion of vocal music with drama. He was the creator of beautiful opera melodies that are sung today. He achieved a perfection of Italian opera that has never been surpassed.

Suggested Listening:

1. Title: *Soldier's Chorus* from *Il Trovatore;*
   March from *Aida*
   Performers: R.C.A. Victor Symphony Orchestra
   Record No.: R.C.A. Basic Record Library, E-74, Vol. 4
   Grade Level: 4 - 8
2. Title: *Overtures and Preludes*
   Performers: London Symphony Orchestra
   Record No.: London 6486
   Grade Level: 7 - 12

Optional Assignments:

1. Do some research on the history of opera and prepare a written report.

2. Attend or view an opera or operetta and present an oral report to the class on the performance.

3. Prepare an operetta for performance by your class.

4. Make a study of the famous painters of the nineteenth century.

5. Do some research on the qualifications, training and education needed for a person to become an opera singer.

RICHARD WAGNER

Composer: (Wilhelm) Richard Wagner
  Born: Leipzig, Germany 1813
  Died: Venice, Italy 1883

Aural Recognition of Themes:
  Composition: *Bridal March* (1850)

General Information about Composer and Compositions:

1. Richard Wagner began the study of piano at the age of twelve. He taught himself composition by studying books on the subject. He completed an orchestral overture at the age of seventeen which was performed publicly in Leipzig. In 1831 he was accepted as a law student at the University of Leipzig, but soon gave this up in order to study music. He was appointed choral director of the Wuerzburg Opera. From 1834 to 1836 he was the conductor of the Magdeburg Opera. In 1843 he was appointed director of the Dresden Opera and he achieved great fame there with the production of his great operas.

2. He was an excellent poet and studied Shakespeare and Greek mythology extensively, thus enabling himself to write, compose and direct all phases of opera production. He was also an avid student of German literature.

3. Wagner brought German operatic form to the highest peak ever achieved in the nineteenth century. He was an expert in the integration of drama, music and scenery. He introduced and developed the use of the Leit-Motif (a melody associated with a specific character, situation or mood).

4. He founded one of the world's most famous dramatic theatres at Bayreuth, Bavaria where his works are still performed at the world-renowned Music Festival every year.

5. The piece *Bridal March* from the opera *Lohengrin* (1850), is still used at many wedding services. This work heralds the entrance of the bride. Some of his famous operas are: *Lohengrin* (1850), *Die Meistersinger* (1868), *Tannhäuser* (1845), and *Tristan und Isolde* (1865).

Composer's Main Contribution to the Art of Music:

1. Richard Wagner brought the medium of opera to its most perfect state of development in Germany. Dramatic writing, musical composition, and method stage production demonstrated his genius. He created a perfect fusion of all these ingredients. Many of the world's most famous cultural centers give credit to Wagner's genius by producing his works yearly.

Suggested Listening:

1. Title: *Lohengrin - Prelude to Act III*
   Performers: National Symphony Orchestra, Washington, D.C.
   Record No.: R.C.A. Victor, LE-1009, Adventures in Music
   Grade Level: 4 - 8

2. Title: *Parsifal Prelude*
   Performers: Columbia Symphony Orchestra - Walter
   Record No.: Columbia MS-6149
   Grade Level: 7 - 12

Optional Assignments:

1. Make a study of the Norse gods and heroes of Wagner's operas and write a report on this subject.

2. Do some research on the denominations that have used or still use the *Bridal March* from *Lohengrin* as part of their wedding services.

3. Wagner became involved in politics. After research in the World Book or any other encyclopedia about this subject and other anecdotal references, give an oral report to the class on your findings.

4. Make up a notebook on the life and music of the composer consisting of pictures, newspaper and magazine articles, concert programs, thematic excerpts, original illustrations and written reports.

5. If you have a recording of one of Wagner's compositions, play it for the class and give an oral report on the piece being played.

CHARLES-FRANÇOIS GOUNOD

Composer: Charles-François Gounod
  Born: Paris, France 1818
  Died: Saint-Cloud, France 1893

Aural Recognition of Themes:
  Composition: Selection from Opera *Mirella* (1864)

General Information about Composer and Compositions:

1. Charles-François Gounod received his first piano lessons from his mother who was a professional pianist. At the age of eleven he was enrolled at the Lycee St. Louis in Paris, where he became soloist in the chapel choir. In 1836 he entered the Paris Conservatory.

2. He studied church music in Rome and in 1839 won the Grand Prix de Rome with his cantata *Fernanda.* His first notable work, an orchestral mass, was performed at the Church of San Luigi de Francesi in 1841. His *Requiem Mass* was performed in 1842 at Vienna.

3. He studied theology for about five years and became known as "l'Abbe Gounod." During this time he was organist and musical director of the Chapel of the Seminary of Foreign Missions.

4. His *Messe Solennelle* was performed in Paris in 1849, and in London in 1851, after he had decided not to become a priest. In 1855 one of his most important compositions *The Mass To St. Cecilia* was produced at St. Eustache Church in Paris. From 1852 to 1860 he directed the Orpheon, an organization of combined choral societies.

In addition, Gounod was director of choral music in the public schools of Paris.

5. One of Gounod's most noted works is the opera *Faust*, which was produced in 1859. He also composed symphonies, religious music, organ works and choral compositions.

Composer's Main Contribution to the Art of Music:

1. Charles-François Gounod introduced in his operas some of the religious ideas and impressions he used in his sacred works. Conversely he brought the dramatic element of opera into his religious works. He began a new era and style of French theater music which influenced the composers who followed him.

Suggested Listening:

1. Title: *Faust* - ballet music
   Performers: N.Y. Philharmonic - Bernstein
   Record No.: Columbia MS-7415
   Grade Level: 4 - 8

2. Title: *Messe Solennelle (Saint Cecilia Mass)*
   Performers: Lorengar
   Record No.: Angel S36214
   Grade Level: 7 - 12

Optional Assignments:

1. Gounod wanted to become a priest. What are the requirements today for entry into the priesthood? Present a list of these requirements.

2. Make a biographical sketch of the composer's life.

3. Compare a typical composition (song) of this period with the popular song of today.

4. Choose one of the topics we have discussed under general information and see what you can learn about it in other books. Then report your findings to the class.

5. If you have attended a concert recently, tell your class about the program you heard and discuss the instrumenta - tionof the performing group.

JACQUES OFFENBACH

<u>Composer</u>: Jacques Offenbach
    Born: Cologne, Germany 1819
    Died: Paris, France 1880

<u>Aural Recognition of Themes</u>:
    Composition: *Can Can* from Opera *Orpheus In The*
          Underworld (1858)

General Information about Composer and Compositions:

1. Jacques Offenbach was a French composer who came from a German-Jewish parenthood. His father was the cantor at the Cologne Jewish Synagogue. Offenbach attended the Paris Conservatory in 1833 where he studied the violoncello. A year later he left the Paris Conservatory and became cellist with the Opéra-Comique Orchestra.

2. He is known as the originator of the Opéra-Bouffe (French Comic Opera). He became the conductor of the orchestra at the Théâtre Français in 1849. He was a great showman, arranging many entertaining concerts.

3. From 1872 to 1876 he was the manager of the Théâtre de la Gaite which went bankrupt. In order to pay his debts, he arranged a tour of America in 1877, which brought him enough money to pay his creditors.

4. He toured England at least four times. During these visits he played violoncello concerts and conducted the Bouffes Parisiens Company at St. James Theatre, London in the performance of his works.

5. He was a prolific composer of operettas. He is best known for his comic-opera *The Tales Of Hoffmann* (1880). He composed only two operas. During his youth Offenbach wrote many songs for the cello. His orchestral piece *Gaîté Parisienne* (1838) is a very popular work today.

Composer's Main Contribution to the Art of Music:

1. Jacques Offenbach was the originator of French comic opera. The libretto or story of his comic operas usually was a satire on the political and social conditions in France. His style of opera composition was simple, light and frivolous.

Suggested Listening:

1. Title: *Music of Offenbach and Orpheus*
   Performers: Boston Pops Orchestra - Fiedler
   Record No.: RCA Victor 1466
   Grade Level: 4 - 8
2. Title: *Tales of Hoffmann* (excerpts)
   Performers: Gedda
   Record No.: RCA Victor LM2310
   Grade Level: 7 - 12

Optional Assignments:

1. Offenbach was the originator of French comic opera. Make a study of this type of opera and write a report.

2. Choose one of the topics we have discussed under general information, and after some research give an oral report on it to the class.

3. Learn a basic dance used during the composer's lifetime and present it to the class.

4. If you play a musical instrument, select a composition of the composer and perform it for the class.

5. Write a report on the history and development of the major instruments of this period.

CÉSAR FRANCK

Composer: César Franck
 Born: Liége, Belgium 1822
 Died: Paris, France 1890

Aural Recognition of Themes:
 Composition: *Panis Angelicus* (1872)

General Information about Composer and Compositions:

1. César Franck received his first instruction in music at the Liége Conservatory and later continued his education at the Paris Conservatory where he studied composition, piano and organ. He received several prizes for his works. He was considered an excellent organist and was advised to become an organ virtuoso.

2. Although he was Belgian by birth, he is known as a French composer because he spent most of his life in France. After the death of Berlioz, French music went into a decline and it was César Franck who revived the old classic forms with a style of his own, and restored French music to its former level of prominence.

3. He was appointed professor of organ in 1872 at the Paris Conservatory. He was also church organist for thirty-two years at St. Clotilde, in Paris. He taught organ, composition and piano privately. Among his students who achieved fame was the composer Vincent D'Indy. Franz Liszt on hearing Franck play the organ, compared him to Johann Sebastian Bach.

4. He achieved eminence as a composer at the late age of fifty-five. He wrote his greatest works during the latter part of his life. He was influenced at first by the music of Beethoven, but he gradually developed his own style.

162

5. His *Symphony In D Minor* (1886) and his organ works are among his most famous compositions. He composed chamber music, piano pieces, religious works and songs. His sacred song *Panis Angelicus* (1872) is still sung by many professional and school choirs.

Composer's Main Contribution to the Art of Music:

1. César Franck studied tirelessly the musical styles and forms of the composers who preceded him in the endeavor to improve and perfect his own style of composition. Among the composers who influenced his style of composition are Bach, Beethoven, Wagner, Liszt and Schumann.

Suggested Listening:

1. Title: *Chorales for Organ*
   Performers: Newman
   Record No.: Columbia M-31127
   Grade Level: 4 - 8

2. Title: *Symphony in D Minor*
   Performers: Boston Symphony Orchestra - Munch
   Record No.: R.C.A. Victor 1034
   Grade Level: 7 - 12

Optional Assignments:

1. Tell the class about an historical event which took place during the lifetime of the composer.

2. Make a study of the famous philosophers who lived during this period and write a report on this subject.

3. Make a notebook on the life and music of César Franck consisting of pictures, newspaper and magazine articles, concert programs, thematic excerpts, original illustrations and written reports.

4. Make a list of organ composers and their most famous compositions.

5. If you play a musical instrument, select a composition by the composer and perform it for the class.

JOHANN STRAUSS II

<u>Composer</u>: Johann Strauss II
   Born: Vienna, Austria 1825
   Died: Vienna, Austria 1899

<u>Aural Recognition of Themes</u>:
   Composition: *Blue Danube Waltz* (1867)

<u>General Information about Composer and Compositions</u>:

1. Johann Strauss's father, Johann Strauss I, was a famous orchestral conductor and composer. He was known as "The Father of the Waltz" having composed over one-hundred and fifty waltzes. Johann Strauss II followed in the footsteps of his father and became known as "The Waltz King" having composed over five hundred waltzes.

2. Johann's father did not wish his son to become a musician, and therefore he sent him to the Gymnasium and Polytechnic Institute to become a bank clerk. Johann, without his father's knowledge, took lessons on the violin and studied composition with Drechsler.

3. He made his orchestral debut at Dormayer's Casino at Heitzing, Germany in 1844 where he performed his own as well as his father's compositions. He then began a series of successful concert tours through Austria, Holland, Poland, Russia and other countries of Europe.

4. From 1863 to 1868 he was the conductor of Court balls in Vienna. In 1869 he came to Boston, Massachusetts for the Gilmore Jubilee where he conducted a chorus of twenty thousand singers and a very large orchestra. He also performed in New York City and then returned to Vienna.

5. Johann Strauss II composed the *Emperor Waltz* (1888) for Emperor Francis Joseph who said to Strauss, "My friend, you too are Emperor. Your music, like yourself, never grows older." Besides waltzes, he composed operettas, the most famous of which is *Die Fledermaus* (1874). His most popular composition, known the world over, is the *Blue Danube Waltz* (1867).

Composer's Main Contribution to the Art of Music:

1. Johann Strauss II gave to the art of dance music an ever-lasting popularity through his famous Viennese waltzes. He can be considered one of the first composers of popu - lar music because of the appeal of his melodious waltzes.

Suggested Listening:

1. Title: *Waltzes*
   Performers: Boston Pops Orchestra - Fiedler
   Record No.: R.C.A. Victor LM-2028
   Grade Level: 4 - 8

2. Title: *Die Fledermaus* - excerpts
   Performers: Boston Pops Orchestra - Fiedler
   Record No.: R.C.A. Victor LM-2130
   Grade Level: 7 - 12

Optional Assignments:

1. If you dance, discuss and demonstrate the Viennese waltz.

2. Make a study of the Viennese waltz orchestra and present an oral talk on this topic.

3. If you have a recording of a composition by Strauss, play it for the class and give an oral report on the selection being played.

4. Make a biographical sketch of the composer's life.

5. Make a study of a popular instrument used during the composer's lifetime.

ALEXANDER BORODIN

<u>Composer</u>: Alexander Borodin
    Born: St. Petersburg, Russia 1833
    Died: St. Petersburg, Russia 1887

<u>Aural Recognition of Themes</u>:
    Composition: *Polovetzian Dances* - 1st Theme (1880)

General Information about Composer and Compositions:

1. Alexander Borodin showed a native talent for music at an
early age, but did not receive formal instruction in
music until he was nine years old. At the age of fourteen
he began to compose music. He entered the Academy of
Medicine in St. Petersburg and graduated with a major in
chemistry in 1856. He became a professor at the Academy
devoting himself to scientific research. He was very prominent in the field of chemistry.

2. Borodin was one of the "Russian Five," a group of five
Russian composers who banded together in the latter half
of the nineteenth century in order to promote and develop
a national style of Russian music. The other members of
this group were: Rimsky-Korsakoff, Balakireff, Cui, and
Moussorgsky.

3. His compositions include folk themes and portrays folk
tales of his native land. His music reflects the life of
the Russian people; it is nationalistic and displays a
contemporary style.

4. In his *Polovetzian Dances* (1880), his music follows the
tradition of the ballad dance. Such dances were popular

in the medieval courts of Russian nobility. From these dances, the Russians later developed ballets.

5. Borodin's music possesses an exotic quality, showing the influence of Oriental rhythm and harmony in his style. He used many modern harmonic and rhythmic effects which were later developed by Debussy and Ravel.

Composer's Main Contribution to the Art of Music:

1. Alexander Borodin was the first composer to introduce a national style of music in Russia. The inspiration for his music was drawn from the culture of his native country. His harmony and rhythm had an oriental flavor which paved the way for further exploration of this style of writing by Debussy and Ravel.

Suggested Listening:

1. Title: *In The Steppes Of Central Asia*
   Performers: National Symphony Orchestra, Washington, D.C.
   Record No.: Victor LE-1006, Adventures In Music
   Grade Level: 4 - 8

2. Title: *Prince Igor - Polovetzian Dances*
   Performers: Boston Pops Orchestra - Fiedler
   Record No.: R.C.A. Victor LM-2202
   Grade Level: 7 - 12

Optional Assignments:

1. After research in the World Book about Borodin, give an oral report on your findings.

2. Study the political events which took place in the United States during Borodin's lifetime and write a report on this subject.

3. If you play a musical instrument, learn one of Borodin's songs and play it for the class.

4. What popular Musical Comedy is adapted from the music of Borodin? Write a short review of this production.

5. Use your imagination and illustrate the *Polovetzian Dances* for bulletin board display.

167

JOHANNES BRAHMS

Composer: Johannes Brahms
    Born: Hamburg, Germany 1833
    Died: Vienna, Austria 1897

Aural Recognition of Themes:
    Composition: *Hungarian Dance No. 5* (1869)

General Information about Composer and Compositions:

1. Johannes Brahms' father was a professional musician who played double-bass in the Hamburg City Theatre. He studied piano with Friedrich Cossel and later studied piano, theory and composition with Edouard Marxsen (who would accept no fee for the lessons). Many years later, Brahms dedicated his *B Flat Piano Concerto* (1881) to Marxsen.

2. Brahms made his debut as a concert pianist and composer at the age of fourteen in Hamburg, where he played his own variations on a folk song. He was a brilliant pianist and he teamed with a well-known Hungarian violinist, Eduard Remenyi, for concert tours throughout Europe.

3. Brahms was proclaimed by Robert Schumann as the "New Messiah of Music." He was a close associate of the Schumanns, and performed many concerts with Clara Schumann. Brahms is thought to be Robert Schumann's successor in the German-Romantic style of composition.

4. From 1863 to 1864 he was the conductor of the Singakademie in Vienna. In 1871 he became conductor of the Gesellschaft der Musikfreunde, a musical organization which is still active today. Brahms, in 1877, was offered the degree of

Music Doctor from Cambridge University in England, which he refused. He accepted the Doctor of Philosophy degree from Breslau University in 1881.

5. His compositions marked the culmination of the Romantic period. His works include almost every form but opera. He wrote four symphonies, two overtures, concertos for piano, violin and cello, all types of chamber music, and many vocal selections. Among the most popular of his songs is his *Lullaby* (1887). His *German Requiem* (1868) is one of his most famous works.

Composer's Main Contribution to the Art of Music:

1. Johannes Brahms revived the style and strict form of the Classical period for which he was criticized by his contemporaries. His larger works reflect the perfect classical form. In his songs he expressed the emotion and feeling typical of the Romantic period through the use of richer harmonies and varied rhythmic treatment. He was influenced by and had a great respect for the music of Beethoven.

Suggested Listening:

1. Title: *Hungarian Dance No. 1*
   Performers: National Symphony Orchestra, Washington, D.C.
   Record No.: R.C.A. Victor LE-1007, Adventures In Music
   Grade Level: 4 - 8

2. Title: *Academic Festival Overture, Op. 80*
   Performers: Royal Philharmonic Orchestra
   Record No.: Sera. S-60083
   Grade Level: 7 - 12

Optional Assignments:

1. Make a list of interesting facts about the composer and write a composition developing one of these.

2. Make a comparison of the songs of Brahms with those of Schubert and Schumann.

3. Make a study of the famous literary geniuses of this period and write a composition on this topic.

4. Tell the class about an historical event which took place during the life of Brahms.

5. Play a recording of a composition by Brahms for the class, and give an oral report on this selection.

MODESTE MOUSSORGSKY

Composer: Modeste Moussorgsky
   Born: Karevo, Russia 1839
   Died: St. Petersburg, Russia 1881

Aural Recognition of Themes:
   Composition: Selection from Opera *Boris Godunov* (1872)

General Information about Composer and Compositions:

1. Modeste Moussorgsky's mother was an accomplished pianist who taught him to play the piano at a very early age. He attended a military academy, Ensigns' School in St. Petersburg. During this period he continued his piano studies and became a virtuoso pianist.

2. He entered the military service at the age of seventeen, where he lived comfortably as an officer. The fact that his military career interfered with his musical aspirations caused him to resign and accept the poverty of a composer's life at the age of twenty-two.

3. In 1857 he became associated with a famous group of composers consisting of Rimsky-Korsakov, Borodin, Balakirev and Cui. This group eventually became known as the "Russian Five," a group of neo-Russian musicians.

4. He had such a precarious financial existence as a composer that he was forced to accept minor governmental positions throughout his life. He was irresponsible in his work and was compelled to change jobs many times.

5. His orchestral work A *Night on Bald Mountain* (1877) has been performed by Leopold Stokowski and the Philadelphia Symphony Orchestra. His piano piece *Pictures at an Exhibition* (1874) was orchestrated in 1922 by Maurice Ravel. His opera *Boris Godunov* (1872), the libretto of which is based on Pushkin's famous historical drama, is considered his best musical work.

Composer's Main Contribution to the Art of Music:

1. Modeste Moussorgsky strived to have his music express the realities of life. He used modern techniques of composition such as unusual harmony, rhythm and orchestration to attain the desired effect. His success at portraying dramatic expression in his operas places him above many of his contemporaries in this area.

Suggested Listening:

1. Title: *Night On Bald Mountain*
   Performers: N.Y. Philharmonic - Bernstein
   Record No.: Columbia MS-6943
   Grade Level: 4 - 8

2. Title: *Pictures At An Exhibition*
   Performers: Philadelphia Symphony Orchestra - Ormandy
   Record No.: Columbia M30448
   Grade Level: 7 - 12

Optional Assignments:

1. If you are artistic, draw or paint a picture of the composer and present it for bulletin board display.

2. After listening to a recording of Moussorgsky's *Pictures At An Exhibition*, draw or paint a scene that the music might suggest to you.

3. Make a study of the Russian military, its historical background and present status, and conduct a class discussion on this subject.

4. Make a collection of current program notices (Concerts: Professional, Schools, Television and Radio). Before placing these notices on the bulletin board, give a brief talk about them to the class.

5. Make up words for the composition written under the Aural Recognition of Themes section, and sing it for the class.

171

CAMILLE SAINT-SAËNS

Composer: Camille Saint-Saëns
   Born: Paris, France 1835
   Died: Algiers, Algeria 1921

Aural Recognition of Themes:
   Composition: *The Swan (Le Cygne)* (1886)

General Information about Composer and Compositions:

1. Camille Saint-Saëns began the study of piano at the age of three. He made his first public appearance at the age of five playing a Gretry opera. He became known as the "New Mozart," a boy wonder. At the age of seven he was accepted at the Paris Conservatory where he studied piano, organ, theory and composition.

2. He has been called the Dean of the French school of composition. In 1851 he produced his first symphony. In 1852 he wrote *Ode à Sainte Cecile* which won first prize at a competition in Paris. He was influenced by Franz Liszt in his style. During the early period of his composing, he continued to perform and was proclaimed the most famous organ virtuoso of his time. In 1853 he was appointed organist at the church of St. Merry in Paris. In 1857 he was appointed organist at the church of the Madeleine. From 1861 to 1865, the only period of his life devoted to teaching, he was Professor of Piano at Niedermayer School of Religious Music.

3. He visited London, England in 1871, giving concert tours there. He received the honorary degree of Doctor of Music from Cambridge University in 1892. He came to the United States in 1906, where he conducted the New York Symphony Orchestra and also appeared as a piano virtuoso in Boston, Cincinnati and other leading cities.

4. In addition to being a fine musician and composer, Saint-Saëns was versatile in other fields, e.g., poetry, astronomy, playwriting, musical criticism, archeology, literature and mathematics. He published many papers and books in these varied fields.

5. His compositions include all areas of music such as: chamber music, piano concertos, symphonic poems, masses, cantatas, oratorios, symphonies, a ballet, operas, operettas, choral works, organ music, incidental music and transcriptions. Some of his most popular works are: *Carnival of the Animals* (1886), *Samson et Dalila* (1877), and *Dance Macabre* (1874).

Composer's Main Contribution to the Art of Music:

1. Camille Saint-Saëns might well be called an international composer. His works are written in the style of all eras and many countries of the world. His works show the influence of many composers such as Wagner, Liszt and Verdi.

Suggested Listening:

1. Title: *The Youth of Hercules* - excerpts
   Performers: R.C.A. Victor Orchestra
   Record No.: R.C.A. Basic Record Library, E-82, Vol. 6
   Grade Level: 4 - 8

2. Title: *Carnival of the Animals*
   Performers: New York Philharmonic Orchestra - Bernstein
   Record No.: Columbia M31808
   Grade Level: 7 - 12

Optional Assignments:

1. Make a list of interesting facts about the composer and his music and write a paper developing one of these.

2. Make a study of the instrumental virtuoso, and give an oral report on what is involved in his training, performance and career.

3. After listening to Saint-Saëns *Carnival of the Animals*, sketch or paint an appropriate picture that the music suggests to you.

4. Do some research and find other composers that were proficient in fields other than music. Write a paper on this subject.

5. Play a recording of one of the composer's compositions for the class and lead a class discussion on the selection.

GEORGES BIZET

Composer: Georges Bizet
   Born: Paris, France 1838
   Died: Bougival, France 1875

Aural Recognition of Themes:
   Composition: *Habanera* from Opera *Carmen* (1875)

General Information about Composer and Compositions:

1. Georges Bizet's father, who was a singing teacher, gave
   him his first music lessons at the age of four. At the
   age of nine he entered the Paris Conservatory of Music
   where he studied piano, organ, harmony and composition.
   During his stay there, he won the Offenbach first prize
   for comic opera. He also won the Grand Prix de Rome.

2. He was a master of the piano at the age of fourteen. His
   pianistic prowess was recognized by Franz Liszt, Berlioz
   and Saint-Saens who encouraged him to write compositions
   for the piano. Bizet wrote piano compositions for two and
   four hands.

3. In 1861, upon his return from a period of study in Italy,
   he taught music for a living in Paris. During this time
   he made piano arrangements of famous operatic airs.

4. In 1872 he composed the incidental music to Daudet's play
   L'Arlesienne which received instant popularity. This music
   is popular today as an orchestral suite.

5. Bizet is recognized as one of the most important of the French composers. His four-act opera *Carmen* (1875) was very successful. His use of Spanish rhythms contributed greatly to the success of this opera. He also composed a symphony, other operas, orchestral suites and songs.

Composer's Main Contribution to the Art of Music:

1. Georges Bizet achieved strong dramatic effects in his operas. His amazing ability in orchestration and composition set the pattern of writing for future composers. His music is expressive and contains the typical French quality of refinement.

Suggested Listening:

1. Title: *Arlesienne Suite No. 1; L'Minuetto*
   Performers: National Symphony Orchestra, Washington, D.C.
   Record No.: R.C.A. Victor LE-1005, Adventures In Music
   Grade Level: 4 - 8

2. Title: *Carmen Suite 1 & 2*
   Performers: Philadelphia Symphony Orchestra - Ormandy
   Record No.: Columbia MS-6051
   Grade Level: 7 - 12

Optional Assignments:

1. Make a study of the Spanish rhythms Bizet employed in his opera *Carmen*, and discuss and demonstrate some of the dances for the class.

2. Write a review of a recent concert which included music of the composer.

3. Lead a class discussion on the composer's life and music. Prepare an outline for this purpose.

4. Make a study of the historical background, cultural achievements and famous people of the Romantic period.

5. Compare a typical composition (song) of this period with the popular song of today.

PETER ILICH TSCHAIKOWSKY

Composer: Peter Ilich Tschaikowsky
  Born: Viatka, Russia 1840
  Died: St. Petersburg, Russia 1893

Aural Recognition of Themes:
  Composition: *Dance Of The Reed Flutes* (1893)

General Information about Composer and Compositions:

1. Peter Ilich Tschaikowsky was given piano lessons at an early age. At the age of ten, his family moved to St. Petersburg where he attended preparatory school and the School of Jurisprudence for nine years. He was educated as a lawyer and did not decide to devote his time seriously to music until he was twenty-three years old. In 1862 he attended St. Petersburg Conservatory graduating in 1865. He was appointed professor of harmony at the Moscow Conservatory.

2. His interesting personality was portrayed in his music: gay and light, sad and moody, fierceful and dynamic. He was influenced by folk music and many of his compositions contain the folk melodies of his native country.

3. The composer Balakirev suggested that Tschaikowsky write a tone poem based on Shakespeare's works. Tschaikowsky complied with the suggestion because of his intense interest in literature, and composed three versions of *Romeo and Juliet* (1870). This overture was inspired by the Shakespearian play of the same name.

4. One of Tschaikowsky's admirers, Madame von Meck, became his patron, and endowed him with an annual salary of six thousand rubles, although she had never met him. The years of her patronage were his most productive years as a composer.

176

5. He composed orchestral music, operas, concertos, songs, overtures and ballet music. Some of his most famous compositions include: *Nutcracker Suite* (1892), *Symphony No. 6 (Pathétique)* (1893), *1812 Overture* (1880), *Italian Caprice* (1880), and *Piano Concerto No. 1 in B Flat Minor* (1874) (Popular version: *Tonight We Love*).

Composer's Main Contribution to the Art of Music:

1. Peter Ilich Tschaikowsky was one of the foremost composers to introduce and popularize Russian music for world recognition and acceptance. The immense popularity of his music is due to his beautiful melodies, brilliant orchestration and dramatic portrayal of the Russian national character. His style of composition is typical of the composers of the Romantic era.

Suggested Listening:

1. Title: *Symphony No.4* - Fourth movement
   Performers: National Symphony Orchestra, Washington, D.C.
   Record No.: R.C.A. Victor LE-1008
   Grade Level: 4 - 8

2. Title: *Nutcracker Suite* - excerpts
   Performers: Boston Pops Orchestra - Fiedler
   Record No.: R.C.A. Victor LM-2052
   Grade Level: 7 - 12

Optional Assignments:

1. Make up a quiz using the information listed under General Information. Give the quiz orally to the class.

2. After studying the life of Tschaikowsky, write a report on his life and music. Include information about his activities in the United States during his visit here.

3. After listening to a composition by Tschaikowsky, write about the type of mood the music portrays.

4. Explain the following phrase: "Tschaikowsky wrote his autobiography in his music."

5. After some research on Anton Rubinstein, write about the influence of this teacher on Tschaikowsky.

ANTONIN DVOŘÁK

Composer: Antonin Dvořák
 Born: Nelahozeves, Czechoslovakia 1841
 Died: Prague, Czechoslovakia 1904

Aural Recognition of Themes:
 Composition: *New World Symphony* (1893)

General Information about Composer and Compositions:

1. At the age of eight, Antonin Dvořák played in the village orchestra with his father. He also sang in the village church choir. In 1857 he was enrolled at the Conservatory of Prague. At this school he majored in organ, theory and voice.

2. He played viola in the Prague Concert Band after graduating from the conservatory. He later played in the Czech National Theatre Orchestra under the leadership of the composer Bedrich Smetana. In 1873 he was appointed church organist at St. Adelbert's Church in Prague.

3. Dvořák had his first real success in the field of composition with his *Hymnus* (1873), a patriotic piece for orchestra and chorus. He was influenced in his composition by Smetana, the founder of the Czech national school of music composition. Johannes Brahms was a great admirer of Dvořák's music.

4. In 1875 he received a government subsidy which permitted him to devote his full time to composition. In 1891 the degree of Music Doctorate was awarded him by Cambridge University in England. From 1892 to 1895 he was the

178

director of the National Conservatory in New York. In 1895 he accepted the post of director of the Prague Conservatory.

5. His popular *Fifth Symphony, Op. 95* (1893) (From the *New World*), was inspired by his visits to America, and received its première at Carnegie Hall, New York, Dec. 15, 1893. He composed operas, symphonies, choral works, concertos, chamber music and songs.

Composer's Main Contribution to the Art of Music:

1. Antonin Dvořák is known in this country mainly for his very popular *New World Symphony* which expresses one important phase of American culture. His chief musical achievement is his skillful incorporation of Czechoslovakian folk melodies in his symphonies.

Suggested Listening:

1. Title: *Slavonic Dance No. 7*
   Performers: National Symphony Orchestra, Washington, D.C.
   Record No.: R.C.A. Victor LE-1005
   Grade Level: 4 - 8

2. Title: *New World Symphony*
   Performers: Boston Symphony - Fiedler
   Record No.: RCA LSC-3315
   Grade Level 7 - 12

Optional Assignments:

1. Dvořák's native land was Czechoslovakia. Make a study of the geographical position and historical background of this country, and prepare a written report.
2. Dvořák was a very good friend of Johannes Brahms. Make a comparison of the music of these composers.
3. Do some research on the *New World Symphony* by Dvořák and prepare an oral report on the folk elements which provided the inspiration for this composition.
4. Do some research into governmental subsidies allowed to composers in the various countries of the world.
5. Lead a class discussion on the composer's life and music, and prepare an outline for this purpose.

JULES MASSENET

Composer: Jules Massenet
  Born: Montaud, France 1842
  Died: Paris, France 1912

Aural Recognition of Themes:
  Composition: *Élégie* (1873)

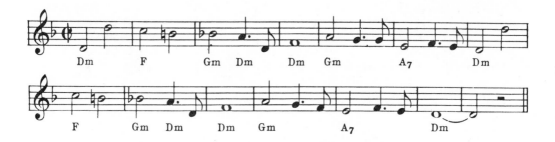

General Information about Composer and Compositions:

1. Jules Massenet's mother was a piano teacher and he received his first music lessons from her. At the age of eleven he entered the Paris Conservatory where he studied piano and solfeggio. Later he studied harmony and composition.

2. During his student days, he was very poor, and had to earn his living by playing in a restaurant orchestra three nights a week. At the conservatory he won first prize for composition of a fugue and also took first prize in piano virtuosity. In 1863 he won the Prix de Rome for his cantata.

3. He met Franz Liszt in Rome, who suggested that he give piano lessons to a girl who later became Massenet's wife. From 1878 to 1896 he was professor of music at the Paris Conservatory. At the age of thirty-six he became the youngest member ever elected to the Académie des Beaux-Arts.

4. Massenet is mostly noted for his operas, having written twenty-eight. He was a brilliant orchestrator. His style of writing is clear, concise and melodious.

180

5. One of his piano compositions *Élégie* (1873), an air from his incidental music to a play, is still used in the standard repertoire of many pianists. He composed many operas, among which *Le Cid* (1885) and *Sapho* (1897) are very popular. He also composed orchestral pieces and songs.

Composer's Main Contribution to the Art of Music:

1. Jules Massenet was the most important French composer of opera during this period. His composition shows the influence of Gounod. His style is lyric, melodic, and reveals beautiful harmonic treatment. His music expresses a refinement of musical structure. His style influenced future composers of opera, among whom may be listed, his pupils Alfred Bruneau, Gabriel Pierné, and Gustav Charpentier.

Suggested Listening:

1. Title: *Le Cid* (ballet suite)
   Performers: Boston Pops Orchestra - Fiedler
   Record No.: R.C.A. Victor LM-2661
   Grade Level: 4 - 8

2. Title: *Arias*
   Performers: Callas - vocalist
   Record No.: Angel 36147
   Grade Level: 7 - 12

Optional Assignments:

1. If you play the piano, study the *Elégie* by Massenet and play it for the class.

2. Lead a class discussion on the composer's life and music. Prepare an outline for this purpose.

3. Make a study of the famous literary geniuses of this period and write a report on this subject.

4. Tell the class about an historical event which took place during the composer's lifetime.

5. If you are artistic, draw or paint a picture of the composer and present it for bulletin board display.

ARTHUR S. SULLIVAN

Composer: Arthur S. Sullivan
    Born: London, England 1842
    Died: London, England 1900

Aural Recognition of Themes:
    Composition: Selection from *H.M.S. Pinafore* (1878)

General Information about Composer and Compositions:

1. Arthur S. Sullivan's father was an army bandmaster, and at the age of eight, Arthur was able to play almost every instrument of the band fairly well. He composed an anthem at the age of eight.

2. At twelve years of age, he became a chorister at the Chapel Royal in London. Two years later he won the Mendelssohn Scholarship to the Royal Academy of Music. He later became an outstanding student at the Leipzig Conservatory of Music in Germany.

4. In 1861 he was appointed organist at St. Michael's Church in London. In 1874 he was appointed conductor of the Leeds Festival and director of the Royal Philharmonic Orchestra.

4. In 1870 he met William S. Gilbert who became his collaborator in the writing and production of their world-famous operettas. In 1871 they produced a comic opera *Thespis* which was unsuccessful. This was followed by *Trial By Jury* (1875) which was very successful.

5. Gilbert and Sullivan made such a perfect team, that although they broke up their partnership many times,
   neither was ever able to write successfully without the
   other. Some of their more popular operettas, which are
   performed by professional companies as well as many
   school groups, include: H.M.S. *Pinafore* (1878), *The
   Pirates of Penzance* (1880), *Iolanthe* (1882), *The Mikado*
   (1885), and *The Yeomen of the Guard* (1888).

Composer's Main Contribution to the Art of Music:

1. Sir Arthur S. Sullivan is known as one of England's best
   composers of comic opera. He achieved his greatest success when he collaborated with the librettist William S.
   Gilbert. In their operettas they gave the world a musical
   and dramatic picture of life in England during the latter
   half of the nineteenth century. Their operettas are satirical masterpieces and are popular throughout the world.

Suggested Listening:

1. Title: *The Mikado* (excerpts)
   Performers: D'Oyly Carte - Godfrey
   Record No.: London 25903
   Grade Level: 4 - 8

2. Title: *Overture di Ballo*
   Performers: Boston Pops - Fiedler
   Record No.: Polydor 245006
   Grade Level: 7 - 12

Optional Assignments:

1. Do some research and write a report on the life of the
   lyricist, William S. Gilbert.

2. If you have seen a Gilbert and Sullivan operetta recently,
   give an oral description of this operetta and its music
   to the class.

3. Select a composition by the composer and either sing or
   play it for the class.

4. For a class project, prepare a performance of a Gilbert
   and Sullivan operetta.

5. If you are artistic, draw or paint some of the background
   scenery needed for one of these operettas.

EDVARD HAGERUP GRIEG

Composer: Edvard Hagerup Grieg
  Born: Bergen, Norway 1843
  Died: Bergen, Norway 1907

Aural Recognition of Themes:
  Composition: *Norwegian Dance* (1881)

General Information about Composer and Compositions:

1. Edvard Hagerup Grieg studied piano with his mother, who
   was an accomplished pianist. He began to compose songs
   at the age of nine. He studied at the Leipzig Conservatory in Germany from 1858 to 1862. He also studied composition in Copenhagen, Denmark.

2. With Richard Nordaak, a Norwegian nationalistic composer,
   Grieg fostered a Norwegian school of composition. In 1867
   he founded and conducted a choral society in Christiania.
   In 1865 and in 1870 he visited Rome, Italy, where he met
   Franz Liszt; the two became friends.

3. He achieved European recognition through the performance
   of his piano concerto at a Gewandhaus Concert in Leipzig
   in 1879. In 1888 he performed his piano concerto and
   conducted two of his pieces for string orchestra at
   London Philharmonic.

4. In 1894 he received the honorary degree of Doctor of
   Music from Cambridge University in England. He gained
   popularity in this country with the performance of concerts with his wife, Nina Grieg, who was an accomplished
   singer.

5. Many of his compositions depict elements of nationalism through the use of Norwegian folk tunes and mythology. One of the most popular of his works *Peer Gynt* (1875) is based on the play by Ibsen. His *Piano Concerto In A Minor* (1868) is probably one of the most popular piano works known today.

Composer's Main Contribution to the Art of Music:

1. Edvard Hagerup Grieg was an ardent nationalist who brought world recognition to himself and his native country through his music. He found his inspiration for composition in the folk lore and melodies of his native land.

Suggested Listening:

1. Title: *Lyric Suite - Norwegian Rustic Dance*
   Performers: National Symphony Orchestra, Washington, D.C.
   Record No.: R.C.A. Victor LE-1004, Adventures In Music
   Grade Level: 4 - 8

2. Title: *Concerto In A Minor* - for piano
   Performers: Pennario - Los Angelos Philharmonic - Leinsdorf
   Record No.: Sera. S60195
   Grade Level: 7 - 12

Optional Assignments:

1. Make a study of Norwegian folklore and write a report on this subject.

2. If you play the piano, learn and perform one of Grieg's works for the class.

3. Play a recording of a composition by Grieg, and conduct an oral discussion with the class on the selection.

4. Write a brief review of a book about the composer, including biographer, title and interesting facts.

5. If you are artistic, draw or paint a picture of the scenery of Norway.

NIKOLAI A. RIMSKY-KORSAKOV

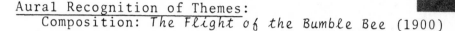

<u>Composer</u>: Nikolai A. Rimsky-Korsakov
   Born: Tikhvin, Russia 1844
   Died: St. Petersburg, Russia 1908

<u>Aural Recognition of Themes</u>:
   Composition: *The Flight of the Bumble Bee* (1900)

<u>General Information about Composer and Compositions</u>:

1. Nikolai A. Rimsky-Korsakov studied piano with his mother at the age of six. He began to write songs at the age of nine. Since he came from an aristrocratic family, he followed family tradition and enrolled in the Naval College of St. Petersburg at the age of twelve. He re-mained in the Russian Navy until he was almost thirty years old.

2. During his years at the Naval College, he took lessons in piano and cello. At this time he met Balakirev, the founder of the new Russian school of composition, who in-fluenced him to join the group of Russian composers called "The Russian Five" which included also Moussorgsky, Borodin and Cui.

3. The purpose of "The Russian Five" was to promote a nationalistic culture of Russian music through the use of folk themes and folk lore. Rimsky-Korsakov used the minor mode of Russian religious music for some of his works.

4. In 1871 he became professor of composition at St. Peters-burg Conservatory. He wrote a book called *The Foundations*

of Instrumentation, and also published a textbook on harmony. He was a member of the Paris Academy of Arts from 1907 till his death in 1908. He became the conductor of the Russian Symphony Concerts in 1886.

5. He composed operas, symphonies, chamber music, piano music, and choral music. One of his most popular works is the symphonic suite *Schéhérazade* (1888).

Composer's Main Contribution to the Art of Music:

1. Nikolai A. Rimsky-Korsakov developed the art of orchestration, instrumentation and harmony to such a high degree of perfection that his textbooks in these areas are used as references by many modern composers and students of composition. In his compositions he utilized Russian folk melodies. He is considered to be the creator of the Russian symphony and tone poem.

Suggested Listening:

1. Title: *Le Coq d'Or Suite - Bridal Procession*
   Performers: National Symphony Orchestra, Washington, D.C.
   Record No.: R.C.A. Victor, LE-1004, Adventures In Music
   Grade Level: 4 - 8

2. Title: *Schéhérazade, Op. 35*
   Performers: New York Philharmonic - Bernstein
   Record No.: Columbia MS-6069
   Grade Level: 7 - 12

Optional Assignments:

1. Do some research on the Russian political history during the Romantic period and write a report on this subject.

2. Make a study of the life and works of one of the other members of the "Russian Five" and present an oral report to the class.

3. Make a biographical sketch of Rimsky-Korsakov's life.

4. Write a report on the United States Navy School of Music including programs and curriculum.

5. Rimsky-Korsakov played the cello. Give an oral report to the class on its history and use in the symphony orchestra.

ENGELBERT HUMPERDINCK

Composer: Engelbert Humperdinck
  Born: Siegburg, Germany 1854
  Died: Neustrelitz, Germany 1921

Aural Recognition of Themes:
  Composition: Selection from *Hänsel and Gretel* (1893)

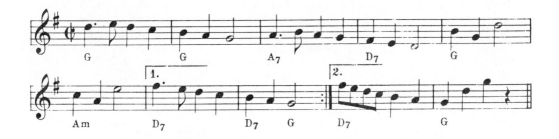

General Information about Composer and Compositions:

1. Engelbert Humperdinck was well known as a composer, critic and teacher. He studied at the Gymnasium at Paderborn and in 1872 was accepted at the Cologne Conservatory. In 1876 he won the Frankfort Mozart Stipendium, an honorary scholarship fund. In 1877 he attended the Royal School of Music in Munich.

2. After winning several prizes, he went to Italy, where he met Richard Wagner who influenced him greatly. Humperdinck became Wagner's assistant in the production of *Parsifal* at Bayreuth.

3. He also travelled to France and Spain, where he taught theory at the Barcelona Conservatory. In 1887 he taught at the Cologne Conservatory, and from 1890 to 1896 he was a professor at the Hock Conservatory in Frankfort.

4. He became the music critic for the local newspaper, Frankfurter Zeitung. In 1900 he went to Berlin to head the master-school for composition at the Academy of Fine Arts.

5. The composition which brought him much fame, and for which he is known throughout the world is the opera: *Hänsel and Gretel* (1893). He composed incidental music for several Shakespeare plays, the best known of which are: *The Merchant of Venice* (1905), *The Tempest* (1906), and *As You Like It* (1907).

Composer's Main Contribution to the Art of Music:

1. Engelbert Humperdinck became known internationally for his fairy-tale opera *Hänsel and Gretel*. He was the creator of a new style of opera based on folk lore which originated with fairy tales. He inspired many contempo-raries and future composers to adopt this style of writing.

Suggested Listening:

1. Title: *Hänsel and Gretel - Prelude*
   Performers: National Symphony Orchestra, Washington, D.C.
   Record No.: R.C.A. Victor, LE-1007, Adventures In Music
   Grade Level: 4 - 8

2. Title: *Hansel and Gretel* - selections
   Performers: Boston Pops - Fiedler
   Record No.: RCA - VCS-7060
   Grade Level: 7 - 12

Optional Assignments:

1. Several composers have written music for Shakespeare plays. Do some research and give an oral report to the class on this subject.

2. Using only a skeleton outline, tell your class about an interesting musical event that you attended recently.

3. Prepare a school performance of the opera *Hänsel and Gretel*.

4. Make up a notebook on the life and music of Humperdinck consisting of pictures, newspaper and magazine articles, concert programs, thematic excerpts, original illustrations and written reports.

5. If you are artistic, draw or paint the background scenery for the production *Hänsel and Gretel*.

RUGGIERO LEONCAVALLO

Composer: Ruggiero Leoncavallo
  Born: Naples, Italy 1858
  Died: Montecatini, Italy 1919

Aural Recognition of Themes:
  Composition: *Vesti la Giubba* from Opera
      I Pagliacci (1892)

General Information about Composer and Compositions:

1. Ruggiero Leoncavallo was the son of the President of the High Court of Justice in Naples. He was a day scholar at the Naples Conservatory of Music at the age of eight. He received his diploma at the age of sixteen and entered the University of Bologna where four years later he received his Doctor of Letters degree.

2. He travelled on a concert tour visiting many foreign countries including Egypt where he was appointed private musician to the Viceroy of Egypt. He played accompaniments at cafe-concerts in France, England, Germany and Holland. He gave concerts in the United States in 1906 and 1913.

3. He was a disciple of Richard Wagner who encouraged him in his composition. Leoncavallo followed Wagner's dramatic style and like Wagner, wrote his own libretti for his operas.

4. He was commissioned by the Kaiser of Germany to write an opera *Roland* in 1904, but it was unsuccessful. In 1906

his opera *La Jeunesse de Figaro* was produced by the Metropolitan Opera Company in New York.

5. He composed a symphonic poem *Nuit de Mai* (1894), a ballet *La Vita d'una Marionetta* (1900), and many operas. His most popular operas are: *I Pagliacci* (1892), *La Bohème* (1894), and *I Medici* (1893).

Composer's Main Contribution to the Art of Music:

1. Ruggiero Leoncavallo is famous throughout the world for his very popular opera *I Pagliacci*. This opera is one of the finest ever written and is included in the repertory of many opera houses in all countries of the world. His style of opera composition had a tremendous influence on that of his contemporaries in both Germany and Italy.

Suggested Listening:

1. Title: *Bohème* - selections
   Performers: San Remo
   Record No.: Everest S-462
   Grade Level: 4 - 8

2. Title: *I Pagliacci* - excerpts
   Performers: Vocal-Orchestra
   Record No.: DG 136281
   Grade Level: 7 - 12

Optional Assignments:

1. *I Pagliacci* is a comic opera. Make a study of comic opera and give an oral report to the class on this subject.

2. Make a study of the famous music schools in Europe and compare their curriculum with that of the music schools in the United States.

3. If you are artistic, draw or paint a picture of one of the leading characters in *I Pagliacci*.

4. Make a list of opera composers and their most popular operas.

5. If you play a musical instrument or sing, perform a selection from one of the composer's works for the class.

GIACOMO PUCCINI

Composer: Giacomo Puccini
    Born: Lucca, Italy 1858
    Died: Brussels, Belgium 1924

Aural Recognition of Themes:
    Composition: Selection from *La Bohème* (1896)

General Information about Composer and Compositions:

1. Giacomo Puccini's father was a music teacher and director of the Lucca Academy of Music. Giacomo studied organ and voice at the Pacini Institute. The Queen of Italy gave him a grant so that he could attend the Milan Conservatory, where he produced his first orchestral work *Sinfonia-Capriccio* which proved very successful.

2. In 1893 he was appointed professor of music at the Milan Conservatory. During this period he composed many operas. His works are considered to be superior to those of Mascagni and Leoncavallo. He achieved a quality of excellence in opera composition that was comparable to that of Giuseppe Verdi.

3. He combined the old, traditional characteristics of Italian opera with modern dramatic style, and used beautiful orchestral coloring. His lyrics are light in charac - ter and easily understood by modern audiences.

4. Puccini in 1916 attempted to write the first musical comedy (operetta) of this time called *La Rondine*. This later was made into a comic opera, but did not receive the recognition that his other operas achieved.

5. Some of Puccini's operas that have received much acclaim throughout the world are: *La Bohème* (1896) (in four acts), *La Tosca* (1900) (in three acts), and *Madame Butterfly* (1904) (in two acts).

Composer's Main Contribution to the Art of Music:

1. Giacomo Puccini was a master of writing melody. He was very adept in the selection of librettos that contained popular appeal. Next to Verdi, he is known to be the most outstanding contributor to the development of an aristocratic style of Italian opera composition.

Suggested Listening:

1. Title: *Madame Butterfly* - selections
   Performers: Boston Pops Orchestra - Fiedler
   Record No.: R.C.A. Victor LM-2604
   Grade Level: 4 - 8

2. Title: *Tosca* - selections
   Performers: Kingsway Symphony - Camarata
   Record No.: London 21019
   Grade Level: 7 - 12

Optional Assignments:

1. Make a comparison between Italian and German opera, and write a report on this subject.

2. If you are artistic, draw or paint a picture of the composer and present it for bulletin board display.

3. Play a recording of one of Puccini's compositions for the class and give an oral report on this selection.

4. Make a study of the political and economic conditions in Italy during the composer's lifetime.

5. Lead a class discussion on the composer's life and music after preparing an outline for this purpose.

ISAAC ALBÉNIZ

<u>Composer</u>: Isaac Albéniz
  Born: Camprodón, Spain 1860
  Died: Cambó les Bains, Spain 1909

<u>Aural Recognition of Themes</u>:
  Composition: *Tango in D* (1895)

General Information about Composer and Compositions:

1. Isaac Albéniz was an infant prodigy. At the age of four, he made his first appearance on the stage as a pianist at the Teatro Romea in Barcelona and also performed in Madrid. Later he performed in Paris while studying piano at the Paris Conservatory with Marmontel.

2. His first composition was a *Pasodoble* (1867) which he wrote at the age of seven. He gave a concert performance as a youth in North and South America. He studied music at the Madrid Conservatory and was awarded a pension by the King of Spain which enabled him to further his musical studies in Brussels, Belgium. He then went to Leipzig where he studied piano with Franz Liszt.

3. He was court pianist at Madrid. In 1881 he toured the United States, England and other European countries with Anton Rubinstein. He then settled down in Madrid, where he taught from 1885 to 1889.

4. From 1890 until his death, he lived in London and Paris. In London he became popular for his comic operas. In Paris he came under the influence of Claude Debussy, and wrote more piano compositions.

5. He composed several operas, none of which are popular in this country. He is mostly noted for his piano works, the most popular of which are: *Malaguena, Iberia* (1906), set of twelve piano pieces, and *Suite Espagnole* (1899).

Composer's Main Contribution to the Art of Music:

1. Isaac Albéniz gave to the musical world, through his compositions, vivid and colorful pictures of Spain. He was the first of Spain's nationalistic composers, and utilized the Spanish folk songs and dance rhythms in his compositions.

Suggested Listening:

1. Title: *Maleguena*
   Performers: Jose Iturbi
   Record No.: R.C.A. Victor LM-1967
   Grade Level: 4 - 8

2. Title: *Iberia*
   Performers: Chicago Symphony Orchestra - Reiner
   Record No.: R.C.A. Victor LM-2230
   Grade Level: 7 - 12

Optional Assignments:

1. Make a study of other Spanish composers, noting in particular any similarities in their works (Ex.: rhythm, form, instrumentation etc.).

2. If you play the piano, perform a selection of the composer for the class.

3. Learn a basic dance used during the composer's lifetime and present it to the class.

4. Do research in the World Book or any other encyclopedia on the composer and report your findings to your classmates.

5. Study the development of the piano, and collect literature and pictures of this instrument for your notebook.

EDWARD A. MacDOWELL

Composer: Edward A. MacDowell
  Born: New York, N.Y. 1861
  Died: New York, N.Y. 1908

Aural Recognition of Themes:
  Composition: Selection from *Woodland Sketches* (1896)

General Information about Composer and Compositions:

1. Edward A. MacDowell was an American composer and pianist of Scotch-Irish descent. He began the study of piano at the age of eight. In 1876 he studied at the Paris Conservatory. In 1879 he studied composition and theory at the Frankfort Conservatory in Germany.

2. He taught at the Darmstadt Conservatory at Hesse, Germany. Later he moved to Frankfort where he gave music lessons and devoted much time to composition. In 1896 he was appointed professor of music at Columbia University in New York City.

3. His wife, Marion Nevins MacDowell, founded the MacDowell Colony for the study of music on their estate at Peterboro, New Hampshire. It is a creative center for young composers.

4. MacDowell's compositions are written in American style, showing European influence. He lived in Boston for a while and played his concertos with the Boston Symphony Orchestra.

5. MacDowell composed mainly for the orchestra and the piano. Some of his well-known compositions include: *Woodland Sketches* (1896) piano piece arranged for orchestra, *Indian Suite* (1892) for orchestra, and *Piano Concerto in A Minor* (1885).

Composer's Main Contribution to the Art of Music:

1. Edward A. MacDowell is well-known for his program music. He was the first composer of serious music in the United States. His style of composition was an inspiration for many other American composers to follow. He was the creator of an individual American style and tried to foster a nationalistic style of American music and achieved this ambition to a certain degree.

Suggested Listening:

1. Title: *Second (Indian) Suite - In Wartime*
   Performers: National Symphony Orchestra, Washington, D.C.
   Record No.: R.C.A. Victor LE-1006, Adventures In Music
   Grade Level: 4 - 8

2. Title: *Woodland Sketches, Op. 51* - excerpts
   Performers: Pennario - piano
   Record No.: Angel 36049
   Grade Level: 7 - 12

Optional Assignments:

1. Do some research on the musical activities of the MacDowell Colony in Peterboro, New Hampshire. Give an oral report of your findings to the class.

2. Lead a class discussion in the composer's life and music, after preparing an outline for this purpose.

3. If you are artistic, draw or paint a picture of the composer.

4. Make a study of the famous literary geniuses of this period and write a composition on this topic.

5. Prepare a skit involving noteworthy incidents in the life of the composer.

CHAPTER 7

THE MODERN PERIOD (1900-   )

Historical Background of the Modern Period:

I. Introduction: The beginning of the 20th century seemed to hold promise for the establishment of peace. Mankind had made remarkable progress in technological and scientific discoveries, in opportunities for education, and in social reforms. However, overshadowing these advances were forces that moved toward war. These included the extremes of nationalism, imperialism, expansionism, militarism and economic rivalries. As a result of these forces of friction, the nations of the world became involved in two major wars within twenty-five years. The persistent turmoil has shown that the motives for war have outweighed the desire and hope for peace and international cooperation.

A. Causes of World War I:

1. Extreme nationalism developed national hatreds. Franco-German rivalry increased over France's desire to re-annex Alsace-Lorraine. The submerged nationalities within the most powerful countries of Central Europe (Germany, Turkey and Austria-Hungary) wanted their independence or union with their mother country.

2. Europe became divided into two armed camps, the Triple Alliance (Italy, Germany, Austria-Hungary) and The Triple Entente (Russia, France, England). The two alliances took opposite sides in various conflicts but succeeded in avoiding a major clash until 1914.

3. The immediate cause of World War I was the assasination of the Archduke of Austria, Francis Ferdinand.

B. World War I:

1. Austria declared war on Serbia, followed by the mobilization of Germany and Russia. France and England entered the war because of their alliance with Russia. Rumania and Italy (1915) joined the Allies, while Turkey and Bulgaria joined the Central Powers. In 1917 the United States entered the

conflict followed by China and much of Latin America.
About forty nations became involved in the war.

2. The Western Front in France was the major battle-
field. Other battles were fought in Belgium, northern
Italy, Polish Russia and Germany. The failure of
Germany's offensive in the Spring of 1918 resulted in
the defeat of her armies. The Armistice was signed on
November 11, 1918.

C. The Russian Revolution of 1917:

1. Russia, under the absolute monarchy of the Tsars, was
beset by political corruption, widespread famine, and
oppression of the people. Nicholas II was overthrown
by the March Revolution of 1917 and a Provisional
Government was formed by the Duma (or legislature).
Administration of the government was instituted by
representatives of liberal parties. This government
was opposed by the "soviets" (or councils) of workers
and soldiers which were communist dominated and opposed to Russian participation in World War I.

2. In October 1917, the Bolsheviks (Communists), under
the leadership of Lenin, Trotsky and Stalin, revolted
and gained control of the government.

D. Period from 1918-1938:

1. In 1918 President Wilson presented his "Fourteen
Points" program to Congress. This included the establishment of the League of Nations which became a part
of the peace treaty.

2. After 1930, the League of Nations could not stop
military aggression. Japan invaded China (1933). In
1934 Hitler was declared Führer and leader of the
Nazi party and government of Germany. Persecution of
Jews and Christian churches, terror of the secret
police, and rearmament followed by aggressive foreign
policy occurred under the Nazi rule. Fascist Italy
under Mussolini invaded Ethiopia (1935). A Civil War
broke out in Spain (1936) between the Insurgents
under Franco and the Loyalists. There was a renewal
of the balance of power alliances.

3. The Fascist governments of Italy, Germany and Japan
formed the Rome-Berlin-Tokyo Axis (1937). By 1938,
Europe was separated into armed camps.

E. Causes of World War II:

  1. By 1938, it was apparent that peace efforts had
     failed. Germany and Italy had acquired colonies.
     Japan planned to seize European and American trade
     in the Far East. The League of Nations had failed to
     stop aggression and nations began to prepare them-
     selves for the eventuality of war.

F. World War II:

  1. In 1939 Hitler's troops invaded Poland, and this
     aggression provided the impetus for France and
     England to declare war on Germany.

  2. From 1933 to 1939, the United States was undecided
     about its foreign policy of either isolation or
     collective security. The Lend-Lease Act (1941) was
     passed by Congress to lend or lease supplies to
     Britain and other countries who were fighting fas-
     cism. The United States assisted England, France and
     China while placing an embargo on important raw ma-
     terials to Japan.

  3. On December 7, 1941 there was a sneak air attack by
     the Japanese on Pearl Harbor, Hawaii. This act
     brought the United States into World War II against
     Japan, Germany and Italy. A federation of nations
     was established for the purpose of defeating the
     Axis. This federation included the United States,
     England, Canada, Soviet Russia, China, Free French,
     Australia, New Zealand, and a number of Latin Ameri-
     can countries. The efforts of all the countries in-
     volved brought about the surrender of the German
     general staff in May, 1945.

  4. A new super weapon, the atomic bomb, developed by
     the United States had a devastating effect on
     Hiroshima and Nagasaki which caused the surrender of
     Japan in August, 1945.

G. Aftermath of World War II:

  1. The United Nations was organized at the San Fran-
     cisco Conference in the Spring of 1945. The purpose
     of the organization is to attempt to maintain an
     international peace and bring about cooperation in
     the solution of economic, social, health, humani-
     tarian and cultural problems.

2. A struggle for power known as the Cold War has been continuing since 1947. Conflicts have been waged precipitating from different political ideologies, competition for power, acquiring of colonies, and monopoly of world trade. A race for armament superiority has given an impetus to technological and scientific developments.

3. The "cold war" has developed into a "shooting war" in some areas of the world. Although these conflagrations have threatened to expand into a major world conflict, they have thus far been confined. The most notable of these crises are the Korean War, the Vietnam conflict, the Cuban crisis, and the Civil War in the Republic of the Congo.

4. The problems of the world are never-ending. Man, with the knowledge that he today possesses, has the potential of remaking a more wonderful and better world.

Studies in Cultural Correlation - Modern Period:

I. Cultural Achievements - Social Studies:

The studies of human behavior by psychologists and sociologists have produced influential intellectual movements in the 20th century. The methods used in social research (which deal with human acts, values and emotions) have been limited by the nature of the subjects being studied and the difficulty of obtaining controlled experiments. Nevertheless, sociological thinkers with their new ideas and methods have influenced literature, art, science and human thought.

Major intellectual revolutions have been instigated by new and profound political theories and ideas. The resultant tensions of capitalism and socialism on the one hand, and democracy and totalitarianism on the other hand, has produced a world torn by conflicting ideologies and cultures.

Several influential thinkers who have dominated human thought in the 20th century include:

1. Émile Durkheim (1858-1917) - French philosopher and psychologist: Durkheim was a pioneer in social psychology. In his work *The Elementary Forms of the Religious Life* (1915), he studied the origins of religions. He concluded that an individual's actions and reactions

were different from those of a group's in quality but
that religion grew from group experiences.

2. <u>Nikolai</u> <u>Lenin</u> (1870-1924) - Russian statesman: Lenin
was the leader of the Russian Revolution and the founder of the U.S.S.R. (Union of Soviet Socialist Republics)
He was a skillful orator, organizer and writer. His
What is to Be Done? (1902), was concerned with trade
unions and socialistic ideology.

3. <u>Oswald</u> <u>Spengler</u> (1880-1936) - German social philosopher:
Spengler's famous *The Decline of the West* (1918) predicted the decline of Western civilization in three
hundred years with the establishment of an oriental culture. His book also served as an intellectual rationali-
zation for Nazism.

4. <u>Sigmund</u> <u>Freud</u> (1856-1939) - Austrian physician and
psychoanalyst: Freud was the founder of psychoanalysis
and one of the great pioneers in psychotherapy. He was
among the first to establish the influence of uncon-
scious motivation in human behavior. His many works
include: *The Interpretations of Dreams* (1900) and *The
Ego and the Id* (1923).

5. <u>John</u> <u>Dewey</u> (1859-1952) - American philosopher, psychologist and educator: Dewey developed the theory of pro-
gressive education which stressed "learning by doing".
His idea of freedom, called 20th century liberalism, was
related to the policies of a "Welfare State" with its
program of public planning and control that aids the
less fortunate classes. His works include: *Art as
Experience, Human Nature and Conduct,* and *Democracy and
Education.* He related his philosophy to economic, sociological, political and educational problems.

II. <u>Cultural Achievements</u> - <u>Physical Sciences</u>:

The Nuclear Age has seen a tremendous drive towards
scientific growth and success in all areas such as the
development of television, plastics, atomic energy, wonder-
working drugs and serums, and powerful insecticides. Jet
aircraft with their great speed have broken through the
sound barrier and affected commercial and military avia-
tion. The achievements are endless.
Except for the restrictions and secrecy imposed upon
atomic research, the majority of scientific studies of the
20th century have been international rather than national
in character. The secrecy surrounding the knowledge and

utilization of atomic energy has produced world-wide
political, economic and cultural problems.
Among the notable scientists and inventors of this
period are:

1. Wilbur Wright (1867-1912) - Orville Wright (1871-1948)
   American inventors: The Wright brothers made the first
   successful ascent and descent in a heavier-than-air
   machine. In 1903 they flew the first airplane with a
   gasoline engine at Kitty Hawk, North Carolina.

2. Wilhelm Roentgen (1845-1923) - German physicist:
   Roentgen won the Nobel Prize in 1901 for the discovery
   of X-rays.

3. Pierre Curie (1859-1906) - French physicist and Marie
   Curie (1867-1934) - Polish physicist: The Curies discovered the element radium and made significant contributions toward the understanding and use of radio-
   activity.

4. Luther Burbank (1849-1926) - American horticulturist:
   Burbank developed new species of flowers, fruits and
   vegetables through selection, crossing and grafting.
   His methods helped revolutionize food production.

5. Albert Einstein (1879-1955) - German and American
   physicist: Einstein won the Nobel Prize in Physics in
   1921 for his work on the photoelectric effect. His
   famous general theory of relativity (1915) sought to
   show that time, motion and space are relative. His
   well-known equation, "Energy equals mass times the
   speed of light," postulated the theory that mass could
   change into energy and energy would change into mass.
   In addition to his scientific treatises, Einstein wrote
   the books *About Zionism* (1930), *The World As I See It*
   (1935) and others.

6. John Logie Baird (1888-1946) - Scottish inventor: Baird
   invented the first functional television system.
   Through his research he later produced three-dimension-
   al and color television, and navigational instruments
   utilizing infra-red television systems.

7. Alexander Fleming (1881-1955) - Scottish bacteriologist: Fleming discovered the antibiotic mold, penicil-
   lin, which has been used successfully for the treatment of many diseases difficult to cure.

8. <u>Enrico Fermi</u> (1901-1954) - Italian physicist: Fermi bombarded uranium with neutrons and transmuted it into a different element, No. 93, neptunium (1934). He produced the first successful nuclear chain reaction (1942) which made nuclear bombs and nuclear reactors possible.

9. <u>Norbert Wiener</u> (1894-1964) - American mathematician: Wiener formulated the mathematical theory of cybernetics. This was a landmark in the Nuclear Age for it made possible the engineering of computers and electronic automation.

III. <u>Cultural Achievements</u> - <u>Literature</u>:

The Modern Period has been an age of great accomplishment and progress in all areas of knowledge. Despite this amazing advancement and growth, many people of the world still experience poverty, hunger and disease. Writers have tried to find solutions to these problems as well as to remedy the hypocrisy and deceit which they believe exists. Some have merely reported life as they perceived it, while others have sought various political, social, economic or mystical solutions. Realism, symbolism and disillusionment have become the forms of expression in literature. The novel has been the dominant literary form of the 20th century.
Some of the major writers of this century are:

1. <u>Guillaume Appollinaire</u> (1880-1918) - French poet, short-story writer and art critic: Appollinaire is credited with introducing many new modern forms which include surrealism (a word he invented), cubism and dadaism. He wrote *The Cubist Painters* (1913) which explained the aims of cubism. He is the author of novels and a drama but his poems are his most famous works. His poems were often written without punctuation. They include: *Alcools* and *Animes in Calligrammes*.

2. <u>Marcel Proust</u> (1871-1920) - French novelist: Proust's masterpiece consisted of a series of novels translated as *Remembrance of Things Past*. His work showed a preoccupation with time. He shifted back and forth in the time medium to develop a picture of a decadent society. He wrote with sensitivity and insight about people and mores. His work, which combined naturalism and symbolism, influenced many modern writers.

3. <u>William</u> <u>Butler</u> <u>Yeats</u> (1865-1939) - Irish poet and dramatist: Yeats won the Nobel Prize for literature in 1923 and is considered one of the greatest poets of modern times. He was one of the leaders of the Irish literary revival. Yeats poetry is known for its rich, varied expression and musical quality. His famous poems include: *The Tower* (1928) and *Last Poems* (1936-1939).

4. <u>James</u> <u>Joyce</u> (1882-1941) - Irish novelist: A main subject of Joyce's writings was man in general. His *Ulysses*, portrays modern man as being a weak version of the heroic figures of Greece. His famous stream of consciousness technique, which originated in his novel *Portrait of the Artist as a Young Man*, has influenced modern literature.

5. <u>George</u> <u>Bernard</u> <u>Shaw</u> (1856-1950) - Irish playwright and critic: Shaw began his literary career as a newspaper critic of plays and music. His reviews are famous. Shaw's dramatic comedies are known for their wit, brilliant satire, ingenuity, and his special brand of fearless intellectual criticism of the modern age. Among his most notable plays are: *Man and Superman* (1903), and *Pygmalion* (1912).

6. <u>Eugene</u> <u>O'Neill</u> (1888-1953) - American playwright: O'Neill is considered one of the greatest contributors to the American theater. He won the Nobel Prize for Literature in 1936. O'Neill introduced new devices and techniques such as masks, systematic use of the aside, and the double appearance of the same character. A few of his fine plays include: *Desire Under the Elms* (1924), *The Hairy Ape* (1922) and *Ah Wilderness* (1933).

7. <u>Thomas</u> <u>Mann</u> (1875-1955) - German novelist: Mann's contribution to the development of the novel was the new dimension which he created which went into the history, civilization and culture as the basis of his fictional world. In all his works, Mann's main subject was "Man and his victory over death and timelessness." His famous *Magic Mountain* (1924), portrays the doubts and conflicts of the modern age. Mann won the Nobel Prize in 1929.

8. <u>Ernest</u> <u>Hemingway</u> (1899-1961) - American novelist and short-story writer: Hemingway bridged the gap between literature and journalism in his style of writing. His *The Sun Also Rises*, *A Farewell to Arms*, and *For Whom the Bell Tolls* are cynical, disillusioned pieces which emphasize the sensual. Some of his books were not

fiction but were concerned with sports such as *Death in the Afternoon* (bull-fighting), and *The Green Hills of Africa* (hunting).

9. William Faulkner (1897-1962) - American novelist, poet and short-story writer: Faulkner received the Nobel Prize award in 1949. Most of his work dealt with the history, life and people of an imaginary county of Yoknapatawpha in Mississippi. His works include the famous *The Sound and the Fury* (a stream of consciousness novel), and *Light in August*. His style and technique have made him one of America's great writers of the Modern Period.

10. Thomas Stearns Eliot (1888-1964) - American born British poet, dramatist and critic: T.S. Eliot's poems were considered the finest of the 1920's. They were compact, free in style, witty, and psychologically intense. His *Poems* (1920) and *The Waste Land* (1922) are famous. His books of criticism include: *The Sacred Wood*, and *The Use of Poetry and the Use of Criticism*. T.S. Eliot won the Nobel Prize in 1948.

IV. Cultural Achievements - Philosophy:

The important progress made in science and technology has resulted in a transformation in attitude toward life and thought. The general tone of the viewpoints of 20th century philosophers appears to be considerably less materialistic than those of the 19th century. Many believe that life would be meaningless if it were to be based solely on an impersonal evolutionary materialism.

Philosophers have developed many new systems of thought in idealism, realism, phenomenology, vitalism, naturalism, mysticism, pragmatism, dualism, intuitionism, and positivism (logical analysis). As in science, art and literature, philosophy of the Modern Age has developed from interpretations of life from individual viewpoints.

Some well-known philosophers of this century include:

1. Henri Bergson (1859-1941) - French philosopher: Bergson is called the French philosopher of vitalism. His *Creative Evolution* (1907) was a rebellion against the materialistic determinism of the time. He believed that philosophy took precedence over science and he made a clear distinction between the two. He instigated two general movements in France: philosophical syndicalism (social revolution) and Catholic Modernism (fusing of Catholic faith, modern science and biblical criticism).

2. George Santayana (1863-1952) - American philosopher, essayist and poet: Santayana detested modern technological culture and idolized ancient Greek society. A critical realist, he emphasized that consciousness reveals reality. His chief works include: *Skepticism and Animal Faith*, and *Realms of Being*.

3. Alfred North Whitehead (1861-1948) - British mathematician and philosopher: Whitehead stressed the idea of one reality based on whatever is given in one's perceptions. In his *Process and Reality* (1929), he formulated a metaphysical system called the philosophy of organism. In *Science and the Modern World*, he emphasized that in order to have continual progress in culture, the over-specialization resulting from our technological age should be avoided.

4. Miguel De Unamuno (1864-1936) - Spanish writer and philosopher: Unamuno's chief work *The Tragic Sense of Life* (1913), stressed his main philosophy. He analyzed the soul of man and found it torn apart by the engulfing threat of over-industrialization.

5. Bertrand Russell (1872-1970) - British mathematician and philosopher: Russell calls his philosophy logical atomism. Using his mathematical logical ability, Russell has explained reality by stating that things can exist apart from one actually perceiving them. His works include: *The Analysis of the Mind, The Analysis of Matter,* and *Principia Mathematica* (co-author A.N. Whitehead). He has also written sociological articles (e.g. the banning of testing nuclear weapons). He won the Nobel Prize Award in Literature in 1950.

V. Cultural Achievements - Fine Arts:

The artists of the Modern Period have cast aside traditional techniques and sought new art forms. Many diversified styles have been developed. Cubism has found expression through arrangement of geometric forms in many colors and textures. The Fauvists have brought an Oriental dash into art with their shocking flat areas of color. Neo-plasticism shuns natural appearances and concerns itself with balancing lines and colored areas. The Expressionists have sought to portray an emotional impact of the artists' inner feelings. Surrealism, influenced by Freud, has reproduced dreams or fantasies by placing illogical objects in unrealistic settings.

Modern sculpture has found expression through concentrating on mass, design and surface. Architecture has stressed the functional as well as the visual effect. Architects have utilized new and various shapes and materials to create an international style.

Life, objects, people and society are interpreted and represented in the individualistic style of the outstanding artists of this period. The most illustrious of these include the following:

1. Pablo Picasso (1881-1973) - Spanish painter, sculptor, engraver and ceramist: Picasso, through his inventiveness, experimentation and creativeness, is considered one of the most influential painters of the 20th century. The cubistic painting *Guernica*, a condemnation of war, is considered to be one of his greatest masterpieces.

2. Henri Matisse (1869-1954) - French painter and sculptor: Matisse, leader of the Fauvists, painted in terms of color patterns which have an oriental effect. He used all the complementary colors. His harmony of color is held together by a linear patterning. Among his famous paintings are: *The Three Sisters*, and *Lux*.

3. Piet Mondrian (1872-1944) - Dutch painter: Mondrian's paintings are known for their modern, abstract, geometric designs in primary colors. He influenced modern design in industry, architecture and interior decorating . One of his most famous paintings is *Composition 2*.

4. Salvador Dali (1904-   ) - Spanish painter: Dali, one of the leading surrealist painters, is noted for his manner of painting illogical objects realistically. His religious paintings are also famous.

5. Henry Moore (1898-   ) - British sculptor and painter: Moore's art shows an African influence. His sculpture is completely abstract. He is best known for his massive, rotund, human forms. *The Reclining Figure*, shows Moore's fascination for solid and void form interchange which gives the effect that the sculpture is always facing one regardless of one's position.

6. Alexander Calder (1898-1945) - American sculptor: Calder is noted for his abstract mobiles created out of paper, pipe, wire, plastic and metal, which are affected by movement of air. In *Lobster Trap and Fish Tail*, Calder achieved a specific type of motion for each part of his mobile.

7. Le Corbusier (1887-1965) - Swiss architect: Corbusier's modern architecture, adapted to its natural setting, is characterized by its plastic and curvilinear form. His beautiful *Chapel of Notre Dame du Haut* (Ronchamp, France, 1955), has been called "almost a piece of sculpture." The *Carpenter Center for the Visual Arts*, located at Harvard University is an example of his pure and unornate beauty in architecture.

8. Frank Lloyd Wright (1867-1961) - American architect: Wright created an "organic" architecture. His buildings correlated the needs of the people inhabiting the structures with the total design. His architecture adapted itself to the natural surrounding terrain. *Falling Water at Bear Run* (Pennsylvania, 1936), *The Robie House*, and *Taliesin*, are examples of his use of a natural setting to determine the form of a house.

Music of the Modern Period:

Developments Which Contributed to the Musical Culture:

A. General Characteristics: It is difficult to be objective in describing the music of this period because we are living in this century; also, the music of this time is in a state of transition and therefore a complete evaluation is not possible. However, certain characteristics stand out.

   1. Experimentation in atonal musical composition has marked the beginning of this century. Free use of dissonance and fluidity of form are some of the qualities of this experimental music.
   2. The invention of the following electronic devices has made possible the ever-increasing size of the listening public:
      a. Radio
      b. Phonograph
      c. Sound movies
      d. Television
      e. Tape recordings and tape recorders

B. Schools of Composition: The following schools of composition have appeared in this century:

   1. Neo-Impressionism:
      a. Impression of external things.
      b. Influence of painting and literature.
      c. Use of whole-tone scale.

2. Neo-Classicism:
   a. Return to Classical style of composition.
   b. Music is intellectual as well as emotional.
   c. Use of mechanical instruments.
3. Neo-Romanticism:
   a. Derived from Romanticism.
   b. Use of Wagnerian style.
   c. Use of oversized orchestras, forms and advanced orchestration.
4. Expressionism:
   a. Expression of the inner self or subconscious.
   b. Use of atonality (abandonment of key center)
   c. Use of polytonality (simultaneous use of two or more keys).

C. Elements of Music:

1. Melody: Dissonance and atonality are common to the melody of this period. Tension, unusual melodic intervals and harsh sounds are characteristic.
2. Harmony: There is a liberal use of dissonant harmony with irregular progressions, polytonality, altered tones and scales.
3. Rhythm: Some of the main characteristics of rhythm of the modern period are: changes of meter throughout the composition, more complex rhythms, use of irregular accents, and use of jazz rhythms.

D. American Popular Music:

1. A comparatively new art still going through many stages of development.
   a. Ragtime: originated in New Orleans.
   b. Blues: improvisation of twelve-measure phrases with use of lowered third and seventh degrees of the scale.
   c. Jazz: written arrangements with improvisation for solo instruments.
2. Popular music has had some influence upon serious music:
   a. Harmony: harmonic freedom and license; altered chords.
   b. Rhythm: complex dance rhythms.
   c. Instrumentation: smaller instrumental groups.

E. Vocal Music of the Modern Period:

1. The instrumental music of this period is more prominent than the vocal music.

2. Interest has been revived in singing of "a cappella" music, (unaccompanied singing).
3. Oratorio: The modern form of the oratorio follows basically the form used by Handel.
4. Opera: George Gershwin introduced the jazz idiom into opera writing. In this century experimentation with various forms and styles has taken place in opera composition.

F. Instrumental Music: Modern technology has brought about many advances in the development of instrumentation and orchestration.

1. Continued improvement of instruments and invention of new electronic devices has made available to the composer many new tonal combinations and sound effects, and has generally influenced all instrumental music.
2. Development of orchestral color in instrumental music.
3. Chamber music revived during this period.
4. Smaller orchestral groups are more practical for playing modern compositions.

G. Instrumental Forms:

1. Few new forms have been developed during this period.
2. Generally, musical forms have been shortened and revised to achieve more clarity and simplicity.
3. On the whole, there is more freedom in the construction of musical form.

H. Electronic Music: Electronic music is initiated and modified through electronic means. It employs the use of many electronic instruments, including tape recorders, synthesizers, oscillators, reverberators, echo chambers and computers. It is basically sound-oriented whereas traditional music is theme-oriented. Electronic music is produced, reproduced and manipulated for various sound effects. The composer of electronic music is unlimited in the type of sounds he wants; he can go as far as his imagination will carry him.

There were three important electronic music centers developed during the 1950's:

1. Music concrete in Paris (1948) led by Pierre Scharffer. Some composers in this school included Pierre Henry, Karlheinz Stockhausen, Darius Milhaud and Edgar Varese.

2. Cologne studio in Germany (1951) led at first by
Herbert Eimert, later by Karlheinz Stockhausen. A leading composer of this school was Ernst Krenek. The Cologne
studio influenced many electronic music studios in
Stockholm, Milan, Tokyo and Warsaw.

3. Collaboration of Otto Luening and Vladimir Ussachevsky
in New York (1952) later resulted in the formation of the
Columbia-Princeton Electronic Music Center (1959).
Luening and Ussachevsky were leaders at this electronic
center. Other composers who worked at this center in-
cluded Muchiko Toyama, Bulent Arel, Mario Davidovsky,
Charles Wuorinen, Milton Babbitt, Roger Sessions and
Edgar Varese. Today the Columbia-Princeton Electronic
Center is one of the best furnished electronic music
centers in the world.

I. Aleatoric Music: Aleatoric music is often called "chance
music". As is suggested in the name, much of the performance in this type of music is left to chance. To perform
aleatoric music, you may choose a familiar song and change
its rhythmic pattern, with performers varying the speed,
note values and melody, or you may create your own music
from a group of numbers (birthday, telephone etc.), and
using middle c as 1, work out the numbers accordingly.
The potentials of this type of music are unlimited. The
composers of aleatoric music vary in their compositions;
some give a lot of directions while others give very
little, allowing the performer a lot of freedom. An example of aleatoric music composition is: "For Five Or Ten
People" by the French composer, Christian Wolff.

Juan Gris : *Le Violon.* Kunstmuseum, Basel.

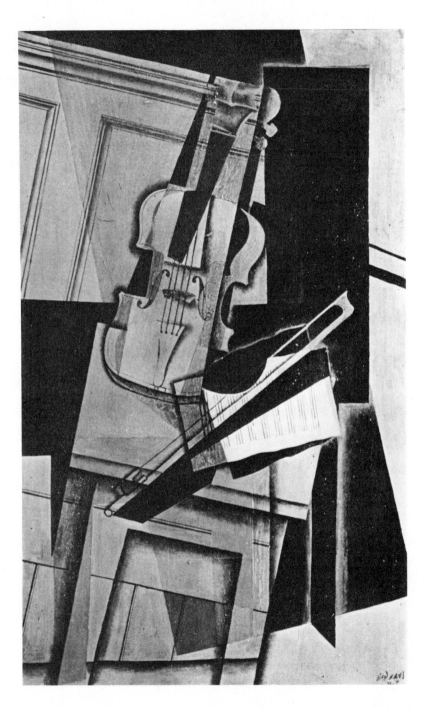

CLAUDE-ACHILLE DEBUSSY

Composer: Claude-Achille Debussy
   Born: St. Germain-en-Laye, France 1862
   Died: Paris, France 1918

Aural Recognition of Themes:
   Composition: _Rêverie_ (1890)

General Information about Composer and Compositions:

1. Claude-Achille Debussy, at the age of nine, studied piano with Mme. de Fleurville who had been a pupil of Chopin. He attended the Paris Conservatory of Music where he studied piano, harmony and composition. He was an excellent student and won many prizes. He visited Rome where he composed the cantata _L'Enfant prodigue_ (1884) for which he received the Prix de Rome.

2. While Chopin created poetry with the piano, Debussy used the piano artistically in painting music. His piano compositions _Clair de Lune_ (1890) and _Images_ (1905) clearly demonstrate this.

3. Debussy is known as the father of impressionistic music (descriptive or pictorial music largely concerned with the scenes of nature). He created sensuous and interpretative effects with the use of simplicity of form, extension of textural patterns and harmonic dissonance.

4. Although he was for many years an admirer and afterwards a critic of Wagner, Debussy composed only one opera, _Pelléas et Mélisande_ (1902). This work is considered by

214

many to be the ultimate in the perfection of opera composition during the modern period.

5. Debussy wrote a piano salon piece *Rêverie* (1890), the theme of which was adapted by Tin Pan Alley in America. This song *My Reverie* became the hit song of the year 1938, and is still included in the standard repertoire.

Composer's Main Contribution to the Art of Music:

1. Claude-Achille Debussy, because of his interest in impressionistic painting and poetry, created a style of impressionistic music. He brought about a revolution in musical composition by expanding the laws of harmony and tonality.

Suggested Listening:

1. Title: *La Mer - Play of the Waves*
   Performers: National Symphony Orchestra, Washington, D.C.
   Record No.: Victor LE-1008, Adventures In Music
   Grade Level: 4 - 8

2. Title: *Clair de Lune*
   Performers: Pennario - piano
   Record No.: Angel 36049
   Grade Level: 7 - 12

Optional Assignments:

1. Obtain the sheet music to *My Reverie* adapted from Debussy. Learn the song and sing it for the class.

2. Play a recording of a composition by the composer for the class and give an oral report of it to the class.

3. Construction of instruments is an interesting topic. Make a study of a popular instrument used during the composer's lifetime.

4. Debussy was the leader of the school of impressionistic music. Make a study of the impressionistic paintings and artists of this period.

5. Listen to a recording of Debussy's *La Mer*, then draw or paint a picture of your impressions of the sea from your interpretation of the music.

RICHARD STRAUSS

<u>Composer</u>: Richard Strauss
   <u>Born</u>: Munich, Germany 1864
   <u>Died</u>: Garmisch-Partenkirchen, Bavaria 1949

<u>Aural Recognition of Themes</u>:
   Composition: *Der Rosenkavalier*, Op. 59 (1910)

<u>General Information about Composer and Compositions</u>:

1. Richard Strauss was in no way related to Johann Strauss,
   "The Waltz King". His musical training began with the
   study of piano at the age of four. Four years later,
   he began the study of the violin, and at the age of six,
   he composed his first composition - a polka.

2. By the time he reached seventeen, he had composed many
   works including the *Serenade for Thirteen Wind Instruments* (1881), which was played by the Meiningen Orchestra
   conducted by the celebrated composer Von Bülow. At this
   time he composed his first symphony which was produced
   and conducted by Hermann Levi, the great Wagnerian
   conductor.

3. Strauss achieved fame as a conductor as well. He held
   such positions as orchestra conductor at Munich Court
   Theater, court conductor at Weimar, musical director of
   the Berlin Royal Opera, and in 1904 he conducted his
   tone poem *Till Eulenspiegel* at Carnegie Hall in New York.

4. The tone poems of Richard Strauss are one of the greatest
   musical achievements of this era. A tone poem is program
   music in one movement that tells a story - narrative; or

216

portrays a scene - pictorial or descriptive. Some of his most famous tone poems are: *Till Eulenspiegel's Merry Pranks* (1894), *Don Quixote* (1897), *Also Sprach Zarathustra* (1895), and *Don Juan* (1888).

5. Strauss was also a famous composer of operas and operettas. Some of the best known are: *Salome* (1905), and *Der Rosenkavalier* (1910).

Composer's Main Contribution to the Art of Music:

1. Richard Strauss is recognized as a genius in the area of tone poem composition. His tone poems are famous and are loved by both children and adults alike. They are included in the record library of most public schools because of their emotional appeal and inventiveness.

Suggested Listening:

1. Title: *Der Rosenkavalier - Suite*
   Performers: National Symphony Orchestra, Washington, D.C.
   Record No.: R.C.A. Victor LE-1009, Adventures In Music
   Grade Level: 4 - 8

2. Title: *Till Eulenspiegel, Op. 28*
   Performers: Philadelphia Symphony - Ormandy
   Record No.: Columbia MS-66678
   Grade Level: 7 - 12

Optional Assignments:

1. Make an historical outline of the modern period. Include industrial, scientific and artistic achievements of this century.

2. Make a study of the famous literary geniuses of this period and write a composition on this subject.

3. Using only a skeleton outline, tell the class about an interesting musical event that you attended recently.

4. Define the symphony and the symphonic tone poem. Listen to recordings of each and write a comparison of these two musical forms.

5. Do some research in the World Book or any other encyclopedia on Strauss; then make a report about his life and music to the class.

JEAN SIBELIUS

Composer: Jean Sibelius
  Born: Tavastehus, Finland 1865
  Died: Jarvenpaa, Finland 1957

Aural Recognition of Themes:
  Composition: *Finlandia* (1900)

General Information about Composer and Compositions:

1. Jean Sibelius, as a boy, taught himself to play the violin. He and his sisters organized a string trio that performed chamber music. His father who wanted Jean to become a lawyer, sent him to the University of Helsinki in Finland. Sibelius left the law school and studied music in Helsinki, Berlin and Vienna.

2. Sibelius' father was a doctor, and his family was very fond of music. Jean was a great admirer of nature and student of Finnish mythology which had a strong influence on his music. Good examples of this are: *Lemminkainen Suite* (four legends) (1893-1899), *Spring Song, Op. 11* (1894), and *En Saga, Op. 9* (1892).

3. Finland, the native country of Sibelius, subsidized and supported him in his works, mainly because he introduced nationalistic elements in his music which portrayed the beauty and historical background of the country. A good example of this is the symphonic poem *Finlandia* (1900).

4. He traveled extensively, and visited the United States where his music was received enthusiastically. In 1914,

Sibelius taught at the New England Conservatory of Music in Boston, Massachusetts.

5. Jean Sibelius was one of the leading symphonic composers of this era. His works are quite individualistic in that he did not depend on the styles and forms of composition that other composers used. He composed symphonies, an opera, symphonic tone poems, violin concertos, chamber music, and songs.

Composer's Main Contribution to the Art of Music:

1. Jean Sibelius was the first modern composer to receive financial support from the government of his native land, Finland, along with national recognition. The folk lore and mythology of Finland was the inspiration for most of his works. He brought international fame both to himself and his beloved country.

Suggested Listening:

1. Title: *Karelia - Alla Marcia*
   Performers: National Symphony Orchestra, Washington, D.C.
   Record No.: Victor LE-1006, Adventures In Music
   Grade Level: 4 - 8

2. Title: *Pelléas et Mélisande, Op. 46*
   Performers: Royal Philharmonic Orchestra - Beecham
   Record No.: Angel 35458
   Grade Level: 7 - 12

Optional Assignments:

1. Make up a notebook on the life and music of the composer consisting of pictures, newspaper and magazine articles, concert programs, thematic excerpts, original illustrations and written reports.

2. Tell the class about an historical or interesting event which took place during the life of Sibelius. (Ex.: World War II).

3. Choose one of the topics we have discussed under general information, do some research on it and report about it to the class.

4. Have the class learn and memorize the words and music of *Finalndia* and sing this song for a special program.

5. Make a comparison between the terms "patriotic music" and "nationalistic music." Lead a class discussion on this topic.

ARNOLD SCHOENBERG

Composer: Arnold Schoenberg
  Born: Vienna, Austria 1874
  Died: Los Angeles, California 1951

Aural Recognition of Themes:
  Composition: *Verklärte Nacht, Op. 4* (1899)

General Information about Composer and Compositions:

1. Arnold Schoenberg took violin lessons as a child, and during this period he composed duets for the violin. He later taught himself how to play the violoncello and composed string quartets which were played by a chamber group of boys which he conducted. At the age of eighteen, he studied counterpoint and composition with Alexander von Zemlinsky, a leading composer among the acquaintances of Johannes Brahms.

2. Schoenberg considered music an exact science and made an exhausting study of all the musical combinations possible. This scientific approach to music eventually led him to the foundation of atonalism (twelve-tone system of composition).

3. In 1911 he wrote a book called *Treatise on Harmony* which he dedicated to his pupils, prefacing the book with the statement "This book I have learned from my pupils." He wrote many other articles and books on music.

4. In 1924 he became a professor of composition at the Berlin Academy of Music. In 1933 he came to the United States and taught in Boston and New York. From 1936 to 1944 he

taught at the University of California. Some of his most famous pupils were: Alban Berg, Anton von Webern and Karl Horowitz.

5. Schoenberg composed a wide variety of music. He composed four operas, orchestra music, chamber music, choral and piano music.

Composer's Main Contribution to the Art of Music:

1. Arnold Schoenberg developed and introduced to the music world the twelve-tone system of composition. He believed that there is little difference between consonance and dissonance. Through the use of atonality he expanded the possibilities for creative composition. There is much controversy among many concerning the value of his music, although his composing techniques have been accepted and used by other contemporary composers.

Suggested Listening:

1. Title: *Three Little Orchestra Pieces, Op. 31*
   Performers: C.B.S. Symphony Orchestra - Craft
   Record No.: Columbia M2S-6
   Grade Level: 4 - 8

2. Title: *Transfigured Night, Op. 4*
   Performers: CBC Symphony
   Record No.: Columbia M2S-694
   Grade Level: 7 - 12

Optional Assignments:

1. Make a study of the various reviews and criticisms of Schoenberg's music. Write a report on this subject.

2. Compare a composition of Schoenberg with a popular song of today. Give an oral report on this comparison to the class.

3. Make a study of the political background of Germany during the years that Schoenberg lived there.

4. Choose one of the topics we have discussed under general information, and after doing outside research on it, give an oral report to the class.

5. During Schoenberg's lifetime, World War II took place. Write an essay describing this war.

221

CHARLES IVES

Composer: Charles Ives
   Born: Danbury, Connecticut 1874
   Died: New York, N.Y. 1954

Aural Recognition of Themes:

Purchase at your local music store one or more of the following piano sheet music arrangements of Charles Ives'
compositions. You may play the main theme with the written
accompaniment, or you may supply your own accompaniment using the chords notated above the melody line (although the
chord symbols are written for guitar, they are easily adapted to the piano). Play each theme of the composition several
times in order to facilitate recognition.

   Variations On America (1949)

   Concord Piano Sonata (1915)

   The Circus Band (1953)

General Information about Composer and Compositions:

1. Charles Ives came from a musical family. His father was a
   Bandmaster during the Civil War period and his mother was
   a music teacher. Young Ives received his early music instruction and inspiration from his parents.

2. He was one of the first American composers who got away
   from the European tradition of composition. Ives was experimental in his music and with Carl Ruggles launched
   the American experimental tradition.

3. Realizing that he could not make a livelihood by composing
   experimental music, Ives became an insurance executive in
   Hartford, Connecticut. He continued to write music during
   his successful business career.

4. The music of Ives employs some tonality, atonality and
   intentional noise. His compositional techniques range from
   simple harmony to the use of the twelve tone system. Ives
   includes many variations of American folk tunes and old
   songs in his symphonic works. An example of this is his
   musical fantasy, *Three Places in New England*. In this composition he incorporates the Revolutionary songs, *Yankee
   Doodle* and *Hail Columbia*.

222

5. Many composers of the American Experimental School were
   followers of Charles Ives. Among these were Henry Cowell,
   Lou Harrison and John Cage. Ives was ahead of his time
   in musical ideas. Some of his compositions, written at
   the beginning of the 20th century, have a very contemporary sound.

Composer's Main Contribution to the Art of Music:

1. Charles Ives was one of the first composers to successfully experiment with harmonics and tonalities, and thus
   made one of the most important contributions to futuristic
   music.

Suggested Listening:

1. Title: *Circus Band March*
   Performers: Bernstein - Instrumental
   Record No.: Columbia M3X-31068
   Grade Level: 4 - 8

2. Title: *Symphony: Holidays*
   Performers: New York Philharmonic - Bernstein
   Record No.: Columbia MS7147
   Grade Level: 7 - 12

Optional Assignments:

1. Make a study of the era during which Charles Ives lived
   and try to discern why he was so far ahead of his time
   in musical composition.

2. After listening to selections by the composer, compare
   his modern concepts of music to the Rock music of today.

3. If you are artistic, paint or sketch a picture of the
   composer and use it for bulletin board display.

4. Write a biographical sketch of the composer's life.

5. After listening to a composition by Ives, write about
   the type of mood this composition portrays.

MAURICE RAVEL

Composer: Maurice Ravel
  Born: Ciboure, France 1875
  Died: Paris, France 1937

Aural Recognition of Themes:
  Composition: *Boléro* (1928)

Permission for reprint granted by Durand et Cie, Paris, France Copyright Owners
Elkan-Vogel Co., Inc., Philadelphia - Sole Agents.

General Information about Composer and Compositions:

1. Maurice Ravel, at the age of twelve, went to Paris where he studied piano and music theory. He later entered the Paris Conservatory of Music where he studied composition with Fauré and counterpoint with Gedalge. He was very interested in contemporary music and made a thorough analysis of the works of the composers of the modern period. He was awarded the Grand Prix de Rome in 1901.

2. Ravel was born and lived near the Spanish border during his childhood. Spanish folk music had a profound influence on his style of composition. Two of his most popular works contain folk themes of Spanish origin: *Rapsodie Espagnole* (1907) and *Boléro* (1928).

3. Ravel was a brilliant orchestrater. He developed impressionistic music beyond Debussy. It is the opinion of some that his music is more colorful, vivid, virile, and contained more depth through the skillful writing and orchestration of unique instrumental effects. Mastery of this ability is displayed in his very popular *Boléro*.

4. Ravel is considered by many to be the greatest French composer of the first half of the twentieth century. Some of his music displays characteristics of popular style

or jazz, through the use of dissonance and complex rhythmic patterns; e.g. *Tzigane* for piano and violin (1924), and *Concerto for Piano in G Major* (1931).

5. Diaghilev, the famed director of the Russian Ballet performed Ravel's ballet *Daphnis et Chloé*. It has since become a very popular concert selection. Ravel composed operas, ballets, piano concertos, works for piano solo, chamber music and songs. He orchestrated many of his piano selections.

Composer's Main Contribution to the Art of Music:

1. Maurice Ravel was a master of impressionistic composition. Though his style was modern, his musical structure was patterned after the format of the classicists. His chamber music was one of the most notable contributions to the art of musical composition. The individuality of his works were an inspiration to the composers who followed him.

Suggested Listening:

1. Title: *Mother Goose Suite - The Conversations of Beauty and the Beast*
   Performers: National Symphony Orchestra, Washington, D.C.
   Record No.: Victor LE-1006, Adventures In Music
   Grade Level: 4 - 8

2. Title: *Boléro*
   Performers: New York Philharmonic Orchestra - Bernstein
   Record No.: Columbia MS-6011
   Grade Level: 7 - 12

Optional Assignments:

1. Write a short book review of a biography of the composer, including author, title and interesting facts.

2. The composers of this period were the first to introduce jazz elements in serious music. Do some research on this subject and present an oral report to the class.

3. If you play drums or other percussion instruments, demonstrate the bolero or other Spanish rhythms to the class.

4. Debussy and Ravel were both impressionistic composers. Make a comparison between them and write a report on this subject.

5. Any student of ballet may create a dance for one of Ravel's ballet selections.

MANUEL DE FALLA

Composer: Manuel de Falla
   Born: Cádiz, Spain 1876
   Died: Alta Gracia, Argentina 1946

Aural Recognition of Themes:
   Composition: *Love, The Magician* - ballet (1915)

General Information about Composer and Compositions:

1. Manuel de Falla, at an early age, became an excellent
   pianist and showed natural music ability. His mother was
   a concert pianist and Manuel received his first instruction from her. Together they performed a four-hand piano
   selection of Haydn at Manuel's first public concert.

2. He is well known as one of the greatest twentieth century
   Spanish composers and his works represent Spanish nationalism in music for this period. He derived many of the
   themes for his works from Spanish folk songs. An example
   of this is: *La Vida Breve (Life is Short)* - opera (1904).

3. In his piano compositions, he was influenced by Domenico
   Scarlatti who originated the Spanish style of keyboard
   music. Examples of this influence are displayed in: *Nights
   In The Gardens Of Spain*, symphonic nocturne, composed for
   piano and orchestra (1909), and *Concerto for Harpsichord
   and Orchestra* (1923).

4. He lived in Paris for seven years, and was a pupil of
   Debussy whose ideas in impressionism influenced his works.

226

5. De Falla composed operas, ballets, songs and several orchestral compositions. One of the most popular of his compositions today is the ballet *Three Cornered Hat* (1919).

Composer's Main Contribution to the Art of Music:

1. Manuel de Falla incorporated Spanish folk melodies in his works. His masterly treatment of Spanish rhythms is unparalleled in musical composition. His use of church modes and oriental figures contributed to the Spanish flavor of his music. He gave to the world a musical portrait of the culture and beauty of Spain.

Suggested Listening:

1. Title: *La Vida Breve - Spanish Dance No. 1*
   Performers: National Symphony Orchestra, Washington, D.C.
   Record No.: Victor LE-1009, Adventures In Music
   Grade Level: 4 - 8

2. Title: *Three Cornered Hat* - excerpts
   Performers: Royal Philharmonic - Rod Zinsky
   Record No.: Seraphim S-60021
   Grade Level: 7 - 12

Optional Assignments:

1. After listening to a selection by the composer, write a critique and compare with other compositions you have heard, or make up an appropriate story that the music might suggest to you.

2. Learn a basic dance of the composer's lifetime and perform this dance for the class.

3. Make a list of composers for the piano, and list their most popular compositions.

4. Make a study of the famous Spanish artists and painters of this period and write a report on this subject.

5. Make a study of the Latin American music used for popular dancing in the United States. Compare this music with that of Manuel de Falla.

ERNEST BLOCH

Composer: Ernest Bloch
    Born: Geneva, Switzerland 1880
    Died: Portland, Oregon 1959

Aural Recognition of Themes:
    Composition: *Concerto Grosso* for String Orchestra
           and Piano (1924)

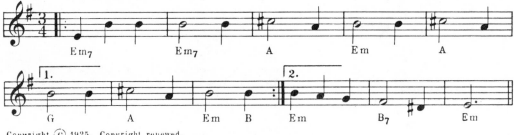

General Information about Composer and Compositions:

1. Ernest Bloch, as a child, studied music with Jaques-
   Dalcroze. At the age of fifteen, he composed a symphony
   and a string quartet. In 1897 he attended the Brussel's
   Conservatory where he studied harmony and composition.
   During this period he composed several songs for piano
   and violin; he also composed orchestral music.

2. In 1900 he studied at the Hoch Conservatory in Frankfort,
   Germany and during this time composed the symphonic poems
   Vicre-Aimen (1900) and his *Symphony in C Sharp Minor*
   (1901).

3. In 1902 he went to Paris and began work on a lyric composition *Macbeth* which was finally produced by the Opera-
   Comique in Paris in 1910. In 1915 he was elected Professor of Music at the Geneva Conservatory in Switzerland
   where he taught aesthetics of music.

4. In 1916 he came to the United States. He taught at the
   Mannes School in New York. In 1917 he conducted the
   Boston Symphony Orchestra in the performance of his works.

228

From 1920 to 1925 he was the director of the Cleveland Institute of Music. He was elected director of the San Francisco Conservatory of Music in 1925.

5. In 1928 he won the first prize in Musical America's contest for a symphonic work with his epic rhapsody *America*. He composed symphonies, operas, orchestral works, chamber and choral music, and piano selections.

Composer's Main Contribution to the Art of Music:

1. Ernest Bloch, a naturalized citizen of the United States, did more to bring about a better understanding of the Jewish character and customs than any other composer. Some of his famous works were inspired by traditional Jewish modes and melodies. The reading of biblical works provided the inspiration for much of his music.

Suggested Listening:

1. Title: *Sinfonia Breve*
   Performers: Minneapolis Symphony - Dorati
   Record No.: CRI S-248
   Grade Level: 4 - 8

2. Title: *Schelomo - Hebrew Rhapsody*
   Performers: Piatigorsky
   Record No.: R.C.A. Victor LM-2109
   Grade Level: 7 - 12

Optional Assignments:

1. Bloch wrote some of his works in the Jewish idiom. Write a report on Jewish or Hebrew music.

2. Prepare a paper comparing the music of Bloch and Schoenberg.

3. Make a study of the famous scientists of this period. Give an oral report to the class on your findings.

4. If you are artistic, draw or paint a picture of the composer, and present it for bulletin board display.

5. Lead a class discussion on the composer's life and music. Prepare an outline for this purpose.

BÉLA BARTÓK

Composer: Béla Bartók
   Born: Nagyszentmiklos, Hungary 1881
   Died: New York, N.Y. 1945

Aural Recognition of Themes:
   Composition: *Rhapsody No. 1* (1904)

General Information about Composer and Compositions:

1. Béla Bartók studied piano with his mother at the age of six. He made his first public appearance on the concert stage at the age of ten as a pianist and composer. From 1899 to 1903 he studied at the Royal Hungarian Music Academy of Budapest.

2. In 1907 he was elected Professor of Piano at the Royal Hungarian Music Academy. He engaged in a series of concert tours of Europe, and he visited the United States (1927-1928). From 1940 to 1941 he taught music at Columbia University in New York.

3. Bartók made a lifetime study of not only Hungarian folk music and legends, but also of the folk music and folklore of other countries. While he taught at Columbia University, he was commissioned to make a study of Ukrainian folk music.

4. Serge Koussevitzky, the conductor of the Boston Symphony Orchestra, commissioned Bartók in 1943 to write a concerto for orchestra. Bartók was not only an excellent composer, but was also a fine concert pianist and musicologist.

230

5. Bartók wrote one opera *Bluebeard's Castle* (1911). He also composed orchestral pieces, chamber music, ballets, choral works and piano music.

Composer's Main Contribution to the Art of Music:

1. Béla Bartók made an extensive study of the folk music of Ukrania and Hungary. His compositions express the strength, barbarity and intense emotions of the primitive culture of these lands. His music contained harmonic dissonances, irregular rhythms, polytonality and complex structures that were not readily accepted by the public. His musical genius is acknowledged by most musicians and composers of the twentieth century.

Suggested Listening:

1. Title: *Hungarian Sketches - Evening In The Village*
   Performers: National Symphony Orchestra, Washington, D.C.
   Record No.: Victor LE-1007, Adventures In Music
   Grade Level: 4 - 8

2. Title: *Bluebeard's Castle*
   Performers: Philadelphia Symphony Orchestra - Ormandy
   Record No.: Columbia MS-6425
   Grade Level: 7 - 12

Optional Assignments:

1. Make a study of the history and government of Hungary. Explain to the class its present status as a country.

2. Choose a country, and write a report on its folk music.

3. Make a list of composers who wrote music for the piano and list their most popular compositions.

4. Serge Koussevitzky was the conductor of the Boston Symphony Orchestra. Lead a class discussion on the life and accomplishments of this famous conductor.

5. Write a review of a recent concert you heard or attended in which the music of the composer was performed.

GEORGES ENESCO

Composer: Georges Enesco
   Born: Dorohoiû, Rumania 1881
   Died: Paris, France 1955

Aural Recognition of Themes:
   Composition: *Roumanian Rhapsody No. 1* - orchestral
      selection (1908)

General Information about Composer and Compositions:

1. Georges Enesco, at the age of four, learned to play the
   violin and wrote compositions for this instrument. At
   the age of seven, he was accepted at the Vienna Conservatory where he studied violin and harmony. He won prizes
   in both of these areas. At the age of eleven, he was ad-
   mitted to the Paris Conservatory where he studied composition.

2. He toured Europe and America extensively as a violin
   virtuoso. He also served as court violinist to the Queen
   of Rumania. He was well known for his interpretation of
   Mozart's violin compositions.

3. He taught violin at the Ecole Normale de Musique in
   Paris. From 1948 to 1950 he taught at the Mannes Music
   School in New York. He was later appointed Professor of
   Music at the University of Illinois.

4. Until World War II, he lived alternately in Rumania and
   France. Later he settled in the United States. He appeared as violin virtuoso and guest conductor with many of
   the symphony orchestras in the United States.

5. Enesco is noted for his Rumanian Rhapsodies in which he uses the folk themes of his native country. In addition he composed symphonies, chamber music, suites, and an opera *Oedipus* (1936).

Composer's Main Contribution to the Art of Music:

1. Georges Enesco is well known for the musical representation of the folk melodies of his native land, Rumania. He incorporated these melodies into his compositions and developed them into artistic works. He was the founder of the Rumanian school of composition.

Suggested Listening:

1. Title: *Roumanian Rhapsody No. 1*
   Performers: R.C.A. Victor Symphony Orchestra - Stokowski
   Record No.: Victor LM-2471
   Grade Level: 4 - 8

2. Title: *Sonata No. 3 in A for Violin and Piano*
   Performers: Ferras - Barbizet
   Record No.: Mace S-9045
   Grade Level: 7 - 12

Optional Assignments:

1. Make a study of the major performing instrument of the composer and collect literature and pictures of this instrument for your notebook.

2. Learn to dance a Rumanian folk dance and perform this dance for the class.

3. Make a study of the political and economic conditions in Europe prior to World War II and give an oral report on this topic.

4. Create a musical crossword puzzle or make up a quiz using information about the composer.

5. Make up words for the composition noted under Aural Recognition of Themes, and sing it for the class.

233

IGOR STRAVINSKY

Composer: Igor Stravinsky
    Born: Oranienbaum, Russia 1882
    Died: New York, N.Y. 1971

Aural Recognition of Themes:
    Composition: *Petrouchka* - ballet suite (1911)

General Information about Composer and Compositions:

1. Igor Stravinsky came from a musical family. His father
   was the leading bass singer in the Imperial Opera Company
   in St. Petersburg. Igor began piano lessons at the age of
   nine, and later studied composition with Rimsky-Korsakov.

2. He composed many compositions for Sergei Diaghilev, the
   director of the Russian Ballet. He was commissioned to
   write orchestral arrangements of two selections by Chopin
   for the ballet *Les Sylphides*. His most famous ballet
   compositions are: *The Firebird* (1910), *Petrouchka* (1911),
   and *The Rite of Spring* (1913).

3. During World War I, he lived in Switzerland and composed
   The Soldier's Tale (1918). During this period, he experi-
   mented with jazz composition and composed the following:
   Ragtime for Eleven Instruments (1918), and *Piano Rag-
   Music* (1919).

4. Stravinsky spent the greater part of his life in the
   United States. He was a music critic for *Show Magazine*.
   In May of 1953, he directed his opera *The Rake's Progress*
   at Boston University School of Fine and Applied Arts in
   Boston, Massachusetts.

234

5. C.B.S. Television commissioned Stravinsky to compose a half-hour composition, *The Flood*, combined opera, ballet, drama, and oratorio, which was shown nation-wide in 1962.

Composer's Main Contribution to the Art of Music:

1. Igor Stravinsky may be considered one of the most prominent composers of twentieth century music. He constantly experimented with new sounds which he produced using polytonality and polyrhythms. His use of dissonance, unorthodox harmonic structure and unusual instrumentation have made him one of the most controversial composers of this century. His works have paved the way for other modern composers who are searching for techniques of creating new musical sounds.

Suggested Listening:

1. Title: *Pieces Faciles*
   Performers: Eden
   Record No.: London 6626
   Grade Level: 4 - 8

2. Title: *Firebird Suite*
   Performers: Boston Symphony - Leinsdorf
   Record No.: RCA LSC-2725
   Grade Level: 7 - 12

Optional Assignments:

1. Make a collection of concert program notices (Concerts: professional, schools, television, and radio). Before placing these notices on the bulletin board, give a brief talk about them to the class.

2. Stravinsky was a music critic. What qualifications are required to become a music critic?

3. Make a biographical sketch of the composer's life, and prepare a skit involving interesting incidents in his life.

4. There is much controversy regarding Stravinsky's music. Why is this so? Write a report on this subject.

5. Make a study of some of the famous scientists of today.

HEITOR VILLA-LOBOS

Composer: Heitor Villa-Lobos
    Born: Rio de Janeiro, Brazil 1881
    Died: Rio de Janeiro, Brazil 1959

Aural Recognition of Themes:
    Composition: *Saudades das Selvas Brasileiras* - piano
        selection (1927)

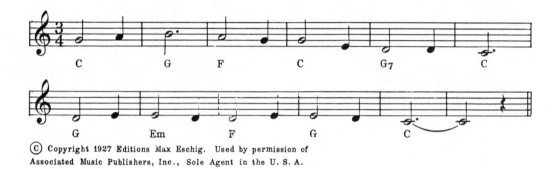

General Information about Composer and Compositions:

1. Heitor Villa-Lobos is one of the best known South
   American composers. His father was a cellist who gave
   him his first lessons on the cello. His father died when
   Heitor was only eleven years old, so that he had to work
   playing cello with theater and restaurant orchestras to
   support his mother.

2. He enrolled in the Rio de Janeiro Institute of Music
   where he studied piano and composition. He made concert
   tours throughout Brazil as a cello virtuoso for a period
   of four years from 1906 to 1910. With financial aid from
   the Brazilian Government he was able to travel throughout
   Europe playing and conducting his own works. He spent six
   years in Paris.

3. In 1930 he was appointed Director of Music Education in
   Rio de Janeiro. In 1932 he was made Director of Brazil's
   Department of Musical and Artistic Education. He was con-
   sidered a national hero by the people of Brazil.

4. He founded a school for music teachers in Rio de Janeiro.
   In 1933 he founded and became conductor of the Rio de

Janeiro Symphony Orchestra. In 1937, he was made an honorary member of the Saint Cecelia Academy in Rome.

5. Villa-Lobos dedicated his composition *Fantasia* (1945) for cello and orchestra to the great American conductor Serge Koussevitzky. He dedicated another composition *Bachiana* (1930) to Aaron Copland, the American composer. Villa-Lobos wrote almost fifteen hundred compositions, including symphonies, symphonic poems, operettas, chamber music, choral selections, operas, piano and cello pieces.

Composer's Main Contribution to the Art of Music:

1. Heitor Villa-Lobos created a national style of Brazilian music. In his compositions he interprets and presents to the listener a tonal image of the culture, folk-lore, and character traits of the people of Brazil. He incorporated in his works the folk tunes, dances, and intricate South American rhythms that were popular among Brazilians.

Suggested Listening:

1. Title: *Prole do bebe* - piano
   Performers: **Artur** Rubinstein at Carnegie Hall
   Record No.: Victor LM-2605
   Grade Level: 4 - 8

2. Title: *Music for the Spanish Guitar*
   Performers: Almeida - guitarist
   Record No.: Capitol STER-291
   Grade Level: 7 - 12

Optional Assignments:

1. Make a study and write a report on Brazilian folk music.

2. Choose one of the topics we have discussed under General Information, do research on it in other books, and give an oral report to the class.

3. Learn a South American dance, and perform it for the class.

4. List some famous musicians and actors of South America. Conduct a class discussion on these people.

5. If you have attended a concert recently which featured Villa-Lobos' works, tell your class about some of the selections you heard.

237

SERGE PROKOFIEV

Composer: Serge Prokofiev
    Born: Ekaterinoslav, Russia 1891
    Died: Moscow, Russia 1953

Aural Recognition of Themes:
    Composition: *March from Music for Children, Op. 65,*
                piano selection (1935)

General Information about Composer and Compositions:

1. Serge Prokofiev's mother gave him piano lessons at an early age; and he composed his first music at the age of five. At the age of thirteen, he studied under Rimsky-Korsakov at St. Petersburg Conservatory. He was awarded the Rubinstein medal and first prize by the Conservatory for his *Piano Concerto No. 1* (1910).

2. In 1918 Prokofiev left Russia and visited London, Paris, Japan and the United States. His opera *The Love For Three Oranges* was produced by the Chicago Opera Association in 1921. In 1933 he made a triumphal return to his native land, Russia, where he was received with great acclaim and given many prizes.

3. His music displays humor, mockery and wit; it especially characterizes a complete disregard for conventionalism. This is demonstrated in his *The Buffoon* (1921) written for Diaghilev's Russian Ballet in Paris. A popular symphonic piece, the fairy tale *Peter and the Wolf* (1936) which was primarily written to introduce the various musical instruments, also is enjoyed by adult audiences.

4. Prokofiev's music was not popular with the members of the Communist party in Russia because it was difficult for them to listen to and understand. Some of his compositions were therefore banned by the Russian government.

5. He was a very versatile composer. He composed background music for movies, and wrote operas, ballets, symphonies, sonatas, concertos, cantatas and chamber music. Among the most popular are: *The Classical Symphony* (1915), *The Love For Three Oranges* - opera (1921), *Romeo And Juliet* - ballet (1936), and *War and Peace* - opera (1942).

Composer's Main Contribution to the Art of Music:

1. Serge Prokofiev was an explorer in the field of composition. He experimented with new tonalities and harmonic dissonances. He included both gay and bizarre emotional qualities in his works. He also made a very important contribution to Russian nationalism in his later works.

Suggested Listening:

1. Title: *Love For Three Oranges* - *March*
   Performers: R.C.A. Victor Symphony Orchestra
   Record No.: R.C.A. Basic Record Library, E-76, Vol. 6
   Grade Level: 4 - 8

2. Title: *Peter And The Wolf*, *Op. 67*
   Performers: N.Y. Philharmonic - Bernstein
   Record No.: Columbia MS-6193
   Grade Level: 7 - 12

Optional Assignments:

1. Listen to the recording of *Peter And The Wolf* and name some of the predominant instruments used.

2. Make a study of Russian composers and list their most popular compositions.

3. The next time you attend a movie, listen carefully to the background music, and present an oral report to the class describing this music and its relationship to the story.

4. Lead a class discussion on the composer's life and music, after preparing an outline for this purpose.

5. Make a study of the political and economic conditions in Russia during Prokofiev's lifetime and write a report on this subject.

FERDE GROFÉ

Composer: Ferde Grofé
  Born: New York, N.Y. 1892
  Died: Santa Monica, California 1972

Aural Recognition of Themes:
  Composition: *Grand Canyon Suite* - orchestral
          selection (1931)

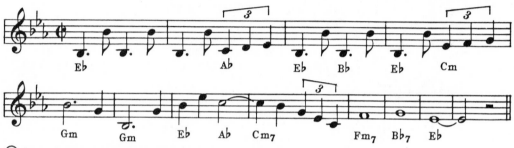

General Information about Composer and Compositions:

1. Ferde Grofé received his early training in harmony and theory from his mother who was a graduate of the Leipzig Conservatory. He also studied with his uncle who was concert-master of the Los Angeles Symphony Orchestra.

2. During his musical apprenticeship he worked at various odd jobs such as bookbinder, truck driver, stage hand and usher. From 1909 to 1919 he played viola in the Los Angeles Symphony Orchestra. He also performed with dance bands and theater orchestras.

3. At the age of sixteen, he published his first composition. From 1920 to 1932 he played piano and wrote musical arrangements for the famous Paul Whiteman Orchestra. During this period he gained fame and popularity by scoring George Gershwin's *Rhapsody In Blue* for orchestra.

4. Grofé's *Grand Canyon Suite* received its premiere by the Paul Whiteman Orchestra in 1931. This established him as a composer of distinction. It is one of the most famous pieces of American program music. He received a Doctor of Music degree from Illinois Wesleyan University in 1946.

5. Grofé's fame as a composer is supplemented by his conducting ability. He has conducted orchestras on radio, television, Carnegie Hall, and the Hollywood Bowl. He uses the jazz idiom in his compositions. Some of his other works are: *An American Biography* - based on the life of Henry Ford, *Hollywood Ballet* (1924), and *Symphony In Steel* (1935).

Composer's Main Contribution to the Art of Music:

1. Ferde Grofé was one of the first composers of serious music to embrace the jazz idiom. His works are mainly program music that describes the American scene. He was one of the few modern composers of serious music who earned his living writing arrangements for a popular dance orchestra. He established a pattern of musical composition for television and radio. His style of composition for these popular media has been adopted and developed by other composers of today.

Suggested Listening:

1. Title: *Death Valley Suite - Desert Water Hole*
   Performers: National Symphony Orchestra - Mitchell
   Record No.: Victor LE-1004, Adventures In Music
   Grade Level: 4 - 8

2. Title: *Grand Canyon Suite*
   Performers: N.Y. Philharmonic - Bernstein
   Record No.: Columbia MS-6618
   Grade Level: 7 - 12

Optional Assignments:

1. Make a comparison between the works of Ferde Grofé and those of George Gershwin, or some other American composer. Write a report on this subject.

2. Compare the Paul Whiteman Orchestra with some of the modern large dance orchestras of today. Conduct a class discussion of these groups.

3. Write a report on program music, and explain how Grofé's music can be included in this category.

4. If you are artistic, draw or paint a picture of the composer, and present it for bulletin board display.

5. Make a list of composers who used the jazz idiom in their music and list their works.

241

ARTHUR HONEGGER

Composer: Arthur Honegger
    Born: Le Havre, France 1892
    Died: Paris, France 1955

Aural Recognition of Themes:
    Composition: *Chant de Nigamon* - orchestral
                 selection (1917)

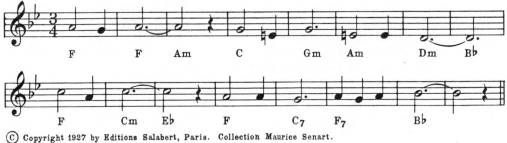

General Information about Composer and Compositions:

1. Arthur Honegger received his general education in the public schools of Le Havre. During his youth, he took private lessons on the violin and harmony. He furthered his musical education by attending the Zurich Conservatory in Switzerland.

2. He returned to France in 1912 and studied harmony and counterpoint at the Paris Conservatory of Music. It was during this time that he met the famous composer Darius Milhaud from whom he received encouragement and inspiration.

3. Honegger was a member of a group of composers who were known as "Les Six" and were exponents of polytonality. His compositions are written in a complex polyphonic style, emphasizing harmonic dissonance.

4. He taught music at the École Normale in Paris. In 1948 he received an honorary doctorate degree from Zurich University. In 1947 he visited the United States and taught composition at the Berkshire Music Center at Tanglewood,

Massachusetts. In 1949 he was elected to the office of President of the International Authors and Composers Association.

5. Honegger composed several types of music, including symphonies, operas, oratorios, chamber music and ballets. His most popular works are: *Pacific 231* - impressionistic musical portrait of a locomotive (1923), *Judith* - biblical opera (1925), and *King David* - cantata with narrator (1921).

Composer's Main Contribution to the Art of Music:

1. Arthur Honegger was a very definite exponent of polytonality. Unlike his contemporaries who experimented with the popular jazz idiom, he preferred to work with serious music. He contributed to the development of impressionistic music composition with his programmatic style of writing.

Suggested Listening:

1. Title: *Pacific 231*
   Performers: N.Y. Philharmonic - Bernstein
   Record No.: Columbia MS-6659
   Grade Level: 4 - 8

2. Title: *Concertino for Piano and Orchestra*
   Performers: Vienna Pro Musica - Klein
   Record No.: Turnabout 34130
   Grade Level: 7 - 12

Optional Assignments:

1. After looking up the definition of polytonality in a music reference book, conduct a class discussion on this subject.

2. Compare Honegger's compositions with the works of another French composer you have studied.

3. Using only a skeleton outline, tell the class about an interesting musical event that you have attended recently.

4. Honegger was an impressionistic composer. Make a study and write a report on impressionistic art.

5. Write a report on the history and development of the major instruments of this period.

DARIUS MILHAUD

Composer: Darius Milhaud
    Born: Aix-en-Provence, France 1892

Aural Recognition of Themes:
    Composition: *Le Boeuf Sur Le Toit (The Nothing Doing Bar)*
        ballet (1924)

General Information about Composer and Compositions:

1. Darius Milhaud, as a youth, studied with local teachers
   at the College in Aix. During this time he played violin
   in a string quartet. From 1910 to 1915, he was a student
   at the Paris Conservatory of Music where he studied
   violin, composition and counterpoint. He won prizes in
   each of these areas of study.

2. While he was at the Conservatory, he composed short songs
   and piano compositions. He later wrote his first opera,
   La Brebis Égarée (1915). In 1917 he became cultural atta-
   ché with the French Legation in Brazil. Here he worked
   with the poet, Claudel, who became his librettist.

3. In 1920 he returned to Paris where he joined the group of
   French composers known as "Les Six". Since the death of
   Ravel in 1937, Milhaud became the leader of this group
   and is known as one of the greatest living French composers. He was one of the first composers to use jazz in art
   forms.

4. In 1937 he was appointed director of the Paris Conservatory. He came to America in 1940 and taught composition
   at Mills College in Oakland, California. During his stay

in America, he conducted the Boston Symphony Orchestra in the performance of his *Symphony No. 2* (1944).

5. Milhaud is a prolific composer. He wrote symphonies, ballets, concertos, operas, chamber music, piano and choral works. Some of his most popular works are: *Le Train Bleu* - ballet (1922), *Christopher Columbus* - opera (1928), and *Symphonic Suite No. 2* (1919).

Composer's Main Contribution to the Art of Music:

1. Darius Milhaud developed the jazz idiom and made an extensive study of African folk lore, rhythm patterns and blues style. He uses polytonality in his jazz works. His music served as the inspiration of the popular American composer, George Gershwin. Milhaud's style of composition is regarded very seriously by contemporary composers, but is not easily accepted by the public because of its complexity and dissonance.

Suggested Listening:

1. Title: *Saudades do Brazil - Copacabana*
   Performers: National Symphony Orchestra - Mitchell
   Record No.: R.C.A. Victor LE-1005, Adventures In Music
   Grade Level: 4 - 8

2. Title: *Création du Monde*
   Performers: Utah Symphony Orchestra - Abravanei
   Record No.: Vanguard 2117
   Grade Level: 7 - 12

Optional Assignments:

1. Make up a notebook on the life of the composer, consisting of pictures, newspaper and magazine articles, concert programs, thematic excerpts, original illustrations and written reports.

2. Make a comparison of the life and music of Ravel and Milhaud. Write a composition on these composers.

3. If you play the violin, perform a violin solo for the class.

4. After listening to a selection by the composer, write a critique; compare this composition with others you have heard, or make up an appropriate story that the music might suggest.

5. Choose one of the topics we have discussed under general information, do some research on it in other books, and present an oral report to the class.

WALTER PISTON

<u>Composer</u>: Walter Piston
   Born: Rockland, Maine 1894

<u>Aural Recognition of Themes:</u>
   Composition: *The Incredible Flutist* (1938)
               ballet suite

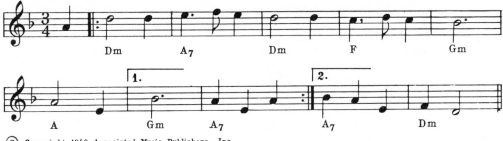

© Copyright 1949 Associated Music Publishers, Inc.
Used by permission.

General Information about Composer and Compositions:

1. Walter Piston, in his youth, was mainly interested in becoming an artist, and attended an art school. He did not seriously consider music as a career until he was in his early twenties.

2. He took private lessons on piano and violin, and studied theory at Harvard University in Cambridge, Massachusetts. He later went to France where he studied harmony with Nadia Boulanger.

3. Piston received his Bachelor of Arts degree from Harvard University in 1924. He became a member of the Harvard College faculty in 1926, and in 1938 was appointed associate professor, a position which he holds at present. He has helped to train many of the promising musical artists of today. His outstanding ability in the field of music has been widely recognized and he was awarded the Pulitzer Prize in 1948 and 1958, the Coolidge Medal in 1935, and has received several other awards.

4. He has written four musical textbooks that are widely used in many colleges and universities: *Principles of*

246

Harmonic Analysis (1933), *Harmony* (1941), *Counterpoint* (1947), and *Orchestration* (1955).

5. Walter Piston has composed symphonies, ballet suites, and chamber music. His style of composition is Neo-Classic (use of strict form).

Composer's Main Contribution to the Art of Music:

1. Walter Piston is one of the few notable modern composers to base his style on the traditional classic idiom of composition. His influence upon the students and present day composers of music is indicated by the acceptance of his text books by many leading music schools and colleges throughout the world.

Suggested Listening:

1. Title: *Incredible Flutist* - (ballet suite)
   Performers: N.Y. Philharmonic - Bernstein
   Record No.: Columbia MG-31155
   Grade Level: 4 - 8

2. Title: *Symphony No. 2*
   Performers: Boston Symphony - Thomas
   Record No.: DG 2530103
   Grade Level: 7 - 12

Optional Assignments:

1. Piston was awarded many prizes for his compositions. Do some research and make a list of these awards.

2. Walter Piston taught at Harvard University. Make a study and write a report on the College of Music at Harvard.

3. After choosing one of the topics we have discussed under general information, do some research on it in other books, then give an oral report on your findings to the class.

4. If you have attended or heard a concert recently which included a work by Piston, tell your class about the composition and some of the selections on the program.

5. Make a study of the major performing instruments of the composer and collect literature and pictures of these instruments for your notebook.

PAUL HINDEMITH

Composer: Paul Hindemith
    Born: Hanau, Germany 1895
    Died: Frankfurt, Germany 1963

Aural Recognition of Themes:
    Composition: *Kleine Kammermusik, Op. 24, No. 2* (1922)
                chamber music for five wind instruments

General Information about Composer and Compositions:

1. Paul Hindemith studied violin at an early age and became
   a virtuoso at the age of thirteen. He attended Hoch's
   Conservatory in Frankfurt where he studied viola and
   composition. While he was at the conservatory, he obtained
   practical experience as a musician playing in theater
   orchestras, movie houses and dance bands.

2. At the age of twenty, he was appointed director of the
   Frankfurt Opera Orchestra. He founded the Amar String
   Quartet in 1922 in which he played viola. This group made
   concert tours throughout Europe.

3. In 1921 he became one of the organizers of the Donau-
   eschingen Chamber Music Festival, a prominent festival of
   twentieth-century music in Salzburg. He achieved recognition as a composer and his music was performed yearly at
   the Salzburg Festival.

4. Hindemith came to the United States in 1938, and was
   appointed Professor of composition at Yale University in
   Connecticut in 1940. In 1953 he was appointed Professor

of music at Harvard University. During interim periods, he held the position of Professor of composition at the University of Zurich, Switzerland.

5. Hindemith composed operas, a ballet, symphonies, chamber music, a requiem, choral, organ and piano works. He was also an author and wrote several music textbooks, the most prominent of which are: *Traditional Harmony* (1941), *Elementary Training For Musicians* (1946), and *The Craft Of Musical Composition* (1937).

Composer's Main Contribution to the Art of Music:

1. Paul Hindemith believed that music should be functional and should be composed with a specific purpose in mind. His works such as chamber songs for the amateur musician, songs to accompany games, demonstrate his views. He rejected the theory of atonality in music during the latter part of his life because of his feeling for fundamental harmony and beauty of tone. His music serves as an inspiration for many contemporary composers.

Suggested Listening:

1. Title: *Sonatas for Organ*
   Performers: Biggs
   Record No.: CSP CMS 6234
   Grade Level: 4 - 8

2. Title: *Kleine Kammermusik, Op. 24, No. 2*
   Performers: New York Woodwind Quintet
   Record No.: Concert - Disc 205
   Grade Level: 7 - 12

Optional Assignments:

1. Make a study of the music courses offered at Harvard and Yale Universities. Report your findings to the class.

2. Write a brief book review of a biography on the composer.

3. Make a study of the famous artists of the Modern period. Write a brief report on the styles of painting used during this period.

4. Write to the Library of Congress and obtain a copy of the music copyright laws. Conduct a class discussion on this subject.

5. Play a recording of one of Hindemith's compositions for the class, and give an oral report on the piece being played.

WILLIAM GRANT STILL

Composer: William Grant Still
　　Born: Woodville, Mississippi 1895

Aural Recognition of Themes:

Purchase at your local music store one or more of the following piano sheet music arrangements of William Still's
compositions. You may play the main theme with the written
accompaniment, or you may supply your own accompaniment using
the chords notated above the melody line (although the chord
symbols are written for guitar, they are easily adapted to
the piano). Play each theme of the composition several times
in order to facilitate recognition.

　　　Your World (1968)

　　　God's Goin' To Set This World On Fire (1968)

　　　Afro-American Symphony (1930)

General Information about Composer and Compositions:

1. Dr. William Grant Still was born to a musical family and
   throughout his childhood he displayed a keen interest
   in music. His mother and grandmother were singers who
   provided a constant musical environment.

2. During his boyhood, he learned to play the violin and
   performed in a college string quartet. He wrote arrangements for the string quartet and college band and
   conducted these groups. He attended Oberlin Conservatory
   in Ohio and the New England Conservatory of Music in
   Boston.

3. Still also studied other instruments of the orchestra
   which contributed to his success as an arranger and
   composer. During his early professional career, he composed and arranged music for CBS and Mutual radio networks.

4. He has written over 50 compositions, including symphonies,
   operas, orchestral suites and symphonic selections for
   band. Still is the first American Negro composer to write
   a symphony, Afro-American Symphony. In his compositions
   he introduced the elements and style of American Negro
   music.

5. Still has conducted many major symphony orchestras in the performance of his compositions throughout the country. He has received many awards for his achievements including four honorary degrees.

Composer's Main Contribution to the Art of Music:

1. William Grant Still is known as the "Dean of Negro Composers". For many years he has contributed a great deal to bringing American Negro music to the forefront of the concert field. The recognition of his accomplishments has inspired many other black composers.

Suggested Listening:

1. Title: *Songs Of Separation*
   Performers: Oakland Youth Orchestra
   Record No.: Desto 7107
   Grade Level: 4 - 8

2. Title: *Festive Overture* (1945)
   Performers: Royal Philharmonic
   Record No.: Composers Recordings, Inc. S-259
   Grade Level: 7 - 12

Optional Assignments:

1. Prepare a biographical sketch of the life and music of William Grant Still.

2. Do some research on other black composers who have achieved success. Write a report on this subject.

3. Still has arranged several Negro spirituals. Learn one of these and perform for your class.

4. Play a recording of a work by Still. Give an oral report and conduct a class discussion on this composition.

5. After some research about present-day black music, give an oral report or write a paper on this topic.

GEORGE GERSHWIN

Composer: George Gershwin
  Born: Brooklyn, New York 1898
  Died: Hollywood, California 1937

Aural Recognition of Themes:

   Purchase at your local music store one or more of the
following piano sheet music arrangements of George Gershwin's
compositions. You may play the main theme with the written
accompaniment, or you may supply your own accompaniment
using the chords notated above the melody line (although
the chord symbols are written for guitar, they are easily
adapted to the piano). Play each theme of the composition
several times in order to facilitate recognition.

   Strike Up The Band (1927)

   Someone To Watch Over Me (1926)

   Of Thee I Sing (1931)

General Information about Composer and Compositions:

1. George Gershwin never had any formal conservatory training in music, but studied with local teachers. He joined
   Remick Publishing Company at the age of sixteen where he
   worked as a song plugger. He became a song-writer in Tin
   Pan Alley.

2. One of his favorite popular composers was Jerome Kern
   from whom he derived his interest in musical comedy. Some
   of Gershwin's more popular musical comedies are: *Of Thee
   I Sing* (1931), and *Strike Up The Band* (1927).

3. George Gershwin made use of the jazz idiom in all of his
   concert orchestral compositions; e.g. *Rhapsody In Blue*
   (1924), *Concerto In F* (1925), *An American In Paris* (1928),
   and the folk opera *Porgy And Bess* (1935).

4. Gershwin appeared as a soloist with the Boston Symphony
   Orchestra under Serge Koussevitzky where he presented
   his *Second Rhapsody* in 1932. Some of the themes of the
   songs that Gershwin wrote for the movie film *Delicious*
   were included in his concert piece *Second Rhapsody*.

5. Paul Whiteman commissioned Gershwin to write a piece that would incorporate the jazz idiom in a serious composition. The result was Gershwin's famous work *Rhapsody In Blue*. In 1925, Walter Damrosch commissioned Gershwin to write the *Concerto In F* which was enthusiastically received.

Composer's Main Contribution to the Art of Music:

1. George Gershwin effected the fusion of jazz and serious music. He attempted to raise the standards of composition of popular music in the United States. His works are the inspiration of many contemporary composers who are adopting elements of his style. This is especially true of the composers of background music for the screen and television.

Suggested Listening:

1. Title: *Rhapsody In Blue*
   Performers: Boston Pops Orchestra - Fiedler
   Record No.: RCA Victor LSC3319
   Grade Level: 4 - 8

2. Title: *Concerto In F*
   Performers: Boston Pops Orchestra - Fiedler
   Record No.: RCA Victor LSC-8
   Grade Level: 7 - 12

Optional Assignments:

1. Make a list of modern jazz musicians according to the instruments they play. Choose one and give an oral report about his life and music to the class. Ex.: Louis Armstrong.

2. Write a report on the history and evolution of jazz in this country.

3. Make a study of the influence American jazz has had on the music of other countries of the world. Write a report on this subject.

4. Trace the origin of musical comedy from its inception to the present day, including in the written report the important composers and musical comedies of this era.

5. After listening to a selection by George Gershwin (ex. *Rhapsody In Blue*), write a critique, comparing it with other compositions you have heard, or make up an appropriate story that the music might suggest to you.

AARON COPLAND

Composer: Aaron Copland
      Born: Brooklyn, New York 1900

Aural Recognition of Themes:
      Composition: *Appalachian Spring* (1944)

General Information about Composer and Compositions:

1. Aaron Copland is well known as one of America's leading
   composers. He was educated in the public schools of
   Brooklyn, New York. He began the study of piano under the
   tutelage of his older sister, and continued with other
   teachers, including Nadia Boulanger. In 1921 he attended
   the Fountainbleau School of Music in France.

2. His first compositions were received with acclaim at
   Paris and Fountainbleau. Copland's style was influenced
   by Ravel and Stravinsky.

3. Copland has also been successful as a conductor, having
   led many prominent orchestras throughout the world, including the Boston Symphony and the New York Philharmonic.

4. His early compositions incorporated the jazz idiom. In
   some of his later compositions he used the American folk
   theme as the basis for his style: *Appalachian Spring*
   (1944) and *Billy The Kid* (1938).

5. Copland composed background music for several Hollywood
   films. He wrote two play-operas for use in the public

schools; e.g. *An Outdoor Overture* (1938) and *The Second Hurricane* (1937). He is versatile in several fields as a composer, teacher, conductor and author. He has written the following textbooks: *Our New Music* (1941), *Music And Imagination* (1952), *What To Listen For In Music* (1957), and *Copland On Music* (1960).

Composer's Main Contribution to the Art of Music:

1. Aaron Copland has probably done more than any other living composer to further the acceptance of modern music. He promoted the cause of modern music as a teacher, composer, author and director of the League of Composers. He has achieved great success in integrating the jazz idiom into his works.

Suggested Listening:

1. Title: *Billy The Kid Ballet Suite - Street In A Frontier Town*
   Performers: National Symphony Orchestra - Mitchell
   Record No.: Victor LE-1009, Adventures In Music
   Grade Level: 4 - 8

2. Title: *El Salon Mexico*
   Performers: Boston Pops Orchestra - Fiedler
   Record No.: RCA LSC3303
   Grade Level: 7 - 12

Optional Assignments:

1. Copland wrote in the jazz idiom. Make a study of the historical development of jazz and conduct a class discussion on this subject.

2. The next time you attend a movie, listen carefully to the background music. Conduct a class discussion on the importance of music in the medium of the screen.

3. Make a comparison of the music of George Gershwin with that of Aaron Copland. Write a report on this topic.

4. After listening to a selection by the composer, write a critique, comparing it with other compositions you have heard, or make up an appropriate story that the music might suggest to you.

5. Make a study of the famous literary geniuses of the period and write a composition on this subject.

KURT WEILL

Composer: Kurt Weill
    Born: Dessau, Germany 1900
    Died: New York, N.Y. 1950

Aural Recognition of Themes:

    Purchase at your local music store one or more of the
following piano sheet music arrangements of Kurt Weill's
compositions. You may play the main theme with the written
accompaniment, or you may supply your own accompaniment
using the chords notated above the melody line (although
the chord symbols are written for guitar, they are easily
adapted to the piano). Play each theme of the composition
several times in order to facilitate recognition.

        Down In The Valley (1948)

        Mack The Knife (1928)

        September Song (1938)

General Information about Composer and Compositions:

1. Kurt Weill was the son of a Jewish cantor who encouraged
   him to study music. Kurt first studied composition with
   Albert Bing, an orchestral conductor in Dessau. At the
   age of eighteen, he went to Berlin, where he studied with
   Humperdinck and Busoni.

2. He achieved his first success in composition in 1923 with
   his *Fantasy, Passacaglia and Hymn*. His first success with
   one-act opera was *Der Protagonist* which was produced by
   the Dresden Opera Company.

3. In 1928 he collaborated with Bertolt Brecht in the writing of his *Three Penny Opera* (taken from *The Beggar's
   Opera* by John Gay). This opera became famous throughout
   the world. The popular song, *Mack The Knife*, taken from
   this opera became a hit song in the United States. This
   opera shows the influence that Stravinsky and Hindemith
   had upon Weill in the use of the jazz idiom.

4. In 1933 he traveled to Paris where he wrote the comic
   opera *My Kingdom For A Cow*. In 1935 he settled in the
   United States, living in both New York and Hollywood.

5. In 1938, Weill composed musical plays for the Broadway stage. His first musical was *Knickerbocker Holiday* (1938). His folk-opera *Down In The Valley* (1948) includes many American folk melodies which are arranged for school choral groups. He wrote background music for Hollywood films and plays.

Composer's Main Contribution to the Art of Music:

1. Kurt Weill developed the use of folk melodies in concert or stage works. He also incorporated the blues and jazz rhythms in his compositions. He was very successful in utilizing the jazz idiom in his stage works. His style shows the influence of Stravinsky and Hindemith.

Suggested Listening:

1. Title: *Down In The Valley*
   Performers: R.C.A. Victor Orchestra and Chorus - Adler
   Record No.: Victor LPV-503
   Grade Level: 4 - 8

2. Title: *Three Penny Opera*
   Performers: Lenya, Theatre de Lys Production
   Record No.: MGM 3121
   Grade Level: 7 - 12

Optional Assignments:

1. Make a study of the popular composers of musical plays, and give an oral report to the class on this subject.

2. Prepare and sing for the class the title song of Kurt Weill's folk opera *Down In The Valley*.

3. Play a recording of the popular song *Mack The Knife* in class, and compare this song with other popular ones.

4. If you are artistic, draw or paint a picture of the composer, and present it for bulletin board display.

5. Make a list of interesting facts about the composer and his music, and write a composition developing one of these.

ARAM KHATCHATURIAN

Composer: Aram Khatchaturian
    Born: Tiflis, Armenia 1903

Aural Recognition of Themes:
    Composition: *Sabre Dance* from ballet *Gayne* (1942)

General Information about Composer and Compositions:

1. Although he was born in Armenia, Aram Khatchaturian is known as a Russian composer because he moved to Russia, in 1921 and has lived there ever since. His father was a bookbinder in Georgia, Armenia and Aram did not start his music studies until he was eighteen years old.

2. He enrolled in the Gnessin School of Music in Moscow in 1921 where he studied cello and composition. He composed his first composition, a *Dance* for violin and piano, in 1926. In 1927, he composed a *Poem* for piano.

3. From 1929 to 1934 he studied composition at the Moscow Conservatory of Music. As proof of his preference for Russia, he composed in 1934 a symphony commemorating the fifteenth anniversary of the Sovietization of Armenia. In 1938 he wrote a musical selection entitled *Poem About Stalin*.

4. His music contains the folk idioms and native folk lore of Armenia which has its origins in the traditional classicism and oriental colorings of Russian music. His music emphasizes the power of rhythm which makes it very dramatic. He uses very effectively the dance rhythms of the East European countries.

258

5. Khatchaturian's ballet *Gayaneh* (1942) won the Stalin Prize. In 1939 he was awarded the order of Lenin for his achievements in the development of Armenian music. He composed symphonies, concertos, and works for piano and violin. One of his best known piano pieces is his *Sabre Dance* (1942) from his ballet *Gayne*.

Composer's Main Contribution to the Art of Music:

1. Aram Khatchaturian successfully incorporates Armenian folk music into the modern style of composition. He uses the oriental modes very effectively. He is expert in developing colorful and masterful works out of simple folk melodies and dance tunes. In the Soviet Union, he has achieved status on a level with two other great composers, Prokofiev and Shostakovitch.

Suggested Listening:

1. Title: *Masquerade Suite - Waltz*
   Performers: National Symphony Orchestra - Mitchell
   Record No.: Victor LE-1005, Adventures In Music
   Grade Level: 4 - 8

2. Title: *Gayne* - ballet suite - excerpts
   Performers: Boston Pops Orchestra - Fiedler
   Record No.: RCA LSC2267
   Grade Level: 7 - 12

Optional Assignments:

1. Make a study of the political and historical background of Armenia and its relationship to Russia. Write a paper on this subject.

2. After research, write a report on the folk music of Russia, Ukrania and Armenia.

3. If you are a pianist, learn and play the *Sabre Dance* for the class.

4. Do some research on Russian architecture and prepare a paper on this topic.

5. After listening to a selection by the composer, write a critique, comparing it with other compositions you have heard, or make up an appropriate story that the music might suggest to you.

DMITRI SHOSTAKOVITCH

Composer: Dmitri Shostakovitch
Born: Leningrad, Russia 1906

Aural Recognition of Themes:
Composition: *Symphony No. 1 in F* (1925)

General Information about Composer and Compositions:

1. Dmitri Shostakovitch was born of musical parents and received his first music lessons from his mother who was an
   accomplished pianist. At the age of thirteen, he entered
   the Conservatory of Leningrad where he studied piano and
   composition.

2. During his first year at the Conservatory, he composed a
   set of eight piano preludes and his piece called *Three
   Fantastic Dances*. For graduation in 1925, he completed
   his *Symphony No.1* which was such a success that he was
   named the "boy genius" of Russia.

3. In 1927, his piano virtuosity was recognized by the award-
   ing of a prize in the International Pianist's Contest
   held in Warsaw, Poland. In Berlin, Germany in 1927, Bruno
   Walter introduced Shostakovitch's *Symphony No. 1* which
   was received with great acclaim. The following year,
   Leopold Stokowski gave it the American premiére with the
   Philadelphia Orchestra.

4. In 1930, he wrote a satirical opera called *The Nose*, for
   which he was reprimanded by the Kremlin for its bourgeois
   decadence. In 1937, he reinstated himself with the Russian

260

leaders with his *Fifth Symphony* (1937). He composed his *Seventh Symphony* which described the heroic defense of Leningrad in 1941. This composition was played for the first time in America by Arturo Toscanini and the N.B.C. Symphony Orchestra in 1942.

5. Shostakovitch received the Stalin Prize of one hundred thousand rubles for the composition of his *Piano Quintet* in 1941. He wrote operas, ballets, symphonies, chamber music, an oratorio and piano pieces.

Composer's Main Contribution to the Art of Music:

1. Dmitri Shostakovitch, during his early years, was influenced by the modern composers and his music expressed abstractions which did not appeal to the public. Under pressure from the Russian government he has written music which shows the influence of Soviet propaganda and militarism.

Suggested Listening:

1. Title: *The Age Of Gold* - polka
   Performers: R.C.A. Victor Symphony Orchestra
   Record No.: R.C.A. Basic Record Library, E-82, Vol. 6
   Grade Level: 4 - 8

2. Title: *Symphony No. 5, Op. 47*
   Performers: New York Philharmonic - Bernstein
   Record No.: Columbia MS - 6115
   Grade Level: 7 - 12

Optional Assignments:

1. Make a list of composers who wrote music for the piano, and list their most famous compositions.

2. Make a comparison between the music of Khatchaturian and Shostakovitch.

3. Learn a Russian folk dance and perform it for the class.

4. Make a study of the life of Josef Stalin and write a report on this subject.

5. Using only a skeleton outline, tell your class about an interesting musical event you attended recently.

SAMUEL BARBER

Composer: Samuel Barber
   Born: West Chester, Penn. 1910

Aural Recognition of Themes:

   Purchase at your local music store one or more of the following piano sheet music arrangements of Samuel Barber's compositions. You may play the main theme with the written accompaniment, or you may supply your own accompaniment using the chords notated above the melody line (although the chord symbols are written for guitar, they are easily adapted to the piano). Play each theme of the composition several times in order to facilitate recognition.

   Commando March

   Rain Has Fallen

   Nocturne

General Information about Composer and Compositions:

1. Samuel Barber began the study of piano at the age of six, under the tutelage of his mother. He was the nephew of Mme. Louise Homer, the leading contralto of the Metropolitan Opera. He composed his first piano work at the age of seven. He was appointed organist of his hometown church at the age of twelve.

2. He attended the Curtis Institute of Music in Philadelphia where he studied voice, piano and composition. In 1935 he won the American Prix de Rome with his overture to *The School For Scandal*. The first American work ever performed at the Salzburg Festival in Austria was Barber's *Symphony In One Movement* (1935).

3. The first American works conducted by the great conductor Arturo Toscanini was Barber's *Adagio For Strings* (1937) and *Essay For Orchestra* (1937). He was also honored by the famous violin virtuoso, Albert Spaulding, who played his *Concerto For Violin And Orchestra* with the Philadelphia Orchestra in 1941.

4. During World War II, while he was in the Army Air Force, he composed his *Second Symphony* (1943), which he

dedicated to that organization. During this period, he also composed his *Commando March* (1943).

5. Barber has a native talent for writing a colorful melody line. Literary works and poetry influenced his style of composition. A good example of this is his *Music For A Scene From Shelley*, introduced by the New York Philharmonic in 1935.

Composer's Main Contribution to the Art of Music:

1. Samuel Barber is one of the more conservative of the modern composers. He doesn't experiment with dissonance and cacophony but rather emphasizes pure harmony and beautiful and poetic melodies. His music has influenced many contemporary composers.

Suggested Listening:

1. Title: *Commando March*
   Performers: Harvard University Band
   Record No.: INC-7
   Grade Level: 4 - 8

2. Title: *Concerto For Violin And Orchestra, Op. 14*
   Performers: Stern, Bernstein
   Record No.: Columbia MS-6713
   Grade Level: 7 - 12

Optional Assignments:

1. After research, prepare an outline for class discussion on the historical background of World War II.

2. Make a study of the choral and instrumental music organizations of the various branches of the United States Armed Forces. Write a report on these groups.

3. Write a biographical sketch of the composer's life.

4. Play a recording of one of Barber's compositions for the class, and give an oral report on the piece being played.

5. Make a study of the major performing instruments of the composer, and collect literature and pictures of these instruments for your notebook.

<u>GIAN-CARLO MENOTTI</u>

<u>Composer</u>: Gian-Carlo Menotti
   <u>Born</u>: Cadigliano, Italy 1911

<u>Aural Recognition of Themes</u>:

   Purchase at your local music store one or more or the following piano sheet music arrangements of Menotti's compositions. You may play the main theme with the written accompaniment, or you may supply your own accompaniment using the chords notated above the melody line (although the chord symbols are written for guitar, they are easily adapted to the piano). Play each theme of the composition several times in order to facilitate recognition.

   Select excerpts from the following operas:

   Amahl And The Night Visitors (1951)

   Amelia Goes To The Ball (1936)

   The Telephone (1947)

<u>General Information about Composer and Compositions</u>:

1. Gian-Carlo Menotti was born into a musical and wealthy family. His parents participated in opera productions. He started piano lessons at the age of four, and five years later began writing his own plays.

2. He began his musical education at the Conservatory of Milan in Italy. At the age of seventeen, he came to the United States and continued his musical education at the Curtis Institute in Philadelphia. He has remained in this country ever since.

3. Menotti was a protégé of Arturo Toscanini, the world famous conductor. Toscanini encouraged Menotti and assisted him in his musical works.

4. His famous opera *Amahl And The Night Visitors* (1951), was written especially for production on television. Like Wagner, Menotti writes both the music and text for his operas.

5. Menotti is chiefly an opera composer, although he has also composed ballets, concertos, and other orchestral compositions.

Composer's Main Contribution to the Art of Music:

1. Gian-Carlo Menotti has a genuine interest in social problems of the modern world. He develops the social theme in the libretti of his operas which give us a musical picture of modern living. In addition, he has written several plays for radio and television. These works have influenced his contemporaries.

Suggested Listening:

1. Title: *Amahl And The Night Visitors* - Shepherd's Dance
   Performers: National Symphony Orchestra - Mitchell
   Record No.: Victor LE-1005, Adventures In Music
   Grade Level: 4 - 8

2. Title: *The Medium* - ballet (1946)
   Performers: Washington Op. Soc.
   Record No.: Columbia MS-7387
   Grade Level: 7 - 12

Optional Assignments:

1. Obtain an opera libretto from the library for study. Show it to the class and lead a short discussion of the opera and its libretto.

2. Make a study of the life of Arturo Toscanini, and write a report about him.

3. Make up a notebook about the life and music of Menotti, consisting of pictures, newspaper and magazine articles, concert programs, thematic excerpts, original illustra- tions and written reports.

4. Since both Menotti and Wagner wrote their own librettos, make a comparison of the operas of each of these compos- ers.

5. Do some research on the qualifications, training and education needed to become an opera singer.

JOHN CAGE

<u>Composer</u>: John Cage
    Born: Los Angeles, California 1912

<u>Analysis of Composer's Works</u>:

   Purchase at your local music store the music and recording of the following composition by John Cage. The piece is written for piano. Listen to the melody and follow its pattern by drawing a diagram of its movement.

    Dream (1960)

<u>General Information about Composer and Compositions</u>:

1. John Cage is considered one of America's greatest composers in the field of electronic music. He has studied with notable musicians, including Henry Cowell and Arnold Schoenberg.

2. He was valedictorian of his class in high school at Los Angeles. Cage studied briefly at Pomona College. He considered the fields of ministry, architecture, painting and writing before he finally decided to concentrate on music.

3. Cage is not interested in harmony in his music. Instead, he likes startling sounds created by environmental objects such as electric buzzers, flower pots, brake bands and sounds from Chinese, Oriental and Indian percussion instruments. His ideas and music have been accepted by hippies and highbrows alike.

4. Cage was a follower of Charles Ives and a great admirer of Edgar Varèse. He likes to experiment with junk instruments. His prepared piano contains the following objects, used as dampers between the strings: rubber, plastic, screws, bolts, spoons, leather, felt, aspirin boxes and clothespins. Cage has called his prepared piano a percussion ensemble performed by one player.

5. John Cage was ahead of his era as far as electronic composition is concerned. In a 1937 lecture, he spoke of the synthetic production of sound through the recording of environmental noise, radio static, the blending of film sounds and the controlled variations of amplitude and frequency.

Composer's Main Contribution to the Art of Music:

1. John Cage was instrumental in creating a new era of music through the use of electronic instruments. He added another dimension to musical tonality by creating new aesthetics of sound.

Suggested Listening:

1. Title: *Aria With Fontana Mix*
   Performers: Berberian - tape
   Record No.: Mainstream 5005
   Grade Level: 4 - 8

2. Title: *Music For Keyboard*
   Performers: Kirstein - prepared piano
   Record No.: Columbia M2S-819
   Grade Level: 7 - 12

Optional Assignments:

1. Listen to recordings of each and compare the music of John Cage with that of Stravinsky and Schoenberg.

2. Learn and perform one of his selections arranged for the piano.

3. John Cage was a futurist. Do some research on this subject and report on the composers and music of this medium.

4. Select a group of students to compose and perform an original composition using home-made instruments.

5. Read about his prepared piano and experiment on your own using implements to change the sound of your piano.

BENJAMIN BRITTEN

Composer: Benjamin Britten
 Born: Lowestoft, England 1913

Aural Recognition of Themes:
 Composition: *Peter Grimes* (1945) - opera

General Information about Composer and Compositions:

1. Benjamin Britten was educated at Gresham's School in
   Holt, England. During his early years, he studied piano
   and composition privately. He received a three-year
   scholarship to the Royal Conservatory of Music. In 1933
   he won the virtuoso pianists award.

2. At the age of nine, Britten composed a piano suite and
   sonata. While in college, he composed a *Sinfonietta* for
   chamber orchestra which was published. He wrote a unique
   composition entitled *Simple Symphony* in 1934, in which he
   incorporated themes he had written between the ages of
   nine and twelve.

3. He was influenced by Rossini, and in 1936 composed an
   orchestral suite *Soirées Musicales* based on Rossini's
   works. At the Salzburg Festival of 1937, his *Variations
   On A Theme Of Frank Bridge For String Orchestra* was performed by the Boyd Neel Orchestra. This composition became very popular, and during the next two years was performed throughout Europe and America.

4. From 1939 to 1942, Britten resided in the United States.
   During this period he was commissioned to compose several

works. Among these are: *Sinfonia da Requiem* (1939), and *Seven Sonnets of Michelangelo* (1941).

5. Britten wrote chamber music, concertos, operas and piano and vocal works. One of his most popular operas was *Peter Grimes* (1945). In 1939, he composed the *Ballad For Heroes* and dedicated this composition to Britons who died fighting in the Spanish Civil War.

Composer's Main Contribution to the Art of Music:

1. Benjamin Britten has a talent for adapting his composition to any medium, and has written background music for documentary films, theatre productions and radio programs. One of his greatest contributions to the field of music education is *The Young Person's Guide To The Orchestra*, (*Variations And Fugue On A Theme By Purcell*) (1953). This composition was originally composed for an educational film. Recordings of this composition are used as an integral part of the music appreciation program of many public schools in the United States and England.

Suggested Listening:

1. Title: *Young Person's Guide To The Orchestra*
   Performers: London Symphony Orchestra - Britten
   Record No.: London 6671
   Grade Level: 4 - 8

2. Title: *Peter Grimes* (excerpts)
   Performers: Royal Opera House
   Record No.: London 26004
   Grade Level: 7 - 12

Optional Assignments:

1. Do some research on Britten's most recent compositions and write a critique on this.

2. Lead a class discussion on the composer's life and music. Prepare an outline for this purpose.

3. Listen to Britten's *Young Person's Guide To The Orchestra* and give an oral report telling why you think the title of this selection is appropriate.

4. Make a study of the famous scientists of this period. Write a paper on this subject.

5. If you play a musical instrument, select a work of the composer, and perform it for the class.

CHAPTER 8

THUMBNAIL SKETCH OF
THE HISTORY OF AMERICAN POPULAR MUSIC

I. Early American Music 1620-1750

   A. Music of the Pilgrims in New England: The first popular music introduced in New England by the Pilgrims were religious melodies that were brought from England. These psalms and hymns were not only the music for religious services, but became the melodies used for social and official functions as well.
     1. In 1620 the Pilgrims brought from England the *Book of Psalms* by Henry Ainsworth.
     2. In 1640 they published the first American hymn book, *Bay Psalm Book*.
       a. Popular hymn melodies were not written down, but were orally passed on from one generation to the next.
       b. The early hymns were sung in a slow tempo and the rhythmic interpretation was generally musically inaccurate.

   B. Music of the colonies outside of New England: Popular songs, taken from ballad operas and performed by singing actors who traveled around with their English repertory, spread through the colonies. From these ballads the folk literature of this new country was developed.
     1. In Virginia the *English Ballads* were sung from which the people gradually developed a folk music of their own. This was the folk music of the Appalachian and Cumberland Mountains:
       a. *Barbara Allen*
       b. *Chevy Chase*
       c. *Sourwood Mountain*
     2. Ballad Opera stage productions imported from England:
       a. *The Beggar's Opera* by John Gay
       b. *Artaxerxes* 1762 by Thomas Arne

   C. Instruments used during the Colonial Period: The instruments brought to this country by the colonists were products of Europe. Because of the newness of the colonies, instrumental music education was lacking, and performance was on an elementary level.

1. Used as accompaniment for singing and dancing:
   a. Viols, flute, fife, oboe, horns, virginal, spinet, harpsichord, organ and guitar.
2. Used for playing of folk songs and dances at folk parties and festivals.

II. Music of the Revolutionary and Post-Revolutionary War Periods: Although the colonists adopted many English melodies during the Revolutionary War, they wrote patriotic lyrics to these tunes.

A. Popular songs of the American Revolution:
   1. *Yankee Doodle* (1775) by Dr. Richard Schuckburg.
      a. A British song adopted by the American colonists. It was one of the most widely circulated songs in the colonies.
   2. Other English songs adapted by the American colonists:
      a. *God Save the King* changed to *God Save the Thirteen States*.
      b. *The British Grenadiers* changed to *Free America*.
      c. *Rule, Britannia* changed to *Rise, Columbia*.

B. Campaign songs were composed for many years after the Revolutionary War:
   1. *A Toast to Washington*
   2. *The Aristocracy of Henry Clay* (1824)
   3. *Tippecanoe and Tyler Too* (1840)
   4. *Lincoln and Liberty* (1860)
   5. *The Clay Minstrel* - a songbook
   6. *The Polk Songster* - a songbook

C. War songs and current events: Special songs were composed to popularize current events:
   1. *Decatur's Victory* by W. Strickland
   2. *Erie and Champlain* by Samuel Woodworth
   3. *Perry's Victory* by Joseph Hutton
   4. *The Acquisition of Louisiana* by Michael Fortune
   5. *The Star-Spangled Banner* (1814) by Francis Scott Key and John Stafford Smith

D. Origins of American Folk Music:
   1. The influence of the English, Irish and Scotch folk music in Virginia, Kentucky, Tennessee, North and South Carolina.
   2. The influence of the French in Louisiana.
   3. The influence of Spanish folk music in southwestern United States.
   4. Original American folk songs came from the work songs of the Negro, Indians, Cowboys, Railroad workers, etc.

III. Music of the Civil War Period: Most of our best patriotic songs were composed during this period. The first native American musical entertainment medium, the minstrel show, originated during the Civil War.

A. Song writers (composers) of the Civil War Period:
1. John Hill Hewitt (1801-1890) - wrote sentimental ballads:
a. *The Minstrel's Return from the War*
b. *All Quiet Along the Potomac Tonight*
2. Henry Russell (1812-1900) - composer of sentimental ballads:
a. *The Old Family Clock*
b. *The Old Spinning Wheel*
3. *We Are Coming Father Abraham* by Stephen Foster
4. *The Battle Hymn of the Republic* (1861) by William Steffe and Julia Ward Howe
5. *Marching Through Georgia* by Henry Clay Work
6. *Tenting on the Old Camp Ground* (1862) by Walter Kittredge

B. Minstrel shows, composers and songs: The minstrel show achieved a great deal of popularity as stage entertainment during and after the Civil War. Many of the popular songs of this period were part of these musical productions.
1. Daniel Decatur Emmett (1815-1904) - wrote songs for the Virginia Minstrels.
a. *Dixie*
b. *The Blue Tail Fly*
c. *Old Dan Tucker*
2. The Christy Minstrels directed by Ed Christy:
a. Popularized the minstrel show in America and England.
b. *Camptown Races* written by Stephen Foster for Ed Christy's minstrel group.

C. Stephen Foster: (1826-1864) - the most popular composer of minstrel songs and ballads of the South:
1. *Oh, Susanna* (1848)
2. *The Old Folks At Home* (1851)
3. *My Old Kentucky Home* (1853)
4. *Jeannie With the Light Brown Hair* (1854)

IV. Music of the Post-Civil War Period:

A. The sentimental ballad became very popular after the Civil War, and has remained a popular art form to this day. Some of the early writers of ballads and their works are:

1. Henry Clay Work (1832-1884)
   a. *Grandfather's Clock* (1876)
2. William Shakespeare Hays (1837-1907)
   a. *Mollie Darling* (1871)
3. Septimus Winner (1826-1902) - published songs under the name of Alice Hawthorne:
   a. *Listen to the Mocking Bird* (1854)
   b. *Whispering Hope* (1868)
4. Thomas Paine Westendorf
   a. *I'll Take You Home Again Kathleen* (1875)
5. James A. Bland (1854-1911)
   a. *Carry Me Back to Old Virginny* (1871)
   b. *In the Evening by the Moonlight* (1879)
   c. *Oh, Dem Golden Slippers* (1879)
6. Paul Dresser (1857-1906)
   a. *On the Banks of the Wabash* (1899)
   b. *My Gal Sal* (1906)

B. Composers of Light Opera and Operettas: At the end of the nineteenth century, light opera and operetta became popular with the production of operettas by Gilbert and Sullivan in America. The American composers adopted this music form which was very well received by the general public.
   1. Victor Herbert (1859-1924) composer of light opera:
      a. *Babes in Toyland* (1903)
      b. *Naughty Marietta* (1910)
   2. Reginald DeKoven (1861-1920) composer of light opera:
      a. The very popular song *Oh Promise Me* from the opera *Robin Hood* (1890).
   3. Rudolph Friml (1879-1972) musical comedy:
      a. *Rose Marie* (1924)
   4. Sigmund Romberg (1887-1951) light opera:
      a. *Desert Song* (1926)
      b. *The Student Prince* (1924)
      c. *The New Moon* (1928)
   5. George Gershwin (1898-1937) folk opera:
      a. *Porgy and Bess* (1935)
   6. Jerome Kern (1885-1945) American folk opera:
      a. *Showboat* (1927)
   7. Kurt Weill (1900-1950) jazz opera:
      a. *The Three Penny Opera* (1928)

C. Transition from Minstrel Show to Vaudeville (Variety Shows - individual acts): The main difference between Minstrel and Vaudeville stage production exists in the size of group performance. In the Minstrel show the emphasis is on a group performance, whereas in the Vaudeville (Variety) show the single performer or small group work is of prime importance. Some of the famous vaudeville companies and performers are:

1. Sargent's Great Vaudeville Company from Chicago (1871).
2. Tony Pastor's Variety Theatre in New York (1866).
3. Tony Pastor's Music Hall in Union Square (1881).
   a. These shows helped to make famous the following stars of the musical stage:
      (1) Lillian Russell
      (2) Pat Rooney
      (3) Eddie Foy
      (4) The Four Cohans

D. Beginnings of Burlesque (stage shows with slapstick comedy sketches about the Negroes, Italians, Germans, and Irish):
1. *The Mulligan Guard* produced by Harrigan and Hart (1873):
   a. Comedy sketch ridiculing the use of military uniforms by civilian organizations.
2. Charles Hoyt's burlesque show *A Trip to Chinatown*:
   a. A comical satire on woman suffrage and temperance league.
   b. Songs from the show that are still popular: *The Bowery* and *After the Ball*.

E. Band Music Composers: During the early part of the 20th century a strong feeling of nationalism developed, which reflected the pride of the American people in their achievements in industrial production, invention, military prowess, foreign trade, educational and artistic growth. One of the results of this feeling was the development of military bands, and the performances of these bands became a very popular entertainment medium. Band concerts became a part of the social activities of many communities. Some of the most popular composers of band music are:
1. Patrick S. Gilmore (1829-1892) - Conductor of the Twenty-second Regimental Band; also perfected the Concert Band and its music.
2. Edwin Franko Goldman (1878-1956) - Adapted a symphonic repertoire to the medium of the Concert Band.
3. John Philip Sousa (1854-1932) - World-famous composer of band music, was known as the "March King." Some of his best known marches are:
   a. *Stars and Stripes Forever*
   b. *High School Cadets* - written for a Washington, D.C. school.
   c. *King Cotton March* - written for the Louisiana Exposition.
   d. *Semper Fidelis* - composed for his own United States Marine Band.

274

F. Tin Pan Alley: Tin Pan Alley is an area of New York where many song publishing firms are located. During the late nineteenth and early twentieth centuries this group of publishers set the standards and influenced the development of the popular song in America.
   1. Developed patterns of writing and techniques of publicizing, distributing and selling popular songs.
   2. These same methods were adopted in other large cities such as Chicago, Milwaukee, Boston, etc.
   3. Song pluggers (promoters) sang and played their selections in music stores, theatres and department stores. Professional entertainers plugged songs:
      a. Eddie Cantor
      b. George Jessel
      c. George M. Cohan
   4. James Thornton - a singing waiter who published and plugged his own songs:
      a. *When You Were Sweet Sixteen* (1898)
   5. Other popular songs written during this period:
      a. *Daisy Bell* (1892) by Harry Dacre
      b. *The Band Played On* (1895) by Lawlor and Blake
      c. *Sweet Rosie O'Grady* (1896) by Maude Nugent

V. Popular Music of the Twentieth Century:

   A. Jazz: (unorthodox improvisation of a "blues" theme). During World War I, a popular form called "jazz" originated in New Orleans. Its source was the songs and dances, religious chants and rhythmic accents of the Negroes.
      1. This style of music, based upon improvisation, gradually spread throughout the country.
         a. New Orleans was the first center of jazz music.
      2. Two styles of jazz predominated:
         a. Ragtime - rhythmic, syncopated dance style, and improvised melody.
         b. Blues - slow, rhythmic, sorrowful music adopted from the Negro spirituals.
      3. Jazz performers:
         a. Buddy Bolden - cornet
         b. "Jelly Roll" Morton - piano
         c. Jod "King" Oliver - trumpet
         d. Louis Armstrong - trumpet
         e. Sidney Bechet - clarinet
         f. Earl "Father" Hines - piano
         g. "Fats" Waller - piano

4. <u>Boogie-Woogie</u> - a piano style featuring the osti-
   nato bass figures (repeated bass pattern) against
   a blues melody. The following are some of the
   original composers and their compositions:
   a. *Pinetop's Boogie-Woogie* by Pinetop Clarence
      Smith.
   b. *State Street Special* by Jimmy Yancey.
   c. *Honky Tonk Train Blues* by Meade Lux Lewis.
5. <u>Swing</u> - organized notated improvisation with definite melody and rhythm. The leading performers
   and specialists of the swing style are:
   a. Benny Goodman - clarinet
   b. Gene Krupa - drums
   c. Tommy Dorsey - trombone
   d. Lionel Hampton - vibraharp and piano
   e. Artie Shaw - clarinet
   f. Duke Ellington - piano, and composer of the
      following:
      (1) *Sophisticated Lady*
      (2) *Solitude*
      (3) *Mood Indigo*
6. <u>Composers and music of the Ragtime and Blues era:</u>
   a. *Alexander's Ragtime Band* by Irving Berlin
   b. *Twelfth Street Rag* by Euday L. Bowman
   c. *Kitten on the Keys* by "Zez" Edward Confrey
   d. *Hello Ma Baby* by Joe Howard
   e. *Ballin' the Jack* by Chris Smith
   f. *Dardenella* by Felix Bernard and John S. Black
   g. *Darktown Strutters Ball* by Shelton Brooks
   h. *St. Louis Blues* and *Beale St. Blues* by W.C.
      Handy
   i. *Wabash Blues* by Fred Meinken

B. <u>Dance Bands of the twentieth century</u>: The dance band
   of this century has held a prominent place in the
   social life of most Americans. The type of music
   played by dance orchestras has undergone many changes
   in style:
   1. <u>Instrumentation:</u>
      a. Brass section: 3 trumpets and 2 trombones
      b. Reed section: 2 alto saxophones and 2 tenor
         saxophones
      c. Rhythm section: double bass, guitar, piano and
         drums.
   2. <u>Bands that played sweet, smooth music:</u>

a. Guy Lombardo	b. Wayne King
c. Rudy Vallee	d. Ted Lewis
e. Paul Whiteman	f. Vincent Lopez
g. Jan Garber	h. Ted Weems

3. Jazz and Swing bands:
   a. Duke Ellington   b. Count Basie
   c. Jack Teagarten   d. Woody Herman
   e. Fletcher Henderson f. Jimmy and Tommy Dorsey
   g. Benny Goodman   h. Cab Calloway

C. Musical Comedy and its composers: The Broadway Musical
   Comedy was an outgrowth of the operetta and musical
   revue. After World War I, this form of entertainment,
   a product of Broadway and Tin Pan Alley, became the
   most popular form of stage production. It is accepted
   today as an integral part of our music culture. The
   following is a list of composers and their most important Broadway productions:
   1. Richard Rodgers (1902) and Oscar Hammerstein II
      (1895-1960)
      a. *South Pacific* (1949) b. *Oklahoma* (1943)
      c. *Carousel* (1945) d. *The King and I* (1951)
      e. *The Sound of Music* (1959)
   2. Irving Berlin (1888)
      a. *Annie Get Your Gun* (1946)
      b. *Call Me Madam* (1950)
      c. *This Is the Army* (1942)
      d. *Holiday Inn* (1942)
   3. George Gershwin (1898-1937) and Ira Gershwin (1896)
      a. *George White Scandals* (1925)
      b. *Lady Be Good* (1924)
      c. *Strike Up the Band* (1930)
      d. *Of Thee I Sing* (1931)
   4. Cole Porter (1893-1964)
      a. *Kiss Me Kate* (1948)
      b. *Anything Goes* (1934)
      c. *Can Can* (1953)
      d. *Mexican Hayride* (1944)
   5. Jerome Kern (1885-1945)
      a. *Sunny* (1925)
      b. *Roberta* (1937)
      c. *Music In the Air* (1932)
   6. Leonard Bernstein (1918)
      a. *On The Town* (1944)
      b. *Wonderful Town* (1953)
      c. *West Side Story* (1957)
   7. Alan Jay Lerner (1918) and Frederick Loewe (1904)
      a. *Brigadoon* (1947)
      b. *My Fair Lady* (1956)
      c. *Gigi* (1959)
      d. *Camelot* (1960)
   8. Meredith Wilson (1902)
      a. *The Music Man* (1957)
      b. *The Unsinkable Molly Brown* (1960)

D. <u>Latest Musical Productions and Composers</u>: Many notable
composers of musicals have risen during the past decade.
The following list includes the most successful productions:

The Fantasticks by Tom Jones and Harvey Schmidt (1960)
Mary Poppins by Richard M. and Robert B. Sherman (1963)
Fiddler On The Roof by Sheldon Harnick and Jerry Bock (1964)
Man Of La Mancha by Mitch Leigh and Joe Darion (1965)
Mame by Jerry Herman (1966)
Hello Dolly by Jerry Herman (1968)
Promises, Promises by Burt Bacharach (1968)
Hair by Galt McDermot (1968)
Oh Calcutta by The Open Window (1969)
Dear World by Jerry Herman (1969)
Jesus Christ Superstar by Andrew L. Webber and Tim
    Rice (1970)
Don't Bother Me, I Can't Cope by Micki Grant (1970)
Godspell by Stephen Schwartz (1971)
Grease by Warren Casey and Jim Jacobs (1971)
Pippin by Stephen Schwartz (1972)
Irene by Wally Harper and Jack Lloyd (1973)
A Little Night Music by Stephen Sondheim (1973)

E. <u>Rock Music</u>:

  Rock music had its origins in various forms of the blues.
This musical form originated in the music of the Negro and
was an integral part of his culture. In the late 1930's
and early 1940's, the blues and variations of it were
adopted by the white musicians and bands. Some of the blues
forms that emanated from this era were jazz, boogie-woogie,
swing, be-bop, etc.

  By 1949, this music, vitalized with the introduction of
the electric guitar, was identified with the title "Rhythm
and Blues". This musical form combined new blues ideas with
the best of traditional music.

  In 1951, Alan Freed, a disk jockey, writer and concert
promoter, introduced a new idea and title which he called
"Rock and Roll". The youth of America were immediately attracted to this music because it represented for them a
different and new means of communication which separated
them from the adult musical culture.

The movie *Blackboard Jungle* and its theme song *Rock Around the Clock*, sung by Bill Haley and his Comets, was released in 1954 and was an important contribution to the early development of rock music. The instrumentation of this group consisted of electric guitar, bass guitar, tenor saxophone, vibes and drums. Amplification of sound became one of the most important ingredients of rock music at this time.

Rock music received a tremendous impetus with the introduction of Elvis Presley, a white singer from Memphis. His amazing career as a rock singer in motion pictures not only catapulted him to world-wide fame and recognition, but served to further the entrenchment of the rock idiom as part of our culture. For ten years, beginning in 1956, he was the idol of the youth of our nation. Some of his best-known songs include: *Love Me Tender, Hound Dog, Blue Suede Shoes* and *Heartbreak Hotel*.

In 1964, one of the most popular rock groups in history captured the imagination of the American public. This exciting quartet, called the Beatles, emigrated from England to the United States. Composing their own songs and performing musical arrangements of a very high quality, the Beatles brought about a nationwide acceptance of this art form. The Beatles expressed love and human relationships in the following songs: *I Want To Hold Your Hand, Eleanor Rigby, She Loves You, Hey Jude* and *Yesterday*.

One of the most popular exponents of Folk Rock during the 1960's was Bob Dylan. He composed protest songs using the rock medium to try to effect social reform and changes. Some of his compositions are: *Blowing In The Wind* (the integration movement), *With God On Our Side* (the horror of war), *A Hard Rain's Gonna Fall* (world annihilation) and *The Times They Are A-Changing* (the generation gap).

Rock music continues its growth with the development of new styles and techniques of composition introduced by various song writers and performers of the present day. Rock has been and continues to be used to influence the political scene, but has achieved more success as a sociological force.

279

PABLO PICASSO. *Three Musicians.* 1921

CHAPTER 9

COMPOSERS OF AMERICAN POPULAR MUSIC

Introduction: In this chapter, American popular music has been divided into four main categories: (1) folk music, (2) instrumental music, (3) operettas, (4) Broadway musicals. The historical development of popular music evolved in pretty much the same order. The evolutionary stages and writers of popular music are too numerous to list here, so the authors have selected the following composers and their works to give you a representative view of the development of this art form.

A. Composers of American Folk Music:

    1. Daniel Decatur Emmett (1818-1904)
    2. Stephen Collins Foster (1826-1864)
    3. James A. Bland (1854-1911)

B. Composers of Instrumental Music:

    1. Patrick Sarsfield Gilmore (1829-1892)
    2. John Philip Sousa (1854-1932)
    3. Leroy Anderson (born: 1908)

C. Composers of American Operettas:

    1. Victor Herbert (1859-1924)
    2. Rudolph Friml (1879-1972)
    3. Sigmund Romberg (1887-1951)

D. Composers of Broadway Musicals:

    1. Jerome Kern (1885-1945)
    2. Irving Berlin (born: 1888)
    3. Cole Porter (1893-1964)
    4. Richard Rodgers (born: 1902)
    5. Frederick Loewe (born: 1904)
    6. Leonard Bernstein (born: 1918)
    7. Burt Bacharach (born: 1928)

E. Composers of Rock Music: The Beatles

    1. John Lennon (born: 1940)
    2. Paul McCartney (born: 1942)
    3. George Harrison (born: 1943)
    4. Ringo Starr (born: 1940)

DANIEL DECATUR EMMETT

Composer: Daniel Decatur Emmett
   Born: Mt. Vernon, Ohio 1815
   Died: Mt. Vernon, Ohio 1904

Aural Recognition of Themes:
   Composition: *Dixie* (1859)

General Information about Composer and Compositions:

1. Daniel Decatur Emmett was one of the most famous minstrel show performers of his time. As a boy, he played flute in the Army Band. He also worked as an apprentice in a printing shop.

2. In 1835, he joined a circus troupe as drummer boy. Later, he performed as a minstrel entertainer in "Daddy" Rice's Minstrel Company. He was very adept and successful as a minstrel performer, and his intense interest in this medium inspired him to write minstrel songs.

3. Emmett became well known as a composer of minstrel songs, and received contracts from many minstrel companies to write songs for their shows. One of the most famous groups with which he was connected as performer and composer was the Virginia Minstrels.

4. Emmett's most famous minstrel song, perhaps, is *Dixie*, composed in 1859. He performed with Bryant's Minstrels at Mechanics Hall in New York in the first successful production of this song on April 4, 1859. It became the official song of the Confederate Army during the Civil

War. It was also used as a campaign song in the 1860 elections.

5. The song *Dixie* became popular with minstrel groups throughout the country. Some of his other popular minstrel songs are: *The Blue Tail Fly (Jim Crack Corn)*, *Old Dan Tucker*, and *The Boatman's Dance*.

Composer's Main Contribution to the Art of Music:

1. Daniel Decatur Emmett was one of the most famous composers of minstrel songs in the United States. As a performer and composer of minstrel songs, he contributed to the establishment of the minstrel form of music and entertainment as an integral part of the American scene and culture during the latter half of the nineteenth century.

Suggested Listening:

1. Title: *The Blue Tail Fly*
   Performers: Vocal and Instrumental Group
   Record No.: Golden Record Library - Vol. 5
   Grade Level: 4 - 8

2. Title: *Dixie* (Americana Album)
   Performers: The Capitol Symphony Orchestra - Dragon
   Record No.: Capitol P-8523
   Grade Level: 7 - 12

Optional Assignments:

1. Write a report tracing the background and use of the song *Dixie* from its origin up to the present date.

2. In a brief oral report to the class, make a comparison of Stephen Foster and Dan Emmett.

3. The banjo is the most popular instrument for accompaniment of minstrel singing. Write a paper tracing the origin, structure, and development of this instrument.

4. Write a review of a minstrel show that you have attended recently. Tell about the songs, instruments, costumes and scenery used in the show.

5. If you play a musical instrument, or sing, perform one of Emmett's songs for the class.

STEPHEN COLLINS FOSTER

Composer: Stephen Collins Foster
  Born: Pittsburgh, Pa. 1826
  Died: New York, N.Y. 1864

Aural Recognition of Themes:
  Composition: *Beautiful Dreamer* (1864)

General Information about Composer and Compositions:

1. Stephen Collins Foster began his academic education at the Academy in Allegheny, Pennsylvania. He continued his studies and graduated from Jefferson College. He had little formal musical training, but showed a great deal of natural ability in playing the piano and flute. He also had a beautiful singing voice.

2. He studied the works of the great German composers. At the age of fourteen, he wrote his first composition which was a waltz for four flutes. In 1842 he composed his first published song, *Open The Lattice, Love*. It was one of the few songs for which he wrote only the music.

3. Foster's music contributed a great deal to the repertoire of the traveling minstrel shows of that era. He composed many of his songs to fill the needs of the negro minstrel companies who used his songs in their shows. He sold one of his songs *Swanee River* to the negro minstrel Edward Christy, who claimed authorship of this song.

4. His songs were very popular during and after the Civil War. His music was so popular and so typified the era

during which he lived, that it was adopted by the American public as true American folk music.

5. Stephen Foster composed one hundred and seventy-five songs, many of which have been forgotten. A number of these were sentimental love songs. His better-known songs are: *Beautiful Dreamer* (1864), *Camptown Races* (1850), *Jeannie With The Light Brown Hair* (1854), *Oh! Susanna* (1848), *My Old Kentucky Home* (1853), and *Old Folks At Home* (1851).

Composer's Main Contribution to the Art of Music:

1. Stephen Collins Foster was one of the most important contributors to the popularity of songs about the Negro. His music portrays the life and work of the Negro during and after the Civil War. Many of his melodies have become a part of the folk culture of America. The popularity of his songs over a period of the past hundred years is a tribute to his success as a composer of folk music.

Suggested Listening:

1. Title: *Songs*
   Performers: Shaw Chorale
   Record No.: RCA LSC-2295
   Grade Level: 4 - 8

2. Title: *My Old Kentucky Home*
   Performers: R.C.A. Victor Orchestra - Vocalist: Marian
                 Anderson
   Record No.: R.C.A. Victor 18314
   Grade Level: 7 - 12

Optional Assignments:

1. After a study, write a report on the Civil War period in American history.

2. Learn one of Stephen Foster's songs and perform it for the class.

3. Stephen Foster played the flute. Do some research on this instrument and give an oral report to the class.

4. Compare a typical composition (song) of this period with the popular song of today. Write a report on this subject.

5. After some research, write a paper on the origin and development of the minstrel shows of this period.

JAMES A. BLAND

Composer: James A. Bland
    Born: Flushing, N.Y. 1854
    Died: Philadelphia, Pa. 1911

Aural Recognition of Themes:
    Composition: *Oh! Dem Golden Slippers* (1878)

General Information about Composer and Compositions:

1. James A. Bland was educated in the public schools of Washington, D.C. After graduation from high school, he attended Howard University where he studied law. He taught himself to play the banjo and sing minstrel songs.

2. His father held an official position in the United States Patent Office in Washington D.C. While studying at Howard University, Bland worked in the House of Representatives as a page boy. In this capacity, he often entertained important people at Washington with minstrel songs, singing and playing his own accompaniments on the banjo.

3. He became a professional entertainer and joined Callender's Original Georgia Minstrels. He began writing songs for minstrel companies, and traveled as a minstrel performer and composer throughout the United States and Europe.

4. He became known as the "Prince of Negro Songwriters." While not having achieved any great measure of popularity in the United States, he became well known in England, giving command performances for Queen Victoria and other members of the Royalty. His two most popular songs are:

286

Oh! Dem Golden Slippers (1878), and *In The Evening By The Moonlight* (1879).

5. Many of James Bland's compositions were not copyrighted and were claimed by other performers. Although he composed almost seven hundred songs, only thirty-seven are credited to him. His song *Carry Me Back To Ol' Virginny* (1878) was given belated official recognition in 1940 by the Virginia State Legislature when they designated it as the official state song.

Composer's Main Contribution to the Art of Music:

1. James A. Bland did much to spread the popularity of American minstrel music throughout Europe. He became known as the "American Ambassador of Minstrel Music" through his performances in many countries of the world. He received official recognition for his compositions both in America and England.

Suggested Listening:

1. Title: *Oh! Dem Golden Slippers*
   Performers: Chorus-Orchestra
   Record No.: Golden Records GLP-53
   Grade Level: 4 - 8

2. Title: *Carry Me Back To Ol' Virginny*
   Performers: Helen Traubel with male quartet and orchestra
   Record No.: Columbia 72104D in Album M-639
   Grade Level: 7 - 12

Optional Assignments:

1. Write a report comparing the lives and music of Stephen Foster and James Bland.

2. Learn to sing or play one of the songs of the composer, James Bland, and perform it for the class.

3. Make a list of the various state songs of the United States.

4. Learn a basic dance used during the composer's lifetime and perform it for the class.

5. Make a comparison of the folk music and folk singers of today with the folk music of James Bland and Stephen Foster. Conduct an oral discussion of this subject with the class.

PATRICK SARSFIELD GILMORE

Composer: Patrick Sarsfield Gilmore
  Born: County Galway, Ireland 1829
  Died: St. Louis, Missouri 1892

Aural Recognition of Themes:
  Composition: *When Johnny Comes Marching Home* (1863)

General Information about Composer and Compositions:

1. While a youth, Patrick Sarsfield Gilmore migrated to Canada where he joined the military band. Around 1855, he came to Salem, Massachusetts to direct a military band. In 1859, he organized the famous Gilmore Band in Boston, Mass.

2. During the Civil War, he was appointed conductor of the Federal Army Band. During this period, he composed the popular song *When Johnny Comes Marching Home* in 1863, for the returning veterans of the Civil War, under the pseudonym of Louis Lambert.

3. He organized two large music festivals, the first of which was called "The National Peace Jubilee" (1869) in Boston, Mass. at which an orchestra of one thousand instrumentalists and a chorus of ten thousand voices performed. The second festival, which took place in Boston, was called "World's Peace Jubilee" (1872), at which an orchestra of two thousand players and a choral group of twenty thousand voices performed.

4. In 1873, Gilmore went to New York City, where he organized

a brass band which became famous for its concert tours throughout the United States and Europe.

5. Gilmore is the originator of the American concert band. He is also the first conductor to organize large band festivals in this country. He arranged numerous works for band, and wrote a study on scales for the cornet. He also wrote a history of the first Peace Jubilee.

Composer's Main Contribution to the Art of Music:

1. Patrick Sarsfield Gilmore is America's first musical messiah of the peace theme. He organized and conducted mammoth peace jubilees in the larger cities of the United States. He was the originator of the American concert band and toured the United States and Europe with his world-famous group.

Suggested Listening:

1. Title: *When Johnny Comes Marching Home*
   Performers: Mormon Tabernacle Choir
   Record No.: Columbia MS-6259
   Grade Level: 4 - 12

Optional Assignments:

1. Make a comparison between the lives and music of John Philip Sousa and Patrick Sarsfield Gilmore. Give an oral report on this subject.

2. Make a study of the history and development of the concert band in the United States up to the present day. Write a report on this topic.

3. Tell the class about an interesting event which took place during the life of the composer.

4. After research, report to the class on the Peace Jubilees that Gilmore conducted in Boston, Mass.

5. Make a study of the world-famous conductors of today and give an oral report to the class.

JOHN PHILIP SOUSA

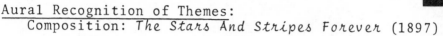

Composer: John Philip Sousa
   Born: Washington, D.C. 1854
   Died: Reading, Pa. 1932

Aural Recognition of Themes:
   Composition: *The Stars And Stripes Forever* (1897)

General Information about Composer and Compositions:

1. John Philip Sousa studied violin and band instruments with John Esputa in Washington, D.C. from 1864 to 1867. At the age of eight, he played the violin for a dancing school. At the age of sixteen, he led an orchestra for a variety theater.

2. In 1867, he played with the Marine Band. During this time he studied theory and composition with G.F. Benkert. In 1872, he became director of a traveling theatrical company. Afterwards he played in an orchestra directed by the composer, Offenbach. Sousa composed the *International Congress Fantasy* for this orchestra which gave the composition its first performance on July 4, 1876.

3. In 1879, he became conductor and composer for the Church Choir Company, for which he wrote the comic opera *The Smugglers*. He also wrote *Our Flirtations* for Mackey's Comedy Company which he conducted.

4. From 1880 to 1892, he was the director of the United States Marine Band. He helped this band achieve world-wide acclaim. In 1892, he formed the famous Sousa Band which traveled around the world.

5. Sousa became known as the "March King" because of the many popular marches he composed. He composed almost one hundred marches. His other works include comic operas, symphonic poems and suites, dances, songs and the oratorio *Messiah Of The Nations*. Sousa also published two books, one on military band instruments and the other entitled *Marching Along*.

Composer's Main Contribution to the Art of Music:

1. John Philip Sousa became world famous as a composer of marches and as a conductor of the symphonic band. As the director of the Sousa Band, he toured the world and brought world wide recognition and acclaim to American band music. His textbooks on military bands are widely used as a guide by band directors of the present day.

Suggested Listening:

1. Title: *El Capitan*
   Performers: Band of the Grenadier Guards
   Record No.: London SP-44103
   Grade Level: 4 - 8

2. Title: *Semper Fidelis*
   Performers: Band of the Grenadier Guards
   Record No.: London SP-44103
   Grade Level: 7 - 12

Optional Assignments:

1. Make a study of military bands and their music from early times to the present day, and write a report on this subject.

2. John Philip Sousa made the United States Marine Band one of the world's best musical organizations. Write to Washington, D.C. and collect information about this famous band. Report your findings to the class.

3. Play a recording of a composition by the composer for the class, and give an oral report on the selection being played.

4. The sousaphone was named after Sousa. Do some research on the history and development of this instrument and write a report on this topic.

5. Lead a class discussion on the composer's life and music.

LEROY ANDERSON

<u>Composer</u>: Leroy Anderson
<u>Born</u>: Cambridge Mass. 1908

<u>Aural Recognition of Themes</u>:

Purchase at your local music store one or more of the following piano sheet music arrangements of Leroy Anderson's compositions. You may play the main theme with the written accompaniment, or you may supply your own accompaniment using the chords notated above the melody line (although the chord symbols are written for guitar, they are easily adapted to the piano). Play each theme of the composition several times in order to facilitate recognition.

Blue Tango

The Syncopated Clock

Sleigh Ride

<u>General Information about Composer and Compositions</u>:

1. Leroy Anderson came from a musical family. His mother was a church organist, and Leroy received his first lessons in music from her. He attended the public schools of Cambridge, Massachusetts, and graduated from Cambridge High and Latin School.

2. He attended the music school at Harvard University where he studied music under Walter Piston and Georges Enesco. While a student at Harvard University, he conducted the Harvard Band. He graduated in 1929.

3. Anderson taught music, and played professionally for a short period; then he was appointed director of the band at Harvard for three years. During the years 1929 to 1935, he served as choir director and organist at a Congregational Church.

4. In 1935, he established himself as an independent composer and arranger. He wrote and orchestrated music for the Boston Pops Orchestra, and received much encouragement from the conductor of this orchestra, Arthur Fiedler who helped popularize his compositions.

5. Leroy Anderson composed in a symphonic jazz vein. On a simpler scale, his style reflects that of George Gershwin. His *Blue Tango*, an instrumental piece without lyrics, was the first song of this type that achieved first place on the American Hit Parade of 1952. Some of his other successful selections are: *Fiddle Faddle, Jazz Pizzicato, Jazz Legato, The Typewriter, The Syncopated Clock,* and *Sleigh Ride.*

Composer's Main Contribution to the Art of Music:

1. Leroy Anderson is recognized as a successful composer of semi-classical music. He has attempted to create a stylistic fusion of serious music and the popular song of today. In doing this, he is developing the style of composition which Gershwin originated. His instrumental selections have received world wide recognition and are part of the standard repertoire of many orchestras.

Suggested Listening:

1. Title: *Syncopated Clock*
   Performers: Boston Pops Orchestra - Fiedler
   Record No.: RCA Victor LSC-2638
   Grade Level: 4 - 8

2. Title: *Irish Suite - The Girl I Left Behind Me*
   Performers: National Symphony Orchestra - Mitchell
   Record No.: Victor LE-1007, Adventures In Music
   Grade Level: 7 - 12

Optional Assignments:

1. Leroy Anderson attended the Harvard College of Music. Write or apply at this school for information about its curriculum of studies and prepare a written report.

2. Anderson was an associate of Arthur Fiedler, the conductor of the Boston Pops Orchestra. After research, present an oral report on the life and activities of this conductor and his orchestra to the class.

3. If you play a musical instrument, select a composition of the composer and play it for the class.

4. Write a report on the life and music of Leroy Anderson and George Gershwin, making a comparison of their styles.

5. Play a recording of a work by Leroy Anderson. Give an oral report, and conduct a class discussion on the selection being played.

VICTOR HERBERT

Composer: Victor Herbert
  Born: Dublin, Ireland 1859
  Died: New York, N.Y. 1924

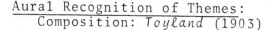

Aural Recognition of Themes:
  Composition: *Toyland* (1903)

General Information about Composer and Compositions:

1. Victor Herbert's mother was a pianist, and he received his first piano lessons from her. He attended the Stuttgart Conservatory of Music in Germany, where he received an excellent musical education. He studied the cello and became a virtuoso cellist, performing with German and Austrian orchestras. He composed the following works at this time: *Suite* (1887) for cello and orchestra, and *Concerto* (1887) for cello and orchestra.

2. In 1886, he married a German opera star, Therese Foerster, who was hired by the Metropolitan Opera Company in New York to play the title role in Karl Goldmark's *The Queen Of Sheba*. Victor Herbert played the cello in the Opera Orchestra.

3. He played cello in many major symphony orchestras in the United States. He became conductor of the 22nd Regimental Band, and was later appointed conductor of the Pittsburgh Symphony Orchestra, 1898-1904. During this period he composed several excellent works, among which are: *American Fantasia* (1909) for orchestra, and *Natoma* (1911), an opera.

4. He is considered one of the best composers of operettas in American history. He had an amazing genius for creating hundreds of beautiful melodies which could express

the whole gamut of human emotions, from gaiety to sadness, from love to turbulence. Some of his most beautiful songs are: *Ah, Sweet Mystery Of Life* (1910), *Thine Alone* (1917), and *Italian Street Song* (1910).

5. In 1949, a motion picture biography, *The Great Victor Herbert*, was made by Paramount Pictures in Hollywood. Many of his operettas have been made into films. Some of his most popular operettas are: *Babes In Toyland* (1903), *Naughty Marietta* (1910), and *Sweethearts* (1913).

Composer's Main Contribution to the Art of Music:

1. Victor Herbert was America's first composer of operettas. He achieved great success in this art form. His operettas are still performed by many amateur and professional stage companies throughout the United States. The beautiful melodies of his operettas are part of the standard listening repertoire of the American public.

Suggested Listening:

1. Title: *Music Of Victor Herbert*
   Performers: Boston Pops Orchestra - Fiedler
   Record No.: R.C.A. Victor LM-2677
   Grade Level: 4 - 8

2. Title: *Babes in Toyland*
   Performers: Vocal-Instrumental
   Record No.: Golden Records LP-78
   Grade Level: 7 - 12

Optional Assignments:

1. Victor Herbert was a virtuoso cellist. The most famous cellist in the world was Pablo Casals. He died in 1973. Do some research on the life and musical activities of Pablo Casals and write a report on this subject.

2. Make a list of composers of operettas, and cite their most famous works.

3. Make a study of a popular instrument used during the composer's lifetime and write a report on this topic.

4. Draw or paint a picture of the composer and present it for bulletin board display.

5. Tell the class about an historical event (ex. World War I) which took place during the composer's lifetime.

RUDOLPH FRIML

Composer: Rudolph Friml
   Born: Prague, Czechoslavia 1879
   Died: Hollywood, California 1972

Aural Recognition of Themes:

   Purchase at your local music store one or more of the
following piano sheet music arrangements of Rudolph Friml's
compositions. You may play the main theme with the written
accompaniment, or you may supply your own accompaniment
using the chords notated above the melody line (although
the chord symbols are written for guitar, they are easily
adapted to the piano). Play each theme of the composition
several times in order to facilitate recognition.

   Song of the Vagabonds (1925)

   Giannina Mia (1912)

   March of the Musketeers (1928)

General Information about Composer and Compositions:

1. Rudolph Friml studied at the Prague Conservatory from
   1900 to 1903 with Josef Jiranek and Anton Dvorak. He
   studied piano seriously and soon became a virtuoso
   pianist. He toured Europe and America as piano accompanist
   for the renowned violinist Jan Kubelik.

2. In 1906 Friml came to America as a piano virtuoso. He gave
   many solo concerts and also appeared as soloist with most
   of the major symphony orchestras in the United States. He
   gave the world premiere of his own *Piano Concerto* (1904)
   with the New York Symphony Orchestra.

3. After many years as a pianist and composer of songs, he
   was called upon to compose an operetta which Victor
   Herbert had started. The result of this was *The Firefly*
   (1912) which became an outstanding success.

4. He composed the music for the *Ziegfield Follies of 1921,
   1923, 1924, 1925*. His operettas were made into movies
   and Friml went to Hollywood to supervise their production.
   Some of his most famous operettas are: *Rosemarie* (1924),
   The Firefly (1912), *Three Musketeers* (1928), and *The
   Vagabond King* (1925).

5. Rudolph Friml also composed many piano selections, small instrumental works, and many songs. Some of his most popular vocal selections are: *Indian Love Call* (1924). *Only A Rose* (1925), and *Sympathy* (1912).

Composer's Main Contribution to the Art of Music:

1. Rudolph Friml created the musical play format which was the prototype of our contemporary Broadway musical. Many of his light operas were produced in Hollywood and distributed as film entertainment throughout the world. He was also acclaimed as a virtuoso pianist and performed on the concert stage in many countries of the world.

Suggested Listening:

1. Title: *The Music of Rudolph Friml*
   Performers: Orchestral Music
   Record No.: London PS-166
   Grade Level: 4 - 8

2. Title: *The Vagabond King*
   Performers: Lanza
   Record No.: RCA LSC-2509
   Grade Level: 7 - 12

Optional Assignments:

1. Make a study and comparison of the music and lives of the operetta composers Rudolph Friml, Victor Herbert, and Sigmund Romberg. Present an oral report to the class.

2. Make a notebook dealing with the life and music of the composer consisting of pictures, newspaper and magazine articles, concert programs, thematic excerpts, original illustrations and written reports.

3. If you play a musical instrument or sing, select a composition of the composer and perform it for the class.

4. Tell the class about an historical or cultural event which took place during the lifetime of the composer.

5. After a listening session, create an imaginative illustration of a scene from the *March of the Musketeers*. The best art illustration will be displayed on the school bulletin board.

SIGMUND ROMBERG

Composer: Sigmund Romberg
    Born: Szeged, Hungary 1887
    Died: New York, N.Y. 1951

Aural Recognition of Themes:

    Purchase at your local music store one or more of the following piano sheet music arrangements of Sigmund Romberg's compositions. You may play the main theme with the written accompaniment, or you may supply your own accompaniment using the chords notated above the melody line (although the chord symbols are written for guitar, they are easily adapted to the piano). Play each theme of the composition several times in order to facilitate recognition.

      Stout Hearted Men (1928)

      One Alone (1924)

      Auf Wiedersehn (1915)

General Information about Composer and Compositions:

1. Sigmund Romberg's father, a pianist, taught his son to play the piano at an early age. At the age of seven, Sigmund took violin lessons. He also studied music theory, harmony and counterpoint in Vienna. He also attended the University of Bucharest for training as a civil engineer and later served in the Austrian Army.

2. In 1909, he came to America where he was employed as a musician in the various Hungarian restaurants of New York City. He formed his own orchestra and played at Bustanoby's Restaurant in New York for a long period of time.

3. He was commissioned by J.J. Shubert to write the musical score for the first Winter Garden Show *The Whirl of the World* (1914). It was so successful that he composed the musical scores to many future productions for this group. In 1929 he went to Hollywood to write music for several musical productions.

4. He made concert tours of the United States giving a total of at least seven hundred concerts. He also appeared as

guest conductor of many symphony orchestras in the United States including Toscanini's N.B.C. Symphony Orchestra in New York.

5. Sigmund Romberg composed over seventy operettas. The most popular of these are: *The Desert Song* (1926), *Maytime* (1917), *The Student Prince* (1924), and *The New Moon* (1928).

Composer's Main Contribution to the Art of Music:

1. Sigmund Romberg was a very prodigious composer of operettas. His operettas are very popular today and many of the songs of these plays have become standards in the repertoire of American popular music. He also composed music for many movie productions which are still shown today throughout the world.

Suggested Listening:

1. Title: *The Student Prince*
   Performers: Roberta Peters, Jan Peerce, Giorgio Tozzi
   Record No.: Columbia OS-2380
   Grade Level: 4 - 8

2. Title: *The Desert Song*
   Performers: Hockridge and Bronhill
   Record No.: Angel S-35905
   Grade Level: 7 - 12

Optional Assignments:

1. Play a recording of one of Sigmund Romberg's compositions for the class, and conduct a discussion of the music.

2. Make a list of interesting facts about the composer and his music. Write a composition about one of these facts.

3. Construct a drawing of the string instruments of the orchestra.

4. After some research on the history of operetta, prepare a written report about it.

5. Present an oral report to the class about the performance of an opera or operetta which you have heard or seen.

JEROME KERN

Composer: Jerome Kern
   Born: New York, N.Y. 1885
   Died: New York, N.Y. 1945

Aural Recognition of Themes:

    Purchase at your local music store one or more of the
following piano sheet music arrangements of Jerome Kern's
compositions. You may play the main theme with the written
accompaniment, or you may supply your own accompaniment
using the chords notated above the melody line (although
the chord symbols are written for guitar, they are easily
adapted to the piano). Play each theme of the composition
several times in order to facilitate recognition.

     Make Believe (1927)

     Smoke Gets in Your Eyes (1933)

     Look for the Silver Lining (1920)

General Information about Composer and Compositions:

1. Jerome Kern took private piano lessons as a youth and
   later attended the New York College of Music. He was one
   of the many composers of this period who received their
   most intensive experience playing and writing songs for
   the publishers of Tin Pan Alley.

2. In 1903 he spent a year in London, England composing
   songs for Charles Frohman, a show producer. Kern's big-
   gest song hit was *Mr. Chamberlain* from the production
   The School Girl. In 1904, he worked as a song plugger
   and pianist for many publishers in Tin Pan Alley.

3. From 1905 until his death, he maintained a close friend-
   ship and business arrangement with Harms Publishing Company of Tin Pan Alley. When he was first employed by
   this company, his job consisted of selling sheet music
   and playing songs on the piano for demonstration purposes
   in Five-And-Ten Cent Stores.

4. From 1904 to 1912, he wrote almost one hundred songs for
   various Broadway musicals. His first complete score *The
   Girl from Utah* (1914), was a great success on Broadway
   and featured one of his prettiest songs *They Didn't
   Believe Me*. His most popular Broadway musical was the

production *Show Boat* produced in 1927. One of the songs
from this show *Ol' Man River* contains the qualities of
an American folk song. The production *Show Boat* has been
used three times for motion pictures by Hollywood. He
also wrote other songs for motion pictures.

5. Some of Jerome Kern's other well-known Broadway Musicals
and songs are: *Sunny* (1925 - popular song from this show:
Who), *Roberta* (1933 - song: *Smoke Gets in Your Eyes*),
and *Music in the Air* (1932 - song: *The Song Is You*).

Composer's Main Contribution to the Art of Music:

1. Jerome Kern was one of the most successful composers of
music for Broadway productions in the world. His melodies
which have become an integral part of the American popular music repertoire are the best of this art form. Their
success is due to his creative ability and the unusual
harmonic and rhythmic treatment which his works display.

Suggested Listening:

1. Title: *Ol' Man River*
   Performers: Allers
   Record No.: RCA LSO-1126
   Grade Level: 4 - 8

2. Title: *Roberta*
   Performers: Roberts and Cassidy
   Record No.: Columbia SP-COS 2530
   Grade Level: 7 - 12

Optional Assignments:

1. Jerome Kern wrote songs for English stage productions.
   Make a study of the English stage shows and write a
   report on this subject.

2. If you have occasion to go to New York, visit Tin Pan
   Alley, interview the various publishers and song writers,
   and prepare an oral report on your findings for the class.

3. Draw a picture of the "Show Boat" as you imagine it in
   the musical play.

4. Try to compose a popular song, and either sing or play
   it for the class.

5. After listening to a composition by the composer, conduct
   a class discussion about the composer and his music.

IRVING BERLIN

Composer: Irving Berlin
    Born: Temun, Russia 1888

Aural Recognition of Themes:
    Composition: *God Bless America* (1918)

General Information about Composer and Compositions:

1. Irving Berlin was born into a poor family in Russia. His father was a rabbi, who moved with his family to the United States when Irving was only four years old. Irving's father died when he was only eight years old, and although he wanted to take music lessons, he was unable to afford this luxury. He learned to play the piano by ear, but never became an accomplished pianist. To this day he can play only in one key, the key of F sharp. He possessed a natural ability to create beautiful melodies and enchanting lyrics.

2. As a boy he sang on street corners and local bars of the bowery for pennies. He worked as a song plugger for the music publishers of Tin Pan Alley. Since World War I, he has been the owner of a very successful music publishing company in New York. He began writing lyrics in collaboration with melody writers. His first successful song *Marie from Sunny Italy* was published in 1907.

3. In 1910, Irving Berlin wrote the lyrics and performed the songs of the musical production *Up and Down Broadway*. He began to compose his own melodies in 1911 and achieved much success with ragtime songs including the still popular *Alexander's Ragtime Band*. He wrote the music and lyrics to many other memorable songs: *Always* (1925), *The Song Is Ended* (1927), and *How Deep Is the Ocean* (1936).

4. He became world famous during World War I for his army show, *Yip, Yip, Yaphank* which featured the very popular song: *Oh, How I Hate To Get Up In The Morning*. Later on he composed the music and lyrics for many successful Broadway shows. Some of the best known of these are: *Annie Get Your Gun* (1946), *Miss Liberty* (1949), *Call Me Madam* (1950), and *Mr. President* (1962).

5. During World War II, Irving Berlin wrote and produced the popular show *This Is the Army* (1942). He received the Medal of Merit from the United States government for this great contribution to the war effort. In 1954 President Eisenhower presented him with a special Congressional Medal as an award for composing the song which has become our second national anthem *God Bless America*. Some of his other popular songs are: *Give Me Your Tired, Your Poor* (1949), *Count Your Blessings*, *Sayonara*, *Russian Lullaby* (1927).

Composer's Main Contribution to the Art of Music:

1. Irving Berlin is one of the most renowned composers of popular music living today. His patriotic songs are played and sung at almost every public gathering. Some of his songs have become the accepted musical material for the commemoration of national and festive holidays.

Suggested Listening:

1. Title: *God Bless America*
   Performers: Robert Shaw Chorale
   Record No.: RCA LSC-2662
   Grade Level: 4 - 8

2. Title: *Give Me Your Tired, Your Poor*
   Performers: Mormon Tabernacle Choir
   Record No.: Columbia MS-6419
   Grade Level: 7 - 12

Optional Assignments:

1. The lyrics of the song *Give Me Your Tired, Your Poor* are inscribed on the Statue of Liberty. After some research, make a report to the class about the origin and meaning of these words.

2. Five prominent composers of Tin Pan Alley and Broadway, New York have become known as the "Mighty Five". They are Irving Berlin, Jerome Kern, Cole Porter, George Gershwin, and Richard Rodgers. Give an oral report on each of these musicians.

3. Perform a selection by the composer for the class.

4. Prepare a biographical sketch on the life and music of Irving Berlin.

5. Draw or paint a picture of the composer.

COLE PORTER

<u>Composer</u>: Cole Porter
  <u>Born</u>: Peru, Indiana 1893
  <u>Died</u>: Santa Monica, California 1964

<u>Aural Recognition of Themes</u>:

   Purchase at your local music store one or more of the
following piano sheet music arrangements of Cole Porter's
compositions. You may play the main theme with the written
accompaniment, or you may supply your own accompaniment
using the chords notated above the melody line (although
the chord symbols are written for guitar, they are easily
adapted to the piano). Play each theme of the composition
several times in order to facilitate recognition.

   Begin the Beguine (1935)

   Night and Day (1932)

   Don't Fence Me In (1944)

<u>General Information about Composer and Compositions</u>:

1. Cole Porter studied violin and piano at an early age. He
    began composing at the age of ten and wrote an operetta.
    At the age of eleven, he wrote piano pieces, one of which
    was published. While pursuing his education at Yale
    University, he composed the still famous *Yale Bull-Dog
    Song*. After graduating from Yale, he attended Harvard
    Law School for one year.

2. Porter began an adventurous episode in his life when he
    joined the French Foreign Legion in North Africa. At the
    outbreak of World War I, he was transferred to duties at
    the Officers School in Paris, France. Here, he continued
    to write songs and he entertained lavishly.

3. Around 1920, he studied composition with the well-known
    composer Vincent d'Indy at the Schola Cantorum in Venice.
    Having been born into a wealthy family, he had the finan-
    cial resources that enabled him to live extravagantly,
    traveling from the United States to France and Italy, and
    leading a gay and carefree existence. During this period
    he continued composing popular music and lyrics.

4. Porter was a fine composer of beautiful, sensual, and
    exciting melodies. His lyric talent is manifested in his
    sophisticated style in which there is a blend of text and

melody, which still retains a popular appeal. Some of his most popular Broadway musicals are: *Anything Goes* (1934), *Kiss Me Kate* (1948), and *Can-Can* (1953).

5. He was a prodigious composer of popular hit songs. One of his hit songs *Night and Day* was the title and theme of a biographical movie of his life. Some of his other hit songs are: *Don't Fence Me In* (1944), *In the Still of the Night* (1937), *Begin the Beguine* (1935), and *True Love* (1946).

Composer's Main Contribution to the Art of Music:

1. Cole Porter is renowned as one of the most successful composers of Broadway musicals. He was a serious student of composition and his songs contain complex harmonies that were considered unique in the musical comedy style. His productions and songs are performed frequently throughout the United States and many other countries of the world.

Suggested Listening:

1. Title: *Night and Day*
   Performers: Chacksfield and Orchestra
   Record No.: London SP-44185
   Grade Level: 4 - 8

2. Title: *Begin the Beguine*
   Performers: Chacksfield and Orchestra
   Record No.: London SP-44185
   Grade Level: 7 - 12

Optional Assignments:

1. Cole Porter joined the French Foreign Legion. Write a report on the history of this famous fighting organization.

2. If you have seen the biographical movie of Cole Porter's life, give an oral report to the class on this subject.

3. Cole Porter was born into a wealthy family. Tell the class about other composers who came from a wealthy family environment.

4. Porter was able to play the violin and piano. If you play either of these instruments, perform a solo for the class and give a talk about your instrument.

5. Make a biographical sketch of the composer's life and present it to the class.

DUKE ELLINGTON

Composer: Duke "Edward Kennedy" Ellington
   Born: Washington, D.C. 1899

Aural Recognition of Themes:

   Purchase at your local music store one or more of the
following piano sheet music arrangements of Duke Ellington's
compositions. You may play the main theme with the written
accompaniment, or you may supply your own accompaniment
using the chords notated above the melody line (although
the chord symbols are written for guitar, they are easily
adapted to the piano). Play each theme of the composition
several times in order to facilitate recognition.

   Mood Indigo (1930)

   Sophisticated Lady (1932)

   Take The A Train (1941)

General Information about Composer and Compositions:

1. Duke Ellington, the famous jazz pianist and composer,
   began to study piano at the age of seven. He attended
   Armstrong High School in Washington D.C. where he had a
   keen interest in music, drawing and art. His father was a
   butler in Washington, his work included some service in
   the White House. The name "Duke" was given to Ellington
   at the age of eight by a neighbor named Ralph Green.

2. It was during his high school days that Duke developed
   his piano playing and arranging technique. At this time he
   was studying music both in school and privately. He also
   developed a zealous interest in ragtime piano and studied
   this style in an intricate manner. Duke began playing for
   parties during his high school years and became very successful. He also composed his first piece entitled, *Soda
   Fountain Rag* during this time.

3. Duke married his childhood sweetheart, Edna Thompson, in
   1918. He went on to New York in 1922 to join Wilbur
   Sweatman. This was the beginning of a great career which
   later brought Ellington to all parts of the world.

4. Ellington has written many compositions, including several
   suites. The suite *Togo Brava* was written with the African
   nation Togo in mind. He also wrote the music for the film
   Anatomy of a Murder (1959).

5. Duke's greatest contribution to the field of jazz has been in the capacity of an orchestra leader. His band has always been well established and stable, with a group of veteran players. Duke has been very successful with his recordings and films. He is also famous for his live concerts throughout the world.

Composer's Main Contribution to the Art of Music:

1. Duke Ellington has contributed more to jazz, as part of our culture, than any other musician of our time. As a composer and orchestra conductor, he has presented many innovative techniques that have made jazz a permanent part of the American musical scene.

Suggested Listening:

1. Title: *Greatest Hits*
   Performers: Duke Ellington
   Record No.: Harmony H-30566
   Grade Level: 4 - 8

2. Title: *Golden Broom and the Green Apple*
   Performers: Ellington, Cincinnati Symphony
   Record No.: Decca 710176
   Grade Level: 7 - 12

Optional Assignments:

1. Do some research on the life and compositions of Duke Ellington. Give an oral report on your findings to the class.

2. If you play an instrument, select a composition by the composer and play it for the class.

3. Write a report on a black musician or composer.

4. Play a recording of a composition by the composer for the class, and give an oral report on the selection being played.

5. Make a notebook dealing with the life and music of Duke Ellington. Include pictures, newspaper and magazine articles, concert programs, thematic excerpts and original illustrations.

RICHARD RODGERS

Composer: Richard Rodgers
    Born: Averne, Long Island, N.Y. 1902

Aural Recognition of Themes:

   Purchase at your local music store one or more of the
following piano sheet music arrangements of Richard Rodgers'
compositions. You may play the main theme with the written
accompaniment, or you may supply your own accompaniment
using the chords notated above the melody line (although
the chord symbols are written for guitar, they are easily
adapted to the piano). Play each theme of the composition
several times in order to facilitate recognition.

   You'll Never Walk Alone (1945)

   Do - Re - Mi (1959)

   It's a Grand Night for Singing (1945)

General Information about Composer and Compositions:

1. Richard Rodgers began to play and study piano at the age
   of four. At the age of nine, he began writing songs. He
   had a compulsive interest in Broadway musicals, and was
   especially attracted to the music of Jerome Kern. Most of
   his spare time and allowance money was spent on atten-
   dance at Broadway musical productions.

2. At the age of fifteen, he began to write scores for
   several amateur productions. While attending Columbia
   College, he and lyricist Lorenz Hart wrote the score for
   the school varsity show. Rodgers and Hart collaborated
   in the production of musicals for almost twenty-five
   years. In 1923, Rodgers attended the Institute of Musical
   Art in order to further his musical talent.

3. Some of the musicals and songs which were produced by
   Rodgers and Hart are: *The Girl Friend* (1928 - popular
   song from this show: *The Blue Room*), *A Connecticut Yankee*
   (1928 - song: *My Heart Stood Still*), and *Spring is Here*
   (1929 - song: *With a Song in My Heart*).

4. In 1943 Oscar Hammerstein II, a celebrated lyricist and
   librettist joined Rodgers and they collaborated until
   the death of Hammerstein in 1960. This writing team made

an important innovation in musical productions, by integrating the solo songs, background music, dance routines and production numbers with the play or story.

5. Rodgers and Hammerstein produced the following popular Broadway musicals: *Oklahoma* (1943), *Carousel* (1945), *South Pacific* (1949), *The King and I* (1951), and *The Sound of Music* (1959). Richard Rodgers also composed the music for two television series concerned with World War II: *Victory at Sea*, and *The Valiant Years - Winston Churchill* (1960).

Composer's Main Contribution to the Art of Music:

1. Richard Rodgers has an amazing gift for composing songs to fit any character or situation required. He has the ability to create beautiful melodies spontaneously with the result that many of his songs have become part of the standard repertoire of professional musicians and vocalists all over the world.

Suggested Listening:

1. Title: *Oklahoma, Carousel, King and I*
   Performers: Movie Soundtrack Cast
   Record No.: Capitol STCL 1790
   Grade Level: 4 - 8

2. Title: *Sound of Music*
   Performers: Movie Soundtrack Cast
   Record No.: RCA LSO D-2005
   Grade Level: 7 - 12

Optional Assignments:

1. Create and perform a dance to the music of Rodgers' Ballet *Slaughter on Tenth Avenue*.

2. Prepare a written report about the two television series *Victory at Sea* and *The Valiant Years*.

3. After doing research, prepare an outline on the origin of the story of *The Sound of Music* and present an oral report to the class.

4. After a study, write a report on the life of Oscar Hammerstein, the lyricist.

5. Learn to sing or play a selection by Richard Rodgers and perform it for the class.

FREDERICK LOEWE

<u>Composer</u>: Frederick Loewe
     Born: Vienna, Austria 1904

<u>Aural Recognition of Themes:</u>

Purchase at your local music store one or more of the following piano sheet music arrangements of Frederick Loewe's compositions. You may play the main theme with the written accompaniment, or you may supply your own accompaniment using the chords notated above the melody line (although the chord symbols are written for guitar, they are easily adapted to the piano). Play each theme of the composition several times in order to facilitate recognition.

   I Could Have Danced All Night (1956)

   Camelot (1960)

   The Heather on the Hill (1947)

<u>General Information about Composer and Compositions:</u>

1. Frederick Loewe's father was an accomplished operetta singer. Frederick studied piano with two famous pianists, Ferruccio Busoni and Eugene D'Albert. At the age of thirteen, he appeared as soloist with the Berlin Symphony Orchestra. At the age of nineteen, he was awarded the coveted Hollaender Medal for piano virtuosity.

2. In 1924, he came to the United States with the hope of earning a living as a piano virtuoso. When these aspirations proved fruitless, he abandoned music and earned his living at various odd jobs, including boxing, punching cattle, truck driver, and other jobs. He finally returned to music, and accepted playing engagements in the night clubs of New York.

3. While playing New York night clubs, he performed many of his own compositions which attracted the attention of the lyricist, Alan Jay Lerner. These two talented men formed a team that has produced many successful Broadway musicals. Their first musical *Brigadoon,* produced in 1947, met with great success. The story of this musical has a setting in Scotland, and beautiful songs from this show included *The Heather on the Hill,* a musical adaptation of this setting.

4. In 1956, they wrote the musical *My Fair Lady* which they adapted from George Bernard Shaw's *Pygmalion*. This musical is one of the most popular Broadway shows ever written. Many of the songs from this show are still popular today: *I Could Have Danced All Night*, *On the Street Where You Live*, *Get Me to the Church on Time*, and *With a Little Bit of Luck*.

5. Their next venture was the very successful musical *Gigi* written for screen production in 1959. In 1960, they wrote the Broadway musical *Camelot*, a musical version of King Arthur and the Knights of the Round Table. This musical production has been performed by many professional and amateur groups. Some of the hit songs of this show are: *If Ever I Would Leave You*, *Camelot*, and *How to Handle a Woman*.

Composer's Main Contribution to the Art of Music:

1. Frederick Loewe was a foreign born composer who received much of his music training in Europe under the tutelage of composers of serious music. Many of his compositions are modern musical versions of subjects taken from classical literature. This style of composition serves as an inspiration to contemporary composers of this music form.

Suggested Listening:

1. Title: *My Fair Lady*
   Performers: Movie Soundtrack Cast
   Record No.: Columbia KOS-2600
   Grade Level: 4 - 8

2. Title: *Camelot*
   Performers: Original Broadway Cast
   Record No.: Columbia OS-2031
   Grade Level: 7 - 12

Optional Assignments:

1. After some research, write a historical review of musical comedy in the United States.

2. Make a study of musical comedy and comic opera, then give an oral report to the class, comparing these two art forms.

3. If you play a musical instrument, learn one of the songs composed by Frederick Loewe, and perform it for the class.

4. Consult with the Art, Music, Drama, and Home Economics Departments in your school. Write a report on the activities required of each department for the production of a Broadway musical.

5. Give an oral report to the class on a performance of a musical comedy which you have recently attended.

LEONARD BERNSTEIN

<u>Composer</u>: Leonard Bernstein
   <u>Born</u>: Lawrence, Mass. 1918

<u>Aural Recognition of Themes</u>:

   Purchase at your local music store one or more of the
following piano sheet music arrangements of Leonard
Bernstein's compositions. You may play the main theme with
the written accompaniment, or you may supply your own accompaniment using the chords notated above the melody line
(although the chord symbols are written for guitar, they
are easily adapted to the piano). Play each theme of the
composition several times in order to facilitate recognition.

   Tonight (1957)

   I Feel Pretty (1957)

   Maria (1957)

<u>General Information about Composer and Compositions</u>:

1. Shortly after Leonard Bernstein was born, his family
   moved from Lawrence to Boston. When he was very young,
   he played piano by ear. He taught himself to play many
   popular and concert pieces. He attended Boston Latin
   School where he produced and directed shows as a student.
   He graduated in 1935.

2. He attended the Harvard University School of Music where
   he studied composition with Walter Piston and Aaron
   Copland, who influenced him in his decision to become a
   composer. He also studied piano with Helen Coates and
   Heinrich Gebhard. On graduating from Harvard in 1939, he
   attended Curtis Institute of Music in Philadelphia, where
   he studied conducting and orchestration.

3. In 1942, he became assistant to Serge Koussevitzsky at
   the Berkshire Festival School in Tanglewood, Mass. In
   1943, he became assistant conductor of the New York
   Philharmonic Symphony Orchestra and is presently the
   conductor of this famous orchestra. He has appeared as
   piano-virtuoso in many concerts and has conducted many
   well-known orchestras in the United States and Europe.

312

4. From 1951 to 1956, he was professor of music at Brandeis University in Waltham, Massachusetts. His work with children as a lecturer and demonstrator of music has gained him considerable esteem. He produced and directed the very informative and popular *Omnibus* series of lectures in music on television. His book *The Joy of Music* published in 1959, is a very popular work on music appreciation.
5. Leonard Bernstein's music contains many of the folk idioms of America. This is probably due to the influence of Aaron Copland. His diversified compositions include: symphonies, opera, incidental theatre music, ballets, choral works, chamber music, film scores, piano pieces, and songs. He is also well-known for his Broadway musicals: *On the Town* (1944), *Peter Pan* (1950), *Wonderful Town* (1953), and *West Side Story* (1957).

Composer's Main Contribution to the Art of Music:

1. Leonard Bernstein is known as "the salesman of serious music". Through his amazing skill as a piano virtuoso, conductor, lecturer, author and composer, he has brought serious music into the lives of millions of people.

Suggested Listening:

1. Title: *Music of Leonard Bernstein*
   Performers: Kostelanetz
   Record No.: Columbia M-30304
   Grade Level: 4 - 8

2. Title: *Symphony No. 3 (Kaddish)*
   Performers: New York Philharmonic, Camerata Singers,
              Columbus Boys Choir - Bernstein
   Record No.: Columbia KS-6605
   Grade Level: 7 - 12

Optional Assignments:

1. Leonard Bernstein is the conductor of the New York Philharmonic Symphony Orhcestra. After research, write a paper on the history of this orchestra.
2. Make a comparison of the contributions of Leonard Bernstein and George Gershwin and give an oral report to the class on this subject.
3. Learn one of the songs from the musical *West Side Story*, and sing or play this song for the class.
4. Read Bernstein's book *The Joy of Music* and write a book report on it.
5. After some research, write a report on the musical activities of the Berkshire Festival School at Tanglewood.

BURT BACHARACH

Composer: Burt Bacharach
    Born: Kansas City, Missouri 1928

Aural Recognition of Themes:

Purchase at your local music store one or more of the following piano sheet music arrangements of Burt Bacharach's compositions. You may play the main theme with the written accompaniment, or you may supply your own accompaniment using the chords notated above the melody line (although the chord symbols are written for guitar, they are easily adapted to the piano). Play each theme of the composition several times in order to facilitate recognition.

    Raindrops Keep Falling On My Head (1969)

    Alfie (1966)

    What The World Needs Now Is Love (1965)

General Information about Composer and Compositions:

1. Burt Bacharach's mother initiated his interest in music by arranging for Burt to take piano lessons. His father, Bert Bacharach, is the nationally famous syndicated columnist. Until he joined the local band in Forest Hills, New York, Burt was interested in playing football. Bop-Jazz was his main interest during his teen years, and he launched his professional career as a jazz pianist, in the middle part of the 1940's, on a USO tour of army hospitals.

2. Burt was drafted into the army in 1950. Prior to this he spent three years studying at several colleges, including McGill University in Montreal, New School for Social Research in New York, and the Mannes School of Music. He also studied for a while with Darius Milhaud and Henry Cowell.

3. In 1952, after Bacharach's discharge from the army, he spent some time playing piano in leading night clubs in New York. It was during this time that he met his music collaborator, Hal David. Burt has been piano accompanist for many famous people, including Vic Damone, Ames Brothers, Polly Bergen, Steve Lawrence and Imogene Coca.

4. The Bacharach and David team, as song writers, began in the early 1950's. They have had a very successful and fruitful association, composing one hit after another. They have written over two hundred songs. Their work, as song writers for films, began in 1963 with the movie, *What's New, Pussycat?*. They were firmly established as movie song writers in 1966 with the title song of the film *Alfie*.

5. In recent years, Bacharach has become nationally famous and popular through his television specials. Bacharach and David are prolific writers, who have written a pro-digious number of songs. Many of their songs have been recorded by leading artists and groups. Burt has been called this generation's Irving Berlin and George Gershwin.

Composer's Main Contribution to the Art of Music:

1. Burt Bacharach is one of the most successful composers of popular songs and Broadway musicals. His compositions hold a prominent place in the musical repertoire of the American people. His success is due to the imaginative use of me-lodic and harmonic innovations.

Suggested Listening:

1. Title: *Burt Bacharach*
   Performers: Burt Bacharach
   Record No.: A&M 3501
   Grade Level: 4 - 8

2. Title: *Promises, Promises*
   Performers: Original Cast
   Record No.: United Artists 9902
   Grade Level: 7 - 12

Optional Assignments:

1. Burt Bacharach performed as a popular pianist during the 1940's and 1950's. Do some research and write on the qualifications necessary for this type of work.

2. Perform a selection by the composer for the class.

3. Make a study of his career as a composer for films and prepare an oral report on this topic.

4. Bacharach has been called this generation's Irving Berlin and George Gershwin. Compare the three composers.

5. Hal David wrote the lyrics to their songs. Write a report on the life of this lyricist.

THE BEATLES

Composers:

John Lennon
   Born: Liverpool, England 1940

Paul McCartney
   Born: Liverpool, England 1942

George Harrison
   Born: Liverpool, England 1943

Ringo Starr
   Born: Liverpool, England 1940

Aural Recognition of Themes:

   Purchase at your local music store one or more of the following piano sheet music arrangements of the Beatle's compositions. You may play the main theme with the written
accompaniment, or you may supply your own accompaniment
using the chords notated above the melody line (although
the chord symbols are written for guitar, they are easily
adapted to the piano). Play each theme of the composition
several times in order to facilitate recognition.

   Michelle (1965)

   Yesterday (1965)

   I Want To Hold Your Hand (1963)

General Information about Composers and Compositions:

1. The Beatles became popular in the early part of the 1960's.
   They are composers as well as performers, and have had an
   enormous influence in the field of popular music. They
   made their American debut on the Ed Sullivan show in 1964.

2. Their style in music include a wide variety of musical
   forms: rock, rhythm and blues, country-western, ballad,
   folk, classical and culture of India. Some of their recordings include the language, instruments and culture of
   other countries. Their musical style was international in
   that it was performed and received in all parts of the
   world.

3. The Beatles were very successful with electronic effects
   in their music, including the use of electric guitars.
   They introduced to rock music a number of different instruments: the Indian sitar, harmonica, tenor banjo, tuba,
   etc.

4. John Lennon and Paul McCartney composed a great deal of music performed by the Beatles. Their song lyrics heralded the social revolution that was beginning in the United States. Each song conveyed a special message concerning life. They questioned the credence of social laws and behavioral standards established by society.

5. The Beatles recorded in all styles of music and they performed before an enormous amount of live audiences and on television programs. This, of course, brought them wealth and made them famous throughout the world.

Composers' Main Contribution to the Art of Music:

1. The Beatles were unique as a popular music group in that they introduced electronic sound effects in their compositions, using unorthodox instruments for rock playing. Their varied styles and techniques of composition have been and are an inspiration to many contemporary song writers.

Suggested Listening:

1. Title: *Beatles*
   Performers: The Beatles
   Record No.: Apple SWBO-101
   Grade Level: 4 - 8

2. Title: *Beatles and Other Sounds From England*
   Performers: The Beatles
   Record No.: Atco S-33-169
   Grade Level: 7 - 12

Optional Assignments:

1. Make up a notebook on the musical career of the Beatles, consisting of pictures, newspaper and magazine articles, concert programs, thematic excerpts and original illustrations.

2. After listening to one of their recordings that utilizes the Baroque style, write a critique, comparing their music with that of composers of the Baroque period.

3. If you play a musical instrument or sing, perform one of their songs for the class.

4. After choosing one of the topics we have discussed under general information, do some research on it in other books, then give an oral report on your findings.

5. Make a study of rock, folk and country-western music and write a report on this subject.

CHAPTER 10

DESCRIPTIVE SUMMARIES
OF WELL-KNOWN COMPOSITIONS

The authors have selected fifty-two works of the various composers and have written a brief review of each composition. These compositions are chosen from the works of composers of each period in music history - from Palestrina (Polyphonic Period) to Bloch (Modern Period). Some of these selections are over three hundred years old, while others are less than fifty years old. All of them have stood the test of time; this is one basic criterion by which the worth of music may be judged.

Most recordings of serious music include program notes about the music and composer. The authors of this book have presented a digest of these program notes in this chapter. This information can enhance your listening experience with a knowledgeable background and interpretation of each work.

At the beginning of each descriptive summary, you will find page references that contain more information about the composer and his music.

A suggested procedure for the use of these descriptive summaries is:

1. For necessary background information about the composer and his music, refer to pages indicated under the composer's name.

2. Study the statements included under Descriptive Summary of Composition in this chapter.

3. Obtain the recording of the composition from your library.

4. Refer to Chapter I, Suggested Procedures For Music Appreciation Lessons, for further information concerning procedures for presenting lessons in music appreciation along with correlated activities and experiences.

If at the present, or at some future time, you may be interested in purchasing a collection of records for your listening library, you will do well to select recordings of some of the compositions noted in this chapter.

Composition: *Brandenburg Concerto No. 2 in F*

Composer: Johann Sebastian Bach
        (For further information refer to pages 80-81)
Descriptive Summary of Composition:

1. This concerto is written in three movements for solo
   flute, oboe, trumpet, violin and string orchestra.
2. In 1719, Bach was commissioned to write six concertos
   for Christian Ludwig, Margrave of Brandenburg. Thus
   originated the name of Brandenburg concertos.
3. Bach exploited in these concertos the complete range
   of instruments available to him at this time, and
   used different solo and instrumental combinations for
   each of his concertos.
4. The first movement, allegro moderato, displays clarity
   and simplicity of construction. He uses his instruments very tastefully as heard in the brilliant sound
   effects of the trumpet part.
5. The second movement, andante, features the trio of
   flute, violin and oboe, accompanied by the harpsichord
   and cello.
6. The third movement, allegro, is written in the free
   contrapuntal style of an accompanied fugue.

Composition: *Essays, No. 1 and 2 for Orchestra*

Composer: Samuel Barber
        (For further information refer to pages 262-263)
Descriptive Summary of Composition:

1. The *Essays for Orchestra* are related to literary
   essays in their form; both are concise and clearly
   written. Literary works and poetry influenced Barber's
   style of writing.
2. *Essay No. 1* was written in 1937. It had its première
   on November 5, 1938 by the N.B.C. Symphony Orchestra
   directed by Arturo Toscanini.
3. The first essay has three principal themes, developed
   logically and briefly. The composition opens with an
   Andante Sostenuto which proceeds to an Allegro followed
   by a Scherzando section. The piece ends with a re-
   iteration of the first measures of the opening section.
4. *Essay No. 2* was written in 1942 and was given its
   first performance on April 16, 1942 by the New York
   Philharmonic-Symphony Orchestra directed by Bruno
   Walter.
5. The second essay is made up of three main themes which
   are brought together in a fugue at the end of the composition.

Composition: *Symphony No. 9 in D Minor*

Composer: Ludwig van Beethoven
    (For further information refer to pages 116-117)
Descriptive Summary of Composition:

1. This symphony contains four movements. Beethoven
   scored it for piccolo, two flutes, two clarinets, two
   oboes, two bassoons, one contra bassoon, two trumpets,
   four horns, three trombones, tympani, cymbals, bass
   drum, triangle and strings.
2. In this composition Beethoven found that instruments
   of the orchestra alone were insufficient to express
   fully his emotions, so he employed a chorus in the
   last movement.
3. The first movement, Allegro ma non troppo, displays a
   great deal of mystery, restlessness and discontent.
4. The second movement, Molto vivace, Presto, is partly
   in the form of a fugue.
5. The third movement, Adagio molto and cantabile, displays a mixture of moods.
6. The fourth movement, Allegro assai, is fiery at times.
   It was in this final movement that Beethoven turned to
   the human voice to express fully his deep feelings and
   convictions. Here he uses Schiller's poem, *Ode To Joy*
   for the text.

Composition: *Rakoczy March*

Composer: Hector Berlioz
    (For further information refer to pages 144-145)
Descriptive Summary of Composition:

1. This march is perhaps the most popular of Berlioz's
   compositions. It is written for piccolo, two flutes,
   two clarinets, two oboes, four bassoons, two cornets,
   two trumpets, four horns, three trombones, tuba, snare
   drum, bass drum, timpani, cymbals, triangle and
   strings.
2. Berlioz was commissioned to write this march for a
   special concert held at Pesth in 1846.

3. The main theme of this composition is a well-known
   Hungarian tune. It is a very exciting and dynamic
   piece.

Composition: *Carmen* - opera

Composer: Georges Bizet
(For further information refer to pages 174-175)
Descriptive Summary of Composition:

1. The opera *Carmen* is in four acts. Its libretto was written by Henri Meilhac and Ludovic Halévy. It was first performed on March 3, 1875 in Paris at the Opéra-Comique Theater.
2. Today it is one of the favorite operas throughout the world. Much of the music from the opera is performed as orchestral solos. The instrumental score is rich and colorful with a variety of Spanish rhythms. A group of favorite orchestral selections from the opera is known as the *Carmen Suite*.
3. Bizet used Spanish folklore and rhythms to give the opera a Spanish atmosphere although the style in which he wrote *Carmen* is French.
4. *Carmen* is a romantic opera which depicts gypsy and peasant life in Spain. The opera is named after its main character, Carmen, a gypsy girl.

Composition: *Schelomo (Solomon)* - Hebrew Rhapsody

Composer: Ernest Bloch
(For further information refer to pages 228-229)
Descriptive Summary of Composition:

1. *Schelomo* is a Hebrew rhapsody for solo cello and orchestra and is Bloch's musical interpretation of the Biblical Jewish King Solomon.
2. King Solomon in this rhapsody is represented by the cello. The cello plays the part with great warmth and sincerity.
3. The music of *Schelomo* is oriental and the melodies have a Biblical flavor. We might say that Bloch wrote this composition in the Hebrew idiom.
4. *Schelomo* has two main themes, the first one announced by the cello and the second theme introduced by the woodwind instruments before it is taken over by the cello.

Composition: *Polovetzian Dances* from opera *Prince Igor*

Composer: Alexander Borodin
(For further information refer to pages 166-167)

Descriptive Summary of Composition:

1. The *Polovetzian Dances* are part of the second act of the opera, *Prince Igor*. Borodin left portions of this opera unfinished. The dances in other parts of the opera were·completed by Rimsky-Korsakov, a friend of Borodin.
2. The dances are scored for strings, piccolo, flutes, clarinets, oboes, bassoons, English horn, trumpets, trombones, French horns, timpani, bass drum, snare drum, tambourine, cymbals, triangle, glockenspiel and harp.
3. These dances follow the style and tradition of the ballad dance. The ballad dances were popular in the medieval courts of Russian nobility. At a later period, these dances were adapted to Russian ballets.
4. The music of the recent Broadway Musical *Kismet* was adopted from the themes of Borodin's *Polovetzian Dances*.

Composition: *Hungarian Dances Nos. 1, 5, 6*

Composer: Johannes Brahms
       (For further information refer to pages 168-169)
Descriptive Summary of Composition:

1. The *Hungarian Dances* are based on folk songs and gypsy music of the Hungarians.
2. These tunes were not original with Brahms; he merely arranged them for the piano.
3. The most popular of the *Hungarian Dances* are:
   a. *Hungarian Dance No. 1 in G Minor*
   b. *Hungarian Dance No. 5 in F# Minor*
   c. *Hungarian Dance No. 6 in Db Major*

Composition: *Peter Grimes* - opera

Composer: Benjamin Britten
       (For further information refer to pages 268-269)
Descriptive Summary of Composition:

1. *Peter Grimes* is an opera in two acts which is based on a poem, *The Borough* by George Crabbe.
2. This composition was commissioned by the Koussevitzky Foundation for the Berkshire Festival at Tanglewood, in Lenox, Mass.
3. The American première of *Peter Grimes* took place at the Berkshire Music Festival on August 6, 1946. It had its first performance at the Sadler's Wells Theater in London, England on June 7, 1945.

4. The story of *Peter Grimes* deals with a fisherman who engages boy orphans to help him in his work. The story tells how the boys were enslaved and eventually killed through abuse. Soon, the village people, except for two, all turn against Peter Grimes. The two persons who understand him are a retired sea captain, Balstrode, and a widowed school mistress. Later, the village people rebel against Peter Grimes, and on the advice of his friend, Balstrode, Peter goes out to sea to sink his boat.

5. The purely orchestral portions of the opera consist of instrumental interludes which introduce the acts and scenes of the opera.

Composition: *El Salon Mexico*

Composer: Aaron Copland
(For further information refer to pages 254-255)
Descriptive Summary of Composition:

1. The title of this composition refers to a famous dance-hall (ballroom) in Mexico City.
2. The composition describes the atmosphere of the dance-hall as well as the spirit and emotions of the Mexican people at the ballroom.
3. The music contains elements of jazz. Copland also used native Mexican folk songs in this composition.
4. *El Salon Mexico* received its first performance on August 27, 1937 in Mexico City. It is one of Copland's most popular and frequently performed orchestral works.

Composition: *La Mer (The Sea)*

Composer: Claude Debussy
(For further information refer to pages 214-215)
Descriptive Summary of Composition:

1. *La Mer* is a symphonic composition in three parts called *Three Symphonic Sketches*:
   a. *The Sea from Dawn until Noon*
   b. *Sport of the Waves*
   c. *Dialogue of the Wind and the Sea*
2. The American première of *La Mer* was given by the Boston Symphony Orchestra on March 2, 1907.
3. *La Mer* is a brilliant composition, and is typical of Debussy's style of orchestral writing.
4. Debussy creates a colorful impression of the sea through skillful orchestration.

Composition: *Symphony No. 5 in E Minor (From The New World)*

Composer: Antonin Dvořák
(For further information refer to pages 178-179)
Descriptive Summary of Composition:

1. The *New World Symphony* contains phrases and suggestions of American folk tunes and spirituals as well as Bohemian folk songs.
2. The symphony is intended to give impressions of the New World.
3. The four movements of the symphony are:
   a. Adagio; Allegro molto
   b. Largo
   c. Scherzo
   d. Allegro con fuoco
4. The large movement contains a beautiful solo for English Horn.
5. The first movement contains a theme developed by Dvorak using the familiar melody *Swing Low, Sweet Chariot*.
6. The Scherzo starts with a theme played by flutes and oboes. The Bohemian peasant and gypsy music is evident.
7. The last movement - Allegro con Fuoco, is full of vitality. The horns and trumpets play the first major theme.
8. The familiar song *Going Home* is taken from one of the main themes of this symphony.

Composition: *Nights in the Gardens of Spain*

Composer: Manuel de Falla
(For further information refer to pages 226-227)
Descriptive Summary of Composition:

1. *Nights in the Gardens of Spain* is a composition for piano and orchestra written in three parts:
   a. *At Generalife*
   b. *Far-off Dance*
   c. *Sierra of Cordoba*
2. This orchestral piece written in 1916, is an expressive, impressionistic composition. Its impressionistic style shows the influence of de Falla's teacher, Debussy.
3. The three movements are often referred to as symphonic impressions. De Falla sought to depict sentiments, sensations and places as suggested by the different titles.

4. The various musical themes are based on the rhythms, figures, cadences and modes of the popular Spanish music of Andalucia. The music is brilliant, festive and very colorful.
5. This composition is regarded as de Falla's most poetic work. It is scored for piccolo, flutes, oboes, clarinets, bassoons, English horn, trumpets, trombones, tuba, timpani, celesta, triangle, cymbals, piano, harp and strings.

Composition: *Symphony in D Minor*

Composer: César Franck
    (For further information refer to pages 162-163)
Descriptive Summary of Composition:

1. The *Symphony in D Minor* is written in three movements as follows:
   a. Lento; Allegro non troppo
   b. Allegretto
   c. Allegro non troppo
2. César Franck's only symphony is a masterpiece and a favorite work in the symphonic repertoire.
3. The première of this symphony at the Paris Conservatory of Music on February 17, 1889, was a fiasco. Everyone was against it, musicians and public alike. They felt that the music was unconventional and had too many innovations, among which included the English horn being featured for the first time in a symphony.
4. The first movement of the symphony, Lento, opens with the main theme played by the basses and celli. This same melody had been used by Wagner and Liszt.
5. The second movement, Allegretto, features the English horn. Pizzicato in the strings and harp form a background to the English horn melody.
6. The Finale, Allegro non troppo, is a joyful and brilliant movement. It recalls the main themes of the first two movements.

Composition: *Rhapsody In Blue*

Composer: George Gershwin
    (For further information refer to pages 252-253)

Descriptive Summary of Composition:

1. Paul Whiteman commissioned Gershwin to write *Rhapsody In Blue* in 1924 for a concert of works by American composers. It was written with the intention of integrating the jazz idiom with concert music.
2. This composition achieved popularity very quickly and has since become well known in almost all parts of the world.
3. *Rhapsody In Blue* is idiomatic American music written in genuine jazz style.
4. Ferde Grofé orchestrated the Rhapsody for concert performance. Gershwin earned over a million dollars from performances, record sales and sheet music of his *Rhapsody In Blue*.
5. The music is essentially made up of five principal themes with many variations of the themes throughout the composition.
6. The changing rhythmic patterns of the music make it very dynamic. The music offers a great variety of moods and can be described as beautiful, charming, dramatic, brilliant, exciting, and manifesting vitality.

Composition: *Ballet Suite*

Composer: Cristoph Willibald von Gluck
        (For further information refer to pages 106-107)
Descriptive Summary of Composition:

1. *Ballet Suite* is an orchestral arrangement by Felix Mottl. It is made up of excerpts taken from leading operas by Gluck.
2. The first two pieces of the suite are taken from the opera, *Iphigenia in Aulis*.
3. The second part of the suite, *Dance of the Blessed Spirits*, is taken from *Orpheus*.
4. *Musette*, making up the next part of the suite, is a selection from Gluck's opera *Armide*.
5. The final part of the *Ballet Suite*, in moderate tempo, is called *Sicilienne* and is an excerpt from the opera *Armide*.

Composition: *Faust* - opera

Composer: Charles Gounod
        (For further information refer to pages 158-159)
Descriptive Summary of Composition:

1. Gounod's fame is largely due to his opera, *Faust*. It is a tragic opera in five acts. Its libretto was written by Jules Barbier and Michel Carré, based on Goethe's drama.
2. *Faust* received its first performance on March 19, 1859 at the Lyric Theatre in Paris.
3. The story takes place in a German village in the eighteenth century. The principal characters of the cast include:
   a. Faust - a philosopher, tenor.
   b. Mephistopheles - evil one, bass.
   c. Marguerite - a village girl, soprano.
   d. Valentine - brother of Marguerite, baritone.
   e. Students:
      (1) Brander - baritone.
      (2) Siebel - soprano.
4. The story of the opera, taken from Goethe, deals with an old Faust who persuades Mephistopheles (the evil one) to grant him a vision of Marguerite (a village girl) and restore his youth; in return Faust will give him his soul.
   His wish being granted, Faust, now young again, is able to allure Marguerite, but later abandons her. A duel between Faust and Valentine (Marguerite's brother) follows, with Faust being victorious.
   Marguerite is imprisoned for the murder of her child. Faust visits her in prison and tries to persuade her to flee with him; she refuses the offer and accepts death instead.
5. The music of *Faust* is very melodious, appealing and fresh. Some of the more popular selections of the opera include:
   a. *The Flower Song*.
   b. *Waltz* from Act II.
   c. *Soldiers' Chorus* and *Mephisto's Serenade* from Act IV.
   d. *Jewel Song* from Act III.
   e. *Prison Scene* from Act V.

Composition: *Concerto In A Minor*

Composer: Edvard Grieg
       (For further information refer to pages 184-185)
Descriptive Summary of Composition:

1. This concerto is written for piano and orchestra in three movements:
   a. Allegro molto moderato.
   b. Adagio.
   c. Allegro moderato molto e marcato.
2. This concerto is in the standard repertoire of every great pianist. It is a dramatic and brilliant piece.

3. The *Concerto In A Minor* contains Norwegian folk elements. In the last movement, Norwegian influences are found in the rhythm and also in the harmony.
4. The first movement, Allegro molto moderato, begins with a roll of the tympani; then the piano begins with a forceful, downward octave passage.
5. The second movement, Adagio, features a melody in a sombre atmosphere which prevails through most of the movement.
6. The Finale, is again, like the first movement, joyous and forceful. Grieg makes dramatic use of bold octave passages for climactic purposes.

Composition: *Grand Canyon Suite*

Composer: Ferde Grofé
   (For further information refer to pages 240-241)
Descriptive Summary of Composition:

1. The *Grand Canyon Suite* is Grofe's most successful composition. It is a famous example of program music. It had its première on November 22, 1931 by the Chicago Symphony Orchestra conducted by Paul Whiteman.
2. In this composition, Grofé describes musically the various changing beauties of the Grand Canyon.
3. The suite is written in five parts, and the title of each part gives a clue to the musical intentions of the composer. The five sections are:
   a. *Sunrise:*
      (1) Muted trumpets depict the sunrise.
   b. *Painted Desert:*
      (1) As viewed from an airplane.
   c. *On The Trail:*
      (1) Suggests a cowboy song. The most popular piece of the five.
   d. *Sunset:*
      (1) The music is gradually subdued, creating a quiet atmosphere.
   e. *Cloudburst:*
      (1) The full orchestra is masterfully used to suggest the sounds of a thunderstorm.

Composition: *Water Music*

Composer: George Frederick Handel
   (For further information refer to pages 82-83)

<u>Descriptive Summary of Composition</u>:

1. This composition is in the form of a serenade, made up of twenty sections. The *Water Music Suite* consists of six of these pieces arranged by Sir Hamilton Harty. The orchestral suite includes:
   a. *Overture* - Allegro, in French style.
   b. *Air* - old English type song.
   c. *Bourrée* - an old French dance.
   d. *Hornpipe* - an old English dance.
   e. *Andante* - a quiet song.
   f. *Allegro deciso* - a quick finale.
2. According to accounts, true or perhaps partially legendary, *Water Music* was written to entertain King George I on an elaborate barge during a water festival on the Thames River.
3. As the King was being rowed up the river, Handel and his group of musicians followed in a second barge. The composer led the orchestra in his *Water Music*.
4. King George I enjoyed the music very much and in recognition of the occasion he bestowed a life pension of two hundred pounds upon Handel.
5. The music of the composition is very clear, agreeable and offers a great variety of listening experiences in its many parts.

<u>Composition</u>: *Rugby*

<u>Composer</u>: Arthur Honegger
       (For further information refer to pages 242-243)
<u>Descriptive Summary of Composition</u>:

1. *Rugby* is a symphonic work. It and *Pacific 231* are probably the best known orchestral compositions of the composer.
2. Although *Rugby* has been labeled a symphonic piece, it is rather free in form.
3. Honegger once told a newspaperman that he could visualize the various formations and movements of a football game in music. The reporter came out with an article stating that the composer was writing a football symphony. From this misunderstanding, the symphonic piece *Rugby* was born.
4. *Rugby* is a musical representation of the abstract patterns of a football game. The various formations, movements, harsh actions and oppositions of a game are musically depicted in the well-orchestrated work.

Composition: *Hänsel And Gretel*

Composer: Engelbert Humperdinck
        (For further information refer to pages 188-189)
Descriptive Summary of Composition:

1. *Hänsel And Gretel* is a children's legendary opera
   in three acts. Its libretto was written by Adelheid
   Wette. It was adapted from a fairy tale by the
   brothers Grimm.
2. It received its first performance on December 23, 1893
   at the Weimar Opera House in Germany. Richard Strauss
   directed the performance.
3. The story takes place in a German forest in the
   seventeenth century. The principal characters of the
   cast include:
   a. Peter - a broom-maker, baritone.
   b. Gertrude - his wife, contralto.
   c. Hänsel - their son, mezzo-soprano.
   d. Gretel - their daughter, soprano.
   e. The Witch - a mezzo-soprano.
   f. The Sand Man - a soprano.
   g. Also, the Den Man, Angels, Children and Elves.
4. The story of the opera tells about Hänsel and Gretel
   going to the woods to pick berries. They become lost
   in the forest and of course are afraid of meeting the
   witch who eats children. The children are captured
   by the witch who tries to roast them in her big oven.
   They in turn are successful in getting the witch
   herself into the oven. The death of the witch releases
   all the children she had captured.
5. The music of the opera is full of melodies, many of
   which are taken from German folk tunes. Some popular
   selections of the opera include:
   a. *Sandman's Song*.
   b. *Evening Prayer*.
   c. *Witch's Song*.
   d. *Gingerbread Waltz*.

Composition: *Gayaneh* - ballet

Composer: Aram Khatchaturian
        (For further information refer to pages 258-259)
Descriptive Summary of Composition:

1. *Gayaneh* is a patriotic folk ballet replete with folk-
   lore of Khatchaturian's native Soviet Armenia. Its
   first performance was given in Molotov on December 9,
   1942. The ballet won the First Degree Stalin Prize
   in 1943.

2. The libretto for the ballet, *Gayaneh*, was written by K.N. Derzhavin. The story takes place on a farm in Soviet Armenia.
3. Orchestral suites derived from the ballet have become well-known in this country. The famous *Sabre Dance* is a part of one of these orchestral suites.
4. The orchestral suites contain thirteen dances in all. Some of the more popular ones are:
   a. *Lullaby*.
   b. *Russian Dance*.
   c. *Dance of the Rose Maidens*.
5. The rhythms of these various dances are syncopated, exotic and very exciting.

Composition: *Symphonic Poem No. 3 (Les Préludes)*

Composer: Franz Liszt
        (For further information refer to pages 152-153)
Descriptive Summary of Composition:

1. Liszt wrote this piece in 1850. It was inspired by a set of verses *Les Préludes* by Lamartine.
2. The form of this work is determined by the nature of the poetry at hand which the music is supposed to depict.
3. The sections of the music are determined by various changes of mood and rhythm.
4. *Les Préludes* is scored for: piccolo, three flutes, two clarinets, two oboes, two bassoons, two trumpets, four horns, three trombones, tuba, snare drum, timpani, bass drum, cymbals, harp and strings.

Composition: *Indian Suite*

Composer: Edward A. MacDowell
        (For further information refer to pages 196-197)
Descriptive Summary of Composition:

1. The *Indian Suite* is an orchestral suite. It received its première performance by the Boston Symphony Orchestra on January 23, 1896.
2. The composition shows the great love MacDowell had for Indian folk-lore.
3. The principal themes of the *Indian Suite* are taken from Baher's, *Die Musik der Nordamerikanischen Wilden*. Baher's themes have been changed for the sake of greater musical beauty.
4. The Suite includes the following sections:
   a. *Legend* - theme takes place at a sacred ceremony of the Iroquois (Indian tribe).
   b. *Love Song* - a love song of the Kiowas (Indian linguistic stock of western Kansas and eastern Colorado).

    c. *In War Time* - movement inspired by a theme attrib-
       uted to supernatural origin by Atlantic Coast
       Indians.
    d. *Dirge* - taken from a Kiowa tune.
    e. *Village Festival* - a dance and song of Iroquois
       origin.

Composition: A *Midsummer Night's Dream*

Composer: Felix Mendelssohn
       (For further information refer to pages 146-147)
Description of Composition:

1. Mendelssohn's music to Shakespeare's A *Midsummer
   Night's Dream* consists of the *Overture* and twelve
   additional numbers. The four most popular movements
   in this composition are:
   a. *Overture.*
   b. *Nocturne.*
   c. *Scherzo.*
   d. *Wedding March.*
2. Mendelssohn wrote the *Overture* when he was seventeen
   years old. Although there was a lapse of seventeen
   years between the *Overture* and the composition of the
   other pieces, the work has a high level of continuity.
3. The *Overture* is a very good symbol of the spirit of
   Shakespeare's comedy.
4. The *Nocturne* occurs at the end of the third act in the
   play. Everyone is asleep and quiet atmosphere prevails.
   The music depicts this in its expressive and romantic
   passages.
5. The *Scherzo* is supposed to portray musically the
   activities of Fairyland.
6. The *Wedding March* is perhaps the most popular of the
   pieces in this composition. It is still used at Wedding ceremonies.

Composition: *Amahl and the Night Visitors*

Composer: Gian-Carlo Menotti
       (For further information refer to pages 264-265)
Descriptive Summary of Composition:

1. Menotti wrote both the music and libretto to this
   one act opera.
2. The National Broadcasting Company commissioned Menotti
   to write a Christmas opera for a television broadcast;
   Amahl and the Night Visitors was the result. The
   première occurred on Christmas eve, 1951. It was the
   first opera composed especially for television broadcasting and was a great success.

332

3. Menotti found the inspiration for his opera in a Flemish painting, *The Adoration of the Magi*, by Hieronymous Bosch.
4. The story deals with a crippled boy, Amahl, who has invited to his poor hut the Three Wise Men who are going to Bethlehem to see the Holy Child. Amahl notices the beautiful gifts they are bringing to Bethlehem, so he offers his only possession, his crutches for a gift. As soon as the Wise Men have accepted his gift for the Holy Child, Amahl is miraculously cured.
5. The music of the opera is powerful and appealing. The text is simple and easily understood.

Composition: *Symphony No. 41 in C Major (Jupiter)*

Composer: Wolfgang Amadeus Mozart
        (For further information refer to pages 114-115)
Descriptive Summary of Composition:

1. This work is considered by many to be Mozart's best symphony, his last. It is believed that J.B. Cramer was the first person to refer to the composition as the *Jupiter Symphony*. It was given this name to designate it as a god of the symphonies, just as Jupiter, to the ancient Romans meant god of the heavens.
2. The symphony consists of four movements:
   a. Allegro vivace.
   b. Andante cantabile.
   c. Minuetto; Allegro; Trio
   d. Finale: Allegro molto.
3. The first movement, Allegro vivace, opens with the announcement of the first theme.
4. The second movement, Andante cantabile, contains a beautiful melody. The theme of the second movement is the main lyric melody of this symphony.
5. The third movement, Minuetto, is written in the traditional minuet style. The character of this movement is cheerful and playful.
6. Finale, Allegro molto, the last movement, is partly written in fugue form. The music in this movement is considered by many to be the highest point in his art.

Composition: *Pictures At An Exhibition*

Composer: Modeste Mussorgsky (Moussorgsky)
        (For further information refer to pages 170-171)

<u>Descriptive Summary of Composition:</u>

1. *Pictures At An Exhibition* was originally a piano
   composition. It was brilliantly orchestrated by
   Maurice Ravel on a special commission by Serge
   Koussevitzsky. It was given its American première
   by the Boston Symphony Orchestra on December 3, 1926.
2. Mussorgsky wrote the original piano work to honor his
   artist friend, Victor Hartmann. The composition is
   intended to be descriptive of paintings by this artist
   as they were being exhibited at an art exhibition held
   in memory of the painter.
3. The work begins with a piece called *Promenade*. This
   was intended to be a musical self-portrait of
   Mussorgsky himself.
4. The other sections of the composition are:
   a. *The Gnome* - a drawing representing a gnome.
   b. *The Old Castle* - a medieval castle.
   c. *Tuileries* - musical re-creation of the famous
      Paris garden.
   d. *Bydlo* - a Polish oxcart; the music is quite pompous
      and heavy.
   e. *Ballet of the Unhatched Chickens* - the music is
      brilliant and very rhythmical.
   f. *Samuel Goldenberg and Schmuyle* - perhaps a
      caricature of the two named persons.
   g. *Limoges* - the market place.
   h. *Catacombs* - a melancholy piece about the catacombs
      of Paris.
   i. *The Hut on the Hen's Legs* - music of folk-lore
      quality.
   j. *The Great Gate at Kiev* - descriptive music of an
      imaginary gate in the Russian city of Kiev.

<u>Composition</u>: *Missa Papae Marcelli*

<u>Composer</u>: Giovanni Pierluigi da Palestrina
        (For further information refer to pages 36-37)
<u>Descriptive Summary of Composition:</u>

1. The *Pope Marcellus Mass* was written at the request of
   a special commission appointed by Pope Pius IV to
   study and bring about a change in Roman Catholic
   Church music.
2. This mass was to be used as a model for future composers of church music. Palestrina dedicated the mass
   to Pope Marcellus.
3. This mass helped to establish Palestrina as one of the
   greatest composers of church music of his time, and
   this composition served its original purpose as a
   model for future masses.

4. The *Missa Papae Marcelli* is one of the best-known single musical compositions of the Renaissance Period. It is a beautiful and devotional piece of church music and displays artistic perfection.

Composition: *Fantasia for Strings*

Composer: Henry Purcell
        (For further information refer to pages 74-75)
Descriptive Summary of Composition:

1. Purcell wrote three Fantasias (Fantasies) for strings. They are written in the seventeenth century traditional English form of free composition.
2. His first fantasy is written in three voice parts, marked Moderato, and scored for violin, viola and cello. The short composition contains four musical figures.
3. The second string fantasy marked, Fast, is written in four voice parts and scored for two violins, viola and cello.
4. The third fantasy is written in five voice parts, marked, Moderately slow, and is scored for two violins, two violas, and cello. The tempo of this composition varies from slow to fast and the music is sometimes lively and joyous.

Composition: *Boléro*

Composer: Maurice Ravel
        (For further information refer to pages 224-225)
Descriptive Summary of Composition:

1. An orchestral composition, *Boléro* was commissioned in 1928 by a Parisian dancer, Ida Rubenstein.
2. The music of this work has a highly Spanish flavor both in melody and rhythm. It shows the great influence Spanish folk music had upon Ravel.
3. The composition was given its American concert première in 1929 in New York City by the Philharmonic Symphony directed by Arturo Toscanini. It became popular quickly and has since been used on Broadway revues, motion pictures, and is still a favorite piece on concert programs.
4. Ravel displays his mastery of orchestration in this piece. The work consists of two main themes which are intensified by the constantly changing orchestration.

Composition: *Scheherazade*

Composer: Nicholas A. Rimsky-Korsakov
         (For further information refer to pages 186-187)
Descriptive Summary of Composition:

1. *Scheherazade* is a symphonic poem and considered by
   many to be Rimsky-Korsakov's most famous composition.
   It is a descriptive piece based on material from the
   story *The Arabian Nights*.
2. The music has an oriental flavor and is very colorful.
   The orchestration brings out the oriental quality in
   the melody and rhythm.
3. *Scheherazade* is made up of four movements:
   a. *The Sea and the Vessel of Sinbad*
         The main theme of this movement is played in
         unison by the strings, trombone, tuba and
         woodwinds.
   b. *The Tale of the Kalandar - Prince*
         The introductory passage includes the main
         theme of *Scheherazade* which also occurs at the
         beginning of the first movement.
   c. *The Young Prince and the Young Princess*
         The music is made up of two lyrical themes.
         The Prince has his theme played by the violins,
         the tempo marking is Andantino quasi allegretto
         (moderately paced, almost fast). The Princess
         enters with a theme played by the clarinet
         accompanied by a few small percussion instru-
         ments, the tempo marking is Pochissimo più
         moso (with a little more motion).
   d. *The Festival at Bagdad*
         The tempo marking in this movement is Allegro
         molto e frenetico (very lively and frantic).
         The music is very exciting as it describes the
         thundering sea with the vessel being shattered
         by the rise and fall of the waves.

Composition: *The Barber of Seville*

Composer: Giocchino Rossini
         (For further information refer to pages 138-139)
Descriptive Summary of Composition:

1. *The Barber of Seville* is a comic opera in two acts
   with libretto written by Cesare Sterbini. It had its
   première in Rome on February 5, 1816.

2. *The Barber of Seville* is one of the most popular of comic operas. The story takes place in Seville (a city in Spain) in the seventeenth century. The main characters of the cast include:
   a. Figaro - the barber of Seville, baritone.
   b. Count Almaviva - tenor.
   c. Doctor Bartolo - a physician, bass.
   d. Basilio - a music teacher, bass.
   e. Rosina - a ward of Bartolo, soprano.
3. The opera is based on a comedy by Beaumarchais. Doctor Bartolo loves Rosina, who in turn loves Count Almaviva. Doctor Bartolo keeps Rosina carefully guarded, so that it is difficult for Count Almaviva to see Rosina. He finally gets in touch with her and they plan an elopement. Doctor Bartolo tries to prevent the marriage but Rosina and the Count finally succeed.
4. *The Barber of Seville* is filled with many beautiful melodic arias.

Composition: *Danse Macabre*

Composer: Camille Saint-Saëns
        (For further information refer to pages 172-173)
Descriptive Summary of Composition:

1. *Danse Macabre* is a symphonic poem based on a poem by Henri Cazalis. It is written in a fast waltz tempo. Franz Liszt wrote a piano transcription of this piece.
2. Saint-Saens included the following instruments in the original score: piccolo, two flutes, two clarinets, two oboes, two bassoons, four horns, two trumpets, three trombones, bass tuba, timpani, bass drum, cymbals, triangle, xylophone, harp and strings.
3. The first theme which describes a scene taking place at midnight is announced by the harp sounded twelve times. The harp is followed by the violin. The dance begins with a motive played by the flute. Later the xylophone is used to imitate the dance of the skeletons.
4. The second theme is introduced by a plain song, *Dies Irae*.
5. The two themes are finally brought together for a climax. Dawn makes its appearance, signified by the horns and the crows of the cock which are imitated by the oboe.

Composition: *Verklärte Nacht (Transfigured Night)*

Composer: Arnold Schoenberg (Schönberg)
        (For further information refer to pages 220-221)
Descriptive Summary of Composition:

1. This composition was originally written as a sextet for strings. Today it is used often in its transcribed version for string orchestra.
2. *Verklärte Nacht* was written in 1899 and was inspired by a poem by Richard Dehmel.
3. Schoenberg was influenced by Wagner in composing *Transfigured Night*. Schoenberg was a follower of Wagner's drama music and studied *Tristan und Isolde* very closely. He imitated Wagner's dramatic style in his early works.
4. In 1917, Schoenberg transcribed his original string sextet for a string orchestra. In this form, it is a symphonic poem. The composition is full of dramatic power and is rich in color and harmonic texture.

Composition: *Symphony No. 8 in B Minor (Unfinished)*

Composer: Franz Schubert
        (For further information refer to pages 140-141)
Descriptive Summary of Composition:

1. It is known as the *Unfinished Symphony* because it has only two movements instead of the usual four; Schubert never completed the last two movements.
2. The two movements are finished pieces in themselves. The symphony is complete in all aspects.
3. The first movement, Allegro moderato, starts with an introductory theme played by the cellos and string basses. The movement follows the traditional sonata form. The music of this movement is of a lyrical and dramatic quality.
4. The second movement, Andante con moto, starts with an exposition of the first theme played by the strings. The second theme is played by the clarinets. Schubert makes a remarkable use of modulation (the changing of keys) in this movement. The modulations enhance the beauty and color of the music. The concluding theme of the movement is played by the first violins.

Composition: *Symphony No. 1 in B Flat Major (Spring Symphony)*

Composer: Robert Schumann
        (For further information refer to pages 150-151)

Descriptive Summary of Composition:

1. *Symphony No. 1 in B Flat Major* was completed in 1840, the year Robert Schumann married the famous concert pianist Clara Wieck. The title, *Spring Symphony* does not refer to the season of the year, but to the happiness that came with his marriage.
2. The symphony was first performed on March 31, 1841 at Leipzig, Germany under the direction of the famous composer, Felix Mendelssohn. Its American première was at Boston in 1853.
3. *Symphony No. 1 in B Flat Major* consists of four movements:
   a. Andante poco maestoso; Allegro molto vivace.
   b. Larghetto.
   c. Molto vivace, Scherzo.
   d. Allegro animato grazioso.
4. The first movement is well balanced with feelings of gracefulness, vitality, beauty, sadness and brilliance.
5. The second movement has a basic theme, first given to the violins.
6. The beginning of a melody played by the trombones at the end of the second movement is the germ for the main theme of the third movement.
7. In the last movement there is a development of the two main themes. The finale ends with a brilliant coda.

Composition: *Symphony No. 1*

Composer: Dmitri Shostakovitch (Shostakovich)
(For further information refer to pages 260-261)
Descriptive Summary of Composition:

1. Shostakovitch composed his first symphony in 1925 at the age of nineteen. The score of this symphony requires a large modern orchestra including a piano.
2. The symphony received its American première in 1928 by the Philadelphia Orchestra directed by Leopold Stokowski.
3. *Symphony No. 1* is written in four movements and contains startling themes, moving rhythms and brilliant harmonies.
4. The first movement, Allegretto; Allegro non troppo, has its first theme announced by the strings, after a short introduction.
5. The second movement, Allegro, features the piano on the main theme.
6. The third movement, Lento; Largo, features an oboe solo at the beginning giving out the principal theme with string accompaniment.

7. The last movement, Allegro molto, features the clarinet playing the main theme with the accompaniment of strings and cymbals. The symphony is brought to a lively and dramatic end.

Composition: *Finlandia*

Composer: Jean Sibelius
        (For further information refer to pages 218-219)
Descriptive Summary of Composition:

1. *Finlandia* is a tone poem for orchestra written by Sibelius in 1899.
2. Sibelius had a great love for the beauty and history of his native country, Finland. He depicted this in his symphonic poem, *Finlandia*.
3. *Finlandia* is a hymn-like tune which is used by the people of Finland as a national song.
4. Although the music of *Finlandia* sounds very much like Finnish folk music, the melodies of this composition are all original tunes written by Sibelius; there are no Finnish folk tunes included in the music.
5. The composition starts with an introductory theme played by a brass choir, this section is marked Andante sostenuto. The woodwinds followed by the strings enter with a solemn passage. The next part, marked Allegro moderato, features the principal theme played by the strings.
6. The next section, marked Allegro, is the beginning of a movement in sonata form. A joyful theme is introduced by the woodwinds and then followed by the strings. These two themes are developed and this development brings the composition to a dramatic conclusion.

Composition: *Blue Danube Waltz*

Composer: Johann Strauss II
        (For further information refer to pages 164-165)
Descriptive Summary of Composition:

1. Strauss composed *On The Beautiful Blue Danube* in 1867 on a commission from the Vienna Men's Choral Society.
2. The composition was inspired by a set of verses by Karl Beck. The poem was a love song, addressed perhaps to a Viennese lady or possibly the city of Vienna itself. Each stanza of the poem ended with the line, "By the Danube, beautiful blue Danube."

3. The first theme of the waltz is built upon the D major triad. The composition is in five principal parts with an introduction and a coda. There are several short interludes between the main parts.
4. The music of this waltz is graceful, lively and full of joy.

Composition: *Till Eulenspiegel's Merry Pranks*

Composer: Richard Strauss
        (For further information refer to pages 216-217)
Descriptive Summary of Composition:

1. *Till Eulenspiegel's Merry Pranks* is a tone poem in rondo form. It is perhaps Strauss's best known and most popular symphonic work in this form.
2. It was composed in 1895 and received its première at Cologne in the same year under the composer's direction.
3. The composition was inspired by a legendary story of German origin. The main character of the story named Till Eulenspiegel, was a practical jokester who found fun in committing one prank after another.
4. The music contains two motifs (a short musical figure or phrase used to suggest an idea or character). The first motif appears at the beginning of the composition; it serves the same function as the phrase "Once upon a time" in a fairy tale. The second motif is assigned to Till himself.
5. The introductory measures of the piece are played by soft strings, suggesting the "Once upon a time" motif after which follows an enchanting horn solo. The "Till" motif first appears in a short phrase played by the clarinet. The figure later appears in the violins, viola, basses, and the flute.

Composition: *The Firebird* - ballet and symphonic suite

Composer: Igor Stravinsky
        (For further information refer to pages 234-235)
Descriptive Summary of Composition:

1. *L'Oiseau de Feu (The Firebird)* is a ballet in one act, with the book by Michel Fokine. The ballet was completed in 1910.
2. In 1919, Stravinsky wrote the *Firebird (Symphonic) Suite,* in which he adapted some of the important musical pieces from the ballet.

3. The *Firebird Suite* is written in six sections. They are as follows:
   a. Introduction: *Kastchei's Enchanted Garden* and *Dance of the Firebird*.
   b. *Supplication of the Firebird*
   c. *The Princess Play with the Golden Apples*
   d. *Dance of the Princess* and *Berceuse* (a lullaby)
   e. *Infernal Dance of all the Subjects of Kastchei*
   f. *Finale*

Composition: *The Mikado*

Composer: Arthur S. Sullivan
         (For further information refer to pages 182-183)
Descriptive Summary of Composition:

1. *The Mikado* is a comic opera in two acts with the libretto written by William S. Gilbert. It received its first performance in 1885 at the Savoy Theater in London.
2. The courtyard and garden of the Lord High Executioner, Ko-Ko in Titipu, Japan is the location for this operetta. The principal members of the cast include beside Ko-Ko:
   a. The Mikado (Emperor) of Japan
   b. Nanki-Poo, his son, a wandering minstrel
   c. Yum-Yum, Ko-Ko's ward from school
   d. Also: friends, courtiers, citizens and servants.
3. The story of the operetta is as follows:
   a. The Mikado's son, Nanki-Poo, runs away from home to avoid marrying the ugly Katisha, his father's choice for him. Nanki-Poo goes on to the town of Titipu and quickly falls in love with the pretty girl, Yum-Yum. Their marriage is deterred by Ko-Ko, the Lord High Executioner, who wants her for himself. Nanki-Poo and Ko-Ko finally make a bargain. Nanki-Poo can have Yum-Yum if he consents to be beheaded at the end of a month; he agrees and they are married. Finally, the Mikado arrives in town, so Nanki-Poo doesn't have to abide by the original agreement. Ko-Ko, instead marries Katisha.
4. The music of *The Mikado* is filled with oriental and exotic qualities. Japanese costumes add a great deal of color to the operetta.

Composition: *Nutcracker Suite*

Composer: Peter Ilich Tschaikowsky
         (For further information refer to pages 176-177)

Descriptive Summary of Composition:

1. The *Nutcracker Suite* is taken from the *Nutcracker Ballet* which Tschaikowsky was commissioned to write in 1891, by the Imperial Opera Company in Russia. Today, this ballet music is most frequently performed as a concert piece and is a great favorite of music lovers.
2. The inspiration for the *Nutcracker Suite* came from a story, *The Nutcracker and the Mouse King* by E.T.A. Hoffmann. The story tells of a little girl who received a nutcracker for Christmas. In a dream, on Christmas night, the nutcracker turns into a prince charming engaged in a battle with the toys against the mice. The prince takes Claire to his kingdom of sweets where they are entertained by dances and other festivities. Tschaikowsky used the various dance titles for his suite.
3. The suite consists of a short overture and seven dances as follows:
   a. *Miniature Overture*
   b. *March*
   c. *Dance of the Sugar Plum Fairy*
   d. *Russian Dance - Trepak*
   e. *Arab Dance*
   f. *Chinese Dance*
   g. *Dance of the Mirlitons*
   h. *Waltz of the Flowers*
4. The music of the suite is brilliant, appealing, full of exotic rhythm, rich in tonal color and very easily understood.
5. The writing of the *Nutcracker Ballet* was also the occasion for the introduction of the celesta (a percussion instrument played from keyboard) into the orchestra. The celesta can be heard in the *Dance of the Sugar Plum Fairy*

Composition: *Aïda*

Composer: Giuseppe Verdi
          (For further information refer to pages 154-155)
Descriptive Summary of Composition:

1. *Aïda* is a Romantic opera in four acts. Its book was written by Antonio Ghislanzoni. It had its first performance at Cairo, Egypt in 1871.
2. The opera was commissioned by the Khedive (Turkish Viceroy) of Egypt for the dedication of the new opera house in Cairo to celebrate the completion of the Suez Canal.

343

3. The story takes place in Memphis and Thebes, Egypt during the rule of the Pharaohs. The principal members of the cast include:
   a. The King of Egypt - bass.
   b. Amneris - his daughter - contralto.
   c. Rhadames - a General - tenor.
   d. Ramfis - High Priest - bass.
   e. Amonasro - King of Ethiopia - baritone.
   f. Aïda - his daughter, a slave - soprano.
   g. Also: soldiers, citizens and dancers.
4. Briefly, the story deals with Rhadames' love for Aïda, daughter of the King of Ethiopia. The king is later captured when Rhadames engages in battle against the Ethiopians and emerged victorious. Aïda is told by her father, to obtain from Rhadames the plan of battle. When this disclosure is discovered, Rhadames is condemned to death. After his interment, he discovers Aïda, hiding in the tombs, has vowed to die with him.
5. The music of *Aïda* is full of Oriental color. There are several popular arias and selections from the opera; among them:
   a. *Celeste Aïda*
   b. *The Grand March*
   c. *Ballet Music* from Act II
   d. *Ritorna Vincitor* from Act I

Composition: *Die Meistersinger*

Composer: Richard Wagner
        (For further information refer to pages 156-157)
Descriptive Summary of Composition:

1. *Die Meistersinger* (*The Master Singers*) is a comic opera in three acts. Wagner wrote the music as well as the libretto.
2. The Prelude to the opera contains themes taken from the three acts.
3. The plot of the opera takes place in Nuremberg, Germany during the sixteenth century. It deals with contests in verse writing and singing conducted among the tradespeople of the town.
4. The master-singers hold these contests which they govern with strict rules; the winners are given prizes.
5. In the opera, the goldsmith, a tradesman of the town, offers his daughter as prize to the winner of the contest.
6. The town clerk and a nobleman of the town both enter the contest with the hope of winning the hand of Eva, the goldsmith's daughter. An exciting contest follows with the nobleman, Walter, Eva's lover, winning the prize.

Composition: *Invitation to the Dance*

Composer: Carl Maria von Weber
(For further information refer to pages 136-137)
Descriptive Summary of Composition:

1. Although the composition has been transcribed for
   orchestra, Weber wrote it originally for the piano.
   Orchestral transcriptions of the piece have been made
   by Felix Weingartner and Hector Berlioz.
2. *Invitation to the Dance* is written as a waltz with
   several waltz melodies written in a medley form. Weber
   originated the form of the medley waltz, which was
   later used by the two Johann Strausses.
3. According to a story connected with the music, the
   waltz takes place at a grand ball where a young man
   invites a lady to dance with him. They dance, converse
   with each other and then separate.
4. In the music, an introductory phrase is played by
   the cellos; this is intended to signify the man's invitation. There is a short reply by the woodwinds. A
   conversation follows; this is indicated by contrasting
   phrases by the strings and woodwinds.
5. The dance of the couple starts when the whole orchestra begins to play. Further conversations take place
   and finally the dance comes to a lively climax, and it
   is over.
6. After the climax in the music, a brief phrase similar
   to the introduction is heard; this indicates the return of the lady to her place.

Composition: *Symphony In G Major (Surprise Symphony)*

Composer: Franz Josef Haydn
(For further information refer to pages 108-109)
Descriptive Summary of Composition:

1. The nickname "Surprise" comes from the surprise which
   occurs in the second movement of the symphony. The
   surprise is a loud and sudden chord which comes when
   least expected during a quiet passage. It is said that
   Haydn put this loud chord in a soft passage purposely
   to awaken anyone who had fallen asleep.

2. The symphony is written in four movements and scored
   for two flutes, two oboes, two bassoons, two trumpets,
   two horns, tympani and strings.

3. The first movement, Adagio; Vivace Assai, opens with
   a short and stately introduction played by the woodwinds, horn and strings. Most of the movement is very
   fast.

345

4. The second movement, Andante, contains the surprise. The whole movement is in the form of theme and variations.
5. In the third movement, Menuetto, Allegro molto, Haydn uses a society dance of his time, the minuet.
6. The finale, Allegro di molto, is a rondo using two basic themes. It is quite fast.

Composition: *Peter And The Wolf*

Composer: Serge Prokofiev (Prokofieff)
(For further information refer to pages 238-239)
Descriptive Summary of Composition:

1. *Peter And The Wolf* is an orchestral fairy tale. The various characters of this story are each represented by a different instrument. Prokofiev wrote this composition for an educational purpose, viz. to teach children the instruments of the orchestra. The story is usually recited while the music is being played.
2. The composition had its American première by the Boston Symphony Orchestra on March 25, 1938.
3. Today the work is not only used as an educational piece, but as a concert piece as well.
4. Instruments representing the various characters are:
   a. Bird - flute
   b. Duck - oboe
   c. Cat - clarinet
   d. Grandfather - bassoon
   e. Wolf - three horns
   f. Peter - string quartet
   g. Shooting of hunters - bass drum and timpani.

Composition: *Symphony: Holidays*

Composer: Charles Ives
(For further information refer to pages 222-223.)

Descriptive Summary of Composition:

1. The *Symphony: Holidays* was inspired by holidays in Connecticut spent by Charles Ives during his boyhood. Like other Ives compositions, it reflects upon his early days in New England.

2. The symphony consists of four movements which portray New England at different seasons and holidays of the year. The various movements were written at different times.

a. Winter - *Washington's Birthday* (1909)
b. Spring - *Decoration Day* (1912)
c. Summer - *The Fourth of July* (1913)
d. Autumn - *Thanksgiving Day* (1904)

3. The first movement, *Washington's Birthday*, is scored for a chamber group consisting of church bells, chimes, piccolo, flute and horn. The last three movements are written for a full symphony orchestra. The whole score is admirably written.

4. The first three movements are often played and re-corded separately. The symphony is written with a flavor of neo-Impressionist style. In this composition, Ives incorporates variations of American folk tunes in an interesting and colorful manner.

Composition: *Afro-American Symphony*

Composer: William Grant Still
(For further information refer to pages 250-251.)

Descriptive Summary of Composition:

1. The *Afro-American Symphony* was written in 1930 and is one of Still's better-known symphonic compositions. It received its premiere performance at Eastman School of Music at an American Composers' Concert conducted by Howard Hanson.

2. The symphony is scored for full orchestra and is in four movements:

a. *Moderato Assai - Longing*
b. *Adagio - Sorrow*
c. *Animato - Humor*
d. *Lento, con Risoluzione - Aspiration*

3. This composition may be called a tonal symphony because each movement is preceded by a poem written by Paul L. Dunbar. The composer portrays a special mood in each poem. This also makes this piece a programmatic com-position.

4. The symphony is based on Negro idioms. The composer makes use of the Blues scale throughout the composition and employs an original blues theme which appears in various forms throughout the symphony.

5. The harmonic structure of the *Afro-American Symphony* is basically derived from the standard Blues progression with necessary variations. The composer makes skillful use of the banjo in the symphony. All of the elements mentioned above help to give this symphony a unique style and flavor.

CHAPTER 11

INSTRUMENTS OF THE SYMPHONY ORCHESTRA

Introduction:

This chapter, will give the reader basic information about the various instruments of the orchestra. The authors believe that a knowledge of the instruments of the symphony orchestra will enable the student to obtain a fuller appreciation of music.

These instruments were developed and perfected over a period of many centuries. The first step toward the development of the physical layout of the symphony orchestra through the use of instrumental choirs or sections was undertaken by Franz Joseph Haydn. This same format has been maintained on to the present day except for the addition and refinement of instruments. The authors of this book have used this format in the description of the instruments of the orchestra. The description of each instrument is divided into the following four categories:

1. Origin: country, dates, craftsmen

2. Construction: instrument parts, wood, metal, etc.

3. Production of sound: bowing, plucking, blowing, etc.

4. Tone quality: types of tone emitted

Photographs of all of the instruments have been included in this chapter. The reader should eventually be able to recognize these instruments both aurally and visually. For purposes of visual recognition, the student may refer to the photographs in this book, and also to pictures and drawings of instruments contained in other sources.

INSTRUMENTS OF THE SYMPHONY ORCHESTRA

I. The String Section:
   The string choir is the largest section of the four orchestral choirs. The instruments of the string section are: Violin, Viola, Violoncello and Double-bass.

A. Violin:

   1. Origin:

      a. Derived from Greek lyre.

      b. Came from the East, introduced into Spain by the Arabs in the eighth century.

      c. First perfect form of the modern violin came from:

         (1) Amati family 1592-1682.

         (2) Guarneri family 1630-1695.

         (3) Antonio Stradivarius 1650-1737.

   2. Construction:

      a. Except for the strings, the violin is made entirely of wood, and consists of two main parts: body and neck.

   3. Production of sound:

      a. Mainly produced by drawing bow across strings or by plucking the strings.

   4. Tone quality:

      a. Many varieties of tone quality are possible, including: clear, sharp, soft, flutelike, round, mellow, deep, broad and full.

B. <u>Viola</u>:

    1. Origin:

        a. Its predecessor was the viola d'amore, an instrument of the viol family. The viol d'amore was invented in England in the seventeenth century.

    2. Construction:

        a. It is constructed on the same principle as that of the violin with the exception that it is one-fifth larger and is tuned a fifth lower.

    3. Production of sound:

        a. The same as described under violin.

    4. Tone quality:

        a. Tone quality can be dark, melancholy, penetrating, cold, nasal, tender and romantic.

C. <u>Violoncello</u> (<u>'Cello</u>):

    1. Origin:

        a. Traced to Italy during the first part of the 17th century.

        b. Its predecessor was the viola da gamba.

    2. Construction:

        a. The construction of the 'cello is the same as that of the violin; the violoncello is much larger.

    3. Production of sound:

        a. Produced by drawing bow across the string or plucking the string.

4. Tone quality:

    a. Tone quality can be mellow, rich, resonant, brilliant and vigorous.

D. <u>Double-bass</u>:

1. Origin:

    a. The four stringed double-bass appeared in 1800. Its predecessor was the basse de viole of the viol family. It is the largest member of the string family.

2. Construction:

    a. For additional strength it has slanting instead of round shoulders. Where the belly is joined to the neck and fingerboard the double-bass has a decided point, whereas in the violin, viola, and cello, the fingerboard is at right angles to the horizontal part of a wide curve.

3. Production of sound:

    a. The chief difference in sound production between the cello and double-bass is that in the double-bass, the stretches for the fingers are very great due to the long string length, and more pressure is needed on the string.

4. Tone quality:

    a. Tone varies greatly in its degrees of loud and soft. The quality of tone may be described as being rough, very powerful, grand, gigantic, calm, majestic, threatening, rich and weird.

II. <u>The Woodwind Section</u>:
    The woodwind family has the following instruments: piccolo, flute, oboe, English horn, clarinet, bass clarinet, bassoon and contra bassoon.

A. Flute:

1. Origin:

   a. The flute is one of the most ancient instruments. References are made to it in Egyptian, Greek and Roman history and mythology.

2. Construction:

   a. Consists of three joints:

      (1) Head - contains the embouchure, which player blows across.

      (2) Body - contains the holes and keys necessary to produce various tones.

      (3) Foot - contains additional keys necessary to extend the compass.

3. Production of sound:

   a. Flute is held almost horizontally with embouchure turned slightly outward. The performer directs the breath across the opening.

4. Tone quality:

   a. Tone differs greatly in the three registers of the flute:

      (1) Lower register produces a sonorous tone.

      (2) Middle register is full, mellow, sweet, and sorrowful.

      (3) Upper register tone can be brilliant, light and delicate.

B. Piccolo:

Piccolo really means little flute. It has half the dimensions of the flute.

1. Origin:

   a. The piccolo came into use at the end of the 18th century. Its origin is the same as the flute.

2. Construction:

   a. Similar to the flute except that it does not contain the tail-piece with the extra low keys.

3. Production of sound:

   a. Same as with the flute.

4. Tone quality:

   a. Sounds an octave higher than the flute. Its tone quality is shrill, piercing, bright and penetrating.

   b. The piccolo is often used in descriptive music to imitate such sounds as the whistling of the wind.

C. Oboe:

   1. Origin:

      a. The oboe is derived from an ancient instrument which is referred to in Egyptian, Greek and Roman history and paintings.

   2. Construction:

      a. A double-reed instrument.

      b. Composed of a wooden tube with conical bore, widening out to form a small bell, and having at the opposite end a short metal tube, to which are bound by silk the two thin pieces of cane which form the mouthpiece.

   3. Production of sound:

      a. Player breathes gently into the mouthpiece. Notes are produced by the opening and closing of holes pierced in the tube of the instrument. These holes are regulated by a system of keys.

4. Tone quality:

    a. The tone of the oboe is very penetrating, shrill, nasal and sharp.

D. English Horn:
      The name, English Horn, is misleading; it is not a horn, but is a double-reed instrument.

1. Origin:

    a. Derived from an ancient instrument, the alto pommer. The exact date at which it assumed its present form is unknown; it was presumably in the 17th century.

2. Construction:

    a. Slightly different from that of the oboe; it is longer, has a larger globular bell, and the mouthpiece is attached to a slightly bent tube.

3. Production of sound:

    a. Same as oboe.

4. Tone quality:

    a. It is slightly less penetrating than that of the oboe. Its tone can be sweet, melancholy and tender.

E. Clarinet:
      It is a single-reed instrument.

1. Origin:

    a. Its ancestor was an ancient Greek instrument. In 1690, when Johann C. Denner made many improvements on this ancient instrument (shawm), it became known as the clarinet. Further improvements by Theobald Boehm in 1843 resulted in the modern clarinet.

2. Construction:

    a. Consists of a cylindrical tube of wood (ebony or cocus) which comes in sections.

The chisel-shaped mouthpiece or ebonite fits
into a socket in the upper part of the tube.

3. Production of sound:

   a. Tone is produced by breathing into the mouthpiece, causing the reed to vibrate. Tones are
   formed by the opening and closing of holes,
   regulated by a system of keys.

4. Tone quality:

   a. Its tone quality varies according to the
   register. It can produce such tone qualities
   as brilliant, sonorous, sweet, mellow, melancholy, weak, clear, expressive, noble, sombre
   and penetrating.

F. Bass Clarinet:

1. Origin:

   a. Its ancestors are the same as
   those of the clarinet. The instrument in its present form
   was invented about 1772 by G.
   Lot.

2. Construction:

   a. It is twice as long as the
   clarinet and has a turned-up
   metal bell. The tube which ex-
   tends to the mouth-piece is
   serpentine in form.

3. Production of sound:

   a. Produced in the same manner as
   that of the clarinet.

4. Tone quality:

   a. Its tone is less reedy than that
   of the higher-pitched clarinet and
   more hollow. It has a somber, dark, deep,
   and resonant quality.

G. Bassoon:
   A double-reed instrument.

   1. Origin:

      a. Like the clarinet, the bassoon is
         thought to be of great antiquity, its
         prototype being the schalmey or shawm.
         The modern instrument is believed to
         have been invented by Afriano of
         Ferrara in the middle of the 16th
         century.

   2. Construction:

      a. It is a conically-bored pipe doubled
         back upon itself so as to reduce its
         length to about four feet. The full
         length is divided into five pieces
         which are, in their order from the
         anterior end:

         (1) The crook

         (2) The wing

         (3) The double joint

         (4) Bass joint

         (5) The bell

   3. Production of sound:

      a. The player breathes into the mouthpiece. The
         mechanism and fingering of the bassoon are very
         intricate but the basic system of tone produc-
         tion is similar to that of the oboe and clarinet.

   4. Tone Quality:

      a. The tone quality of the bassoon varies according
         to the register. It can produce such tone quali-
         ties as thick, reedy, solemn, sonorous, expres-
         sive, sweet, and humorous. Since it can produce
         gay little tunes and humorous sounds, the
         bassoon is sometimes called the "clown of the
         orchestra."

H. Contra-Bassoon (Double-Bassoon):
A double-reed instrument, pitched an octave
lower than the bassoon.

1. Origin:

a. The contra-bassoon can be traced back
to ancient times. Its immediate
ancestor was the schalmey
family.

2. Construction:

a. The length of its tubing amounts to sixteen feet. The tubing is folded on itself
four or six times.

3. Production of sound:

a. Same as that of the bassoon, but its
fingering is less complicated.

4. Tone quality:

a. The tone is rough, harsh, and nasal. In
the medium and upper register its tone is
like that of the bassoon.

I. Saxophone:
The saxophone is related both
to the woodwinds and brass.

1. Origin:

a. The saxophone was invented about
1840 by Adolphe Sax of Belgium.
Adolphe Sax, at the time, was
trying to produce a clarinet
which would overblow an octave
instead of a twelfth. The new
instrument was named the saxophone.

2. Construction:

a. It is made of brass and is built
in seven sizes. The five most
frequently used are:
(1) Soprano in B flat
(2) Alto in E flat
(3) Tenor in B flat

    (4) Baritone in E flat

    (5) Bass in B flat

  3. Production of sound:

   a. The player breathes into the mouthpiece, this causes the reed to vibrate. Notes are formed by the opening and closing of holes, regulated by a system of keys.

  4. Tone quality:

   a. The tone quality of the saxophone is a blend of brass and woodwind. In the upper register its tone is soft and penetrating; in the middle register it is expressive and amorous; and in the lower register it is full and rich.

III. The Brass Section:

  The brass family consists of the following instruments: cornet, trumpet, French horn, trombone, tuba and bass tuba.

 A. Cornet:

  1. Origin:

   a. An early 19th century instrument which evolved from the keyed bugle and trumpet.

  2. Construction:

   a. Composed of a cylindrical tube of brass or electrosilver which becomes conical near the bell. The tube is doubled upon itself. A cup-shaped mouthpiece is used.

  3. Production of sound:

   a. Sound is produced by blowing through the lips which are stretched across the mouthpiece and vibrate against it. Notes are obtained by means of three valves and from the harmonic series.

4. Tone quality:

    a. The tone of the cornet can be sonorous, blaring and penetrating, but is not as brilliant as that of the trumpet. The cornet is seldom used in the symphony orchestra.

B. Trumpet:

    1. Origin:

        a. It is of ancient origin, having been in use among the ancient Egyptian and the Semetic peoples. Its primitive ancestor was made from horns and tusks of animals. The present form of the trumpet with its three valves evolved in the early part of the 19th century.

    2. Construction:

        a. It consists of a long, narrow tube, doubled twice upon itself and ending in a conical bell. The bore is cylindrical from mouthpiece to bell-joint, including all valve-tubes and the tuning slide.

    3. Production of sound:

        a. Same as cornet.

    4. Tone quality:

        a. It is bright, majestic, brilliant, military and noble.

C. French Horn:

    1. Origin:

        a. The origin of the French horn can be traced back to the old hunting horns. They were used in Egyptian, Assyrian and Indian civilizations. The present form of the horn appeared in 1820 with the invention of the three valves

360

2. Construction:

   a. The French horn includes three principal parts:
      the body, the crooks and the mouthpiece.

   b. The length of the horn tube varies according to
      the key being played. Its length can be from
      twelve to sixteen feet of tubing.

3. Production of sound:

   a. The natural or open notes of the horn depend
      upon the length of the tube being used. Other
      means of obtaining the notes desired include:
      tension of the lips, pressure of breath, depres-
      sion of valves and hand-stopping. Bouché or
      hand-stopping consists of inserting the right
      hand into the bell of the horn.

4. Tone quality:

   a. Its tone quality lies midway between the brass
      and woodwinds. The tone is full, mellow, re-
      sonant, sweet and sonorous.

D. Trombone:

1. Origin:

   a. The
      trombone
      derives from old
      predecessors which were used by the ancient
      Romans. The immediate predecessor of the trombone
      was the sackbut used in the Middle Ages.

   b. The sackbut developed into the trombone of seven
      positions at the beginning of the 16th century.
      At this time Neuschels of Nuremberg made slide-
      trombones as well developed as the modern ones
      of today.

2. Construction:

   a. Consists of a tube doubled twice upon itself,
      with a wide bell at one end, and a cup-shaped
      mouthpiece at the other.

   b. The tubes forming the slide are made double and
      are connected to the lower end of a semi-circular
      tube. The outer tube slides upon the inner tube,
      opening to a greater or lesser length of tube
      depending upon the pitch desired.

3. Production of sound:

   a. Tone is produced by breathing into the mouth-piece. There are seven positions of the slide on the trombone, each giving a fundamental tone and its harmonic series. Various notes are obtained through the use of the seven positions and tensions of the lips and wind pressure.

4. Tone quality:

   a. This varies with the different registers. Its tone can be powerful, penetrating, full, rich, majestic, sonorous and heroic.

E. Tuba:

   There are six types of tubas, ranging from soprano to contrabass.

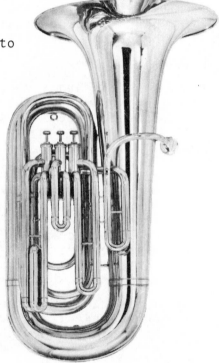

1. Origin:

   a. The tuba was invented in 1835 by Wieprecht. Its ancestor was the keyed bugle.

2. Construction:

   a. It consists of a wide conical brass tube with a wide bore, ending in a wide-mouthed bell. The conical tube is about 18 feet in length. It has four or five valve positions.

3. Production of sound:

   a. Tone is produced by breathing into the mouthpiece. The various notes are obtained through the use of the valves and harmonics.

4. Tone quality:

   a. Its tone quality is deep, rich, sonorous, and powerful.

IV. The Percussion Section:

Instruments which need to be shaken or struck for sound are known as percussion instruments. The main instruments of this section are: timpani, snare drum, bass drum, tom-tom, tambourine, castanets, triangle, cymbals, gong, bells, chimes, glockenspiel, xylophone and piano.

A. Timpani:

1. Origin:

   a. They are of Arabic origin. They were originally quite small and could be conveniently held in one hand and played with the other.

2. Construction:

   a. The timpani is the only drum which can be tuned to a definite pitch.

   b. The timpani consists of a piece of vellum stretched tightly over a hemispherical shell or pan of copper or brass. It is tuned by means of screws working on an iron ring which fits closely around the head of the drum.

3. Production of sound:

   a. Various types of sticks or mallets are used to play it. The end of the stick is usually covered with fine sponge, felt or India-rubber.

4. Tone quality:

   a. Its tone quality is sonorous, resonant, powerful, harsh, and mournful.

   b. Beautiful effects are obtained in rolls, in crescendo and diminuendo passages, or in forte and piano passages. The timpani is often used to produce an effect of fear, surprise and suspense.

363

B. <u>Snare</u> <u>Drum</u>:

    1. Origin:

        a. The
           snare
           drum is
           of early
           Oriental
           origin.
           It was
           used for
           delicate
           rhythmic
           accompani-
           ment; for
           example:
           it sometimes
        supplied the rhythm for flute solos.

    2. Construction:
        a. It consists of a small wooden or brass cylinder
           with a vellum at each end.
        b. The upper head (that on which the player beats)
           is called the "batter-head"; the lower head is
           called the "snare-head".

    3. Production of sound:
        a. The drum is struck by two
           sticks made of hard wood
           with small round tips.

    4. Tone quality:
        a. Its tone quality can be
           crisp, rattling, muf-
           fled, or sharp and mili-
           tary.

C. <u>Bass</u> <u>Drum</u>:

    1. Origin:
        a. The bass drum was first
           introduced into operatic
           music in the 18th century.

        b. It is an enlarged form of
           the snare drum. It was in-
           troduced in the orchestra
           after long use in the
           military band.

2. Construction:

   a. The bass drum consists of a short wooden cylinder, of a very wide diameter, covered at both ends by vellum stretched over small hoops, kept in place by larger hoops.

3. Production of sound:

   a. It is struck near the center with a stick or mallet, which has a large, soft round knob at one end.

4. Tone quality:

   a. Its sound effects are thunderous, climactic, military, full, dull and muffled.

D. Tom-Tom:

1. Origin:

   a. The tom-tom dates back to the ancient and primitive cultures.

   b. The drums were used by American Indians and Orientals.

   c. The tom-tom is sometimes called Hindu-drum or Chinese-drum.

   d. It is a modern derivative of early drums.

2. Construction:

   a. It comes in several sizes and consists of skin membranes stretched tightly on both sides of a cylindrical frame or hoop.

3. Production of sound:

   a. Ordinarily played by being struck with a stick.

4. Tone quality:

   a. Produces a sharp, brief and hollow sound.

   b. Used to obtain the effects of savage and barbaric tribe music.

E. Tambourine:

   1. Origin:

      a. The tam-
bourine
(timbrel)
was used
among the
most ancient nations
of the world, such as Assyria, Egypt and Greece.

      b. It has remained practically unchanged for the
past two thousand years.

      c. It was introduced into orchestral works for
Spanish and gypsy musical effects.

   2. Construction:

      a. It consists of a small wooden hoop, on one side
of which there is a parchment which can be
tightened or loosened.

      b. The hoop is cut away at intervals to allow the
insertion of small tinkling metal discs.

   3. Production of sound:

      a. There are three basic ways of playing the
tambourine: striking the head, shaking the hoop,
and rubbing the thumb on the head.

   4. Tone quality:

      a. Its tingling sound is effective at moments of
rhythmic excitement.

F. Castanets:

   1. Origin:

      a. The instrument
called castanets
is extremely
ancient, and
originated with
the Moors, who
brought it into
Spain, where it
soon became the national instrument of Spanish
dancers.

2. Construction:

   a. Castanets are pairs of small shell-shaped clap-
      pers, made of hard wood or ivory, connected by
      a loop at the upper end.

3. Production of Sound:

   a. The loop is placed over the thumb and the first
      finger of the performer, the remaining fingers
      strike the two halves together.

4. Tone quality:

   a. Its tone consists of short, dry, rhythmical
      beats.

   b. The instrument gives a deep hollow click and
      adds a variety of rhythmical color to the music.

G. Triangle:

   1. Origin:

      a. The triangle probably came
         from the Orient, and ap-
         peared in Europe before
         the 14th century. It
         achieved its triangular
         form in the 15th
         century.

   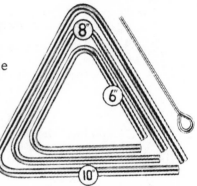

   2. Construction:

      a. It consists of a triangular rod
         of steel which is open and curved slightly at
         one corner. It is suspended on a loop.

   3. Production of sound:

      a. The triangle is played with a beater made of
         steel.

   4. Tone quality:

      a. Its tone is sharp, ringing, tinkling and in-
         cisive.

H. Cymbals:

  1. Origin:

    a. Cymbals are an ancient in-
strument used by the
Assyrians, Egyptians,
Hebrews and Greeks.

  2. Construction:

    a. They are made of two
large circular brass
plates or hammered metal.

    b. They are purposely made to have a saucer-shaped
depression in the center, so that when brought
together, only the edges are in contact.

  3. Production of sound:

    a. They are played by sharply brushing the edges
against each other in a vertical sliding motion.

    b. Sometimes the cymbal is played by hanging it on
a frame and performing a roll on it with two
soft timpani sticks.

  4. Tone quality:

    a. Crashing and harsh are the typical sounds of the
cymbals, useful for climaxes in music.

I. Gong:

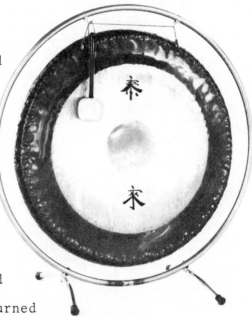

  1. Origin:

    a. The gong originated
in the Far East.
During the period
of the French
Revolution it
found its way
into European
orchestras. In
1804 it was
introduced into
the operatic score
of Lesueur's *Les
Bardes*.

  2. Construction:

    a. It is a bowl-shaped
instrument made of
bronze with an upturned
rim, which is pierced to

take the cord by which the gong is suspended on a frame.

3. Production of sound:

   a. Its center is set into vibration by a mallet or similar beater.

4. Tone quality:

   a. The tone of a large Chinese gong is strange and imposing. The gong may produce a variety of tone qualities which include dark, mysterious, and solemn.

J. Bells: - Chimes:

1. Origin:

   a. Some form of bells were used back in the 4th century by the Romans. Cup-shaped bells were popular in the Middle Ages. The Christian Church has been using some type of bell in its tower since the 6th century.

2. Construction:

   a. Cup-shaped bell:

      (1) It is cast in bronze.

      (2) It is sometimes too heavy for concert work. It is satisfactory if mounted in a wooden frame.

   b. Tubular bells:

      (1) They are made in sets, all of one diameter, (either 1 inch, 1 1/4, 1 1/2, or 2 inches); but different lengths depending upon the pitch desired.

      (2) They are usually hung in a frame.

369

3. Production of sound:

   a. The bells are struck with a mallet.

   b. Tubular bells are tuned to a definite pitch.

4. Tone quality:

   a. Tone quality of the tubular bells is full, sonorous, deep and resonant.

K. Glockenspiel:

1. Origin:

   a. The glockenspiel has the same origin as that of the bells and chimes, and dates back to Roman times of the 4th century.

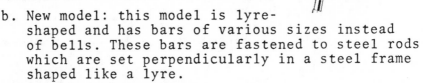

2. Construction:

   a. Old model: was shaped like a pyramid consisting of hemispherical bells, placed one above the other, fastened with an iron rod passing through the center of each bell.

   b. New model: this model is lyre-shaped and has bars of various sizes instead of bells. These bars are fastened to steel rods which are set perpendicularly in a steel frame shaped like a lyre.

3. Production of sound:

   a. The bars are played with a little steel hammer attached to a whalebone stick.

4. Tone quality:

   a. Its tone quality is brilliant, penetrating, clear and sparkling.

   b. Many composers have used the glockenspiel for bell-like effects. Hindemith used it in his symphony *Mathis der Maler*, Gershwin in his *Rhapsody in Blue*, and Mozart in the *Magic Flute*.

L. Xylophone:

1. Origin:

   a. Probably
      originated
      among the
      Russians and
      Tartars. The
      xylophone
      was popular
      in the
      Middle Ages,
      especially
      in Russia
      and Poland.

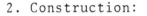

2. Construction:

   a. It is made up
      of small wooden
      bars of definite pitch arranged in two rows,
      similar to the keys of a piano. It has a range
      of about four octaves. There is a metal tubular
      resonator under each bar to provide a fuller
      tone.

3. Production of sound:

   a. It is played with small hard mallets.

4. Tone quality:

   a. Its tone quality is clear, brilliant, brittle
      and quite short.

   b. The tone quality of the xylophone is appealing
      to children. It is often used as a solo instru-
      ment.

V. Instruments for Solo and Accompaniment:

A. Piano:
   The piano is not used very often in the Symphony
Orchestra. It is mainly used as a solo instrument,
or for vocal accompaniment. The piano is considered
one of the most important instruments of the popular
Dance Orchestra of modern times.

1. Origin:

   a. The modern piano was invented in 1709 by
      Bartolomeo Cristofori, a harpsichord maker from
      Florence, Italy. Because earlier models were

inferior to Cristofori's model,
Cristofori is regarded by many
as the true "Father of the
Piano."

b. Its full name is pianoforte, referring to
its hammer action
which makes it
possible to
play the in-
strument
softly or
loudly.

2. Construction:

a. Pianos come
in various
designs and
sizes, such
as the baby grand, concert grand, upright and
spinet.

b. The main parts of the piano are: case and frame,
strings, soundboard, bridges, action, keyboard
and pedals.

c. The modern piano with a full keyboard has eighty-
eight keys which constitute seven and a quarter
octaves.

3. Production of sound:

a. The sound is obtained by depressing a key, which
through a system of levers, raises the hammer
and causes it to strike the strings and rebound.

b. Variations of tone can be obtained through the
use of the pedals. A brief description of the
pedals follows:

(1) Soft pedal (left side): this pedal shifts
the action so that instead of three strings
being struck, only one is struck. This produces a softer tone.

(2) Sostenuto pedal (middle pedal): this pedal
prolongs the tones of certain strings in-
dependently of the others.

(3) Damper pedal (right side; miscalled loud pedal): when this pedal is depressed, the dampers are raised; this causes a sustained vibration of the strings.

4. Tone quality:

   a. The tone quality of the piano varies widely, depending entirely upon the touch of the performer. Some of its effects are: brilliant, dramatic, powerful, poetic, light, rich, soft, full and mellow.

   b. The tone of the piano also varies according to the different piano models. Some manufacturers concentrate on a brilliant and clear tone quality, while others stress a mellow tone.

B. Harp:

   The harp is considered a solo instrument. It is only used occasionally in the Symphony Orchestra and usually supplements the accompaniment with chords and arpeggios.

1. Origin:

   a. The harp is one of the most ancient of all musical instruments. Reference is made to it in the Bible.

   b. Pictures of the harp are found in Egyptian art which dates back to 1300 B.C.

   c. The modern harp of today was perfected by Sebastian Erard; his double-action harp was patented in 1810.

2. Construction:

   a. The main parts of the harp include: column or fore-pillar, body, curving neck, pedals, tuning-pins, ivory pegs and strings.

   b. The strings are vertical and joined to the soundboard at an angle. The strings of the upper and middle registers are made of gut or nylon; the bass strings are made of covered steel wire.

c. Color: the strings of the harp come in three color combinations. A harpist may use any one of these combinations:

   (1) C-green; F-purple; D,E,G,A and B-red.

   (2) C-red; F-purple; D,E,G,A, and B-white.

   (3) C-red; F-purple; D,E,G,A and B-green.

3. Production of sound:

   a. Only thumbs, first, second and ring fingers are used to play or vibrate the strings.

   b. With the use of the seven pedals on the double-action harp, it is possible to change a note a whole tone and therefore the harpist can play in all major and minor keys.

4. Tone quality:

   a. The tone quality of the harp is at its fullest and most brilliant in keys with flats, for then the strings are open. In keys with many sharps its tone becomes more penetrating.

   b. The tone quality is resonant in the bass register; clear and penetrating in the middle and treble registers and very hard and dry in the last octave and a half.

   c. Various effects can be produced on the harp by:

      (1) Harmonics

      (2) Damping

      (3) Glissando

C. Spanish (Acoustic) Guitar:

1. Origin:

   a. Its ancestors were brought to Spain during the middle ages by the Moors. The modern Spanish guitar is derived from the Spanish Vihuela de Mano of the 16th century.

2. Construction:

   a. Fretted string instru-
      ment with an oval body
      and a neck. It is made
      of a light wood.

   b. It has six single
      strings made of metal
      or gut.

3. Production of Sound:

   a. Sound is produced by
      plucking the strings
      with a pick or
      fingers.

4. Tone Quality:

   a. Many varieties of tone quality are possible, in-
      cluding: soft, romantic, tender, harmonious, rich,
      vigorous and brilliant.

D. Electric Guitar:

   1. Origin:

      a. The electric guitar
         came into prominence
         over thirty years ago.
         Leo Fender in America
         invented and intro-
         duced the first solid-
         body electric guitar
         over twenty years ago.

      b. This instrument has
         attained a popularity
         and has become the
         prime instrument of
         rock music.

   2. Construction:

      a. The electric guitar,
         as we know it now,
         is made of a highly
         polished wood frame
         with six strings and
         metal frets.

3. Production of Sound:

   a. The tone is amplified through the use of a small microphone attached to the sound-board which in turn picks up the sound which is amplified through speakers.

4. Tone Quality:

   a. Its tone quality can vary, depending upon the type of sound you wish to produce. It can be sweet, melodious and beautiful or it can be loud, harsh and paralyzing.

E. <u>Electric Bass</u>:

1. The electric bass is the same instrument as the electric guitar except that it has only four strings and is pitched lower.

INSTRUMENTATION USED BY REPRESENTATIVE COMPOSERS
OF VARIOUS PERIODS IN MUSIC HISTORY

INSTRUMENTS	HAYDN 1732-1809	BEETHOVEN 1770-1827	WAGNER 1813-1883	STRAVINSKY 1882-
Strings:				
1st. Violins	8	14	18	18
2nd. Violins	6	12	18	18
Violas	4	10	12	12
Cellos	4	8	12	12
Bass Viols	4	8	8	10
Harps			2	2
Woodwinds:				
Piccolos		1	1	2
Flutes	2	2	3	4
Oboes	2	2	3	4
English Horns			1	1
Clarinets		2	3	4
Bass Clarinets			1	1
Bassoons	2	2	3	4
Contra Bassoon		1	1	1
Brass:				
Trumpets	2	2	3	5
Cornets				2
French Horns	2	4	4	8
Trombones		3	3	3
Bass Trumpet				1
Tubas			1	3
Percussion:				
Timpani	2	2	3	5
Bass Drum		1	1	1
Snare Drum			1	1
Gong			1	1
Cymbals		1	1	1
Triangle		1	1	1
Tambourine				1
Xylophone				1
Glockenspiel			1	1
Celesta				1
Harpsichord	1			
Piano	1	1	1	1
Total number of instruments:	40	77	107	130

Boston Symphony Orchestra
Seiji Ozawa, Music Director

CHAPTER 12

THE ELEMENTS OF MUSIC

Introduction: Information concerning the origin of music and the development of the elements of music in the early stages of history is limited because of a lack of documentation. We must accept the theoretical interpretation of musicologists who have made many studies of early music.

One of the earliest documented sources of music theory and practice originated in the Roman Catholic Church. The basic idiom of Church music was the Gregorian Chant, which can be theoretically summarized in eight scales or modes. These chants form the basic structure of all monophonic music and influenced the form of sacred and some secular music until the beginning of the Baroque period.

The theorists of this time evolved a means by which the composers could notate their music more accurately. Guido of Arezzo, in the eleventh century, developed the musical staff and with it a more exact and scientific approach to the mechanics of music. The basic elements of music were analyzed and its components which include tone, melody, harmony, time and texture now were improved as a means of musical expression.

One major obstacle to the fulfillment of listening to music intelligently is the lack of knowledge of its basic elements. In order to develop the ability to listen discriminatively, the student should learn and understand these basic elements and their parts. In so doing, they will find that the knowledge gained from this chapter will add immeasurably to the joy of creative listening.

The Elements of Music: These elements can be classified as follows: 1. Tone, 2. Melody, 3. Harmony, 4. Time, 5. Texture.

I. Tone: Denotes a sound of a definite pitch caused by regular vibrations (a sound with irregular vibrations is a noise of indefinite pitch).

   A. Musical tone consists of four distinct parts:

      1. Pitch: The "highness" or "lowness" of a musical sound.

      2. Duration: The measured period of time a tone is held in relation to other tones or silence. Musical tone symbols (notes) indicates how long a pitch is

to be held, while other symbols (rests) indicate brief periods of silence.

3. Tone Color: The characteristic tone quality which distinguishes the different instruments and voices.

4. Dynamics: Intensity of tone, i.e. the loudness or softness of tone. Some common terms used to indicate dynamics are:

   a. *Forte* (f) - loud
   b. *Mezzo Forte* (mf) - moderately loud
   c. *Fortissimo* (ff) - very loud

   d. *Crescendo* (⟨=======⟩) - becoming louder

   e. *Piano* (p) - soft
   f. *Mezzo Piano* (mp) - moderately soft
   g. *Pianissimo* (pp) - very soft

   h. *Diminuendo* (⟨=======⟩) - becoming softer.

B. Acoustical properties of musical sound:

1. Musical tone is produced by vibrations resulting from:
   a. Struck, bowed or plucked strings.
   b. Air blown through a reed or metal mouthpiece into wooden or metal sound chambers of an instrument.
   c. Shaken or struck percussion instruments.
   d. Air waves in cylindrical tubes of an organ.
   e. Electronic stimulation through the use of generators.

2. Determination of pitch frequencies:
   a. The level of pitch varies with the number of vibrations per second. The highest limit of sound heard by the human ear is 18,000 vibrations per second. The lowest limit of sound heard by the human ear is 30 vibrations per second.

3. Acoustical relationship of notes of the piano keyboard:
   a. Middle C has 261.6 vibrations per second.
   b. The next C (octave above) has 523.2 vibrations per second, the number of vibrations doubling each consecutive octave above.
   c. The C (octave below middle C) has 130.8 vibrations per second, the number of vibrations halving at each consecutive octave below.
   d. Each note of the keyboard has a specific number of vibrations.

4. The acoustics of tone quality is determined by the composition and structure of the instrument producing the tone.
   a. The volume of tone is dependent upon the size of the sound producing chamber of the instrument.

II. Melody: A succession of pitches arranged to create a linear musical idea. A melody may be compared to a sentence in an English composition; it expresses a complete musical thought.

A. The components of a melody are:

1. Length: A short or long melody.
2. Range: The compass between the lowest and highest notes.
3. Direction: The motion upward or downward in pitch.
4. Pattern: The arrangement in which groups of tones follow one another.

B. Tonality: The relationship which exists between the tones of the melody and the keynote or key of the composition.

C. Scales: All melodies can be tonally summarized into scales. A scale consists of eight consecutive notes in predetermined order of half and whole steps. The most common scales used in music at this time are:

1. Chromatic scale: made up of twelve half-steps.
2. Diatonic major scale: made up of two consecutive four-note groups separated by a whole step. Each group consists of two whole steps followed by a half-step.
3. Minor scales consist of three basic forms:
   a. Natural minor: relative minor scale.
   b. Harmonic minor: raised 7th step.
   c. Melodic minor: raised 6th and 7th step ascending, and lowered 6th and 7th steps descending.

D. Keys and Key Signatures: All melodies and scales are related to specific keys. Every melody is built around a key note and the scale starting on this key note. The keys used today are divided into major and relative minor keys. They consist of the following:

381

Major Keys:	No. of Accidentals:	Minor Keys:
Key of C	No sharps or flats	Key of A
Key of F	1 flat	Key of D
Key of B^b	2 flats	Key of G
Key of E^b	3 flats	Key of C
Key of A^b	4 flats	Key of F
Key of D^b	5 flats	Key of B^b
Key of G^b	6 flats	Key of E^b
Key of C^b	7 flats	Key of A^b
Key of C$^\#$	7 sharps	Key of A$^\#$
Key of F$^\#$	6 sharps	Key of D$^\#$
Key of B	5 sharps	Key of G$^\#$
Key of E	4 sharps	Key of C$^\#$
Key of A	3 sharps	Key of F$^\#$
Key of D	2 sharps	Key of B
Key of G	1 sharp	Key of E

III. Harmony: Harmony may be described as the simultaneous occurrence of two or more musical tones, and involves the relationship of these units to others in succession.

    A. Harmonic Intervals: their relationship to the major scale:

        1. Harmony is based upon the intervallic relationships of the notes of a chord. An interval may be described as the space between two tones. These intervals are based upon the degrees of the scale.

        2. The degrees of the scale are numbered progressively from one through eight:

Degree Name	Letter Name (C Major)	Sol-fa Syllable	Theoretical Name
1st.	C	do	Tonic
2nd.	D	re	Supertonic
3rd.	E	mi	Mediant
4th.	F	fa	Sub-Dominant
5th.	G	so	Dominant
6th.	A	la	Sub-Mediant
7th.	B	ti	Leading Tone
8th.	C	do	Tonic (Octave)

        3. Interval Names: The names of intervals based on the C major scale are:

        a. C (do) to C (do) (same note) - perfect prime
          C (do) to D (re) - major second
          C (do) to E (mi) - major third
          C (do) to F (fa) - perfect fourth
          C (do) to G (so) - perfect fifth
          C (do) to A (la) - major sixth
          C (do) to B (ti) - major seventh
          C (do) to C (do) (octave) - perfect octave

B. Chord: A combination of three or more notes sounded simultaneously.

C. Triad: A three-note chord. The three most common chords of a key, in order of importance, are:

1. Tonic chord: do (1st) - mi (3rd) - so (5th)
2. Dominant chord: so (5th) - ti (7th) - re (2nd)
3. Sub-Dominant chord: fa (4th) - la (6th) - do (8th)

D. Modulation: Use of chords to establish a change of tonality.

E. Consonant Chord: A chord that sounds stable to the ear, and contains no dissonant intervals.

F. Dissonant Chord: A chord that contains dissonant intervals and creates a feeling of instability.

IV. Time: Of all the fine arts, music is the art in which the element of time is of greatest importance to its structure.
    Time consists of the duration and speed of sound within the structure of musical composition. The musical symbol which denotes the division of time in a composition is the time signature (the numerical fraction appearing at the beginning of the composition). The three parts of time include tempo, meter, and rhythm:

A. Tempo: The rate of speed of a composition, ranging from slow to fast.

1. Tempo markings:
   a. *Grave* - slow, solemn.
   b. *Largo* - slowly.
   c. *Adagio* - slow; slower than *Andante*.
   d. *Lento* - slow; between *Andante* and *Largo*.
   e. *Andante* - at a leisurely, easy-going pace; moderate.

f. *Andantino* - literally means slower than *Andante*, but is usually performed slightly faster.

g. *Moderato* - at a moderate pace.

h. *Allegro* - fast; lively.

i. *Allegretto* - not as fast as *Allegro*.

j. *Presto* - very fast.

B. <u>Meter</u>: The arrangement of musical rhythm. The first <u>beat</u> of each measure is usually accented:

  1. Duple meter:

     a. Two beats per measure:

  2. Triple meter:

     a. Three beats per measure:

  3. Quadruple meter:

     a. Four beats per measure:

C. <u>Rhythm</u>: Pertains to the duration and orderly movement of musical sounds. Rhythm contains measured time with the occurrence of regular accents except in syncopated rhythm. In some music the occurrence of accents is irregular as in Gregorian Chant.

V. <u>Texture</u>: The weaving of the horizontal (melodic line) <u>and the</u> vertical (harmony).

A. Three basic types of musical texture:

  1. <u>Monophonic</u>: melody line alone (horizontal).

  2. <u>Homophonic</u>: melody line with chords (horizontal and vertical).

  3. <u>Polyphonic</u>: weaving of more than one melody line (horizontal with a vertical relationship).

CHAPTER 13

MUSICAL FORM

Introduction

Form may be considered the structure or architecture of music. It is the organization of musical ideas woven together to create an artistic entity.

In this chapter the authors have presented definitions of the various types of vocal and instrumental forms plus explanations of the ingredients that make up musical form. The knowledge and understanding of various types of musical forms will enable the listener to appreciate the ideas that the composer sets forth in his music.

The forms of musical structure may be easily compared to the structural units of English composition. The following chart shows the structural comparison of the components of music composition and English grammar, and the equivalents in each subject area:

	English	Music
Grammar:	Syllable	Note
	Word	Motive
	Clause	Phrase
	Sentence	Period (2 phrases)
	Paragraph (short)	Double Period (4 phrases)
Punctuation:	Comma	Semi-cadence
	Period	Complete cadence

A study of the above chart will point out the similarities of expression in both Music and English. The very obvious correlation of music with poetry, may be found in the multitude of poetic verses which have been set to music.

MUSICAL FORM

Form: A complete and balanced musical composition made up
of identical and contrasting phrases, the whole of
which is a balance of variety and unity.

A. Phrase: The most common unit of form.

  1. The phrase, which is the easiest unit of form to
  hear and understand, is a musical thought (not
  necessarily complete) and corresponds to the length
  of a breath (vocal), or to one line of poetry. It
  is usually four measures in length.

B. Ingredients of form:

  1. Repetition: Repetition re-enforces the memory of
  the listener, and thus establishes the basis for
  a comparison with new material. Repetition is
  meaningless under the following conditions:
  a. When musical sound consists only of repetition,
  it becomes monotonous, dull and uninteresting.
  b. Constant changing of phrases without reverting
  back to any point creates disorder, confusion,
  and disinterest.
  2. Contrast:
  a. Introduction of new material to provide more
  variety than simple variation techniques can
  supply, e.g. a contrasting phrase which intro-
  duces a new thought.
  3. Variety: Variety may be achieved through slight
  alterations of the phrase:
  a. Alterations of contour.
  b. Slight changes in rhythm.
  c. Different instrumentation.
  d. Variation in mode and harmonic background.
  e. Changes in dynamics.
  f. Modification of interpretation using staccato
  effect and legato phrasing.
  g. Variance in the tempo.
  4. Unity:
  a. The composition as a whole must be unified. It
  must be symmetrical, balanced, and the parts
  related to the whole composition.
  b. The listener must be able to understand and re-
  member the sections and relate them to the composition as a whole.

386

c. The composer usually has his main theme or a variation thereof recur throughout the composition in order to achieve unity. Also unity is achieved harmonically and rhythmically.

C. Seven basic types of musical form:

1. One-part form: only one theme used in the entire composition (Monothematic form).
2. Two-part form: use of two themes or sections, (Binary form) e.g. letter symbols: A B form.
3. Three-part form: three sections are used, (Ternary form) e.g. letter symbols: A B A form.
4. Rondo form: the main theme continually alternates with subordinate themes, e.g. A B A C A D A.
5. Sonata form: uses highly developed three part form.
6. Variation form: uses one part form with variations.
7. Fugue form: a highly developed form of a round. A short theme is imitated in each part of the fugue, usually in a related key (thus differing from the round in which there is merely exact repetition in the same key).

D. Vocal forms:

1. Short forms - selections:
   a. Hymn: a religious song in praise of God.
   b. Folk song: a popular or national song that has been handed down from an early source and has become a tradition.
   c. Art song: a short song written by a composer which sets a lyric text and contains refinement in melody and accompaniment.
   d. Elegy: a lament;a mournful piece; a funeral march.
   e. Lied: a type of art song in which the music is subordinate to the lyrics, and the music interprets the words.
   f. Ballad: a popular narrative song.
   g. Serenade: evening music; a love song.
   h. Spiritual: a religious song of negro origin.
   i. Recitative: a song in which the melodic pattern follows the inflections of the speaking voice.
   j. Carol: a song that celebrates the Christmas and Easter holidays.
   k. Mattinata: a morning song.
   l. Aria: an elaborate vocal solo with accompaniment. It can be part of an opera, or exist separately as a concert aria.

2. Choral forms - selections:
   a. Round: a short melody that is repeated with different voices or sections beginning and ending at different times.
   b. Canon: a song featuring strict imitation, and containing a subject and an answer.
   c. Chorale: a religious psalm or hymn performed by a choir or chorus.
   d. Madrigal: a pastoral or dramatic secular song in two to eight parts sung without accompaniment.
   e. Motet: an unaccompanied religious composition, based on the sacred text of the Roman Catholic Church services.
   f. Magnificat: a religious song using twelve verses of the bible for Church services.
   g. Passion: a type of oratorio which is a setting of the Passion of Christ. Each Passion is based on one of the four Gospel accounts.
   h. Requiem: usually a Mass for the dead.
   i. Anthem: a sacred English choral composition performed in the Anglican or other Protestant Churches.
   j. Glee: a secular unaccompanied song for three or more voice parts.

3. Large Choral Forms - selections:
   a. Cantata: a composite vocal form resembling a short oratorio. It can be either sacred or secular.
   b. Mass: the polyphonic or homophonic setting of the Roman Catholic Church services divided into five sections: (1) Kyrie, (2) Gloria (3) Credo (4) Sanctus (5) Agnus Dei.
   c. Oratorio: a religious dramatic work similar to opera, but without costumes or scenery.
   d. Opera: a large and complex drama for the stage in which the text is sung instead of spoken. It usually includes an overture and instrumental interludes.

E. Instrumental Forms:

1. Short forms - selections:
   a. Toccata: an improvisatory keyboard piece with elaborate ornamentation.
   b. March: a piece to accompany marching in simple and regularly accented rhythm.
   c. Nocturne: a romantic instrumental song suggesting the night or other romantic situations. Those of Chopin are well-known.
   d. Invention: a short contrapuntal study piece for the piano popularized in Johann Sebastian Bach's works.

e. Etude: a practice exercise or piece to help develop fluency of technique.
f. Scherzo: a light humorous piece; often the third movement of a symphony.
g. Rhapsody: a dramatic and emotional piece usually for solo instrument; Hungarian Rhapsodies of Liszt are very popular.
h. Fantasia: an improvisatory piece written in free form and style; mood music.
i. Caprice: a short humorous piano piece in three part form.
j. Ballade: a piano composition that tells a story and portrays a dramatic mood.
k. Bagatelle: a short piano piece.
l. Barcarolle: a piano composition that suggests a Venetian boat ride or song.
m. Intermezzo: a transitional piece sometimes used between movements of a sonata; an interlude; a short character piece for the piano.
n. Impromptu: an improvisatory piece which may have irregular rhythm; informal folk melody with sharp accents.
o. Arabesque: a highly ornamented and delicate piano piece.
p. Berceuse: a piano piece suggesting a lullaby or cradle song.
q. Novelette: a short narrative piano piece.

2. Dance forms - selections
   a. Waltz: most popular dance in 3/4 time.
   b. Minuet: a French dance in 3/4 time; very dignified and played in moderate tempo.
   c. Pavane: a slow, solemn and dignified dance in 4/4 time.
   d. Polka: a lively Bohemian dance in 2/4 time.
   e. Polonaise: a national Polish dance made popular by Chopin.
   f. Chaconne: a slow Spanish dance in 3/4 time.
   g. Passacaglia: a dance very similar to the Chaconne; written in a minor key; ground bass in 3/4 time.
   h. Ecossaise: originally Scotch, now a lively English country dance in 2/4 time.
   i. Gavotte: a French dance in 4/4 time; begins on the third beat of the measure.
   j. Gigue: a lively English dance in 6/8 time.
   k. Allemande: a German dance in 2/4 time; usually the first dance of the suite.
   l. Courante: a French dance in 3/2 or 6/4 time in two sections.

m. Sarabande: a slow, dignified Spanish dance
   in 3/4 time.
n. Tarantella: a very fast Italian peasant dance
   in 3/8 or 6/8 time.
o. Mazurka: a Polish national dance in 3/4 time
   which Chopin popularized as a piano solo.
p. Habanera: a popular dance of Spain and Cuba in
   3/4 time with syncopation.

3. Large forms - extended selections:
   a. Prelude: an introductory composition; generally
      used as the introduction of first movement of
      some larger form and is not used in any other
      part of the composition.
   b. Overture: an elaborate introductory composition,
      the themes of which are woven into the larger
      form it introduces; also played frequently as a
      complete composition in itself.
   c. Fugue: a highly developed contrapuntal composi-
      tion in which the themes are melodically and
      harmonically imitated.
   d. Sonata: a composition for solo instruments,
      usually in four movements.
   e. Concerto: a sonata for a solo instrument and
      orchestra, usually in three movements.
   f. Symphonic Poem: a composition for orchestra in
      one movement that tells a story in music.
   g. Symphony: a sonata for orchestra in four move-
      ments often preceded by an introduction.
   h. Theme and Variations: the statement of a theme
      followed by variations based on the theme. Some
      composers introduce a second theme with varia-
      tions in their major works.

CHAPTER **14**

PROGRAM MUSIC AND ABSOLUTE MUSIC

I. Program Music - Descriptive Music:

A. Definition:

   1. Musical interpretation of a poetic or extra-musical
      idea. The composer employs musical themes which de-
      scribe a narrative idea, or develop concepts of
      literary, religious, emotional, geographic, or his-
      torical character. Vocal music is obviously pro-
      grammatic because the lyrics contain the program.

B. Three basic types of program music:

   1. Imitative: musical instruments imitate certain
      sounds.
      a. Water music - Harp
      b. Thunder - Tympani
      c. Bird music - Flutes and Piccolos
   2. Narrative: the composer suggests a particular event
      or scene in his music.
   3. Impressionistic: originated among the French paint-
      ers of the nineteenth century. Music that suggests
      a mood or idea; the specific interpretation is left
      to the listener.

C. Titles of compositions:

   1. Sometimes the composer will indicate the program he
      wishes to suggest by the title he gives his compo-
      sition:
      a. *La Mer* - Claude Debussy
      b. *The Typewriter* - Leroy Anderson
      c. *Invitation to the Dance* - Carl Maria von Weber
      d. *Harold in Italy* - Hector Berlioz
      e. *The Butterfly* - Edvard Grieg

D. Program related to nationalistic music:

   1. The composer suggests musical ideas adopted from
      myths, legends and characteristics that often per-
      tain to a specific group of people. Folk themes are
      used for this purpose:
      a. *The Moldau* - Bedrich Smetana

b. *The Swan of Tuonela* - Jean Sibelius
c. *Peer Gynt Suite* - Edvard Grieg
d. *In the Steppes of Central Asia* - Alexander Borodin

E. Suggestions for listening to program music:

1. Listen to the music without reading the program or title.
2. Read the program suggested by the composer.
3. Listen to the music again; this time try to discover how the music portrays the story suggested by the composer.
4. Conduct a class discussion on the manner in which the music interprets the story suggested in the program.
5. Listen to the music again for enjoyment aided by an understanding of the program.
6. Play the selection again at other music appreciation sessions. Repeated hearings will enable the student to develop an appreciation and enjoyment of the music.

F. Suggested Listening:

1. Title: *La Mer*
   Composer: Claude Debussy
   Performers: New York Philharmonic - Bernstein
   Record No.: Columbia MS-6754

2. Title: *Invitation to the Dance*
   Composer: Carl Maria von Weber
   Performers: Philadelphia Orchestra - Ormandy
   Record No.: Columbia MS-6241

3. Title: *Harold in Italy*
   Composer: Hector Berlioz
   Performers: New York Philharmonic - Bernstein
   Record No.: Columbia MS-6358

4. Title: *The Moldau*
   Composer: Bedrich Smetana
   Performers: London Symphony Orchestra - Dorati
   Record No.: Mercury 90214

5. Title: *The Swan of Tuonela*
   Composer: Jean Sibelius
   Performers: Philadelphia Orchestra - Ormandy
   Record No.: Columbia MS-6157

6. Title: *In the Steppes of Central Asia*
   Composer: Alexander Borodin
   Performers: Boston Pops Orchestra - Fiedler
   Record No.: Victor LSC-2202

7. Title: *Peer Gynt Suites Nos. 1 and 2*
   Composer: Edvard Grieg
   Performers: Boston Pops Orchestra - Fiedler
   Record No.: Victor LSC-2125

8. Title: *Ride of the Valkyries* from *The Valkyrie*
   Composer: Richard Wagner
   Performers: Philadelphia Orchestra - Ormandy
   Record No.: Columbia MS-6624

9. Title: *Firebird Suite*
   Composer: Igor Stravinsky
   Performers: Boston Symphony Orchestra - Leinsdorf
   Record No.: Victor LSC-2725

10. Title: *Woodland Sketches*
    Composer: Edward MacDowell
    Performers: Pennario
    Record No.: Angel 36049

11. Title: *Pacific 231*
    Composer: Arthur Honegger
    Performers: New York Philharmonic - Bernstein
    Record No.: Columbia MS-6659

12. Title: *Enchanted Lake*
    Composer: Anton Liadov
    Performers: Ansermet
    Record No.: London STS-15066

13. Title: *Danse Macabre*
    Composer: Camille Saint-Saëns
    Performers: Boston Pops Orchestra - Fiedler
    Record No.: Victor LSC-2745

14. Title: *Funeral March of a Marionette*
    Composer: Charles Francois Gounod
    Performers: Philadelphia Symphony - Ormandy
    Record No.: Columbia MS-6474

15. Title: *Hänsel and Gretel (selections)*
    Composer: Engelbert Humperdinck
    Performers: Philharmonic Orchestra - Klemperer
    Record No.: Angel 36175

16. Title: *Children's Games (Jeux d'enfants)*
    Composer: Georges Bizet
    Performers: Paris Conservatory Orch. - Martinon
    Record No.: London STS-15093

17. Title: *Nutcracker Suite*
    Composer: Peter Ilich Tschaikowsky
    Performers: New York Philharmonic - Bernstein
    Record No.: Columbia MS6193

18. Title: *Overture* from *William Tell*
    Composer: Giocchino Rossini
    Performers: New York Philharmonic - Bernstein
    Record No.: Columbia MS 6743

II. <u>Absolute</u> <u>Music</u> - <u>Pure</u> <u>Music</u>:

A. Definition: Absolute music is music in which the composer writes "Music for the sake of music." There are no extra-musical implications such as a program which suggests a story, scene, action, mood or feeling.

B. Characteristics of absolute music:

   1. Music that adheres to perfection of form, follows a basic pattern, and produces beauty in melody and harmony.
   2. Absolute music usually will not suggest to the listener any specific mood or any definite idea.
   3. Most of the music composed during the Romantic period is program music. Many of the works of the composers of the Polyphonic and Classical periods such as Johann Sebastian Bach and Wolfgang Amadeus Mozart are good examples of absolute music.
   4. It is sometimes very difficult to distinguish between absolute and program music. Some music has many of the characteristics of both types:
      a. Follows a definite pattern or form.
      b. Suggests a definite program.

C. Suggestions for listening to absolute music:

   1. Discuss briefly the form of the piece to be heard. An excellent comparison may be made between the form in art and architecture, and the structure of music.
   2. Absolute music requires uninterrupted listening with the student concentrating on the repetitions, variations and general form of the music.

394

3. After the class has had an opportunity to listen to the music attentively without interruption, the teacher may discuss with the class the form of the selection in more detail.
4. Now that the class has a basic understanding of the structure of the composition, play the recording again so that they may fully enjoy the beauty of the music with knowledge and understanding.
5. Play the selection again at other music appreciation sessions. Through repeated hearings will come greater comprehension and, therefore, more enjoyment.
6. Discuss and compare absolute and program music.

D. Suggested Listening:

1. Title: *Concerto Grosso* , for string orchestra, fourth movement *Finale*
   Composer: Ernest Bloch
   Performers: Eastman-Rochester Symphony - Hanson
   Record No.: Mercury 90223

2. Title: *Toccata and Fugue in F*, for organ
   Composer: Johann Sebastian Bach
   Performers: Biggs - organist
   Record No.: Columbia MS-6748

3. Title: *Symphony No. 1 in D*
   Composer: Franz Josef Haydn
   Performers: Vienna Orchestra
   Record No.: Odyssey 32160006

4. Title: *London Suite*
   Composer: Eric Coates
   Performers: Gould Orchestra
   Record No.: Victor LSC-2719

5. Title: *Overture to the Magic Flute*
   Composer: Wolfgang Amadeus Mozart
   Performers: BBC Symphony - Davis
   Record No.: Philips 6580048

6. Title: *Concerto No. 2 in F*, for piano
   Composer: Frederick François Chopin
   Performers: Rubinstein - Wallenstein Symphony
   Record No.: Victor LSC-2265

7. Title: *Concerto in D*, for violin
   Composer: Johannes Brahms
   Performers: Stern - Philadelphia Orch. - Ormandy
   Record No.: Columbia MG-31418

8. Title: *Concerto in D*, for trumpets, oboes and strings
   Composer: George Frederick Handel
   Performers: Zickler
   Record No.: Turnabout 34295/9

9. Title: *Sonatas for Piano*
   Composer: Muzzio Clementi
   Performers: Crowson
   Record No.: Oiseau S-306/7

10. Title: *Sonata No. 3 in C*
    Composer: Ludwig van Beethoven
    Performers: Rubinstein - pianist
    Record No.: Victor LSC-2812

BIBLIOGRAPHY

MUSIC

Music Appreciation Books:

Austin, W. W. *Music in the Twentieth Century*. New York: W.W. Norton and Co., Inc., 1966.

Bekker, Paul. *The Orchestra*. New York: W.W. Norton and Co., Inc., 1964.

Berlioz, Hector. *Evenings in the Orchestra*. Baltimore, Md.: Penguin Book Co., 1963.

Bernstein, Leonard. *The Joy of Music*. New York: Simon & Schuster Co., 1963.

Cooper, Grosvenor. *Learning to Listen*. Chicago: University of Chicago Press, 1961.

Copland, Aaron. *The New Music 1900-1960*. New York: W.W. Norton and Co., Inc., 1968.

Copland, Aaron. *What to Listen for in Music*. New York: McGraw-Hill Book Co., Inc., 1957.

Dudley, Louise and Faricy, Austin. *The Humanities*. New York: McGraw-Hill Book Co., Inc., 1967.

Ernst, David. *Musique Concrète*. Boston: Crescendo Pub. Co., 1972.

Ewen, David. *Great Men of American Popular Song*. Englewood Cliffs, N.J.: Prentice-Hall, Inc., 1970.

Ewen, David. *Music for the Millions*. New York: Arco Pub. Co., 1950.

Fox, Sidney. *The Origins and Development of Jazz*. Chicago: Follett Ed. Corp., 1968.

Karel, Leon C. *Avenues to the Arts*. Kirksville, Mo.: Simpson Pub. Co., 1969.

Machlis, Joseph. *Introduction to Contemporary Music*. New York: W.W. Norton & Co., Inc., 1961.

Machlis, Joseph. *The Enjoyment of Music*. New York: W.W. Norton & Co., Inc., 1970.

Miller, William H. *Everybody's Guide to Music*. Philadelphia: Chilton Co., 1961.

Milligan, Harold V. *Stories of Famous Operas*. New York: Garden City Pub. Co., 1950.

Moore, Douglas. *A Guide to Musical Styles*. New York: W.W. Norton & Co., Inc., 1962.

Moore, Douglas. *Listening to Music*. New York: W.W. Norton & Co., Inc., 1963.

Ostransky, Leroy. *Perspectives on Music*. New Jersey: Prentice-Hall, Inc., 1963.

Pleasants, Henry. *Serious Music and All That Jazz*. New York: Simon & Schuster, 1969.

Rossi, Nick and Choate, Robert A. *Music of Our Time*. Boston: Crescendo Pub. Co., 1970.

Scholes, Percy A. *The Listener's Guide to Music*. London: Oxford University Press, 1961.

Seaman, Julian. *Great Orchestral Music*. New York: Crowell-Collier Pub. Co., 1962.

Stringham, Edwin J. *Listening to Music Creatively*. New Jersey: Prentice-Hall, Inc., 1959.

Taubman, Howard. *How to Bring Up Your Child to Enjoy Music*. New York: Ballantine Books, Inc., 1962.

Thompson, Oscar. *How to Understand Music*. Conn.: Fawcett Pub. Co., 1962.

Tischler, Hans. *The Perceptive Music Listener*. New Jersey: Prentice-Hall, Inc., 1955.

Ulrich, Homer. *Music: A Design for Listening*. New York: Harcourt, Brace & World, Inc., 1962.

Wilson, N. Emett. *How to Help Your Child With Music*. New York: Collier Pub. Co., 1961.

Music History Books:

Belz, Carl. *The Story of Rock*. New York: Oxford University Press, 1972.

Brockway, Wallace and Weinstock, Herbert. *Men of Music*. New York: Simon & Schuster, Inc., 1958.

Buchanan, Fannie R. and Luckenbill, Charles L. *How Man Made Music*. Chicago: Follett Pub. Co., 1959.

Cohn, Nick. *Rock from the Beginning*. New York: Stein and Day Co., 1970.

Cope, David. *New Directions in Music 1950-1970*. Dubuque: W.C. Brown Co., 1971.

Davies, Hunter. *The Beatles*. New York: McGraw-Hill Co., 1968.

Einstein, Alfred. *A Short History of Music*. New York: Vintage Books Co., 1956.

Ewen, David. *History of Popular Music*. New York: Barnes & Noble, Inc., 1961.

Grout, Donald J. *A History of Western Music*. New York: W.W. Norton & Co., Inc., 1961.

Howard, John Tasker and Lyons, James. *Modern Music*. New York: Thomas Y. Crowell Co., 1957.

Reidel, Johannes. *Music of the Romantic Period*. Dubuque: W.C. Brown Co., 1969.

Schuller, Gunther. *Early Jazz: Its Roots and Development*. New York: Oxford Press, 1968.

Shaw, Arnold. *The World of Soul*. New York: Cowles Book Co., 1970.

Southern, Eileen. *Music of Black Americans*. New York: W.W. Norton Co., Inc., 1971.

Spellman, A.B. *Black Music*. New York: Schocken Books, 1970.

Instrumental Music Books:

Baines, Anthony. *Musical Instruments Through the Ages*. Baltimore: Penguin Books, 1971.

Bellow, Alexander. *Illustrated History of the Guitar*. Rockville Center: Belwin-Mills Co., 1970.

Donnington, Robert. *The Instruments of Music*. New York: Barnes & Noble, Inc., 1962.

Hause, Robert W. *Instrumental Music for Today's Schools*. New Jersey: Prentice-Hall, Inc., 1965.

Keenan, Kent W. *The Technic of Orchestration*. New Jersey: Prentice-Hall, Inc., 1962.

Pace, Robert. *Piano for Classroom Use*. New Jersey: Prentice-Hall, Inc., 1963.

Sheftel, Paul. *Exploring Keyboard Fundamentals*. New York: Holt, Rinehart & Winston, 1970.

Electronic Music Books:

Cage, John. *A Year from Monday*. Middletown, Conn., Wesleyan Press, 1967.

Cowell, Henry. *New Musical Resources*. New York: Small Publishers Co., 1969.

Crowhurst, Norman H. *Electronic Musical Instrument Handbook*. Indianapolis: Sams, Howard W. & Company, 1962.

Dorf, Richard H. *Electronic Musical Instruments*. Mineola, N.Y.: Radiofile Co., 1963.

Gerhard, Roberto. *Concrete and Electronic Sound Composition*. London: Hinrichsen Edition, 1961.

Kostalanez, Richard. *John Cage*. New York: Praeger Publishers, 1970.

Reichardt, Jasia. *Cybernetics Serendipity, the Computer, and the Arts*. New York: Praeger Publishers, 1969.

Russcol, Herbert. *The Liberation of Sound*. Englewood Cliffs, New Jersey, Prentice-Hall, Inc., 1972.

Taylor, C.A. *The Physics of Musical Sounds*. London: English University Press, 1965.

Music Reference Books:

Apel, Willi. *Harvard Dictionary of Music*. Cambridge, Mass.: Harvard University Press, 1970.

Baker's Biographical Dictionary of Musicians. New York: G. Schirmer, Inc., 1971.

Castellini, John. *Rudiments of Music*. New York: W.W. Norton & Co., Inc., 1962.

Groves Dictionary of Music and Musicians. (9 vols.). New York: St. Martins Press, Inc., 5th ed., 1959.

Harman, Alec and Mellers, Wilfred (eds.). *Man and His Music* (4 vols.). New York: Schocken Books, 1971.

Miller, Hugh M. *Introduction to Music*. New York: Barnes & Noble, Inc., 1970.

New Oxford History of Music. (3 vols.). New York: Oxford University Press, Inc., 1967.

Reti, Rudolph. *Tonality in Modern Music*. New York: Collier Pub. Co., 1962.

Roxon, Lillian. *Rock Encyclopedia*. New York: Grosset & Dunlap Co., 1969.

Sacher, Jack. *Music A to Z*. New York: Grosset & Dunlap Co., 1963.

Sandved, K. B. *The World of Music - Illustrated Encyclopedia*. (4 vols.). New York: Abradale Press, Inc., 1963.

Standifer, James A. & Reeder, Barbara. *Source Book of African and Afro-American Materials for Music Educators*. Washington, D.C.: Music Educators National Conference, 1972.

Thompson, Oscar. *The International Cyclopedia of Music and Musicians*. (9th. ed.). New York: Dodd, Mead, 1964.

Taylor, Deems and Kerr, Russell. *Music Lover's Encyclopedia*. New York: Doubleday & Co., Inc., 1954.

HISTORY

History Books:

Blum, Jerome. *The European World, a History*. Boston: Little, Brown and Company, 1970.

Dill, Marshall. *Germany; a Modern History*. Ann Arbor: University of Michigan Press, 1970.

Durant, William James. *The Story of Civilization*. New York: Simon & Schuster, 1961.

Erlanger, Philipe. *The Age of Courts and Kings*. New York: Harper Company, 1967.

Ferguson, W.K. and G. Bruun. *A Survey of European Civilization*. Boston: Houghton Mifflin Company, 1962.

Hayes, C.J.H. and C.W. Cole. *History of Europe Since 1500*. New York: Macmillan Company, 1960.

Herold, Christopher J. *The Horizon Book of the Age of Napoleon*. New York: American Heritage, 1963.

Hicks, John D. *The Federal Union, A History of the United States to 1877*. Cambridge, Mass.: Riverside Press, 1957.

Hicks, John D. *The American Nation, A History of the United States from 1865 to the Present*. Cambridge, Mass.: The Riverside Press, 1955.

Mazour, A.G. and J.M. Peoples. *Men and Nations: A World History*. New York: Harcourt & Hall, 1961.

McNeill, William H. *The Rise of the West*. Chicago: University of Chicago Press, 1963.

Palmer, R.R. and J. Colton. *A History of the Modern World.* New York: Knopf Company, 1965.

Palmer, Robert R. *Twelve Who Ruled.* New York: Atheneum, 1965.

Shenton, James P. *History of the United States from 1865 to the Present.* New York: Doubleday Company, 1964.

Smith D. Mack. *Italy.* Ann Arbor: University of Michigan Press, 1959.

Smith, Goldwin Albert. *A History of England.* New York: Scribner Company, 1966.

Walsh, Warren B. *Russia and the Soviet Union.* Ann Arbor: University of Michigan Press, 1958.

SOCIAL STUDIES

Social Studies Books:

Gillin, John, Editor. *For a Science of Social Man.* New York: The Macmillan Company, 1954.

Laver, James. *The Age of Illusion, Manners, and Morals 1750-1848.* New York: David McKay and Company, Inc., 1972.

McLuhan, Marshall. *Culture Is Our Business.* New York: McGraw Hill Book Company, Inc., 1970.

SCIENCE

Science Books:

Asimov, Isaac. *A Short History of Chemistry.* New York: Doubleday & Company, Inc., 1965.

Bernal, John D. *Science in History.* New York: Hawthorn Books, Inc., 1965.

Crombie, Alistair C. *Medieval and Early Modern Science.* Cambridge, Mass.: Harvard University Press, 1961.

Dampier, Sir William Cecil. *A History of Science and Its Relations with Philosophy and Religion.* Cambridge, England: University Press, 1961.

Forbes, Robert J. and E.J. Dijsterhius. *A History of Science and Technology.* Baltimore: Penguin Books, 1963.

Mason, Stephen Finney. *A History of the Sciences.* New York: Collier Books, 1962.

McKenzie, Arthur and Edward Ellard. *The Major Achievements in Science.* New York: Cambridge University Press, 1960.

Singer, Charles. *A History of Biology.* New York: Schuman Company, 1950.

Taton, Rene, Editor. *History of Science.* (4 vols.). Translated by A.J. Pomerans. New York: Basic Books, 1964-1966.

Taylor, E. Sherwood. *An Illustrated History of Science.* New York: Frederic A. Praeger, Inc., 1955.

Warshofsky, Fred. *The 21st Century: The New Age of Exploration.* New York: The Viking Press, Inc., 1968.

PHILOSOPHY

Philosophy Books:

Brehier, Emile. *The History of Philosophy*. Translated by J.
    Thomas, Chicago: University of Chicago Press, 1963.
Choron, Jacques. *The Romance of Philosophy*. New York:
    Macmillan Company, 1963.
Copleston, Frederick Charles. *A History of Philosophy*.
    Westminster, Maryland: Newman Press, 1963.
Durant, William James. *The Story of Philosophy*. London:
    Benn Company, 1950.
Gilson, Etienne, general editor. *A History of Philosophy*.
    New York: Random House, 1962.
Huxley, Sir Julian, and others. *Growth of Ideas: Knowledge,
    Thought, Imagination*. Garden City, New York: Doubleday
    Company, 1965 and 1966.
Jaspers, Karl. *The Great Philosophers*. New York: Harcourt,
    Brace Jovanovich, Inc., 1962-1966.
Magill, Frank N. and Ian P. McGreal. *Masterpieces of World
    Philosophy in Summary Form*. New York: Salem Press, 1961.
McNeill, William H. *The Contemporary World, 1914/Present*.
    New York: William Morrow & Company, Inc., 1968.
Merton, Robert King. *Social Theory and Social Structure*.
    Glencoe: Free Press, 1962.
Runciman, Hon. Walter Garrison. *Social Science and Political
    Theory*. Cambridge, England: Cambridge University Press,
    1963.
Strauss, Leo, and Joseph Cropsey, Editors. *History of
    Political Philosophy*. Chicago: Rand McNally Company,
    1964.
Untemeyer, Louis. *Makers of the Modern World*. New York:
    Simon & Schuster, Inc., 1962.
Wells, H.G. *The Outline of History; Being a Plain History of
    Life and Mankind*. New York: Doubleday & Co., Inc., 1971.

LITERATURE

Literature Books:

Benet, William Rose, Ed. *The Reader's Encyclopedia: An Ency-
    clopedia of World Literature and the Arts*. New York: Thomas
    Y. Crowell Company, 1965.
Crigson, Geoffrey, Editor. *The Concise Encyclopedia of
    Modern World Literature*. New York: Hawthorne Books, 1963.
Cunliffe, Marcus. *The Literature of the United States*.
    New York: Penguin Pelican Books, 1967.
Day, Martin Steele. *History of English Literature*. Garden
    City, New York: Doubleday Company, 1963.
Diaz-Plaja, Guillermo. *A History of Spanish Literature*. New
    York: New York University Press, 1971.

Friedrich, Werner P. *An Outline History of German Literature.*
New York: Barnes & Noble, Inc., 1961.

Lindstrom, Thais. *A Concise History of Russian Literature,
Vol. I, From the Beginnings to Chekhov.* New York: New York
University Press, 1966.

Nitze, William A. and E. Preston Dargan. *A History of
French Literature.* Translated and revised by S. Griswold
Morley. (3rd ed.). New York: Henry Holt & Co., 1950.

Russell, Bertrand. *A History of Western Philosophy; And Its
Connection with Political and Social Circumstances from
the Earliest Times to the Present Day.* New York: Simon &
Schuster, Inc., 1945.

Thilly, Frank. *A History of Philosophy.* New York: Holt,
Rinehart & Winston, Inc., 1957.

Weatherly, Edward H., and Others. *The Heritage of European
Literature.* (2 vols.). Boston: Ginn and Company, 1948-
1949.

Wilkins, Ernest Hatch. *A History of Italian Literature.*
Cambridge, Mass.: Harvard University Press, 1954.

FINE ARTS

Fine Arts Books:

Hartt, Frederick. *History of Italian Renaissance Art: Painting, Sculpture, Architecture.* New York: Harry N. Abrams,
Inc., 1969.

Janson, H.W. *History of Art.* New York: Harry N. Abrams, Inc.,
1969.

Kuh, Katherine. *The Open Eye; In Pursuit of Art.* New York:
Harper & Row, Publishers, 1971.

Levey, Michael. *A History of Western Art.* New York: Frederick
A. Praeger, Inc., 1968.

Lynton, Norbert. *The Modern World.* New York: McGraw-Hill
Company, 1965.

Meyers, Bernard S. *Art and Civilization.* New York: McGraw-
Hill Company, 1967.

Muller, Joseph E. *Modern Painting from Manet to Mondrian.*
New York: Castle Books, 1960.

Munro, Thomas. *The Arts and Their Interrelations.* Western
Reserve University Press, 1967.

Time-Life Books. *Seven Centuries of Art.* New York: Time,
Inc. Book Division, 1970.

GENERAL REFERENCES

Encyclopedias, Dictionaries, Etc.:

A *Dictionary of the Social Sciences.* New York: The Free
Press, 1964.

Asimov, Isaac. *Asimov's Biographical Encyclopedia of Science and Technology*. Garden City, N.Y.: Doubleday & Company, Inc., 1964.

Cassell's Encyclopedia of World Literature. (2 vols.). New York: Funk & Wagnall's Company, 1954.

Collier's Encyclopedia. (24 vols.). New York: Crowell, Collier and Macmillan, Inc., 1970.

Compton's Pictured Encyclopedia and Fact-Index. (15 vols.). Chicago, Toronto, etc.: F.E. Compton Company, 1969.

Dictionary of American History. (6 vols.). New York: Charles Scribner's Sons, 1961.

Dictionary of Political Sciences. New York: Philosophical Library, Inc., 1964.

Encyclopedia Americana. (30 vols.). New York and Chicago: American Corporation. Plate revisions annually. *Americana Annual* (1923 to date) is an annual supplement.

Encyclopedia Britannica. London and New York: Encyclopedia Britannica, 1970.

Encyclopedia of Science and Technology. (15 vols.). New York, Toronto, etc.: McGraw-Hill Book Company, 1966.

Encyclopedia of the Social Sciences. New York: Macmillan Company, 1930-1935. (15 vols.). Re-issued in 8 vols., 1948.

Encyclopedia of World Art. (12 vols.). New York, Toronto etc.: McGraw-Hill Book Company, 1959.

Johnson, Thomas Herbert. *The Oxford Companion to American History*. New York: Oxford University Press, 1966.

Larousse Encyclopedia of Modern History, From 1500 to the Present Day. New York: Harper & Row Company, 1964.

The Book of Popular Science. (10 vols.). New York: Grolier Inc., 1966.

The Cowles Comprehensive Encyclopedia. New York: Cowles Educational Books, Inc., 1966.

The Lincoln Library of Essential Information. Buffalo, N. Y.: The Frontier Press Company, 1966.

The World Book Encyclopedia. (20 vols.). Chicago: Field Enterprises Educational Corporation, 1973.

Weir, Albert E. *Thesaurus of the Arts*. New York: G.P. Putnam's Sons, 1943.